DRUGS
A FACTUAL ACCOUNT

DRUGS

A FACTUAL ACCOUNT

FIFTH EDITION

Dorothy E. Dusek, Ph.D.
Daniel A. Girdano, Ph.D.

McGRAW-HILL, INC.
New York   St. Louis   San Francisco   Auckland   Bogotá
Caracas   Lisbon   London   Madrid   Mexico   Milan   Montreal
New Delhi   Paris   San Juan   Singapore   Sydney   Tokyo   Toronto

DRUGS
A Factual Account

1 2 3 4 5 6 7 8 9 0 DOC DOC 9 0 9 8 7 6 5 4 3 2

ISBN 0-07-018396-1

This book was set in Times Roman by Better Graphics, Inc.
The editors were Sylvia Shepard and Scott Amerman;
the production supervisor was Annette Mayeski.
The cover was designed by Andrew Canter Design.
R. R. Donnelley & Sons Company was printer and binder.

Library of Congress Cataloging-in-Publication Data

Dusek, Dorothy.
   Drugs, a factual account / Dorothy Dusek and Daniel Girdano. —
5th ed.
      p.   cm.
   Includes bibliographies and index.
   ISBN 0-07-018396-1
   1. Drug abuse.   2. Drug abuse—Physiological aspects.   3. Drug
abuse—Treatment.   I. Girdano, Daniel A.   II. Title.
HV5801.D88   1993
613.8–dc20   92-25036

ABOUT THE AUTHORS

DOROTHY E. DUSEK is a consultant, counselor, and teacher in private practice, an accomplished author in the health and behavior change field, and a motivational speaker for groups through the United States.

She received her Ph.D. from the University of Toledo, and has held health professorships at San Francisco State College, Worcester State College, the University of Maryland, and the University of Utah. These positions offered experience in curriculum planning, training professional students, and supervising graduate research. Dr. Dusek has also been adjunct faculty at Texas A&M, Colorado Mountain College, the University of Northern Colorado, and the Metropolitan State College at Denver.

Currently, Dr. Dusek is consultant to the Wyoming Perinatal Substance Abuse Prevention Program, an Office of Substance Abuse Prevention grant administered through the University of Wyoming School of Nursing.

She has authored major texts with prominent national publishing houses in drug education, nutrition and weight management, stress management, fitness, health behavior change, relationships and interpersonal communication, and other personal and public health topics. As senior editor, she edits and publishes books, pamphlets, and instructional materials for Paradox Publishing.

DANIEL A. GIRDANO is president and co-founder of Paradox Associates, consultants specializing in program planning, evaluation, professional training seminars, materials development, and publishing in the fields of education, medicine, public health, and business. Dr. Girdano is a specialist in developing goals and objectives, strategic planning, analyzing resources, evaluation planning, and research. He is currently a training and evaluation consultant to The Wyoming Perinatal Substance Abuse Prevention Program (OSAP Grant).

Dr. Girdano received his Ph.D. from the University of Toledo. He has an M.A. from Kent State University and a B.S. from West Liberty College.

Professorial positions have been held by Dr. Girdano at the Universities of Utah and Maryland, Boston University, Texas A&M, and Pennsylvania State University.

Dr. Girdano has been widely recognized as an innovative leader in the health professions for almost twenty-five years. He has authored or co-authored twenty health psychology textbooks.

CONTENTS

With the fifth edition of *Drugs: A Factual Account,* we look back to twenty years ago when the first edition was published. In a way, drug taking hasn't changed at all: people have the same motivations for use and abuse that they had back in 1972, they are still trying to withdraw from problems or trying to be something they are not, and some people are still getting caught up in the dependence and addiction cycle. Scientists are still trying to find the "cure" for drug abuse, and the focus still tends to be on the drug(s) rather than on the people who take the drugs and the culture that makes the experience possible. The major illicit drugs of choice have changed from time to time from downers to psychedelics, to stimulants, back to downers, and so on, while the major killers (alcohol and tobacco) retain their prestigious place at the top of the drug-use charts. We all still pay the escalating costs for the hundreds of thousands of deaths that are alcohol- and smoking-related through our automobile, home, and health insurance.

Twenty years ago we didn't call it the War on Drugs, but we put most of our federal money into interdiction, criminalization of possession and sales of illicit drugs, with stiffer and stiffer penalties so that no one in their right mind would buy or use an illicit drug. This effort produced little success, so we began the process of prevention—teaching school-age children about the dangers of drugs, how to recognize illicit drugs, and how to clarify their personal values so they could refuse the drug experience when the offer came. Evaluations of drug education efforts have shown disappointing results.

Only recently have we begun to balance out the supply reduction side of the equation with demand reduction. We are seeing some changes in demand. It is becoming unsocial to smoke cigarettes in many public and private places. Nonsmokers have learned to just say no. The trends of drug abuse in some of the illicit categories are down. Some ethnic/minority groups have announced that they do not want their children to be the targets of major advertising campaigns. Women's groups are demanding that smoking companies not target women, especially those of childbearing age.

We are finally looking at some of the risk factors that come into play in drug abuse, and we are making a case for the abolition of these risk factors: factors such as low self-esteem, nonassertiveness, anger, fear, and stress. Every class in every school can take on the goal of helping young people find success in their lives and, through supportive activities, build their self-esteem. Self-assertiveness, anger management, fear management, and other healthy behaviors are skills that can be learned if we have someone there to teach them.

We still feel that knowledge about drugs is important. In this issue we include an updated factual account of licit and illicit drugs—what they are and what effect they have on the human body. However, in this edition, we focus on motivations, prevention, and treatment across the board rather than making these issues drug-specific, because addiction is *first* a psychosocial problem and *then* a drug problem. When we find solutions to the first part, the second part will no longer be an issue.

Dorothy E. Dusek
Daniel A. Girdano

DRUGS
A FACTUAL
ACCOUNT

DRUG TRENDS, DEFINITIONS, AND PHYSIOLOGICAL FOUNDATIONS

TRENDS

Surveys find less drug use but more abuse.

NATIONAL SURVEYS

Casual drug use is on a downward swing, at least for the middle class. After a few years of experimentation, the generation that popularized the drug culture has grown up to get married, raise children, become doctors, lawyers, parents, teachers. The generation's cocaine use is down. The number of all those who use cocaine dwindled by as much as one-third over the past several years according to household surveys by the National Institute on Drug Abuse (NIDA). Casual use started to decline in 1985, and heavy use started to decline in late 1989, showing the usual three-year lag. However, changes in casual use still leave a hard-core culture, concentrated in inner cities, of violent dealers and addicted victims and their babies. The upswing in use as measured by 1991 surveys is concentrated in this group. The victims are turning up in hospital emergency rooms at a rate five times higher than five years ago. Police departments say they are overwhelmed more than ever by the fallout from drug crimes and overdoses. The drug war is turning into a new form of class conflict. Those waging it see less drug use but more abuse, with the abusers getting worse. Among some groups heavy use remains high. Use and abuse, especially of cocaine, are on the increase in Western Europe and Japan.

Two major surveys provide information on the changing drug scene in America. One is the National Household Survey on Drug Abuse conducted every year by NIDA. The second is the National High School Senior Survey (also conducted by NIDA). These surveys, along with hospital records and other general survey reports, give us the following information about drug taking in the United States.

The National Household Survey on Drug Abuse conducted interviews with thousands of individuals 12 years old and older. Those surveyed are representative of the noninstitutionalized population living in households in the continental United States. In 1985 the survey started to look at minorities, conducting an oversampling of interviews with blacks and Hispanics so that more reliable estimates of drug use by these population groups could be obtained. The 1988 National High School Senior Survey also provided data on college students (Rogers, 1990).

A major component of the High School Senior Survey is an analysis of drug use trends among college students from 1980 through 1990. The percentage of college students reporting *annual use of any illicit drug* decreased from 56 percent in 1980 to 45 percent in 1984. From 1984 through 1986, the percentage of drug users among college students remained level at 45 percent. Between 1986 and 1988, a dramatic drop occurred, from 45 percent to 37 percent. For most classes of drugs, the drop among college students paralleled a drop among the non-college group and among high school seniors (Rogers, 1990; NIDA, 1990).

During 1988, college students generally showed less abuse of most drugs than their non-college peers, though the degree of difference varies considerably by drug. For *past year use of any illicit drug*, 37 percent of college students and 40 percent of their non-college peer group reported use. In 1988, *annual stimulant use* showed the largest difference, with 6.2 percent for college students and 10.7 percent for non-college. A similar lower rate of abuse was found among college students for tranquilizers, barbiturates, LSD, and opiates other than heroin. *Annual use* of tranquilizers also dropped from 6.9 percent of college students in 1984 to 3.5 percent in 1984 and has remained low.

OVERVIEW OF SPECIFIC DRUGS

Alcohol

Alcohol is the most widely used drug in America. More than one-half of the adult population drinks. More than 18 million Americans are believed to have definite problems associated with alcohol. It is estimated that 50,000 deaths occur each year from motor vehicle accidents and that about 50 percent of those are alcohol-related. Cirrhosis of the liver remains the fourth leading cause of death for middle-aged men and fifth for women. The number of homicides and suicides committed under the influence of alcohol is difficult to assess but is believed to be considerable. A greater awareness among pregnant women of the effects of alcohol on the fetus shows promise in reducing the incidence of fetal alcohol syndrome.

With the possible exception of the teenage drinking problem, the number of drinkers, the severity of their problem, and the number of deaths attributed to alcohol have remained fairly constant over the last decade. In addition, little progress has been made in the understanding of the factors that cause alcoholism. As might be expected, little progress has been made in alcohol treatment techniques, and little new information has been uncovered on how alcohol affects the human organism (Hollister, 1983).

The National Household Survey on Drug Abuse (NIDA, 1990) showed a slight drop in alcohol use *at least once in the last month* by adults 26 years of age or older, from 54.4 percent in 1988 to 52.3 percent in 1990. Alcohol abuse remains the number one problem among college students. Although students had an overall lower prevalence of use of most illicit drugs, their annual and monthly prevalence rates in 1988 for alcohol, at 90 percent and 77 percent, respectively, were slightly higher than those of their non-college peers, 87 percent versus 69 percent. Daily use, however, was slightly lower among college students than among their non-college peers. The most important difference was that college students engaged in more heavy drinking, defined by the survey as drinking five or more drinks in a row during the past two weeks. College students reported heavy drinking at a rate of 43 percent, while their peer group reported a rate of 36 percent. This difference is primarily attributed to the relatively low rates of heavy drinking among non-college females. An analysis of differences in drinking patterns by sex shows that male college students engaged in heavy drinking only slightly more often than "other" males, 52 percent versus 48 percent, respectively. Among females, the difference was more pronounced, with 26 percent of non-college females drinking heavily compared to 37 percent of female college students. The National Household Survey on Drug Abuse (NIDA, 1990) showed a slight drop in alcohol use *at least once in the last month* by those of college age, from 65.3 percent in 1988 to 63.3 percent in 1990.

The National Household Survey on Drug Abuse (NIDA, 1990, 1991) showed a slight drop in alcohol use *at least once in the last month* by those 12 to 17 years old, from 25.2 percent in 1988 to 24.5 percent in 1990 and 1991.

Tobacco

Nicotine is the second most widely used drug in the United States. Approximately 55 million Americans smoke daily, and more than 485,000 Americans die prematurely from tobacco-related illness. Smoking annually causes 147,000 cancer deaths, 240,000 deaths from diseases of the circulatory system, 61,000 non-cancer deaths from diseases of the respiratory system, 14,000 deaths from diseases of the digestive system, 4,000 infant deaths due to mothers smoking, 4,000 deaths due to fires and accidents, and nearly 15,000 deaths from miscellaneous and ill-defined diseases. Add to that the deaths caused by the smoking of pipes and cigars, the passive inhalation of environmental tobacco smoke, and the chewing and snuffing of tobacco, which probably raises the total U.S. tobacco death toll to more than a half million—more than one-fourth of all deaths from all causes (Center for Health and Safety Studies, 1985). There has been a slight drop since 1979 in the number of current users of cigarettes. In a breakdown by age group, it is seen that 22 percent of youth and 40 percent of adults are regular smokers. By age 12, one out of five youngsters smokes. One alarming increase in smoking patterns is that of young girls—the smoking pattern of high school girls now approximates that of high school boys.

Nicotine meets the established scientific criteria for being classified as a dependency-producing drug in the same way opiates, stimulants, and sedatives do. Nicotine produces physiological dependence in both animal and human experiments. Under experimental conditions, there is clear evidence of nicotine withdrawal; symptoms when habitual use is discontinued include electroencephalogram (EEG) (brain wave) changes, measurably impaired intellectual and psychomotor performance, irritability, aggressiveness, anxiety, insomnia, and fatigue. Withdrawal symptoms can be relieved by the use of nicotine-containing chewing gum. Use of "smokeless tobacco" results in blood levels of nicotine corresponding to those after cigarette smoking. Preliminary evidence indicates that the use of smokeless tobacco also leads to nicotine dependency. Smoking cessation treatment can result in short-term success rates as high as 70 percent, but these rates significantly decrease as measured by continued nonsmoking a year later.

College students reported daily smoking during 1988 at a rate of 12 percent versus 28 percent for the non-college peer group. This difference is consistent with data reported by the high school survey, which show that college-bound students smoke at a lower rate than students not planning to attend college. A look at sex differences in smoking shows that among college students, women are more likely to smoke than men. The National Household Survey on Drug Abuse (NIDA, 1990, 1991) showed a slight drop in cigarette smoking in the category *at least once in the last month* for the college age population, from 35.2 percent to 31.5 percent.

The household survey (NIDA, 1990, 1991) also showed a slight drop in the use of cigarettes in the category *at least once in the last month* by those in the 12-to-17-year-old range, from 11.8 percent in 1988 to 11.6 percent in 1990. Among the adult population, cigarette smoking decreased from 29.8 percent to 27.7 percent.

Marijuana

Along with the downward trend in the number of current users of alcohol and tobacco, there appears to be a diminishing percentage of youth and young adults using marijuana (*Cannabis sativa*). Over 40 million persons have experienced cannabis, and it remains the most extensively used illicit drug. Marijuana use was widespread during the 1960s and 1970s. In the 1980s, however, marijuana began to lose its popularity, with 2.1 percent of college students reporting daily use in 1986 compared to 7.2 percent in 1980. Beyond 1986, the rate of decline in daily use continued more gradually. Overall, daily marijuana use dropped by more than two-thirds between 1980 and 1988.

Daily use of marijuana was much lower among college students. Only 1.8 percent of college students reported daily use of marijuana during 1988, while 4.8 percent of the non-college group reported daily use. This finding is consistent with the large difference in daily use between college-bound high school students and those not planning to attend college. Substantial differences between the sexes were also observed for daily marijuana use. Males generally smoked marijuana more often than females. Daily marijuana use was reported by 2.9 percent of male college students and 1 percent of college females.

The National Household Survey on Drug Abuse (NIDA, 1990, 1991) showed a drop in use of marijuana in the category *at least once in the last month* for the college-age population, from 15.5 percent in 1988 to 12.7 percent in 1990, with a continued small decrease in 1991. The same survey showed a slight drop in use of marijuana in the category *at least once in the last month* by those 12 to 17 years old, from 6.4 percent of that age group in 1988 to 5.2 percent in 1990. Among the adult population the use decreased from 3.9 percent in 1988 to 3.6 percent in 1990 to 3.3 percent in 1991.

The health hazards of cannabis are of great concern, and this remains an area of interest for researchers. The potency of street samples of marijuana has continued to increase, now averaging over four times what it was a decade ago. There is published evidence that women who use marijuana during pregnancy are more likely than non-users to give birth to lower-birth-weight infants who also more frequently have congenital abnormalities like those associated with fetal alcohol syndrome. Evidence that marijuana reduces the body's immune response in humans seems conclusive.

Marijuana use is associated with greater use of other drugs, with decreased participation in conventional activities, with a history of psychiatric hospitalization, with lower self-perceived psychological well-being, and with greater involvement in other socially deviant activities. A study of marijuana use by adolescents found that it is used as a means of escaping from real-world problems and relieving stress and that it reinforces the subject's unwillingness to face these problems.

Stimulants

Between 1932 and 1946 amphetamines were used medically as a cure-all for many different conditions. The establishment of the dangerous abuse potential of these drugs has led to a marked reduction in their use. The effects of amphetamine use are due to depletion of important neurotransmitter pools. Since drugs of the stimulant type (including cocaine) share many similarities, research on these substances continues to be an important source of insight into their basic mechanisms of action and possible means of preventing their abuse.

The 1982 NIDA survey showed that 6.7 percent of youth (ages 12 to 17), 18 percent of young adults (ages 18 to 25), and 6.2 percent of older adults had used stimulants for nonmedical reasons at least once. Additionally, 2.9 percent of youth, 4.3 percent of young adults, and 12 percent of older adults reported using stimulants for medical reasons at some time in their lives. Stimulant abuse (e.g., of the amphetamines) has generally decreased from the peak levels of the early 1980s.

The National Household Survey on Drug Abuse (NIDA, 1990, 1991) showed a drop in stimulant use in the category *at least once in the last month* by those of college age, from 2.4 percent in 1988 to 1.2 percent in 1990. The same survey showed a slight drop in the use of stimulants in the category *at least once in the last month* by those in the 12-to-17-year-old range, from 1.2 percent in 1988 to 1.0 percent in 1990. Among the adult population, stimulant use decreased from 0.5 percent in 1988 to 0.3 percent in 1990 and continued at this level in 1991.

Cocaine

There has been a remarkable increase in the use of cocaine over the last decade. Cocaine is one of the most reinforcing drugs known, and dependence on the drug is very difficult to break. Heavy users can experience psychosis when high for prolonged periods and severe depression when the drug is withdrawn. The flow of cocaine into the United States seems to be increasing with its demand. Even though the federal government has greatly increased its efforts to stem the tide of cocaine importation, the monetary rewards for this expensive drug are so great that many people are willing to take the risk of dealing in cocaine. Cocaine appears to stimulate the brain's reward system so intensely and directly that profound dependence is readily produced in animals and humans when the drug is habitually used and freely available.

Cocaine that can be smoked is now readily available on the illicit market as "crack." Since crack is easy to produce, not requiring use of dangerously volatile chemicals, and because it is available at low cost, the dangers of increasing use and the likelihood of becoming cocaine-dependent are magnified. Smoking cocaine results in more rapid and more intense effects than snorting, making it more likely to produce dependency rapidly. There is now laboratory evidence that in humans tolerance to the mood-elevating effects of cocaine develops rapidly, requiring increased doses even during periods of "binge" use. Contrary to earlier belief, a true withdrawal syndrome that is physiologically based can develop from cocaine use, including such symptoms as depression, social withdrawal, drug craving, tremor, muscle pain, eating and sleep disturbance, and EEG changes. Irregular heart action and cocaine-related heart attacks have been clinically reported. Brain hemorrhages presumptively related to increases in blood pressure accompanying cocaine use have also been reported.

The purity of street cocaine markedly increased—from 29 percent to 73 percent pure—between 1982 and 1984. Illicit cocaine is now not only significantly purer, it is much less expensive than a decade ago (it is now selling at pre-1977 levels of $60 to $100 a gram—1/28 ounce—despite its greater purity).

Treatment centers that specialize in cocaine dependence are springing up throughout the country. To date no unique mode of treatment for cocaine abusers has been developed, but all programs stress the need for total abstinence, learning to manage impulsive drug-using behavior, and developing insight into the destructive role of the drug in the user's life. Three out of four cocaine users interviewed who called the 800-COCAINE help line reported a loss of control over their use; two-thirds were unable to stop despite repeated attempts. Nine out of ten users interviewed in the 800-COCAINE sample reported serious emotional and physical consequences of use.

Although cocaine use has increased, there has been greater media recognition of the hazards of use and a markedly reduced tendency to glamorize use in recent years. From 1980 to 1986 cocaine use among college students was fairly stable. Annual prevalence started declining in 1986, dropping from 17 percent to 10 percent in 1988. Crack use too was lower among college students, with 1.4 percent of students and 4 percent of the non-college group reporting *use within the past year.*

The *National Household Survey on Drug Abuse* (NIDA, 1990, 1991) showed a drop in cocaine use in the category *at least once in the last month* by those of college age, from 4.5 percent in 1988 to 2.2 percent in 1990. The same survey showed a drop in the use of cocaine in the category *at least once in the last month* by those in the 12-to-17-year-old range, from 1.1 percent in 1988 to 0.6 percent in 1990. The National Institute on Drug Abuse (NIDA) household survey for 1991, based on a sample of more than 32,000 people, reverses a five-year downward trend in cocaine use and represents an unexpected setback for the administrations' anti-drug effort. The number of Americans using cocaine at least once a month rose to an estimated 1.9 million in 1991, an 18 percent jump over 1990. This was caused by substantial increases in drug use among blacks, the unemployed, and persons over 35.

Drug-related emergency room visits, overdose deaths, and serious clinical problems show a higher rate of increase for cocaine than for any other abused drug. However, the number of cocaine-related hospital emergency room visits nationwide dropped by 30 percent between the third quarter of 1989 and the second quarter of 1990, according to data from NIDA's Drug Abuse Warning Network (DAWN). The drop reverses a trend in which such emergencies increased fourfold between 1985 and 1989 (Sobel, 1990). The increase in cocaine use in 1991 was accompanied by a dramatic increase in cocaine-related hospital emergency room visits, which further verifies the increase in hard-core abuse.

Sedatives and Antianxiety Agents

Used for treating anxiety, insomnia, muscle spasms, and convulsion, sedative drugs such as the benzodiazepines (e.g., tranquilizers such as diazepam) are the most widely prescribed class of sedative-hypnotics. Although illicit supplies of sedatives do reach the market, these drugs are largely prescribed. Physicians have become more cautious in prescribing sedatives with the growing recognition of their abuse potential, and there is evidence that they are generally used appropriately and conservatively. Physical dependence upon anxiety-relieving/sedative drugs has been shown in a variety of animal studies and human clinical observations. Symptoms of drug withdrawal after heavy habitual use may include anxiety, insomnia, agitation, loss of appetite, tremor, muscle twitching, nausea and vomiting, hypersensitivity to sensory stimuli, feelings of depersonalization, hallucinations, delirium, grand mal convulsions, and sometimes death. There is now good evidence that prolonged treatment (six months or more) at normal therapeutic doses can produce physical dependence on benzodiazepines. One recent concern has been the problem of low-dose dependence. This occurs when long-term treatment with therapeutic doses seems to create a type of dependence that is difficult to distinguish from symptoms of anxiety. It is now known that receptors for benzodiazepines as well as barbiturates occur naturally in the brain, and the reaction of these receptors to long-term benzodiazepine treatment may bring about dependence (Hollister, 1983).

In 1982, nearly 6 percent of youth, 18.7 percent of young adults, and 4.8 percent of older adults reported that they had used sedatives nonmedically at least once in their lives. For medical use, the corresponding figures were 5.6 percent of youth, 9.7 percent of young adults, and 21.4 percent of older adults. Data from the 1988 National High School Senior Survey indicate a large drop in the use of tranquilizers and sedative-hypnotics.

The National Household Survey on Drug Abuse (NIDA, 1990, 1991) showed a drop in sedative use in the category *at least once in the last month* by those of college age, from 3.4 percent in 1988 to 2.4 percent in 1990. The same survey showed an increase in the use of sedatives in the category *at least once in the last month* by those in the 12-to-17-year-old range of from 1.7 percent in 1988 to 2.8 percent in 1990. Among the adult population the percentage using sedatives decreased from 1.3 percent in 1988 to 0.9 percent in 1990 and 1991.

Hallucinogens

Hallucinogens include the many different natural and synthetic substances such as LSD and mescaline that markedly distort perception and thinking in strikingly vivid ways. Use of these drugs has generally decreased, although it is by no means uncommon—about one in ten high school seniors (Class of 1985) used these drugs at some time. Phencyclidine piperidine (PCP) causes effects that most accurately mimic schizophrenic thinking and is a leading cause of psychiatric admission. PCP has replaced LSD as the most abused hallucinogen, but LSD remains very popular in certain places. The illegal manufacture of PCP is lucrative and relatively easy, its chemical precursors being substances widely used commercially and impossible to control. Although there is an encouraging trend toward decreased use of PCP, use in some populations such as high school seniors has increased from 0.3 percent to 1.4 percent. Whether it will be sustained remains to be seen. Methylenedioxymeth-amphetamine (MDMA), a synthetic hallucinogen that was billed as the ideal hallucinogenic drug, will no doubt add to the incidence of drug taking in this category.

Recent animal research has found a possible neurochemical basis for enduring behavioral change resulting from repeated hallucinogen use. Specific antagonists for some of the hallucinogens have been tested in animals, but it is uncertain whether these will prove useful in treating "bad trips," the acute panic that sometimes results from use.

The National Household Survey on Drug Abuse (NIDA, 1990, 1991) showed a drop in hallucinogen use in the category *at least once in the last month* by those of college age, from 1.9 percent in 1988 to 0.8 percent in 1990. The same survey showed an increase in the use of hallucinogens in the category *at least once in the last month* by those in the 12-to-17-year-old range, from 0.8 percent in 1988 to 0.9 percent in 1990. The percentage of the adult population using hallucinogens decreased from 1.3 percent in 1988 to 0.9 percent in 1990 and remained relatively stable in 1991.

Heroin

It appears that there has been a stabilization of the number of heroin-dependent persons in the last few years, with estimates given at approximately one-half million people. However, reports on heroin use for the second quarter of 1991 indicate that bad reactions to heroin use sent 9,432 people to emergency rooms, up 17 percent from 1990. The abuse of heroin and other narcotics remains a significant public health problem. The ills associated with opiate abuse continue to be more social than medical—thievery and prostitution are the most common consequences of having a habit that is both expensive and debilitating and that precludes useful employment. About 80,000 opiate-dependent persons are in treatment at any given time in the United States. Some centers advocate drug programs, such as methadone maintenance, and some advocate therapeutic communities. There is more proof for the efficacy of methadone programs than for any other modality, but this should not prevent the advocacy of other types of programs.

In recent years advances have been made in understanding the mechanisms of action of the opiates and the role of naturally occurring opiate-like substances that provide a neurochemical basis for believing that opiate addiction is a disease that may involve neurophysiological differences between addicts and non-addicts. Advances in the chemistry of opioids may lead to a practical way of synthesizing morphine and related drugs, simplifying the drug control problem by eliminating the need to grow the opium poppy overseas to meet pharmaceutical needs.

Designer Drugs

An emerging problem in the drug abuse area is that of analogues of drugs of abuse. These are synthetic compounds created by underground chemists and designed to mimic scheduled psychoactive drugs. These chemists change the molecular structure of a drug and thus make a drug similar to the drug that is legally restricted. The changes in chemical structure may also change its potency, length of action, euphoric effects, and toxicity. These newer drugs have also been illegal since the passage of the Anti-Drug Abuse Act of 1986 (P.L. 99-570), which contains the Controlled Substance Analogue Enforcement

Act of 1986 subtitle. It is now required that any analogue of a controlled substance be included in Schedule I of the Controlled Substances Act.

Unfortunately, these analogues have been dubbed "designer" drugs in the media, which may create an impression that they are somehow special or even desirable. However, they often contain contaminants and can have serious adverse side effects. It is impossible to know exactly how many overdose episodes have occurred from use of these drugs and how many fatalities can be attributed to them or even the extent of their use and availability. However, there is ample evidence to generate concern among public health officials about a possible epidemic of drug use from use of these chemical analogues of dangerous substances, especially if the use of cocaine decreases and the use of hallucinogens increases.

OTHER HEALTH PROBLEMS RELATED TO DRUGS

AIDS

It is thought that intravenous drug users (IVDUs) contract the acquired immunodeficiency syndrome (AIDS) human immunodeficiency virus (HIV) primarily by sharing unsterilized needles with other individuals infected by HIV. Of New York City's adult cases of AIDS, 27 percent involve intravenous drug users. For the remainder of the country the figure is 12 percent. Among pediatric cases of AIDS in New York City, either one or both parents of these children are intravenous drug users in 74 percent of the cases, compared to 31 percent of the pediatric cases of AIDS in the rest of the country (Ginzburg & MacDonald, 1986).

It is clear that practices within the drug-using subculture in each city have an impact on the spread of AIDS within that community. Renting or sharing needles and other equipment for the intravenous injection of drugs has long been common practice in New York City. This accounts, in part, for the fact that over one-third of all AIDS cases in the United States are in New York. In San Francisco, it is estimated that approximately 10 percent of AIDS cases are intravenous drug users, but the drug subculture in San Francisco is different with regard to the sharing or renting of equipment, which may account for the lower rate. In Miami and in other cities, the fear of contracting AIDS because of dirty needles seems to have led to a shift in the route of administration for cocaine, from intravenous injection to a greater reliance on free basing. Clearly, intravenous use of drugs is one of the leading risk factors for AIDS.

Drugs and the Neonate

It is known that drugs used by a mother cross the placental barrier and affect the fetus. There is a long-standing and rich research tradition concerning the effects of heroin on neonates (i.e., neonatal heroin addiction). A substantial body of research exists concerning the effects of cigarette smoking and alcohol use by the mother on the newborn. Recently, research has emerged suggesting that the symptoms usually attributed to fetal alcohol syndrome (FAS) are also found when the new mother is a heavy user of marijuana. With extremely heavy use of marijuana, it is very difficult to clinically differentiate fetal alcohol syndrome from fetal marijuana syndrome. Likewise, research and clinical evidence has clearly shown the devastating effects of cocaine and crack on the fetus. AIDS transmitted to the fetus is among the greatest tragedies of modern life.

Attitudes Toward Drugs

Americans have reported increasingly negative attitudes toward drug use over the past four years, according to an annual survey by the Partnership for a Drug-Free America. The survey, first conducted in 1987, is the nation's largest measure of attitudes toward drug use, with 8,000 respondents in 1990. It has found increasingly antagonistic attitudes toward drug use among children aged 9 to 12, teenagers 13 to 17, and adults 18 and over. The 1990 survey found that more than 70 percent of both teenage and adult respondents now think that even occasional use of marijuana is risky, and 71 percent of teens fear using cocaine; this is up 9 percentage points from 1989 (Sobel, 1990b). Capitalizing on this trend toward a changing attitude to drug use, a national initiative to denormalize drug use has begun. This campaign seeks to change the public image of "the non-user is a loser" to "the user is a loser." Only time will tell if this will be successful and the downward trend will continue.

REFERENCES

APA (1980). *Diagnostic and Statistical Manual of Mental Disorders*, 3d ed. (DSM-III). Washington, D.C.: American Psychological Association.

Center for Health and Safety Studies (1985). Smoking and health. *Health Reporter*, 2(3): 8.

Ginzburg, H. M., and MacDonald, M. G. (1986). The epidemiology of human T-cell lymphotropic virus, Type III (HTLV-III disease). *Psychiatry Annals*, 16: 153–157.

Hollister, L. (1983). Drug abuse in the United States: The past decade. *Drug and Alcohol Dependence*, 11: 49–55.

NIDA (1990, 1991). *National Household Survey on Drug Abuse*. Washington, D.C.: U.S. Department of Health and Human Services.

Rogers, S. (1990). NIDA's high school senior survey also provides data on college student's drug use. *NIDA Notes*, 5(4): 16–18. DHHS Pub. (ADM) 90-1488. Washington, D.C.: U.S. Department of Health and Human Services.

Sobel, K. H. (1990a). Cocaine-related hospital emergency room visits drop 30 percent. *NIDA Notes*, 5(4): 6–7. DHHS Pub. (ADM) 90-1488. Washington, D.C.: U.S. Department of Health and Human Services.

Sobel, K. H. (1990b). NIDA-funded survey finds American's antidrug attitudes on the rise. *NIDA Notes*, 5(4): 15. DHHS Pub. (ADM) 90-1488. Washington, D.C.: U.S. Department of Health and Human Services.

DEFINITIONS AND DRUG TERMINOLOGY

Models are created to help explain phenomena in a logical format. There are numerous models used to study drug abuse. One is the moral-legal model, which operates from the premise that the answer to drug abuse problems is to keep drugs away from people. In this model drugs are classified as either safe or dangerous. The "dangerous" category includes not only drugs that are physically dangerous but also those that are not socially or legally sanctioned. Drugs are the active ingredient; people are the deviant victims who must be protected. Protection comes in the form of legal controls on cultivation, manufacture, distribution, and possession. The deterrents are punishment and fear of harm. The major difference between the legal-moral model and the disease or public health model is that the latter dwells less on the legality of the substance and more on its potential harm and assumes that drug use or abuse occurs from the interaction of host, agent, and environment and, over time, becomes a disease or epidemic.

Two additional models, the psychosocial model and the sociocultural model, operate from the premise that the object is to keep people away from drugs. The psychosocial model tends to put major emphasis on the individual rather than on the substance as the active agent. Drug use is seen as another behavior that persists because it serves some purpose for the individual. This model makes important distinctions among different use patterns, attitudes, and behaviors.

The sociocultural model views drug use and the problems associated with drug abuse in the social context, emphasizing environmental and socioeconomic conditions. Poverty, poor housing, discrimination, lack of opportunity, urbanization, and so on are all seen as the breeding ground of the personal factors that ultimately lead to drug use.

In each model the tactics designed to reduce drug use are slanted toward the specific philosophical bias of the model. The main tactic may be punishment, control, threat, reduction of need, or restructuring of the environment. Each model defines the goals of specific attempts to influence drug use. Although the recognized bias in this book is toward the psychosocial approach, the other models do receive attention so that the reader can realize the place and importance of each and put together a composite picture of drug use and abuse.

DRUG TERMINOLOGY

The scientific definition of a *drug* is that it is a substance that, by its chemical nature, affects the structure or function of a living organism. This definition covers almost everything that people ingest, inhale, inject, or absorb. It includes medicines, over-the-counter drugs, illegal drugs, beverages, cigarettes, food additives, industrial chemicals, and even food. Therefore, any discussion of drugs must be somehow limited. For this book the emphasis will be on *psychoactive drugs,* drugs that alter behavior. The taking of drugs to the extent that they cause social or medical harm to the taker is termed *drug abuse*.

Medicine denotes a drug taken into the body to prevent or cure a disease or disabling condition.

Addiction and Dependence

Opiate dependence was one of the earliest problems associated with drug abuse in the United States, and much of the early drug terminology came from defining and treating that problem. The World Health Organization (WHO) described addiction as a condition in which the addict is committed to a drug physically and mentally, has developed tolerance to the drug, and is a societal problem. It was learned, however, that some of the new drugs did not produce the same physical dependence as the depressant drugs (and thus did not present the same classic withdrawal as seen with the opiates), but the mental drive to take them was still overpowering. Hence, the term "psychological dependence" (or "psychic dependence") was coined. *Psychological dependence* was defined as a strong desire or compulsion to continue the use of a psychoactive drug, a craving for repetition of the pleasurable, euphoric effects of the substance. There are no commonly used psychoactive drugs that are not capable of producing psychological dependence.

During the 1970s and 1980s efforts were made to substitute the words "chemical dependency," "physical dependency," and "psychological dependency" wherever possible in order to disenfranchise the term "addiction." Discouragement of the use of the latter term was meant to help change society's stereotyped picture of the addict as a criminal so that we would begin to treat dependence on drugs as a disease. The terms "addict" and "addiction" are once again common in the literature, being related not only to drugs, but also to eating, gambling, exercise, working, relationships, and other behaviors that may fall within the psychiatric definition of addiction or dependence.

According to the American Psychiatric Association (APA, 1980) definition of addiction, if individuals meet three or more of the nine criteria listed below, they should be classified as "addicted."

1 The individual takes a substance (or does the behavior) more than originally intended.

2 The individual wants to cut back or has tried to cut back but failed.

3 The individual spends a great deal of time trying to get the substance or set up the activity, taking the substance or doing the activity, or recovering.

4 The individual is often intoxicated or suffers withdrawal symptoms when expected to fulfill obligations at work, school, or home.

5 The individual curtails or gives up important social, occupational, or recreational acts because of the substance or activity.

6 The individual uses the substance or does the activity despite persistent social, psychological, or physical problems caused by the substance or activity.

7 The individual needs more and more of the substance or activity to achieve the same effect (tolerance).

8 The individual suffers characteristic withdrawal symptoms when the activity or substance is discontinued (cravings, anxiety, depression, jitters).

9 The individual takes the substance or does the activity to relieve or void withdrawal symptoms.

Figure 1 diagrams the pattern of addiction.

Stanley Peele, in *Love and Addiction* (Peele, 1975), gave an in-depth description of addiction as a human reaction to drugs and many other experiences as well. He described addiction as an attachment to an object, person, or sensation that is so strong that the person's appreciation of and ability to attend to other things in the environment or within the self diminishes to such a degree that he or she becomes dependent on that experience as the sole source of gratification.

FIGURE 1
The pattern of addiction.

PSYCHOLOGICAL DEPENDENCE
Escape

TOLERANCE
Adaptation
Enzyme production
Neurohormone production
Learning process

PHYSICAL DEPENDENCE
Depression of CNS
Depression of neurohormone production
Depression of stress reaction

ADDICTION

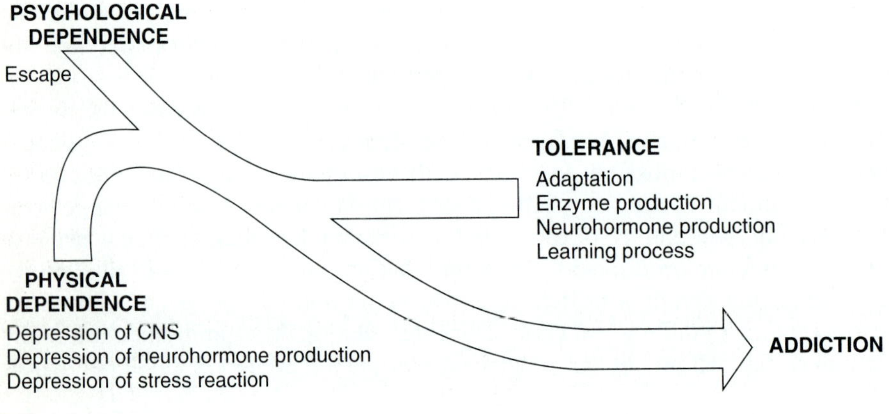

It is becoming increasingly apparent that drug addiction has at least four basic aspects.

1 *The drug.* Drugs that produce the most instantaneous euphoria, a shorter period of effects, a long period between the effects and any negative consequences, and a painful crash are those most likely to be highly addicting. Nicotine, crack (smoked cocaine), and Ice (smoked methamphetamine) are highest on the addictiveness scale.

2 *Biological makeup.* Individuals who have an alcoholic parent, use drugs for chronic pain, and have a particular sensitivity to a drug (or drugs) are more vulnerable to addiction. This may be genetically linked.

3 *Mental and emotional makeup.* Personalities that show lack of self-control, brash impulsiveness, low self-esteem, powerlessness, depression, and a lack of values that constrain drug use are more likely to succumb to addiction (Franklin, 1990).

4 *Environment.* People who live in barren surroundings (e.g., slums, prisons), have few social guidelines for acceptable use of drugs, have easy access to drugs, are isolated or aliented from family and friends, and/or whose friends are drug abusers are more likely to use drugs in excess.

Once the mental form of dependence (or addiction) was designated, the term "physical dependence" also came into being. This denoted that the body developed a cellular demand for a specific drug. (Physical dependence can be discovered when the drug is taken away from the user and the user then develops withdrawal symptoms.) The terms "harmful abuse" and "chemical dependency" have also been used to describe drug addiction. Harmful abuse has been described by three characteristics: (1) a pattern of pathological use, (2) impairment in social or occupational functioning due to substance use, and (3) minimal duration of disturbance of at least one month. Chemical dependency is a more severe form of substance abuse because it includes evidence of either tolerance or withdrawal. Both harmful abuse and chemical dependency are possible with alcohol, barbiturates and other similar sedatives or hypnotics, tranquilizers, opiates, amphetamines, cannabis, cocaine, phencyclidine piperidine (PCP) or others with similar actions, hallucinogens, and tobacco.

Tolerance and Physical Dependence   Tolerance is an important phenomenon in the study of drug abuse. *Tolerance* is a reduction in response to repeated administration of a drug (or other addictive behavior). Traditionally, tolerance has been explained as a reduced physiological or behavioral response to the same dose of a drug with a need to increase the dose to obtain a constant effect. One important mechanism of tolerance that is understood is that the presence of a particular drug, such as a barbiturate, stimulates an increase in drug-metabolizing enzymes in the liver. As the rate of metabolism of the drug increases, the activity of the drug diminishes. This is known as *metabolic tolerance.*

Cellular tolerance has also been observed. This is due to some unknown cellular adaptation in the brain whereby the receptors responsible for the drug action become less sensitive to the drug.

The concept of *learned tolerance* (also referred to as *behavioral tolerance*) stresses the importance of corollary processes, such as environmental cues, associated with the consumption of any particular drug. Individuals in the drugged state can learn to overcome some of the effects of the drug by overcompensation.

Cross-tolerance has been observed between drugs of the same general class of action. That is, consumption of one depressant drug often produces a tolerance to another depressant drug.

An enzyme theory of tolerance was proposed by Shuster (1961), who indicated that initial depression of neurohormone-producing systems (systems for production of norepinephrine, serotonin, dopamine, etc.) caused the body to overproduce these hormones so that the natural, normal (predrug) levels could be maintained. Therefore, increased drug doses would be necessary to overcome the increased levels of neurohormones. Withdrawal symptoms, then, are due to the high level of neurohormones that would be present when the depressant drug was no longer there to counteract them. As the neurohormone level diminished—or returned to normal, preaddiction levels—withdrawal symptoms would also diminsh (Goldstein, 1989).

Physical dependence is a unique biological phenomenon characterized by a metabolic demand for a particular substance. It has been described as a state of pseudohomeostasis—a hyperexcitability that develops in the cells of the central nervous system after prolonged use of depressants such as heroin, alcohol, or barbiturate-like substances or a state of depressed activity after prolonged use of cocaine. However, this phenomenon can be seen only when the drug is withheld, and symptoms known as the *abstinence syndrome* or the *withdrawal syndrome* emerge.

Theories presented to explain physical dependence generally center on (1) the production, release, and/or destruction of neurohormones. (such as norepinephrine, dopamine, or acetylcholine), (2) neuronal sensitivity, and (3) depression of endocrine function.

Because of similarities in the abstinence syndromes caused by such chemically dissimilar agents as alcohol, barbiturates, meprobamate, paraldehyde, chlordiazepoxide, and others—and because these substances have the capacity to stave off signs of withdrawal in users of other depressants, including heroin, due to cross-tolerance—one mechanism for physical dependence seems to be the depression of nervous activity in similar central nervous system pathways. This may be initial depression at the synapse followed by a gradual limiting of the production of neurohormones. As one pathway becomes depressed, other parallel, or redundant, pathways may enlarge their function and continue body processes at a somewhat depressed level. The body's amazing homeostatic or equilibrium-maintaining mechanisms (centered primarily in the hypothalamus) allow for continued functioning without triggering stress reactions. This results in a sort of disease of adaptation. This adaptation affects the endocrine glands, which are depressed and therefore do not produce the stress reactions that usually accompany altered homeostatic conditions.

Upon withdrawal from a depressant there is extreme hyperexcitability, due in part to release of depressed stress reactions and in part to restoration of depressed neural pathways. In essence, the body is now able to realize to what extent its homeostasis or equilibrium has been altered, and violent stress reactions (the classic withdrawal symptoms) are now experienced. These first appear as a sense of apprehension and general weakness, which soon develops into muscle fasciculations, tremors of the hands, hyperactive reflexes, insomnia, abdominal cramps, nausea, and vomiting. There is extreme dehydration and rapid loss of weight accompanied by increases in heart rate, blood pressure, and respiratory rate. Disorientation in time and space, hallucinations, and death are not uncommon results of withdrawal.

Some of the other terms that are useful in understanding the drug education literature are as follows:

Minimal dose: The smallest dose that is sufficient to produce an effect.

Maximal dose: The largest dose that produces an effect without producing a toxic reaction.

Average dose: The dose used successfully by the majority of people; the dose eliciting average response in the average person who is not sensitive or allergic to the drug.

Codependent: One who has a relationship with a troubled, needy, or dependent person and tries to control the behavior of that other person. The other person is often drug-dependent. The codependent continually takes care of or rescues the other person, keeping him or her from developing growth skills.

Drug effects: Multiple effects, which vary from dose level to dose level, from person to person, are greatly influenced by time and setting. Drug effects are a function of the interaction between the drug and the individual's physical, psychological, and social milieu. All drugs are dangerous for some individuals at some dose levels under some circumstances. Some drugs are more dangerous than others; some individuals are more susceptible to drugs than others.

Food and/or alcohol consumption, cigarette smoking, food additives, exposure to household or occupational chemicals, and physical activity, can alter the effect of drugs.

Genetic determinants: Biological differences influenced by genetics that are responsible for much of the physical variation in response to drugs. Such factors as drug metabolism, drug receptor synthesis, and activity that affects response may differ among individuals and may be predominant in specific races of people. Specific genetic differences in response to alcohol consumption are currently a very active area of research.

Concomitant drug use: Simultaneous use of several drugs. This can influence the absorption, distribution, metabolism, or excretion of a drug because of competition for protein binding sites or depletion of the enzymes necessary for biotransformation.

Route of administration: When a drug is injected intravenously, a high level in the blood is achieved almost immediately, but the concentration remains high for a relatively short period of time. Intramuscular (into muscles) or subcutaneous (under the skin) injections provide for a slower rise in plasma drug levels. Oral administration produces an even slower rise in plasma drug level because of the slower rate of absorption from the digestive tract. Inhalation results in a rapid onset of the drug effect.

Loading dose: A dose that "fills" the body with a drug quickly. The user obtains maximal effects without having to wait for the drug to accumulate over time from smaller doses. Once this concentration is achieved, an effective dose can be maintained by smaller maintenance doses given at regular intervals (Wartak, 1983).

Other factors related to dose: There are numerous factors that alter the response to drugs and must be considered when using drugs. Some of the most important factors are:

Age: Children show significant differences in absorption, distribution, metabolic sensitivity, and excretion of most drugs. Likewise, persons over 60 require lower dosages of most drugs.

Size: Underweight and overweight adults also show differences in drug effect. The average effects are often measured on a 70-kilogram (154-pound) adult. The same dose consumed by a 100-pound and a 200-pound person will produce markedly different effects. Body composition is also important. Those individuals with a higher percentage of adipose tissue will have less body water; therefore, smaller amounts of the drug will be bound, and larger amounts of the drug will be free to act on sensitive tissue.

Disease: Renal disease is an important factor in that elimination of the drug or its harmful metabolites will be slowed. Liver disease also slows the biotransformation of most drugs, allowing for increased concentrations to act on sensitive tissue.

Other conditions that will affect an individual's response to drugs are heart disease, electrolyte imbalance, hypoproteinemia, thyroid disease, and gastrointestinal disorders.

The use of any drug involves risks; the choice of risk depends on the cost versus worth equation constructed by each individual. The elements that must be considered are the substance, the individual, and the socio-cultural milieu. Action based exclusively on any one element increases the risk.

REFERENCES

APA (1980). *Diagnostic and Statistical Manual of Mental Disorders*, 3d ed. (DSM-III). Washington, D.C.: American Psychiatric Association.

Franklin, Deborah (1990). Why isn't everyone an addict? *In Health,* November/December, pp. 39–52.

Goldstein, A. (Ed). (1989). *Molecular and Cellular Aspects of the Drug Addictions.* New York: Springer-Verlag.

Peele, Stanley (1975). *Love and Addiction.* New York: Signet.

Shuster, L. (1961). Repression and derepression of enzyme synthesis as a possible explanation of some aspects of drug action. *Nature,* 189: 314–315.

Wartak, J. (1983). *Clinical Pharmacokinetics.* New York: Praeger.

MOTIVATIONS FOR DRUG USE AND ABUSE

Life is a series of choices. Why so many people choose to use drugs is a question with many theories and few distinct answers. In other words, there is no one reason why people use and abuse drugs. Humans have used drugs and become dependent on them throughout history, but this century has seen drug use and abuse reach epidemic proportions. Theories that seek to explain drug-using behavior center on the predisposition certain people have to particular drugs. This may take the form of genetically determined physical factors such as metabolism, or involve problems in psychological development derived from childhood environment, or involve learning and conditioning responses and/or issues that relate to coping with the stress of living in our fast-paced high-expectation society.

STRESS AND DRUGS

Researchers have found that each drug group produces a particular psychological ego state and that chronic users choose a specific drug because of the state it induces. The drug gives them the illusion of overcoming or escaping specific kinds of problems. Although people take drugs (including alcohol) for various reasons, a common motivation is to get "high" or experience an altered state of consciousness, often in an attempt to reduce the excess stress of coping with life. Coping with stress can be considered either competent or incompetent depending on one's success. *Competent coping* is defined as remaining in control and in optimal health while meeting the demands of life. *Incompetent coping* is the inability to meet demands, or sacrificing health or control in the coping attempt. Incompetent coping is usually unhealthy physically and psychologically, as it exhausts energy reserves. Incompetent coping requires that

21

an individual recruit physical or psychological help, which often comes in the form of drugs such as stimulants (amphetamines or cocaine) for extra bursts of energy and optimism, tranquilizers and depressants to block out negative feelings, or even steroids to become bigger and stronger.

There are numerous examples of unhealthy psychological recruitment, most notably rationalization, denial, and withdrawal. Withdrawal from the world with chemical substances (mainly alcohol, marijuana, tranquilizers, and sedatives) is an easy way to alter one's state of consciousness. An *altered state* can be defined as a deviation from the "normal" state of consciousness, in which most of us communicate, are goal-directed, and have rational, cause-and-effect thinking.

When one is in an altered state of consciousness, there has been a shift from a normal, "taking-care-of-business" state to another level of consciousness. Drugs can alter states of consciousness through a continuum ranging from stimulation to depression. Depressants such as alcohol, cannabis, inhalants, barbiturates, tranquilizers, and narcotics promote withdrawal and the inability to deal with reality. Stimulants, which include cocaine (and derivatives like crack) and amphetamines (and derivatives such as Ice and "crystal meth"), promote a period of increased activity with a sense of unreal capabilities, followed by depression when reality returns. Hallucinogens like LSD, PCP, and mushrooms promote a sense of unreality, a kind of "time out" with interesting sights, sounds, and unrelated thoughts.

Figure 2 illustrates the continuum of states of consciousness.

Drugs can alter present reality. They are taken to help *do* something one feels incapable of doing or *be* something one is not. When people are comfort-

FIGURE 2
Drug and nondrug states of consciousness.

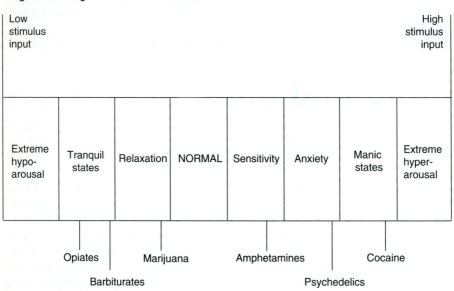

able with who they are (known as self-acceptance), they are better able to accept their performance as it is without the performance negatively impacting on the way they feel about themselves. Conversely, people who master most of life's tasks will feel good about themselves and be less inclined to alter their true perception of themselves.

People with low self-concept are uncertain and ambivalent about what they want, what they deserve, and what they can achieve. They exhibit diminished capacity to take an active role in improving their situations. In these conditions, preservation of ego necessitates survival adaptations, and they often alter their perceptions of themselves with drugs.

Children learn to use drugs as a coping mechanism the same way they learn everything else—by imitating parents, role models, and peers. Part of adopting drug-taking behavior is the expectation of and conditioning for instant gratification. Pain and discomfort are viewed as abnormalities that can and should be relieved immediately, most often with drugs. Some health authorities suggest that Americans attempt to numb themselves out of the range of normal aches and pains as well as the physical and emotional distress that occurs in the course of a normal day (Esmay & Wertheimer, 1979).

Ivan Illich (1981) pointed out that in more primitive times pain was accepted as a normal part of existence. However, in contemporary society, the medical community has attacked pain and sickness on all fronts with the promise of a pain-free existence. Being perceived as unnecessary, pain has become unbearable. This new attitude causes our culture to escape pain rather than face it. This includes psychological as well as physical pain. Thus, if we do not feel perfectly happy, we know there are drugs available for instant relief.

The contemporary practice of medicine is part of the drug promoting social learning process. Most patients expect a prescription each time they visit a physician's office, and the physician usually accomodates them. This frequently occurs because the prescription serves to legitimize the patient's illness. For example, if the patient is absent from school, work, or some other social responsibility in order to see a physician, the prescription is tangible evidence that the patient had a legitimate excuse to be absent. In the absence of a prescription, most Americans will self-medicate with over-the-counter medications. Almost every practicing pharmacist sees patients misusing prescription and over-the-counter drug products on a daily basis. This "legitimate" misuse does not go unobserved by children. Additionally, adults turn to coffee, cigarettes, and other drug products to help them cope with the difficulties of everyday life. The message that is communicated is very clear: drugs are effective, necessary, and appropriate coping mechanisms.

Drug advertising conditions potential customers from an early age. Children are given the impression that medicine has magical qualities. In a single one-minute commercial, children see the use of a drug product transforming a victim's face from distress to relief almost instantly. Parents, by their behavior, introduce their children to drug products and drug-taking behaviors. Studies of "high drug users" have indicated a higher recall of more medications in the childhood home than was reported for "low drug users." And when parents used a particular product, about 71 percent of their children also used it (Esmay & Wertheimer, 1979).

THE IRONY OF DRUG ABUSE

The irony of drug abuse is that for all the reasons people take drugs there is only one real effect, which is self-deception. Even as medication, drugs are a disappointment. It has been estimated that 80 percent of all illness episodes are self-limiting and do not require professional intervention or drugs (Hartzema, 1982). Drugs can, and usually do, provide a temporary refuge from the responsibility of "thinking and doing" during the "I am normal" state of consciousness.

A drug-induced state of consciousness is often a pleasant experience. The intensity or quality of the drug experience depends on many factors, such as when and where the drug is taken, quantity and quality of the drug, mood when taking the drug, motivation for taking the drug, general state of health (especially emotional well-being), personality, and expectations. Frustration and disappointment may develop if expectations are not met; and fear, apprehension, and injury can result if the drug is too strong or is dangerously adulterated. In either case, the drug-taking person is not really in control of the experience and is, in a sense, imprisoned in an altered state of consciousness until the drug has been metabolized. More important, drugs change but do not stop the flood of sporadic thoughts that bombard the consciousness. Consequently, the goal of quieting the mind is usually not realized.

The psychoactive drugs, both legal and illegal, that we typically consume to promote relaxation do not solve our problems. Our problems are still present and continue to stress the system. The only difference is, we have temporarily blocked the situation from the present, active, here-and-now thoughts.

Drugs can fulfill a limited goal, producing an altered state of consciousness, but they cannot fulfill the dream—that the experience would somehow give the user greater insights and the ability to transcend the ego and live a calmer, more relaxed, and more enlightened life.

The passivity of the drug experience is itself a drawback. Passive experiences in which the individual just rides along are not as satisfying or as lasting or growth-inducing as experiences in which the individual is the active, creative center. Creative activities enhance feelings of self-esteem and in turn increase motivation and readiness for future unknown ventures and provide a basis of knowledge and success for new experiences.

Altered states can be induced through such activities as meditation, daydreaming, and drug taking. They can also be induced by hypoarousal or hyperarousal of the central nervous system. It is healthier to induce these states by mind direction than by drug use. Currently, there are many popular techniques that induce a self-transcendent, altered state of consciousness through mind direction or control. Yoga, meditation, muscular relaxation, autogenic training, and biofeedback are a few examples. These techniques are a more positive option than drugs, not only because they are less dangerous, more socially acceptable, and more controllable but also because they are active and creative, requiring and promoting self-control and self-discipline. These learning exercises provide the foundation and motivation needed to reeducate and retrain thoughts and coping skills. Illich (1981) concluded that dealing with illness and pain teaches us to cope with uncertainties in life and helps us maintain a sense of individuality.

CHOOSING DRUGS

Most drug users experience an altered state of consciousness from the drug, especially if they enter the experience with that expectation. From the initial experience of an altered state the person may or may not choose to seek that experience again. If the reason for initial drug use is "just to see what it's like," the person's motivation is likely to be explained as experimental or as curiosity. If the altered state is repeatedly sought, the motivation changes—it may be for pleasure or to "be like the other kids," or perhaps to escape from a world that seems stressful. At the other end of the continuum of involvement within each class of drugs is the compulsive user or abuser. Compulsive users find that virtually every aspect of their lives revolves around obtaining, maintaining, and using a supply of the drug. These individuals (described as being drug-dependent) are controlled physically, psychologically, and socially by their drug habit. Failure to obtain the supply of drugs necessary to meet their psychological (and often physical) needs provides a strong reminder of how intensely dependent they are on the drug. Their willingness to exploit others, including those who love them the most, is a vivid reminder of how socially and psychologically dependent users can become.

Between the one-time user whose motivation is curiosity and the daily user/abuser is a continuum that can be described in terms of motivation and frequency of use (Table 1). Drug use here is motivated by peer and social pressures, a continuing need for new experiences, or heightened stimulation of pleasure. The casual user will use a drug occasionally but has no intention of

TABLE 1
TYPES OF DRUG USERS ACCORDING TO MOTIVATION, FREQUENCY OF USE, AND IMPACT

	Experimenting	Casual	Compulsive
Frequency	One or two times	Once a month to once or twice a week	Once or more per day
Motivation	Curiosity Boredom	Peer influence Pleasure Social alienation	Psychological alienation Apathy Lack of identity
Impact*	Less ◀--▶ More		

*The impact on individual, society, legal and medical establishments, and rehabilitation need.

going beyond that level of involvement. This type of person is involved in drug use but often makes a continuing conscious effort never to lose control over his or her occasional use of the drug.

Experimentation

One end of the continuum represents those who report that they have used drugs once or twice and have not engaged in any further drug experimentation. The motivator of this abbreviated drug behavior is probably curiosity, and although good preventive education may remove curiosity as a motivator, drug rehabilitation is not necessary. There exists in all of us an intrinsic desire to experience the unknown, and this desire is especially pronounced during the ages of strong peer influence, when many of a youngster's friends are experiencing drugs. Contradictions regarding psychological effects and medical hazards that are constantly seen in news reports also enhance the desire to discover something of the unknown. Experimental users are much less likely than casual or heavier users to use multiple drugs.

Casual Use

The next category is casual use, and the motivation is that of peer influence, pleasure, and perhaps social alienation (see Table 1). Pleasure or recreation can be viewed as the antithesis of boredom. One could say that these individuals take drugs to have fun, to escape from boredom, and to experience a different kind of awareness. The frequency paralleling this motivation falls between once a month and once or twice a week. Pleasure motivation can be viewed in two ways:

1 *Drugs* for *pleasure:* The use of drugs at a social affair as refreshments or for the purpose of augmenting sociability. In this situation, social interaction is the main goal or pleasure being sought; that is, the drug is a means to an end. One would no longer be able to enjoy the party if a disabling high developed.

2 *Drugs* as *pleasure:* The use of drugs for pleasure and as an end in itself, such as the heightened sensitivity one might experience from smoking marijuana.

If either pleasure-motivation form were to become compulsive, it would depart from the realm of recreation.

Peer Influence

According to theories of social conformity, peer influence is the degree to which persons or groups influence the behavior or attitudes of others. This may take the form of mere compliance, which is outward action without consideration of private conviction; or it may take the form of private acceptance, which is a change of attitude in the direction of group attitudes (Kiesler & Kiesler, 1970). The formation of private acceptance resulting from group compliance is subtle and not readily discerned, nor is it readily admitted by the individual that his or her attitude toward drugs and drug-taking behavior patterns developed from the influence of peers.

Adolescents whose friends use drugs are much more likely to use them than those whose peers do not. Having friends who are drug users is one of the strongest predictors of drug use, as initiation into drug use is usually through friends. Adolescents who are not interested in scholastic or academic achievement are more likely to use drugs than those who are. Adolescents who feel alienated and strongly rebellious, at odds with the dominant social values during early adolescence, and who exhibit a low sense of social responsibility and engage in school misbehavior, fighting, and other types of aggression, have been found to be more common among drug abusers.

It is recognized that locus of control is an important aspect in drug dependency. Locus of control is determined by exploring how one links behavior with reward. People who are internally directed believe that rewards are due to their own behavior. Their motivation comes from within and is based on personal values and satisfactions. The source of inner direction seems to originate early in life, fostered by parents and further influenced by others in authority as the child develops. People who are externally directed believe that rewards are independent of their own actions and are controlled by forces outside themselves, so they are motivated by the drive to perform to meet the needs, expectations, and values of others in the hope of being rewarded. Approval by others becomes their highest goal, and their primary method of obtaining it is by manipulation.

In analyzing peer-influenced use of drugs, it should be noted that the weaker the ego structure of the individual, the more externally motivated he or she becomes. In this case, motivation may subtly shift from social alienation to a deeper problem of self-identity; hence, treatment becomes necessary for that individual.

Compulsive Use

Although compulsive users constitute only a small proportion of the overall population, they consume a disproportionate share of the drugs and constitute a disproportionately large part of the "drug problem." The etiology of a compulsive user may be followed from the drug experimenter who likes the effects of the drug, begins as a casual user who finds psychological needs being met, and then drifts or charges into compulsive use. The psychological motivations usually are not the original reasons for drug experimentation, but they persist as the motivation for abuse once a susceptible individual has experimented with various types of drugs. Susceptibility is a key factor in determining whether any one individual will end up abusing drugs or just being a casual user.

Susceptibility may result from the powerlessness some individuals feel arising from race, sex, age, and social-class discrimination. Discrimination may be seen in the negative response some individuals have toward the handicapped, poor children, and minority children. This response can initiate the endless self-fulfilling prophecy of defeat and powerlessness. These are but a few of the cultural maladies thay may form the backdrop for the deep-seated psychological problems we see in drug abusers. Drug takers who reach this stage generally follow a pattern of alcohol and/or marijuana use, then speed, cocaine/crack, sometimes psychedelics, and then the strong depressants such as barbiturates and nonbarbiturate sedatives, alcohol, and/or opiates. The most common type of problem user is a person who uses multiple drugs, often simultaneously.

Although different individuals may be affected differently by any given drug, each drug has a range of fairly predictable specific pharmacological effects. Thus, when we think of marijuana, we think of the calming effect described by users as "mellowing out." Taking depressants such as alcohol or opiates may symbolize depression or withdrawal from the world. When we think of cocaine we usually think of its ability to stimulate, sometimes described by users as "being wired" on cocaine. However, a compulsive cocaine user often uses other drugs, such as alcohol and marijuana, simultaneously with cocaine to moderate or counteract its undesired effects. It is this drug use pattern that makes it difficult to link the use of a specific drug with one motivation or one personality type.

Drug rehabilitation research throughout the country has clearly documented the lack of self-identity as a deep-seated aspect of drug abuse, and many rehabilitation programs in the United States are aimed specifically at the formation of a positive identity within the individual. Another psychological problem—call it alienation, estrangement, indifference, or anomie—is the withdrawal of an individual into a lonely, hopeless inner world. To the psychologically alienated, drugs become a suicide equivalent, and unless society somehow intervenes, these individuals eventually subject themselves to a lethal overdose.

It is clear that the two psychological problems of apathy and lack of identity dominate the drug rehabilitation treatment efforts. They are the most difficult of drug-taking motivations to treat because therapy involves the reshaping of a personality that is as old as the individual being treated. "Rehabilitation" seems a misnomer in such a case, because it is hard to prove that "habilitation" preceded this state. Motivation for most of life's endeavors can be viewed on a continuum between achievement motivation at one pole and fear-of-failure motivation at the other. From repeatedly challenging and experiencing, we grow and learn to be independent. On the other hand, when we are motivated out of fear of failure, we isolate ourselves from experiencing and growing because we do not see new situations as opportunities to succeed and accomplish—we see them, instead, as threats and as the disgrace that will befall us when we fail. This motivation feeds on itself because the more we withdraw from growth experiences, the less capable we become of handling new situations. Peele (1975) pointed out that drugs are usually not addictive when they serve as a means of fulfilling a larger purpose in life, such as increased self-awareness, expanding consciousness, or just plain enjoyment. But drugs are addictive when they are taken in order to hide from life or to remain untouched by the social order, and they become the sole source of gratification for the person who has chosen not to grow and not to control his or her own destiny. In reality, increased self-awareness and expanding consciousness are *not* outcomes associated with drug use.

REFERENCES

Esmay, Julie B., and Wertheimer, Albert I. (1979). A review of over-the-counter drug therapy. *Journal of Community Health,* 23:54.

Hartzema, Abraham G. (1982). Self-medication. *Pharmacy International,* February, pp. 57–59.

Ilich, Iran (1981). *Medical Nemesis, the Nation's Health.* San Francisco: Boyd and Fraser.

Kiesler, C. A., and Kiesler, S. B. (1970). *Conformity.* Reading, Mass.: Addison-Wesley.

Peele, S. (1975). *Love and Addiction.* New York: Signet.

PHYSIOLOGICAL BASIS OF DRUG ACTION ON THE CENTRAL NERVOUS SYSTEM

Normal function of the nervous system makes it possible for the reader to pick up this book, maneuver its pages, coordinate eyesight, be aware of the book's weight, and, most important, decipher the meaning of the words, which have been arranged in statements and ideas. Were it not for the integrative function of the brain controlling the action of the billions of nerve cells throughout the body, neither action nor thought would be possible. One's behavior is the result of the brain's interpretation of all incoming nerve impulses. These impulses can be depressed, intensified, or distorted by chemical substances—substances known as drugs. A basic facet of the study of drugs is the action of these substances on the central nervous system.

THE NERVE CELL

The nervous system, like every other system in the body, is composed of specialized cells. The specialized cell of the nervous system is the nerve cell, or neuron. The neuron is an electrochemical unit with its action dependent on the constant flow of chemical-carrying electric charges. The action of many drugs can be explained merely by their presence inside the nerve cell. The chemical similarity between some of the currently popular drugs and natural body chemicals may explain how drugs get inside the nerve cell.

To better understand how these foreign chemicals alter nerve cell function, consider the basic structure and function of nerve cells. Although these cells vary in shape and size according to their location and basic neural function, they typically consist of a number of impulse-receiving branches called dendrites and one impulse-sending branch, the axon. The body of the cell also receives stimuli from other axons (Figure 3). One nerve cell may receive

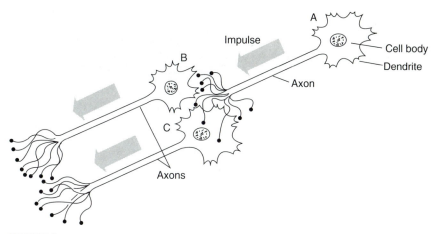

FIGURE 3
Nerve Cell A receives an impulse through its dendrites and/or cell body and sends it on through the axon. The axon of Cell A sends its impulses to Cell B via a dendrite, and to Cell C via the cell body. Cells B and C send impulses via their axons to other cells.

impulses from hundreds of different axons, some of them excitatory and some of them inhibitory. Summation of like impulses (excitatory or inhibitory) then causes the nerve cell to "fire" or remain inactive.

TRANSMISSION OF THE NERVE IMPULSE

A unique feature of nerve cells is that they do not come into direct physical contact with one another. They are separated by a microscopic space. This space, known as the synaptic cleft, prevents the continuous flow of impulses and becomes the focal point of the discussion of drug action on the nervous system (Figure 4).

By analogy, the synapse serves as a switch for electric current. If conditions at the synapse are biochemically correct for the regular propagation of the nerve impulse, the switch is "on." Some drugs turn this switch on themselves, and extra nerve impulses are emitted. If conditions are not normal—for example, because of the presence of a depressant drug or fatigue—the switch is "off."

At the end of the axon (the bouton) there are certain chemicals located in small pockets called vesicles that appear to be crucial in transmitting the nerve impulse to the next nerve cell. These chemicals are called *neurohormonal transmitter substances*. Some of these substances that have been identified are acetylcholine, norepinephrine, serotonin, dopamine, and γ-amino butyric acid, or GABA. In addition to these neurotransmitters, there are a number of CNS (central nervous system) hormones that may act as neurohormonal transmitters as well as carry out their roles as hormones. It is also suggested that various polypeptides (groups of amino acids) called endorphins, enkephalins, and Substance P may function in the brain as neurotransmitters.

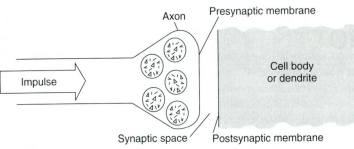

FIGURE 4
The synapse is a microscopic space between the axon and the next nerve cell. The nerve impulse coming down the axon must jump the synaptic space if the impulse is to be carried on.

Each nerve axon contains one of these transmitter substances, and the hypothesized action of the neurotransmitter is as follows. The incoming nerve impulse causes the vesicles containing the transmitter substance to join with the membrane at the end of the axon (the presynaptic membrane), as shown in Figure 5. Upon fusing with the presynaptic membrane, the vesicles open up and release the neurohormone into the synaptic cleft, the space between the presynaptic membrane and the membrane of the next cell, the postsynaptic membrane (Figure 6).

The neurohormone has within its chemical makeup the ability to alter the postsynaptic membrane. When this alteration takes place, electrochemical reactions occur, which recreate a nerve impulse of the same intensity as the one that came through the preceding axon.

Nerve impulses, then, are due to electric current that proceeds through the cell body to the axon, where it causes chemical events to occur due to movement of electrically charged ions such as sodium and potassium. These chemical events at the synapse in turn re-create the electrical activity necessary to carry the impulse to the next cell.

Proper function of the CNS may depend on the interaction of the various peptides and neurotransmitter systems that control pituitary secretion, functions of the limbic system and motor centers, and other parts of the brain that govern the overt responses that we call "behavior."

FIGURE 5
The electric nerve impulse causes the vesicles to move toward the presynaptic membrane.

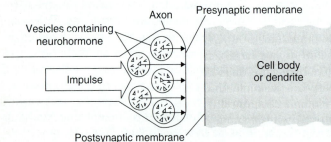

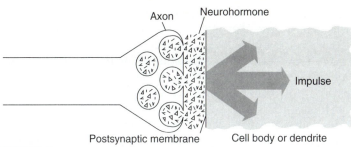

FIGURE 6
Neurohormonal transmitter substance is released into the synaptic space and alters the post-synaptic membrane, allowing electrochemical events to occur which re-create the nerve impulse.

DRUGS AND NERVE TRANSMISSION

Even though we generally understand that each part of the brain serves a specific function and we are beginning to understand what some of those functions are, there are two large pieces of the puzzle that need to be in place in order for us to understand CNS functioning: (1) how these various parts of the brain relate or communicate and (2) how they are activated or inhibited. The latter is of primary interest to the study of the behavioral effect of drugs. Generally speaking, drugs act on the CNS because of their ability to mimic or displace the naturally occurring neurotransmitters. Understanding the presence, nature, and action of neurotransmitters and the "look-alike" drugs should help in understanding the behavioral effects of specific drugs.

Since the synaptic events are chemical in nature, they are vulnerable to foreign chemicals such as drugs. Looking at the synapse, consider what would happen if a drug could (1) inhibit the production of the neurohormone, (2) cause the neurohormone to be broken down more rapidly than normal, or (3) alter the postsynaptic membrane so that neurohormones would not affect it. In any of these cases, it is apparent that the nerve cell action would be inhibited because either there would be no neurohormone or it would not be allowed to work normally (Harper, 1990). It appears that this is the action of the depressant drugs (such as alcohol, narcotics, and barbiturates) when they come into contact with nerve cells in special parts of the brain (Fields, 1989).

On the other hand, consider the drugs that cause excess production and release of neurohormonal transmitter substances or have the ability to mimic the action of the neurohormone or not allow its reuptake. In these cases, the neurons involved would be stimulated at a greater than normal rate. This is the action of the stimulatory drugs on nerve cells within the brain (Higgins et al., 1989).

Neurotransmitters

Neurotransmitters are those substances that act with immediate effect on synaptic receptors to produce excitatory or inhibitory postsynaptic potentials.

Another class of substances comprises the neuromodulators. These are small peptides in the neuronal system that act as local hormones or act to aid neurotransmitters, thus giving a finer level of control.

Recent studies have found large concentrations of more than one neurotransmitter at many sites, which leads to the hypothesis that in many brain structures, perhaps in all of them, there exists a concurrent modulation by more than one neurotransmitter. Such a system of multiple neurotransmitters acting in combination, which questions the one-neuron–one-transmitter theory known as Dale's principle, gives further evidence of the versatility and redundancy of the CNS (Chronister & DeFrance, 1981).

The reason for this multiplicity of neurotransmitters is not known; however, one hypothesis is that it represents a mechanism for increasing the fine control over thoughts and actions. The synaptic junction is more than an on-off switch. It is more like a dimmer switch that has hundreds of potential set points. Some neurotransmitters are degraded rapidly, whereas others stay at the site longer. Thus, excitatory or inhibitory responses evoked by neurotransmitters can vary from fractions of a millisecond to hundreds of milliseconds. The result is the flexibility and precision exhibited by the CNS (Iversen & Iversen, 1981).

The following are the neurotransmitters and neuromodulators thought to be most important in those parts of the CNS that are especially reactive to drugs.

1 Acetylcholine: especially active in the hippocampus, neocortex, and caudate nucleus
2 Biogenic monoamines: norepinephrine, epinephrine, dopamine, and serotonin
3 Amino acids: glutamate, aspartate, GABA, and glycine
4 Neuroactive peptides (Lane et al., 1983; Donnerer et al., 1987): Substance P, VIP (vasoactive intestinal polypeptide), CCK (cholecystokinin), neurotensin, somatostatin, β-endorphin, and the enkephalins

The list of neurotransmitters and modulator substances is constantly being updated as methods of identification become more sophisticated. Examples of some recent additions are aspartic acid, which has an excitatory action similar to that of glutamate; the amine histamine, which exists in small amounts in specific locations in the CNS; Substance P and somatostatin, found in the primary sensory fibers; and the enkephalins and β-endorphins, widely distributed in the CNS areas associated with the control of pain (Emson, 1983; Hughes, 1978).

Immunotransmitters

The discussion of neurotransmitters is incomplete without a brief look at immunotransmitters and how the neurohormones of the brain work back and forth with the immune system. Stem cells in the bone marrow are released through the blood to the lymph tissues and to the thymus (the control center of the immune system). In the thymus the stem cells become T-lymphocyte cells, which directly attack antigens (foreign agents in the body, such as a bacteria). T-cells have receptor sites that are sensitive to neurotransmitters and hormones of the nervous system and other parts of the body (Rossi, 1986).

Psychoneuroimmunology (PNI) is the study of how the mind and nerves communicate with the immune system. PNI research in the 1980s clearly identified that behavior and mood states have an effect on the strength of the immune system: negative moods, stress, anxiety, and depression diminish the strength of the system, while positive, energetic moods enhance the strength of the immune system (Solomon, 1985). The T-cells "speak" to the other parts of the body, especially the hypothalamus and the autonomic and endocrine systems, through immunotransmitters such as ACTH (adenocorticotropic hormone, the hormone that alerts the adrenal glands during times of stress), TSH (thyroid-stimulating hormone), endorphins, and thymosins. It is through these hormones that the immune system tells the rest of the body to "gear up" for an attack, and they are perhaps responsible for that unnamed feeling of knowing when you are getting sick (Wechsler, 1987).

The stem cells that migrate to the lymph tissues become B-cells, which are also sensitive to neurotransmitters and hormones of the nervous system and other parts of the body. In the blood, when B-cells come into contact with an antigen, they become plasma cells that produce antibodies specific to the invading antigen. The antibodies attack the antigens and render them harmless. T-cells stimulate or suppress B-cells via immunotransmitters, thereby giving the thymus full control of both cellular and humoral immunity (Rossi, 1986).

ORGANIZATION OF THE NERVOUS SYSTEM

Every system of the body is involved in behavior, and every system is at least partially regulated by the brain. Sometimes this regulation is direct, through innervation of an organ; at other times it is indirect, through neural stimulation of the endocrine glands. But the brain is always involved, and thus it becomes the logical starting point in the study of the effect of drugs on behavior.

To understand the brain, it may help to use the analogy developed by noted researcher Dr. Paul Maclean of the National Institute of Mental Health, who likens the brain to an archeological site revealing three distinct layers. Each of these layers not only indicates a stage in evolutionary development but also describes units of functional differentiation, each of which demonstrates a distinctly different type of behavior that the body is capable of exhibiting.

Phylogenetically, the oldest part of the brain is found in the lower centers, nearest the spinal cord. For simplicity's sake, these will be referred to as the *brainstem* or *hindbrain*, although this discussion refers more to functional units, which transcend the anatomical boundaries typically found in anatomy textbooks. These are simple structures (if there is such a thing in the brain) in the sense that they are reflex in nature, with the primary function of preserving the self and the species. We are referring here to structures such as the spinal cord; the coordination centers of the cerebellum; the medulla oblongata with its cardiovascular, respiratory, and vasomotor centers; the transmitting network of the pons; the integrating interconnecting network of the thalamus; and the visceral regulating centers for hunger, thirst, body temperature, rage, pain, and pleasure of the hypothalamus.

If humans resemble any other animal species, it is due to basic programs stored within these lower centers. The actions or behavior governed by these centers are natural, direct, and open, without learned inhibition. Activities centered on keeping alive, procreating, preparing a home site, establishing and defending territory, hunting, hoarding, forming simple social groups, and performing daily activities are instinctive and exist in lower animals as well as in humans.

Perhaps to ensure survival, a new layer of brain tissue that enabled a modification or refinement of the basic instincts evolved or appeared in the so-called higher animals. This new layer, called the *limbic system* (from the Latin for "border"), is wrapped around the old layer and is often referred to as the interbrain, since it has structures that communicate with both the higher and lower brains.

Animals that evolved to the second layer, or limbic system, were further ensured of survival, for not only did they have basic survival instincts, but now they added a measure of freedom from ancestral stereotyped behavior. They could think and act on emotions and approach new situations with additional abilities. Primarily, the limbic system added feeling and emotion, which further ensured attendance to basic survival activities, ostensibly by making some activities pleasurable and others unpleasurable. Feelings such as fear, anger, and love attached to external situations guided behavior toward that which protected and away from that which was threatening. Understandably, two of our major neural pathways (those governing oral and genital behaviors) have intricate connections to the pleasure and displeasure centers of the limbic system. The concepts of reward-pleasure and punishment-unpleasure are important to drug-related behavior and seem, to a large extent, to be centered in this area. Numerous researchers have been able to stimulate electrically various parts of the limbic system and elicit both the pleasure and unpleasure responses.

The brain continued to develop with the addition of a third layer called the *cortex, neocortex,* or *forebrain* and reached the ultimate of development in humans. The addition of the vast number of cortical cells allowed the development and storage of analytical skills, verbal communication, writing ability, empathy, fine motor control, additional emotion, memory, learning, and rational thought and gave a new dimension to problem-solving and survival abilities. New dimensions were added to basic oral and sexual behaviors, and vision replaced olfaction as the primary sense. Reactions could be more than reflex, and, for better or for worse, reality could be determined by perception, which is unique to each individual. Behavior could be measured in relation to possible outcomes. Symbolism, goals, motivation, and anticipation became part of the functioning human being.

DRUGS AND THE BRAIN

The brain controls and integrates all human movement and behavior, and nearly all drugs of abuse modify behavior by their action on the brain and brainstem. Behavior modifications caused by drugs, resulting in uncontrollable emotions, restricted information storage, limited capability for decision making, and other uncontrolled behavior, have led us to the study of how the various areas of the brain react to drugs. If one understands what events are taking place at the cellular level and at higher, more sophisticated levels, one can understand more easily why certain behavior occurs.

The brain and brainstem consist of a number of different structures concerned with the control of specific actions, thought, and emotions. Figure 7 depicts the brain and brainstem down to the spinal cord. Alteration of the nerve cell transmissions within these areas affects both mental and physical behavior. Drugs are known to affect these areas, but many drugs are specific to certain structures; thus, each drug causes particular behavioral characteristics. Drug dosage is an important consideration; light doses of a drug may cause little or no behavioral change, whereas very large doses may cause death.

Drugs reach the central nervous system by way of the circulating blood, in general (depending on the physical properties of the drug itself), the faster the drug enters the bloodstream, the more rapidly its effects are felt. Drugs injected into a vein travel directly to the heart and are circulated throughout the system immediately. Inhaled drugs enter the bloodstream a little less rapidly because the chemicals involved must enter capillaries in the lungs. In general, ingested drugs take even longer, because they must first dissolve and are often mixed with food products, thus slowing absorption into the blood supplying the digestive area.

Once the drug enters the nervous tissue of the brain, various reactions may occur, because different drugs appear to have different target areas. Because of this specificity of drug action on the various parts of the central nervous system, the following paragraphs are designed to elaborate on the main func-

FIGURE 7
The brain and brainstem.

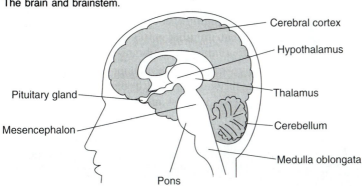

tions of each major area of the brain and brainstem. Once the normal function is known, it becomes easier to determine logically what would happen if the action of a specific area were depressed by alcohol or a barbiturate, or if the cell action of that area were stimulated with cocaine or an amphetamine.

The Brainstem (Vital Centers)

Medulla oblongata, pons, and mesencephalon—these three structures are mainly nerve fiber bundles, or tracts, that carry messages between the spinal cord and the brain.

The medulla is of special interest because it contains the respiratory, cardiac, and vasomotor centers. When drugs completely depress this area, death occurs as a result of respiratory failure. It is now known that opioid recepter sites are located in the medulla, making this a site of pain modulation (Fields et al., 1988).

The Thalamus (Stimulus Relay)

The thalamus is the "switchboard" of the brain; all "incoming" and "outgoing" calls pass through this area. The thalamus serves four important "switchboard" functions (Figure 8).

1 It serves as a transmitter of sensory impulses from other parts of the body to the sensory areas of the brain. Specialized groups of cells do this work. These cells are analogous to switchboard operators who take incoming calls and know to what specific department (or specific sensory brain cells) to transfer the calls.

FIGURE 8
Schematic illustration of thalamic function.

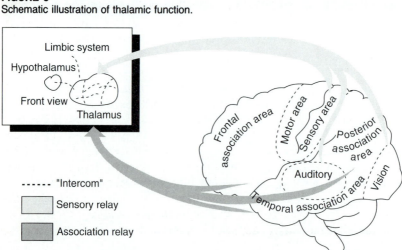

2 Another special task of the thalamus is much like the first except that the "incoming calls" are put through to the association areas of the brain. Again, specialized cell groups (called nuclei) send specific messages to specific brain areas.

3 The third function is communication among subcortical areas. In our analogy this is the "intercom system." In reality, these specialized cells communicate with other thalmic areas, the hypothalamus, and the limbic system.

4 In addition to the other three functions, the thalamus serves as a relay of motor impulses back to the body.

Because of the nerve tracts, or bundles of nerve fibers, that serve as direct connections between the thalamus and the cerebral cortex, it is thought that the neocortex is the evolutionary outgrowth of the thalamus.

The Hypothalamus (Homeostasis)

This interesting structure may hold the answers to many of the mysteries concerning behavior. The hypothalamus continuously maintains body temperature, regulates the production of hormones, maintains water balance in the body, and gauges nutritional needs, sexual needs, and countless other automatic bodily functions. Exciting investigations regarding the endorphins and enkephalins, morphinelike substances of the brain, lead us to believe that this portion of the CNS produces its own analgesic (Fields, 1989). The level of these naturally occurring painkillers appears to be exceptionally high in the hypothalamus and limbic structures—areas involved in emotionality and stress responses (Doane & Livingston, 1986). These substances appear to produce the same pharmacological responses in animals as do various opiates and hold promise in the treatment of mental illness (Fields, 1989).

Perhaps the two most important areas of interest concerning the hypothalamus in relation to drug abuse are those of (1) pleasure and pain and (2) hunger and satiety. It has been found through experimental studies that there are specific areas of the hypothalamus that elicit a quite distinctive pleasure sensation when experimentally stimulated, and there are cells that elicit pain when stimulated. These pleasure and pain areas are very important in drug use and abuse, for some drugs elicit an intense euphoria that is thought to be the result of the stimulation of cells in these hypothalamic pleasure areas or the depression of cells in the corresponding pain centers.

Just as there are pleasure and pain areas in the hypothalamus, it has been found that there are also hunger and satiety centers. As one would expect, when hunger cells are stimulated the body feels the desire for food. When electrodes are implanted in these areas in experimental animals, repeated electrical stimulation causes the animal to eat itself into obesity. Conversely, if this area is destroyed, the animal starves itself to death. It appears that amphetamine diet pills work on both the hypothalamic satiety centers and the pleasure areas, because they depress hunger and pep up the individual (Griffith, 1988).

Integrated emotional behavior is controlled to some extent by the hypothalamus; in fact, it has been shown through animal experimentation that unless the hypothalamus is intact, fully developed rage cannot be elicited. Electrical stimulation of the medial portion of the hypothalamus provokes affective defense reactions, including direct attack on the object closest at hand; upon termination of the stimulation, this action ceases immediately (Bloom et al., 1985). In addition to controlling the emotional reaction of rage, the anterior hypothalamus appears to produce fear behavior, and stimulation of the posterior area yields alertness and curiosity.

Whereas stimulation of some areas of the hypothalamus has been found to bring about fear, pain, defense, and escape reactions, it is of great interest and importance to discover that stimulation of other areas soothes an animal. Stimulation of these areas brings about reactions akin to pleasure in experimental animals; hence, these areas have been dubbed the "pleasure" or "reward" centers. Experimentation has shown that when animals are allowed to self-stimulate this center, they often choose this self-stimulation over various delectable rewards. Experimental animals have been known to repeat self-stimulation of the pleasure center up to 4,000 times an hour! However, experimental stimulation of pain centers can inhibit the pleasure centers; indeed, prolonged stimulation of pain centers may cause severe illness and may eventually lead to the death of the animal (Bloom et al., 1985).

In relating the hypothalamic pleasure–pain control centers with the hypothalamic autonomic control centers (control over blood pressure, hydrochloric acid secretion, etc.), it becomes apparent how so-called psychosomatic diseases might be brought about. Chronic stimulation of pain centers in monkeys has produced ulcers in those animals.

The scientific study of drug action on the pleasure center could be very important in studying psychological dependence on certain drugs. For example, amphetamine action on the pleasure center has been found to facilitate the self-stimulation responsiveness of rats. Control studies showed that facilitation was due to the greater reinforcement value of the stimulus rather than just heightened bodily activity, which is known to occur as a result of amphetamine administration. It has been hypothesized that the amphetamine mimicked the action of (or affected the release of) norepinephrine, the chemical transmitter substance of nerve endings in this hypothalamic area. This illustrates that amphetamines do excite the pleasure area and thus makes it easier to understand why individuals may desire to take this type of drug repeatedly (Fields, 1989).

It is difficult to summarize the function of this underrated structure, the hypothalamus, because it is so all-encompassing, controlling such aspects of bodily behavior as homeostasis, feeding and drinking behavior, emotional behavior, wakefulness, sexual behavior, combinations of these, and perhaps many unknown aspects. It is beyond anyone's ability to specify detailed hypothalamic reactions to the various drugs of abuse and the human behavior resulting from these reactions, because science has not yet provided much information. However, if one applies his or her knowledge of the action of depressant drugs, stimulants, or hallucinogens to the general knowledge of hypothalamic function presented here, greater insight into drug-induced behavior is possible.

The Limbic System (Emotional Memory and Behavior)

The limbic system (Figure 9) is a rim of cortical tissue associated with deep rhinencephalic structures. It is phylogenetically the oldest portion of the cerebral cortex, with few direct connections with the neocortex, the newest portion of the brain. In drug studies, the areas comprising the limbic system have often shown a high concentration of the drug and thus are thought to be effective in altering behavior. This system is in direct neural contact with the thalamus and the hypothalamus, which are often included in discussions as parts of the limbic system (Doane & Livingston, 1986).

Early scientific investigation of the limbic system showed that electrode stimulation in various areas of the system would elicit changes in blood pressure, heart rate, sexual behavior, eating patterns, and many other physiological responses. This information led to a belief that the limbic system also possesses (along with the hypothalamus and other old-brain structures) specific autonomic nervous system nuclei. It is now believed that excitation of limbic areas causes efferent stimulation of lower brain centers, especially the hypothalamus, which control the various physiological responses that accompany emotion.

It has become apparent in only the last decade that the limbic system is the memory area of emotions. As certain situations evoke particular emotions, it is this system that provides the memory and synchronization of feelings with physiological response. If a child is afraid of the dark, this memory pattern of fear takes form in the limbic cortex, and thereafter (perhaps even into adulthood) a dark house or dark street, for example, may trigger this memory, complete with rapid heartbeat, increased breathing rate, and feelings of fear or anxiety.

FIGURE 9
The limbic system (amygdala, hippocampus, cingulate gyrus, and fornix). This system is made up of large groups of nuclei in and around the temporal areas of the cortex.

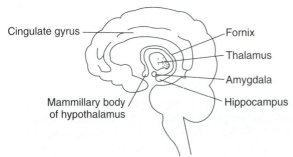

As the hypothalamus is involved when one uses pleasure-producing drugs, so too is the limbic system. If one takes a drug in a pleasurable setting or receives pleasurable feelings from the experience, its emotional content is stored in the limbic system and may become a stimulus to repeat the experience.

The Cerebral Cortex (Thought Process)

The cerebral cortex, the most recent evolutionary development of the vertebrate nervous system, is divided into a number of areas according to function (Figure 10). The two association areas are responsible for responding logically to time, environment, and social climate. The temporal association area is involved in learning processes and memory; the frontal association area is especially implicated in drug use, as this area is the first to be depressed by alcohol and other depressant drugs, thus removing social inhibitions. London (1989) found that drugs such as morphine and cocaine may temporarily disable the cerebral cortex by reducing the electrical activity of cells that serve inhibitory functions. This interferes with the ability of the cerebral cortex to govern lower areas of the brain, resulting in acting out of aggressive, sexual, or other urges, drives, and desires that are usually inhibited.

The sensory area receives impulses from the body via the thalamus and responds via the motor cortex. The visual and auditory areas integrate sight and sound into meaningful images.

Ornstein (1973) studied the role of the right cerebral hemisphere versus that of the left side and found that a unique control is elicited by each side. The functions of the right and left are dichotomized into automation and time–space orientation, respectively. That is, the left hemisphere is highly active (and the right hemisphere inactive) when one is writing, thinking through logic or math problems, conducting scientific ventures, or translating and speaking a particular language. The reverse neurological situation occurs (that is, the right hemi-

FIGURE 10
Functional areas of the cerebral cortex.

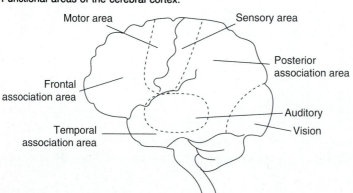

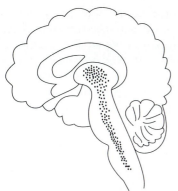

FIGURE 11
The reticular activating system (dotted area).

sphere is active and the left side inactive) when one is involved in fantasy, art, dance, and music or art appreciation. It has been suggested that drugs, meditation, and other such altered states of consciousness erode the automation through which we protect our physical and mental being and shift us into time–space orientation. The newness of this experience and the extension of one's ego boundaries make right-brain dominance a pleasurable and sought-after state.

It is obvious that drugs alter behavior, thought processes, and other reactions controlled by cortical cells. Drugs may work directly on the cortical cells, on the thalamic areas that supply information to and relay information from the cortex, or perhaps on other brain structures (such as the hypothalamus) that may be associated with cerebral function.

The Reticular Activating System (Arousal)

Even though the brain developed in three stages phylogenetically, the three areas do not function independently. Although the lower centers do attend primarily to biological survival and the higher centers permit the existence of a complex society, one cannot view the lower centers as primitive or negative, requiring control by the higher consciousness thought centers. While it is difficult to understand drug-altered behavior without knowledge of the function of each specific structure, it is impossible to conceptualize that behavior as anything but total brain integration.

The concept of upper-center–lower-center integration may be perceived best by understanding the action of the reticular system. The reticular system, often referred to as the reticular activating system or RAS because it generally controls attention and wakefulness of the brain, consists of two neural pathways. These pathways should not be conceptualized as nerve tracts, since the boundaries are not delineated in the usual anatomical sense. Functionally, the RAS is part of the neural transmitter network, which is neither sensory nor motor but internuncial and thus is a two-way street, transmitting impulses from brain to body and from body to brain (Figure 11). Nearly all signals coming to the cortex travel into the RAS; that is, impulses come into the reticular formation, synapse there, and are sent on or damped out. The function of the lower two-thirds of this system is that of arousal only. Like an alarm clock, it awakens the brain (or if awake, the brain is alerted) but gives no explanation of why it has done so. Most of us have awakened at night to find our covers off— sensations of chilliness synapse in the RAS, and this wakes up the brain. Upon first awakening, we are not sure what is wrong. Then we assess the situation for meaning and pull the covers back on. The RAS has said "Wake up," not "Wake up; your covers are off."

In the upper third of the RAS, called the thalamic portion, the decision to send on the impulse is conditional, according to whether the message is new, different, or threatening. The ability of this portion of the RAS to damp out monotonous stimuli is extremely important to our ability to concentrate on one thing at a time. Theoretically, hyperkinetic activity denotes that the neurologic function of the hyperactive person is not up to par; that is, unimportant signals are not damped out, so every sight, sound, smell, or other sensory input is sent on to the brain for attention. This produces an individual with a limited attention span who continually reacts to all new stimuli. It surprises many that stimulant drugs such as amphetamines or Ritalin are given to the hyperactive, but they are given to stimulate underactive cells of this area to produce this damping or selectivity function.

In addition to using amphetamines for this medical purpose, many take them to keep themselves awake because the RAS is aroused by their action. The continuous activation of cells in this area by impulses from muscles, sense receptors, or stimulatory drugs will keep an individual awake and alert. This is why muscle tension due to anxiety or fear may cause insomnia—the tension of the muscles neurologically stimulates the RAS, which in turn arouses the brain. Since the brain can arouse the RAS, worrying or thinking about the past or what tomorrow may bring can also cause insomnia. The theories on neuro-muscular relaxation are based on the importance of damping our RAS activity. Likewise, this is naturally the target of the sedative-hypnotics (Griffith, 1988).

The Cerebellum (Coordination)

The cerebellum controls balance and coordination of body movements by integrating the incoming messages from the motor area of the cortex, the spinal sensory nerves, the balance system of the ear, and the auditory and visual systems. Removal of the cerebellum will not cause paralysis, but rather un-coordinated movement.

DRUG ACTION: A SYNTHESIS

To summarize the hypothesized action of various drugs on the central nervous system, it is helpful to categorize some representative drugs by the action they produce.

Drugs Affecting Arousal

Amphetamines   These drugs probably mimic the effects of norepinephrine by displacing this amine from peripheral adrenergic nerve endings. In the brain they act to release both norepinephrine and dopamine from nerves containing these amines. Amphetamines may also act by displacing catecholamines from storage sites. Dopamine release is correlated with rewarding stimulation, and since these drugs release dopamine, their use can be self-rewarding.

Cocaine   Cocaine inhibits the reuptake of dopamine after it has been released into the synapse, leaving it there to continue to stimulate other cells.

Barbiturates and Nonbarbiturate Sedative-Hypnotics   These drugs probably act by slowing oxidative metabolism and depression of synaptic transmission. They generally act throughout the brain with a specific inhibition of synaptic action of the neurohormone GABA. In large doses, they suppress ongoing behavior and induce sleep. In small doses, they may increase behavioral output due to improved discriminative behavior in certain activities by blocking the overstimulation of the reticular activating system.

Alcohol   Ethanol, as a depressant capable of interacting with nerve cell membranes, can profoundly alter central nervous system function. Ethanol acts in a biphasic, dose-dependent manner. Low doses cause a state of disinhibition, whereas higher doses produce the better-known sedative effects. Many laboratory studies, attempting to define the primary sites of ethanol's short-term effect within the brain, have supported a regional hierarchy of susceptibility ranging from primary sensory neurons as least affected to association cortex and reticular formation as most affected. However, a general disruptive effect at synapses throughout the brain has not been ruled out.

Disruption of membrane protein function by changes in the enveloping lipid may be the mechanism for intoxication.

Drugs Affecting Mood

Antianxiety Drugs   The tranquilizers (i.e., the benzodiazepines) are thought to affect the brain at various levels owing to their action on the inhibitory neurotransmitter GABA. Tranquilizers narrow the range of behavioral responses to adverse stimuli.

Antidepressants   These drugs, which include the MAO inhibitors, probably act by producing a long-lasting rise in the concentration of norepinephrine (NE), dopamine (DA), and serotonin. Although the presence of more neurohormone in storage does not necessarily mean that more will be released, it is known that the monoamine oxidase (MAO) inhibitors result in a potentiation of NE and/or serotonin on the synapse.

Drugs Affecting Perception

Psychedelics The psychedelics include lysergic acid diethylamide (LSD), mescaline, and cannabis. LSD may mimic the effect of serotonin at certain synapses in the brain or slow the rate of serotonin turnover in the brain. Psychedelics can replace the present world reality with an alternative that is equally real but different. Both the drug-induced and nondrug worlds can be attended to at the same time, and there is memory for the drug-induced reality after the drug effect diminishes. Other drugs in this class, such as mescaline, bear a structural resemblance to the catecholamine transmitters.

Cannabis In addition to producing its own effects, cannabis can potentiate the depressant effects of barbiturates or the excitatory action of amphetamines. Less is known about the physiological action of cannabis itself, but it is believed that the subjective feeling of being stoned is the result of the direct action of tetrahydrocannabinol (THC) on brain cells that have a special affinity or chemical attraction for cannabinoids.

REFERENCES

Bloom, F., Lazerson, A., and Hofstadter, L. (1985). *Brain, Mind, and Behavior*. New York: W. H. Freeman.

Chronister, R. B., and DeFrance, J. F. (1981). Functional organization of monoamines. In G. C. Palmer (Ed.), *Neuropharmacology of Central Nervous System and Behavioral Disorders*. Orlando, Fla.: Academic, pp. 26–43.

Doane, B., and Livingston, K. (1986). *The Limbic System*. New York: Raven.

Donnerer, J., et al. (1987). Chemical characterization and regulation of endogenous morphine and codeine in the rat. *Journal of Pharmacology and Experimental Therapy*, 242:583–587.

Emson, P. (1983). Peptides as neurotransmitter candidates in the mammalian CNS. *Progress in Neurobiology*, 13:61–116.

Fields, H. L. (1989). Pain modulation: opiates and chronic pain. In L. S. Harris (Ed.), *Problems of Drug Dependence 1989*. NIDA Research Monograph 95. Washington, D.C.: U.S. Government Printing Office, pp. 326–331.

Fields, H. L., Barbaro, N. M., and Heinricher, M. M. (1988). Brain stem neuronal circuitry underlying the antinociceptive action of opiates. *Progress in Brain Research*, 77.

Griffith, H. W. (1988). *Complete Guide to Prescription and Non-prescription Drugs*. Los Angeles: The Body Press.

Harper, H. A. (1990). Protein and amino acid metabolism. In H. A. Harper (Ed.), *Review of Physiological Chemistry*. Los Altos, Calif.: Lange Medical Publications.

Higgins, S. T., Huges, J. R., and Bickel, W. K. (1989). Human psychopharmacology of intranasal cocaine. In L. S. Harris (Ed.), *Problems of Drug Dependence 1989*. NIDA Research Monograph 95. Washington, D.C.: U.S. Government Printing Office.

Hughes, J. (Ed.), (1978). *Centrally Acting Peptides*. London: Macmillan.

Iversen, Susan D., and Iversen, Leslie (1981). *Behavioral Pharmacology*. Oxford: Oxford University Press.

Lane, John, Smith, James E., and Fagg, Graham E. (1983). The origin and termination of neuronal pathways in mammalian brain and their putatic neurohumors. In T. E. Smith and J. D. Lane (Eds.), *The Neurobiology of Opiate Reward Processes*. Amsterdam: Elsevier Biomedical Press, pp. 158–172.

London, E. D. (1989). The effects of drug abuse on glucose metabolism. *Journal of Neuropsychiatry*, 1:S30–S36.

Ornstein, R. E. (1973). Right and left thinking. *Psychology Today*, May, pp. 87–93.

Rossi, E. (1986). *The Psychobiology of Mind-Body Healing*, New York: W. W. Norton.

Solomon, G. (1985). The emerging field of psychoneuroimmunology with a special note on AIDS. *Advances*, 2 (Winter):6–19.

Wechsler, R. (1987). The new prescription: mind over malady. *Discover*, February, pp. 51–61.

SECTION **2**

BASIC FACTS

ALCOHOL

HISTORY

Fermentation occurs naturally when sugar, water, yeast, and warm temperatures meet and continues until the sugar is used up or until the alcohol content reaches a point where it kills the yeast (at about 12 to 14 percent). In warm climates, nature may produce alcohol in the wild from fermented honey or berries, and in those places it is not uncommon to see animals seek out and partake of nature's brewery. Because of this natural process, alcohol is probably the oldest mind-altering drug used by humankind. Since earliest recorded history the drinking of fermented beverages has been known. Greek, Roman, and Egyptian mythological characters were honored for introducing wine to their respective ceremonies, and the Bible contains numerous references to the production and drinking of various kinds of fermented drinks. Literature through the ages has blessed and cursed the use of alcohol, and now alcohol is the number one drug problem in the United States, France, Russia, and many other countries around the world. Indications are that more than 18 million Americans are either alcoholics or problem drinkers whose drinking habits have adverse effects on themselves, their families, their employers, the police, and society in general. On the average, each alcoholic or problem drinker affects the lives of four family members and more than sixteen friends and business associates in the community.

CLASSIFICATION

Alcohol is classified as a depressant, and it is this depressant action that brings about most of the commonly observed consequences of drinking. A drinker may initially feel stimulated because the brain cells have been depressed, causing a release of inhibitions.

HOW TAKEN INTO THE BODY

Alcohol is ingested in the form of beers and ales, wines, and distilled spirits.

CHARACTERISTICS OF DEPENDENCE

As with all depressant drugs, tolerance builds as alcohol is ingested more often and in greater quantities, and physiological dependence may occur over a period of time. The taking of any mind-altering drug, including alcohol, may result in psychological dependence. Alcoholism, a condition that involves classical depressant dependency, affects about one in seven people in the United States. Alcoholism is considered fully in Section 3, Drug-Related Diseases and Conditions.

PHARMACOLOGY

Chemically, an alcohol is an alkyl group with a hydroxyl (OH) group attached. The representative of this chemical group that has produced a good deal of social and medical concern and detailed study is ethanol (ethyl alcohol), which is contained in all commonly ingested alcoholic beverages. Ethanol is highly fat-soluble, so it easily crosses all cell membranes, including the cells of the brain and the placenta.

Whether ethanol is produced from fermenting grapes or grains or distilled from fermented molasses, as rum is, or from fermented grains, as bourbon is, makes little difference in its effects on the body. However, if the proof of one beverage is higher than that of another, the beverage with the higher proof will be more highly intoxicating if both are drunk in equal quantities: 2 ounces of whiskey is more intoxicating than 2 ounces of beer.

The proof of a distilled beverage is its alcohol content and is expressed as roughly twice the given alcohol percentage (100 proof equals about 50 percent alcohol). A 100 proof spirit is an alcoholic beverage in which the alcohol has a specific gravity of 0.93426 at 60 degrees Fahrenheit. This is the weight of the substance compared to the weight of the same volume of water. It is said that in the early testing of alcoholic beverages the distiller mixed the whiskey with gunpowder. If the alcohol content was too low, the mixture would not light; if the whiskey was too strong, the gunpowder flamed up wildly; but if the alcohol content was near that desired, it would burn with an even, bright blue flame— this kind of flame was "proof" of good whiskey.

EFFECTS ON THE BODY

Ethanol has within its structure the chemical power to depress the action of the central nervous system. There is still much to discover regarding the way in which alcohol causes depression of central nervous system cells, but it appears to researchers that alcohol interferes with the sodium-potassium pump that is responsible for setting up the postsynaptic membrane potential. If the membrane cannot hold or reestablish its integrity, an impulse cannot pass through it—hence, the depressant action on the cell and/or system.

When alcohol is ingested, it is immediately absorbed into the bloodstream, and a rich supply of blood (15 percent of the total blood pumped per minute) is sent to the brain. In the brain, alcohol's first effects are manifested in the cerebral area and are due to the depressant action on the central nervous system. As the tissues of the brain become exposed to ethanol, the first cells to be depressed are those of the highest cortical areas, including the association areas of the cerebral cortex that house the centers of judgment, self-control, and other learned inhibitions. Thus, even small amounts of alcohol bring about some loss of inhibition. When learned inhibitions are removed from the government of behavior, antisocial behavior may occur, because inhibitions are a result of the socialization process. As children learn to live in society, they learn to control their excretory processes, their tempers, and other reactions to social and physical stimuli. They learn that it is not wise to fight with older and bigger children—not acceptable, indeed, to fight at all. They are constantly being conditioned to the sexual and moral code of those around them and are expected to behave in a certain manner. The association areas of the brain act as the guardians of logical, social behavior, so when these particular cells are removed, damaged, or chemically rendered inoperable by alcohol or other drugs, they will cease to guard learned social behavior, and drinkers will revert to more primitive behavior, the degree of reversion depending on the amount of alcohol ingested and on the drinker's temperament.

The first noticeable effects of alcohol result from depression of higher brain centers. As drinking continues, this depression spreads downward through deeper motor areas to the emotional centers buried beneath the cortex, and further down the brainstem to the most primitive areas of the brain (Figure 12). Thus, control over social inhibitions, motor coordination, speech and vision, and the waking state is progressively lost as greater amounts of alcohol are consumed. The final areas affected are those of respiration and heart rate control. Although most deaths attributed to alcohol are the result of long-term physical deterioration caused by many years of alcohol abuse, death from alcohol toxicity can also be caused within a short period of time by depression of the respiratory centers located in the medulla. The lethal level of blood alcohol in most humans is between 0.40 and 0.60 percent.

In addition to its effects on the central nervous system, alcohol has a local effect on the tissues with which it comes into contact. As alcohol is taken into the body through the digestive tract, that system is subjected to irritation and degeneration. Alcohol can damage the esophagus by direct irritation of the cellular lining, which interferes with normal muscular functioning, thereby causing stomach acid to be released up into the esophagus. The major complications are hemorrhage and difficulty in swallowing. Alcohol has also been associated with a variety of inflammatory and bleeding lesions in the stomach.

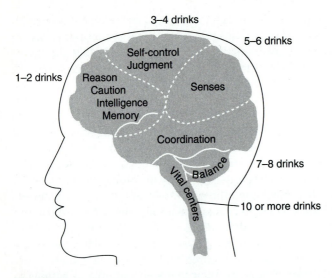

FIGURE 12
Alcohol's effects on the brain. The effects of the number of drinks are dependent on factors such as the period of time over which the drinks are consumed, the weight of the drinker, and other individual considerations. This graphic shows the general depressive effects of alcohol on the brain.

The degree of damage to the lining of the stomach appears to be related to the concentration of alcohol, with damage to the cells occurring rapidly after ingestion of especially highly concentrated drinks. In the intestines, alcohol can change the rate of peristaltic and propulsive waves. Diarrhea is frequently a problem for habitual drinkers. Intestinal malabsorption contributes to nutritional deficiencies as the uptake of calcium, iron, and vitamins is impaired. Problems associated with the pancreas and liver will be discussed later.

Ingestion and Absorption

Because alcohol is already in liquid form, it is ready for absorption into the blood immediately after ingestion. It is changed chemically in the stomach by gastric alcohol dehydrogenase, and some absorption occurs in the stomach but most of it takes place in the first foot of the small intestine. In contrast, most food has to pass far into the latter two-thirds of the small intestine before absorption takes place (Figure 13). It appears that males have more enzyme or greater enzyme activity in the stomach, which neutralizes some of the ingested alcohol. When a man and a woman drink the same amount in proportion to their size and weight, about 30 percent more alcohol enters the woman's bloodstream. The consequence of this is that women who drink heavily show more serious physical conditions (such as cirrhosis) earlier in life than men who drink heavily (Lang, 1991).

Absorption of alcohol is very rapid because it has a low molecular weight, because it is highly fat- and water-soluble, and because the bloodstream in most instances has a lesser concentration of alcohol than the stomach or intestines so it simply flows down the diffusion gradient. This rapid absorption gives the blood of the portal circulation a much higher initial concentration of alcohol than that in the remaining vascular system; however, tissues with a rich blood supply, such as the brain, liver, and kidney, quickly reach a storage equilibrium with the blood. After a period of time, other tissues of the body, such as the muscles, will reach this equilibrium also.

Alcohol diluted to 10 percent or less, as in highballs, is absorbed slowly. The most rapid absorption usually occurs with wines and the stronger mixed drinks such as martinis and manhattans, in which the percentage of alcohol is somewhere between 10 and 40 percent. Under most conditions, the drink with 40 percent alcohol would be absorbed more rapidly than the one with 10 percent because of the concentration being higher in the stomach than in the blood.

When the blood alcohol level exceeds that of the tissues, alcohol is absorbed into the tissues and exerts its depressant effect there. Even though muscle tissue absorbs alcohol, the resulting depression of muscular activity is minor; the muscle tissue, in effect, stores the alcohol. Alcohol is not absorbed in fat tissue to the same degree as in muscles, probably because of the low water and protein content of fat.

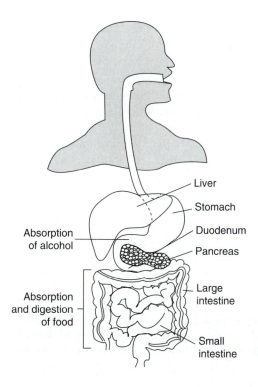

Absorption of alcohol

Absorption and digestion of food

Liver

Stomach

Duodenum

Pancreas

Large intestine

Small intestine

FIGURE 13
Absorption of food and alcohol.

TABLE 2
ALCOHOL CONTENT AND CALORIE VALUE OF VARIOUS ALCOHOLIC BEVERAGES

Beverage	Alcohol content	Approximate calories
Beer (4.5%), 12-oz can	0.54 oz	105
Highball, 1 oz whiskey, 4 oz ginger ale	0.50 oz	140
Manhattan, 1½ oz whiskey, ¾ oz sweet vermouth	0.75 oz	145
Martini, 1½ oz gin, ½ oz 12% vermouth	0.75 oz	150
Tom Collins, 1½ oz gin, lemon, sugar, mix	0.75 oz	154
100 proof scotch, gin, etc., 1 oz	0.50 oz	100
80 proof scotch, gin, etc., 1 oz	0.40 oz	80
Dinner wine (12%), 4 oz	0.50 oz	100
Dessert wine (22%), 4 oz	0.80 oz	160

Alcohol is considered a high-calorie food. Alcohol yields 7 calories per gram, which makes it more caloric than carbohydrates (4 calories per gram) but less caloric than fats (9 calories per gram). A 1-ounce shot glass of whiskey (50 percent alcohol) yields approximately 100 calories. A 12-ounce can of beer (4.5 percent alcohol) contains 105 alcohol calories, and a 4-ounce glass of dry table wine has about 100 calories. For a more detailed listing of the caloric value of alcoholic beverages, see Table 2. The alcoholic who consumes more than a fifth of whiskey per day will take in more than 2,200 calories from the alcohol alone. This may amount to as much as 75 percent of his or her normal daily intake of calories.

Metabolism of Alcohol

Like foods, alcohol must be metabolized into a chemical substance that the cells can utilize. This biochemical process begins in the stomach with gastric alcohol dehydrogenase (ADH). It has been shown that ingestion of aspirin increases blood alcohol levels because it hinders first-pass metabolism of alcohol in the stomach (Roine et al., 1990). The bulk of the beginning oxidation process occurs in the liver, where the ADH changes ethanol into a common biological substance called acetaldehyde, which can be used for energy or converted into fat and stored.

The breakdown of alcohol in the liver proceeds at a rate that varies somewhat from one individual to another, but the range of variation is quite small. Alcohol is metabolized at an average rate of 8 grams per hour, thereby taking about two hours to reduce the blood alcohol level back down to zero (DHHS, 1990). A standard drink—one 12-ounce bottle of beer or one mixed drink—contains about 15 grams of alcohol. Within each person this phase of alcohol metabolism is quite uniform, and little can be done to speed up the process. There are some individual differences in the amount of alcohol that can be stored in the body, but sooner or later this stored alcohol must be metabolized. Until that time, alcohol will continue to affect the central nervous system. Since the major initial phase occurs in the liver at a constant rate, the process of "sobering up" is dependent on the liver. This concept is extremely important for individuals who must drive or perform other activities after drinking.

The second phase of alcohol metabolism, that of oxidation of acetaldehyde into acetic acid, takes place not only in the liver but also in many cells of the body, including the cells of the brain and nervous system. The rate of this oxidation is very important because the accumulation of large amounts of acetaldehyde in the cell can have adverse effects on normal cell function.

Under normal circumstances, acetaldehyde is metabolized rapidly and does not interfere with cell function. However, the large amounts of acetaldehyde that accumulate after ingestion of large quantities of ethanol are significant in the development of headaches, gastritis, nausea, dizziness, and other symptoms, which, when they occur together, are commonly known as a hangover (DHHS, 1990).

The problem of the accumulation of acetaldehyde is compounded by the effects of alcohol on cellular metabolism. Ethanol is a general depressant of several endocrinological processes and associated metabolic events. This decrease in general metabolism also slows down the rate at which acetaldehyde is utilized (Modell, 1990).

The third phase of alcohol metabolism is the energy phase, where acetic acid, the metabolic product of acetaldehyde, enters into the normal chemistry of energy production. It is biochemically used to produce energy, just as other foodstuffs are (Figure 14). When alcohol is in the system it is used preferentially for fuel, *leaving* the foodstuffs to be stored as fat. With this a twofold problem occurs—weight gain and an accumulation of fats that are not removed from the liver. The latter is instrumental in the liver disease that is seen in habitual drinkers.

The Hangover

The nausea, headache, gastritis, dizziness, and vomiting that often accompany excessive consumption of alcohol appear to be caused not only by high alcohol

FIGURE 14
Energy production from food and alcohol.

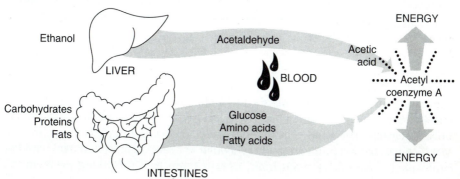

concentration in the blood but also by the increased amounts of acetaldehyde in the tissues. Accumulation of excess amounts of alcohol and acetaldehyde further depresses metabolic activity, thus increasing the amount of lactic acid and acetic acid in the body. Large amounts of lactic acid diminish alkali reserves and the alkali-binding power of the blood. Thus, impaired respiratory exchange, which decreases normal elimination of lactic acid and carbon dioxide, combines with increased acid accumulation due to decreased alkali-binding power to accentuate the symptoms of the hangover.

There remains some controversy as to the value of food substances in speeding up the oxidation of alcohol and elimination of acetaldehyde and lactic acid buildup. Proteins have been shown to speed up the metabolism of alcohol in individuals whose rate of metabolism is not at a maximum. A diet low in protein will tend to diminish the metabolic rate through depletion of the enzymes necessary for alcohol metabolism. Diets high in either fat or carbohydrates have not been shown to have any significant effect on the rate of metabolism of alcohol. Investigators found some increases when glucose or insulin was given, but these increases occurred only in individuals who exhibited a lower-than-maximum alcohol metabolism. It can be concluded that individuals with normal alcohol metabolism cannot increase this metabolism by prior consumption of any dietary substance (DHHS, 1990).

It is generally assumed that alcohol metabolism is independent of overall metabolism and is not sensitive to the overall metabolic demands of the body. Conditions such as hyperthyroidism, physical activity, or exposure to low temperatures (all of which are capable of doubling overall metabolism) have little if any effect on the metabolism of alcohol and on the sobering-up process (Goldberg et al., 1985).

The practice of drinking black coffee to aid the sobering-up process has been followed for many years. However, sobering up or regaining control of the cells depressed by alcohol is entirely dependent on the breakdown of alcohol by the liver. The caffeine contained in coffee is a stimulant and increases the activity of cells in the central nervous system, but it does not speed up the metabolism of alcohol. Even though drinking coffee does not actually speed the sobering-up process, it still remains a sound practice·as long as its effects are not mistaken. Because the caffeine in the coffee is a central nervous system stimulant, it may give the depressed person somewhat of a lift. But because sobering up is a function of time, the time spent in drinking the coffee may be its most valuable asset!

SPECIAL DANGERS

Ten to fifteen percent of the nearly 150 million adults in the United States who are 18 years of age or older have problems with alcohol. If we were talking about measles or the flu, that number would indicate an epidemic of historic significance, calling into action every available health resource to deal with the problem. Of the adults who drink, one in three has a drinking problem. In addition to these adult problem drinkers, there are an estimated 3.3 million problem drinkers among youth between the ages of 14 and 17. It is estimated that alcohol-related deaths may run as high 105,000 per year in the United States. Alcohol contributes to slightly over 50 percent of our traffic accidents and causes in excess of 28,000 fatalities, countless injuries, and immeasurable property damage each year. It is conservatively estimated that our national alcoholic problem costs us $90 billion annually.

Probably the greatest danger and cost to health and personal prosperity in the United States due to alcohol is the disease of alcoholism. This disease and the other alcohol-related diseases of cirrhosis, Wernicke–Korsakoff syndrome, cardiovascular disorders, endocrine disorders, cognitive impairment, fetal alcohol syndrome, and fetal alcohol effects are discussed in detail in Section 3 of this book, Drug-Related Diseases and Conditions.

Drinking and Driving

There are numerous ways of regarding what exactly constitutes the so-called drug problem in the United States. However, one topic on which the vast majority of people agree is the problem of drinking and driving a car, flying an airplane, or operating a boat (Modell & Mountz, 1990). Traffic crashes are the leading cause of death in the United States for all age groups from 1 to 34 (NCHS, 1988).

Safety experts use the term ''problem drinker'' to describe about two-thirds of the drinking drivers who cause fatalities on the highways, not only because their consumption of alcohol is far beyond normal levels but also because they have experienced problems with alcohol in the past. Studies of drivers responsible for alcohol-related fatal accidents show that as many as two-thirds of these drivers have had a problem with alcohol before, as indicated by previous arrest, hospitalization, or a social agency contact in which excessive drinking played a role.

Experts disagree on their estimates of the number of problem drinkers who drive, but most agree that fewer than 7 percent of registered drivers have a drinking problem. In numbers, this still leaves about 8 million problem drinkers on the road responsible for alcohol-related deaths and serious injuries. That is about one out of every fifteen drivers, yet they are involved in two-thirds of all alcohol-related traffic deaths.

From 1982 through 1989 the estimated number of fatalities that involved an intoxicated driver or nonoccupant (pedestrian) decreased by 12 percent, the estimated number of drunk drivers in fatal crashes decreased 13 percent, and the estimated number of drivers with low-level blood alcohol concentration (BAC) involved in fatal crashes decreased 9 percent. Factors that may be related to these decreases include stricter state laws and greater enforcement of them, an increase in the minimum legal drinking age in thirty-five states, increased media attention and public awareness, and an increase in the number of programs that encourage responsible behavior and alternatives to drinking and driving (Fell & Nash, 1989).

Consider these facts about drinking and driving:

• Alcohol is involved in about one-half of all highway deaths. About 22,000 people a year (400 a week) die because some people choose to drive while intoxicated (NHTSA, 1989a).

• An estimated 40 percent of all persons in the United States may be involved in an alcohol-related traffic crash sometime during their lives (NHTSA, 1989b).

• About one-half of those killed each year are not the ones who have been drinking.

• Sixty percent of highway deaths of young adults (16 to 24 years old) are related to alcohol use. In other words, if it were not for drinking drivers, six out of ten young adults killed in automobile accidents would still be alive.

• As many as 60 percent of all alcohol-related accidents are single-vehicle crashes. These accidents usually involve running off the road or running into something. The problem seems to involve judgment, vision, and car control.

• Alcohol-related accidents tend to involve speeding. About one-fourth of all accidents involving young adults are caused by speeding, usually over 40 miles per hour. The problem here is often emotional control and/or judgment.

• Alcohol-related accidents tend to occur at night and on weekends, usually after 10 p.m. As many as 70 percent of all alcohol-caused crashes involving young adults occur on weekends.

The necessary skills of driving are (1) good judgment, (2) good emotional control, (3) ability to see well, and (4) skill and coordination. Alcohol impairs a driver's judgment, making the necessary complex decisions even more difficult. For example, drivers need to gauge their own speed and that of other cars. They must assess carefully whether there is time to pass, whether there is room to merge, stop, or turn, and whether to slow down when other cars seem to be slowing down.

Alcohol has been called "optimism in a bottle," because it causes drunk drivers to overestimate their ability to handle a car. They fail to critically evaluate their own performance. They truly do not realize that their driving performance has deteriorated. The inability of intoxicated drivers to see as well as sober drivers is an often overlooked hazard of drunk driving. Eye muscles relaxed by alcohol do not focus as well or as quickly. Visual acuity diminishes, and things start to look fuzzy. Night vision is a major problem for intoxicated drivers. Both glare vision and glare recovery are impaired by alcohol. Finally, peripheral vision and depth and distance perception are also impaired.

The most common alcohol-related driving errors are driving too fast, changing from fast to slow without reason, running over curbs, driving on the wrong side of the road or in the wrong lane, weaving, straddling lanes, starting in a quick or jerky manner, running stop signs, not signaling turns, and giving the wrong signal. Intoxicated drivers seldom allow someone else to do the driving, because they are unable to see their own mistakes.

Although individuals differ in their reactions to ingested alcohol, one cocktail will usually not interfere with one's driving skill. For instance, a small person drinking a cocktail on an empty stomach may be adversely affected by the drink, but for most people the approximate blood alcohol content (0.02 to 0.03 percent) resulting from one cocktail is not high enough to make a difference in driving ability.

Blood alcohol levels are given in milligrams of alcohol per 100 milliliters of blood. If a person has 50 milligrams of alcohol per 100 milliliters of blood, he or she will have a blood alcohol content of 0.05 percent. Roughly speaking, 4 to 5 ounces of whiskey in an average-weight individual (154 pounds) ingested over a period of one hour will produce a blood alcohol concentration of about 0.10 percent in two hours.

It is generally found that at a blood alcohol level of 0.02 percent there is no discernible intoxication. Between the levels of 0.05 and 0.09 percent there are various signs of intoxication, but these levels would not be legal proof of drunken driving in most states. Most individuals are, however, unmistakably drunk at a level of 0.15 percent, and at a level of 0.3 percent any drinker would be intoxicated. At 0.45 percent, intoxication is severe, and further ingestion of alcohol could well result in death; indeed, levels as low as 0.35 to 0.45 percent have been known to cause death. Levels above 0.55 percent are usually fatal in untreated patients. For a thorough summary of the effects of various levels of blood alcohol concentration, see Table 3.

This is one drug-related topic where the statistics speak loudly and clearly, leaving no room for misinterpretation. Studies have firmly established a significant relationship between blood alcohol concentration (BAC) and relative risk of accident. Below 0.05 percent BAC, the risk of having an accident, on the average, remains at essentially the same level as for drivers who have not been drinking. Between 0.05 percent and 0.10 percent BAC, the curve rises to about seven times that of nondrinking drivers. Above this BAC level, risk rises very rapidly to 20 to 50 times that of drivers who have not been drinking.

Table 3 summarizes the psychological and physical effects of various BAC levels. This information is important enough to be put another way and displayed again. Figure 15, prepared by the National Highway and Traffic Safety Administration (NHTSA), can serve as a usable, ready reference for your own weight and drinking situation. Find your weight and memorize how many drinks you can safely handle before you drive (for most people this is one or two). It could save your life and the lives of others.

Alcohol and Domestic Violence

Although the disease of alcoholism and the behavior disorder of battering are of differing etiology, alcohol and domestic violence are linked. Domestic violence is often perpetrated by the alcoholic spouse on the sober spouse and vice versa. About one-fourth of all homes in the United States have alcohol-related family problems (Randall, 1990). A study by the National Institute on Alcohol Abuse and Alcoholism (NIAAA, 1987) on family violence reported that 63 percent of

TABLE 3
PSYCHOLOGICAL AND PHYSICAL EFFECTS OF VARIOUS BLOOD ALCOHOL CONCENTRATION LEVELS *

Number of drinks †	Blood alcohol concentration	Psychological and physical effects
1	0.02–0.03%	No overt effects, slight feeling of muscle relaxation, slight mood elevation.
2	0.05–0.06%	No intoxication, but feeling of relaxation, warmth. Slight increase in reaction time, slight decrease in fine muscle coordination.
3	0.08–0.09%	Balance, speech, vision, and hearing slightly impaired. Feelings of euphoria. Increased loss of motor coordination.
4	0.11–0.12%	Coordination and balance becoming difficult. Distinct impairment of mental facilities, judgment, etc.
5	0.14–0.15%	Major impairment of mental and physical control. Slurred speech, blurred vision, lack of motor skill. Legal intoxication in all states (0.15%).
7	0.20%	Loss of motor control—must have assistance in moving about. Mental confusion.
10	0.30%	Severe intoxication. Minimum conscious control of mind and body.
14	0.40%	Unconsciousness, threshold of coma.
17	0.50%	Deep coma.
20	0.60%	Death from respiratory failure.

* For each 1 hour time lapse, 0.015% blood alcohol concentration, or approximately one drink.
† The typical drink—ounce of alcohol—provided by:
  a shot of spirits (1½ oz of 50% alcohol—100 proof whiskey or vodka)
  a glass of fortified wine (3½ oz of 20% alcohol)
  a larger glass of table wine (5 oz of 14% alcohol)
  a pint of beer (16 oz of 4½% alcohol).

FIGURE 15
Effect of number of drinks on responsible driving. The unshaded area shows the number of drinks that may not affect responsible driving, depending on one's weight. Beyond that, the probability of being seriously affected becomes much greater.

Drinks Two-Hour Period
Weight   1½ oz 86° Liquor or 12 oz Beer

Weight												
100	1	2	3	4	5	6	7	8	9	10	11	12
120	1	2	3	4	5	6	7	8	9	10	11	12
140	1	2	3	4	5	6	7	8	9	10	11	12
160	1	2	3	4	5	6	7	8	9	10	11	12
180	1	2	3	4	5	6	7	8	9	10	11	12
200	1	2	3	4	5	6	7	8	9	10	11	12
220	1	2	3	4	5	6	7	8	9	10	11	12
240	1	2	3	4	5	6	7	8	9	10	11	12

Be careful   Driving   Do not drive
BAC to .05%   impaired   10% & Up
                     .05 – .09%

the husbands were drinking alcohol when they were violent. An estimated 38 percent of child abuse cases are alcohol-related, and more than 80 percent of prison inmates admit that alcohol was involved in their crimes (Atwood, 1991).

Randall (1991) cautions that the tendency to "alcoholize" wife assault can diminish the seriousness of the offense in the eyes of the perpetrator and the rest of society. Randall calls this "the drunken bum" theory of wife beating, which tends to relieve the batterer of responsibility for his actions. Although alcohol consumption and family violence are highly correlated, the strongest risk factor for wife and child abuse is the batterer's belief that society condones violence by men against women and children.

REFERENCES

Atwood, J. D. (1991). Domestic violence: the role of alcohol. *JAMA,* 265(4):23.

DHHS (1990). *Seventh Special Report to the U.S. Congress on Alcohol and Health from the Secretary of Health and Human Services.* DHHS Pub. (ADM) 281-88-0002. Rockville, Md.: U.S. Department of Health and Human Services, pp. 12–41, 163–79.

Fell, J. C., and Nash, C. E. (1989). The nature of the alcohol problem in U.S. fatal crashes. *Health Education Quarterly,* 16:335–343.

Goldberg, S. R., Prada, J. A., and Katz, J. L. (1985). Stereoselective behavioral effects of $N(6)$-phenylisopropyl-adenosine and antagonism by caffeine. *Psychopharmacology,* 87:272–277.

Lang, S. S. (1991). When women drink. *Parade,* January 20, p. 20.

Modell, J. G. (1990). Behavioral, neurologic and physiologic effects of acute ethanol ingestion. In D. Fassler (Ed.), *The Alcoholic Patient: Emergency Medical Intervention.* New York: Gardner, pp. 220–245.

Modell, J. G., and Mountz, J. M. (1990). Drinking and flying—the problem of alcohol use by pilots. *New England Journal of Medicine,* 323(7):455–461.

NCHS (National Center for Health Statistics). (1988). *Health, United States.* Public Health Service, CDC, 2989; DHHS Pub. no. (PHS) 89–1232. Washington, D.C.: U.S. Department of Health and Human Services.

NIAAA. (1987). *Sixth Special Report.* Washington, D.C.: National Institute on Alcohol Abuse and Alcoholism.

NHTSA (National Highway Traffic Safety Administration). (1988). *Fatal Accident Reporting System, 1988. A Review of Information on Fatal Traffic Accidents in the United States in 1988.* Washington, D.C.: U.S. Department of Transportation.

NHTSA (National Highway Traffic Safety Administration). (1989a). *Highway Traffic Fatalities.* Pub. HS-807-507. Washington, D.C.: U.S. Department of Transportation.

NHTSA (National Highway Traffic Safety Administration). (1989b). *Drunk Driving Facts.* Washington, D.C.: U.S. Department of Transportation.

Randall, T. (1990). Domestic violence intervention calls for more than treating injuries. *JAMA,* 264:939–940.

Randall, T. (1991). Domestic violence: the role of alcohol. In reply. *JAMA,* 265(4):23–30.

Roine, R., et al. (1990). Aspirin increases blood alcohol concentrations in humans after ingestion of ethanol. *JAMA,* 264(18):2406–2410.

TOBACCO

Next to caffeine, nicotine is the most widely used stimulant in the United States. A cup of coffee and a cigarette is "dessert" to many Americans, even though the use of these stimulants, especially nicotine (and the other constituents of tobacco smoke), is strongly related to premature death and increased morbidity.

HISTORY

Native Americans used tobacco and the leaves of other plants in their ceremonial pipes to symbolize putting their thoughts and words out into the world. In a ceremonial context, smoking the pipe meant communing with the spirits. The smoke was taken into the mouth, integrated with the energy of the individual, and then released to the universe. To "swallow" the smoke was to hide one's spiritual intent.

When the Native Americans shared tobacco with their new European neighbors (as early as Columbus), the newcomers quickly discovered the stimulatory effect of tobacco and began the fashion of taking snuff, chewing tobacco, smoking a pipe, and, later on, smoking cigarettes. During World War I, American soldiers began the epidemic of cigarette smoking that 20 to 30 years later translated into a heart and lung disease epidemic in this country.

"Cigarette smoking is currently recognized as the largest single preventable cause of premature death and disability in our society." This now familiar quote from the Surgeon General's 1983 report summarizes the voluminous research results that have clearly documented the health hazards of smoking cigarettes. The death rate for people who smoke two or more packs of cigarettes a day is twice as high as that for people who do not smoke. The Centers for Disease Control (1988) projected differences of between 7 and 9 years in life expectancy between continuing smokers and nonsmokers. More recent studies indicate that men who smoke cigarettes throughout their lives will die nearly eighteen years earlier than men who never start. The data from the present research indicate that a 30-year-old man who smokes will reduce his life expectancy, on average, by about one-fourth (U.S. Surgeon General, 1989).

A report compiled by The National Center for Health Statistics summarized epidemiological data on deaths caused by oral and pharyngeal cancer in the United States in 1987 (Centers for Disease Control, 1990a). This report indicated that more than 9,700 deaths in the United States were caused by cancers of the oral cavity and pharynx. Many of these deaths could have been prevented by reduction of personal risk behaviors such as tobacco use and heavy alcohol consumption. On the average, smokers have a risk of death from lung cancer that is ten times greater than that of nonsmokers, a risk of fatal heart attack that is two times greater, and a risk of death from chronic obstructive lung disease that is six times greater than that for nonsmokers (Centers for Disease Control, 1989).

Translated into numbers of individuals, it has been estimated that cigarette smoking contributes to 400,000 deaths each year in the United States from lung and other cancers, cardiovascular disease, emphysema, and chronic bronchitis. That is more than the number of deaths caused by heroin, crack, powder cocaine, marijuana, Ecstasy, Ice, barbiturates, and LSD combined. It is more than one-fourth of all deaths from all causes (National Interagencies Council on Smoking and Health, 1985). In addition, the U.S. Surgeon General's office (1989) suggests that second-hand smoke (passive smoking) is causing 3,800 lung cancer deaths in the United States every year and as many as 46,000 deaths if illnesses like heart disease and respiratory ailments are included.

CLASSIFICATION

Nicotine is a stimulant of the central nervous system that produces distinct physiological and psychological changes in humans.

HOW TAKEN INTO THE BODY

Tobacco is smoked, snuffed, or chewed to introduce nicotine into the bloodstream. The amount of tar and nicotine in tobacco is determined by such factors as plant strain, processing, origin of the plant, growth conditions, heat and humidity, and the aging process used. How much of the tar and nicotine gets into the system depends on how the tobacco is used—whether it is chewed, taken as snuff, or smoked.

There has been a great resurgence in the use of all forms of smokeless tobacco in the United States. The sales of smokeless tobacco have increased about 11 percent each year since 1974, with an estimated 22 million users in the United States—approximately 29 percent of the population (Drexler, 1990).

There are several forms of tobacco that are either chewed or sniffed. Snuff is a finely ground tobacco sold in small cans. The most common method of ingestion is by placing a pinch of snuff between the lip and gum. Snuff is also placed on the back of the hand and sniffed through the nose. Chewing tobacco is loose-leafed and sold in a pouch. It is also placed between the lip and gum for a period of time and then expectorated. Another type is the plug that is sold in brick form, from which the user cuts or bites off a piece.

CHARACTERISTICS OF DEPENDENCE

Tobacco use may produce both psychological and physical dependence. Smoking cessation appears to be one of the more difficult health behaviors to accomplish, perhaps because it was an "acceptable" societal behavior for so long and smokers tend to begin their habit at such an early age and continue it for decades.

In an animal laboratory setting, most drugs abused by humans are self-administered because the effects of the drug itself is rewarding when separated from other social rewards. Nicotine has now been added to the list of drugs whose effects serve as a reinforcer for animals. This is similar to what is observed with cocaine. Tobacco use, like the use of other abused drugs, is often peer-initiated. There is usually social support for tobacco use, which allows for tolerance and habitual use patterns to develop with repeated use (Mittlemark et al., 1987). As with other dependence-producing drugs, dependence occurs in stages. In the first stage, use gradually increases. In the second stage, perhaps several weeks or even years later, the use pattern becomes stable. Although many factors cause this intake pattern, learning factors and tolerance are believed to account for the gradual acceleration. A ceiling is reached when the drug's increasingly adverse effects offset the rewards from further increasing the level of use.

Dependent smokers usually smoke their first cigarette within a half hour of awakening and find it difficult to abstain for more than a few hours. If smoking is relatively unconstrained, regular patterns develop that closely resemble laboratory animal self-administration of stimulants (Centers for Disease Control, 1989).

PHARMACOLOGY

At least 1,200 different toxic chemicals have been identified as constituents of tobacco smoke. Tobacco smoke is a mixture of hot air and gases that suspend small particles called tars. Many of the particles contain carcinogens, substances that are known to cause cancer. One such chemical, benzpyrene, is among the most potent carcinogens known. Also contained in the particulate matter are chemicals called phenols, which are thought to speed up or activate dormant cancer cells.

Another component of tobacco smoke is the drug nicotine. The behavioral effect attributed to nicotine has been observed for many years, and recently an intense research effort has been aimed at determining nicotine's mechanism of action. Just as with opiates, cannabinoids, and cocaine, it has been found that neurons have specific receptors for nicotine. It is hypothesized that these receptors may be identical to those for the neurotransmitter acetylcholine (Holloway, 1991). Nicotine may have two phases of action, mimicking cholinergic activity in small doses but with large doses first stimulating and then blocking the firing of cholinergic neurons (Volle & Koelle, 1990). Several investigators have suggested that nicotine, mimicking acetylcholine, releases norepinephrine peripherally and perhaps centrally. This action may result from a release of adrenal hormones, perhaps through the stimulatory action of nicotine on adenocorticotropic hormone (ACTH). Nicotine may also stimulate the release of β-endorphin and the enkephalins, and these may produce a tranquilizing effect. Nicotine and other drugs of abuse are thought to produce gratifying feelings by ultimately acting on the mesolimbic system, one theoretical reward pathway in the brain (Holloway, 1991).

Pharmacologically, nicotine seems capable of producing both stimulation and arousal reduction, and such effects underlie the maintenance of smoking behavior. The determining factor may be the arousal state of the smoker. That is, those who smoke in high-arousal situations derive a relaxing effect, whereas those who smoke mainly in low-arousal situations are assisted in maintaining alertness (Escobedo et al., 1990).

EFFECTS ON THE BODY

Normally, small particles in the air that are inhaled are not problematic because the air passageways are cleansed constantly as millions of tiny hairlike whips (cilia) escalate mucus up the respiratory tract. If small particles get past the nasal trap (specially constructed wind tunnels that trap particles), they are snared by the sticky "mucal escalator" and are taken upward, there to be either swallowed or expectorated (see Figure 16). If particles happen to get past this protective mechanism, there is a third line of defense within the lungs. Here white blood cells attack foreign particles and destroy or immobilize them. In an individual without constant overload on these protective devices, the lungs are normally cleared of dangerous materials. However, if a smoker constantly overloads this system, or if an individual works amid coal dust or other constantly inhaled particles or lives in an air-polluted environment, the system cannot remove particles effectively and there is danger of deleterious effects. Then as cigarette tar is deposited on normal respiratory tract cells, some chemicals in the smoke irritate the cells, some bring about the cancer process, and still others speed up this process.

Aiding the tars in their damaging effects on the respiratory system is the action of various gases within cigarette smoke. The gases of importance here are ammonia, formaldehyde, acetaldehyde, and hydrogen cyanide (a strong poison in itself). These four gases combine to immobilize the cilia of the air passageways for 6 to 8 hours, and it is obvious what happens to the mucal escalator when the ciliary movement ceases. No longer can particles be nor-

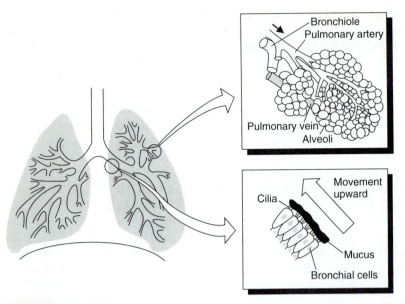

FIGURE 16
The respiratory tree.

mally removed; hence, when they enter the respiratory tract, they can directly affect the mucus-producing and ciliary cells. It is as though two protective coverings have been removed and the underlying cells laid bare to the irritation of cigarette tars. Some of the cilia-producing and mucus-producing cells, then, are completely destroyed over a period of time. In an occasional smoker (one who smokes a pack or less a week) there may be sufficient time after each cigarette for the cilia to recover; however, a heavy smoker (a pack or more a day) rarely allows this recovery time, and permanent damage occurs. The absence of the cilia–mucus protective coating and clearing device makes the ''smoker's cough'' a necessity to clear phlegm, or particles large enough to affect the coughing mechanism, from the air passageways. The damage to these cells of the respiratory tract also makes the smoker more susceptible to upper respiratory infections and chronic bronchitis.

Another gas, carbon monoxide, produced by the incomplete oxidizing of carbon, is perhaps the most hazardous of the substances in tobacco. Physiological studies have shown the involvement of carbon monoxide in the atherosclerosis process (which is discussed in Section 3), and statistical studies have indicated that the concentration of carbon monoxide is the one factor most responsible for linking smoking and diseases of the cardiovascular system.

The maintenance of a smoking habit, like any other drug addiction, is due partly to the positive reinforcing properties of the pharmacological agent, in this case nicotine, and the negative reinforcing properties of its absence. It has been observed that a variety of psychological, behavioral, and physiological disturbances follow the discontinuance of smoking. Among them are a craving for tobacco, irritability, restlessness, dullness, sleep disturbance, gastrointestinal disorders, drowsiness, headache, amnesia, and anxiety as well as impairment of concentration, judgment, and psychomotor performance (Centers for Disease Control, 1990b). These effects seem to be primarily the result of the withdrawal of nicotine, although conclusive evidence is still lacking. Despite this lack of conclusive evidence, much of the research seems to be pointing in the direction of high nicotine involvement. It has been well documented that smokers are able to sense the lack of nicotine in their systems and act to regulate that level. This phenomenon leads smokers to smoke more when low nicotine cigarettes are substituted for their usual brand (if their original brand was higher in nicotine content) (Glynn et al., 1990).

With the use of smokeless tobacco, hemodynamic changes (primarily increases in heart rate and blood pressure) have been observed within 3 to 5 minutes. These physiological changes have not been shown to increase performance, contrary to claims by the leading proponents of its use (male athletes). A review of the literature reveals that the use of smokeless tobacco has the potential for causing cancer of the oral cavity, pharynx, larynx, and esophagus. Smokeless tobacco can produce significant detrimental effects on the soft and hard tissues of the mouth, causing bad breath, discolored teeth, gum recession, and periodontal destruction. Smokeless tobacco can contribute to cardiovascular disease in the same manner as smoked tobacco and is especially contraindicated in individuals with high blood pressure (Farquhar et al., 1990).

Nicotine seems to be the best candidate as the constituent in tobacco smoke that is most capable of producing central nervous system–mediated behavioral effects. Thus, smoking can be seen as a technique for self-administering the drug nicotine. The stimulation or high can result in a psychological dependence that may be a significant factor in habituation to cigarette smoking. Nicotine effects on the cardiovascular system are responsible for the strong statistical link between cigarette smoking and diseases of the cardiovascular system.

Administration of most drugs of abuse results in neuroadaptation, defined as tolerance to the repeated administration of the drug, and a subsequent rebound (withdrawal) when drug use is terminated (Centers for Disease Control, 1990b). Tolerance is defined as either a diminished response to repeated doses of a drug or a need for increasing doses to achieve the same response.

Physiological dependence on drugs is evidenced by the fact that stopping use produces a syndrome of effects, generally opposite in direction to those produced by taking the drug, and that these symptoms can be reversed (at least in their early stages) by administering the drug. Prolonged drug abstinence ("detoxification") ultimately results in a return to baseline ("normal") behavioral and physiological functioning. The American Psychological Association (APA, 1980) has described the tobacco withdrawal syndrome as a characteristic withdrawal syndrome.

Psychological Effects

Most people start smoking for social reasons and continue out of habit or to satisfy a psychological need. Statistics reveal that most heavy smokers take up the habit before the age of 20.

Smoking fits several of the most popular models designed to explain the use and abuse of drugs. The sociocultural model explains drug use in terms of the meaning and significance a given society assigns to the use and users of drugs. It is obvious that the initial use of cigarettes and smokeless tobacco by teen-agers has less to do with the pharmacology of tobacco than with the so-ciocultural milieu surrounding its use. Smoking, at least in the initial stage of the habit, is a sociological phenomenon. Many people need oral gratification, but mainly those who have been oriented to smoking by family and/or friends who accept it as part of their lives. Research helps substantiate this by showing that ninth-graders exhibit smoking behavior identical to that of their best friends, and that children have a 50 percent greater chance of starting to smoke if their parents smoke (Drexler, 1990). As students progress through high school and the sanctions against smoking are lessened, friendships among smokers and nonsmokers become commonplace. Even though high school students are better able to accept individual differences and are more internally motivated, parents, teachers, siblings, and peers still influence many to start smoking. Likewise, one cannot disregard smoking as a symbol of independence or rebellion or of being grown-up.

Even without these common motivators, a very forceful one—that of adver-tising—is left. Apart from television advertising, cigarette manufacturers spend more than $300 million each year not only promoting one particular brand over another but also generally promoting the acceptance of smoking. A closer look at cigarette advertising clearly shows that very few facts about the cigarette are presented. The words are rather trite and meaningless. The ads appeal to the individual's needs and memory of good feeling by presenting a picture of a pleasant and happy situation. Because there exists a universal need for love and companionship and a desire for escape and adventure, the scene often portrays an attractive couple obviously enjoying themselves, or shows the rugged man out in the wilds of nature or the woman taking a much deserved minute of relaxation. The ads are designed to reduce the viewer's anxieties about growing old, being alone, losing one's health or one's sex drive. Or they may attempt to appeal to the reader's ego, by implying that he or she has something more than the next person. The impact of such advertising on potential smokers is substantial, and it has been shown that sales are directly related to capital expenditure for advertising. Most smokers, when blindfolded, cannot even distinguish their favorite brand, which makes a taste factor highly questionable in choice of brand. A particular brand is chosen because of identification with the feeling portrayed by the advertisement or perhaps with someone who also smokes that particular brand.

However, smoking must satisfy a need of the smoker, or smoking behavior would be extinguished. Nicotine as a stimulant causes a slight elevation in mood, which is usually interpreted as relaxation, a feeling of ease, of being in control of one's nervous energy. But the need to continue smoking goes deeper than that. Smoking satisfies a need for oral gratification, it is a dependence-producing habit, and this habit is tightly tied up with emotional and psychological needs. Although theories on the deeper psychological motivations are not well developed, studies on teenage smokers suggest a relationship between the need to smoke and feelings of insecurity and low self-esteem.

The psychosocial model of drug use tends to put a major emphasis on the individual as the active agent in the drug–individual relationship. Drug use and drug users demonstrate a complex, dynamic interrelationship of psychological need and actual or perceived effects of the drug. Smokers continue to smoke primarily because of the perceived benefit derived from smoking. One theory postulates that smoking affects the stress–relaxation continuum. One group of smokers has been identified as the mood control group. It may be that these individuals possess certain personality variables that interact with nicotine and thus affect mood in a variety of ways.

The relationship between stress and smoking has been frequently investigated. Smokers score consistently higher than nonsmokers on nearly all anxiety measures (Drexler, 1990). In addition, smokers are often seen as especially sensitive to stress because as a group they lack coping resources and resort to smoking in an attempt to cope (Centers for Disease Control, 1990b). Subjective distress is one of the most frequently reported cues for smoking. Highly anxious smokers likewise have been found to have lowered expectations that they can produce desired outcomes, which translates into a lowered self-confidence. Although failure to meet one's internal expectations is difficult to measure, it often results in low self-esteem, which has been observed more in smoking teenagers than in nonsmoking ones. Since failure often results in the diversion of efforts from assigned tasks, it is little wonder that teenage smokers seem to experience more failure in school than do nonsmokers. Smokers generally perceive themselves as not meeting the expectations of their parents. This perception gives rise to a certain amount of alienation, and it is not surprising that teenage smokers are more apt to give "non-establishment" responses to questionnaires. It has also been found that teenage smokers tend to get lower grades, create more discipline problems, and participate less in school activities than do their nonsmoking counterparts. In a sociological milieu in which smoking is acceptable (in the teenage world, often encouraged), smoking often becomes an unconscious attempt to gain acceptance.

Another classification of smoking behavior describes smoking as a dependence disorder (APA, 1980). Such models as the addiction model and the maladjusted coping model view smoking as meaningless and as an unpleasant escape from withdrawal.

The Horn Smoking Motives Questionnaire at the end of this chapter addresses most schools of thought on motivations for smoking by assessing six factors identified as sensory motor manipulation, stimulation, pleasure, tension reduction, habit, and addiction, with sensory motor stimulation being the weakest motivator and addiction the strongest. In general, it appears that women and men differ in their main motivation for smoking. Men tend to smoke more for positive affect or pleasure, and women smoke more to alleviate negative affect or reduce tension (Delaney, 1990).

SPECIAL DANGERS

The two main health dangers of dependence on smoking tobacco are cardiovascular disease and cancer, especially cancer of the lungs, mouth, and air passageways between. These conditions are discussed in detail in Section 3, Drug-Related Diseases and Conditions.

Although 41.8 million American adults are former smokers, approximately 29 percent of adult Americans continue to smoke. Smoking is both a sociological and psychological phenomenon. It is a learned behavior, but satisfaction of psychological need and oral gratification create a positive reinforcement to continue. Reports have established beyond a doubt that smoking is harmful to the health of smokers and suggest that it is harmful to the persons around the smoker. Smoking-related diseases are the most preventable diseases known to our society, but knowledge of successful cessation methods still provides little competition against the seemingly strong motivation to smoke.

The benefits of quitting smoking can be major and immediate, regardless of age, but someone who stops smoking before age 50 is only half as likely to die within the next 15 years as a person who continues to smoke (U.S. Surgeon General, 1989). According to the Centers for Disease Control (1990b), the major benefits of smoking cessation include those listed below.

Stroke: Risk 5 to 15 years after quitting is reduced to that of those who never smoked.

Cancers of the mouth, throat, and esophagus: Risk 5 years after quitting is half that of those who still smoke.

Cancer of the larynx: Risk is lower by an undetermined amount compared to those who still smoke.

Coronary heart disease: Risk after 1 year is half that of those who keep smoking. After 15 years, risk is equal to that of those who never smoked.

Chronic obstructive pulmonary disease: Risk after "long-term quitting" is reduced by an undetermined amount compared to those who still smoke.

Lung cancer: Ten years after quitting, the risk may drop to about half that of those who keep smoking.

Pancreatic cancer: Risk is reduced by an undetermined amount 10 years after quitting.

Ulcer: Risk is reduced by an undetermined amount after quitting.

Bladder cancer: Within a "few years" of quitting, the risk is half that of those who keep smoking.

Cervical cancer: Risk a "few years" after quitting is reduced.

Low-birth-weight baby: Risk is reduced compared to that of those who never smoked if a woman quits smoking before pregnancy or during the first trimester.

Peripheral artery disease: Risk is reduced by an undetermined amount after quitting.

Passive Smoking

The use of tobacco cigarettes in public is a strongly disputed issue centering on individual rights: the rights of the smoker to smoke versus the rights of the nonsmoker to breathe air unpolluted by smoke. Recent scientific studies clearly show that nonsmokers in the presence of smokers—especially small children who live in a household of smokers—are also affected by the smoke. The smoking of one cigarette releases into the air surrounding the smoker approximately 70 milligrams of particulates and 25 milligrams of carbon monoxide. The level of carbon monoxide in smoke-filled rooms often reaches 80 parts per million and is considered to be hazardous by the Environmental Protection Agency and to exceed the limits set for occupational exposure. Thus, very often, smoke-filled automobiles and smoke-filled rooms are in violation of pure air quality standards. To make matters worse, often the sidestream smoke is more potent than that inhaled by the smoker, since the sidestream temperatures are cooler and some constituents of the smoke are not completely oxidized.

An increased knowledge of the hazards of smoking in general and the definitive studies of sidestream smoke, combined with an increased sensitivity to air pollution problems and the movement toward individual rights, have led to pressure against smoking in public. Domestic airlines have severely limited smoking on airplanes, and smoking has been banned in many municipal buildings and in many public places. In most hotels, motels, eating establishments, and other privately owned enterprises, the customer is now given the choice of enjoying a nonsmoking room or section.

REFERENCES

APA. (1980). *Diagnostic and Statistical Manual of Mental Disorders,* 3d ed. (DSM-III). Washington, D.C.: American Psychological Association, p. 176.

Centers for Disease Control. (1988). *Smoking and Health: A National Status Report.* Rockville, Md.: U.S. Department of Health and Human Services.

Centers for Disease Control. (1989). *Reducing the Health Consequences of Smoking: 25 Years of Progress.* Atlanta, Ga.: U.S. Department of Health and Human Services.

Centers for Disease Control. (1990a). Deaths from oral cavity and pharyngeal cancer— United States in 1987. *Morbidity and Mortality Weekly Report,* 39:27.

Centers for Disease Control. (1990b). *The Health Benefits of Smoking Cessation.* Rockville, Md.: U.S. Department of Health and Human Services.

Delaney, Sue. (1990). *Women Smokers Can Quit: A Different Approach.* Evanston, Ill.: Women's Healthcare Press.

Drexler, Madeline. (1990). Smoke and mirrors. *Boston Globe Magazine,* May 27, pp. 29–31.

Escobedo, L., et al. (1990). Sociodemographic characteristics of cigarette smoking initiation in the United States. *JAMA,* 264(12):1550–1555.

Farquhar, J. W., Fortmann, S. P., and Flora, J. A. (1990). Community education on cardiovascular disease risk factors: the Stanford five-city project. *JAMA*, 264: 359–365.

Glynn, T. J., Boyd, G. M., and Gruman, J. C. (1990). Essential elements of self-help/ minimal intervention strategies for smoking cessation. *Health Education Quarterly*, 17:329–345.

Holloway, Marguerite. (1991). Trends in pharmacology: Rx for addiction. *Scientific American*, March, pp. 95–103.

Mittlemark, M. B., et al. (1987). Predicting experimentation with cigarettes: the Childhood Antecedents of Smoking Study (CASS). *American Journal of Public Health*, 77:206–208.

National Interagency Council on Smoking and Health (1985). *Smoking and Health Reporter*, 2(2), pp. 14–18.

U.S. Surgeon General. (1989). *Reducing the Health Consequences of Smoking: 25 Years of Progress—A Report of the Surgeon General*. Rockville, Md.: Office on Smoking and Health.

Volle, R. L., and Koelle, G. B. (1990). Ganglionic stimulating and blocking agents. In L. S. Goodman and A. Gillman (Eds.), *The Pharmacological Basis of Therapeutics*. New York: Macmillan, pp. 479–491.

SELF-TEST

WHY DO YOU SMOKE?*

Here are some statements made by people to describe what they get out of smoking cigarettes. How often do you feel this way when smoking? Circle one number for each statement. Important: *Answer every question.*

		Always	Fre-quently	Occa-sionally	Seldom	Never
A.	I smoke cigarettes in order to keep myself from slowing down.	5	4	3	2	1
B.	Handling a cigarette is part of the enjoyment of smoking it.	5	4	3	2	1
C.	Smoking cigarettes is pleasant and relaxing.	5	4	3	2	1
D.	I light up a cigarette when I feel angry about something.	5	4	3	2	1
E.	When I have run out of cigarettes I find it almost unbearable until I can get them.	5	4	3	2	1
F.	I smoke cigarettes automatically without even being aware of it.	5	4	3	2	1
G.	I smoke cigarettes to stimulate me, to perk myself up.	5	4	3	2	1
H.	Part of the enjoyment of smoking a cigarette comes from the steps I take to light up.	5	4	3	2	1
I.	I find cigarettes pleasurable.	5	4	3	2	1
J.	When I feel uncomfortable or upset about something, I light up a cigarette.	5	4	3	2	1
K.	I am very much aware of the fact when I am not smoking a cigarette.	5	4	3	2	1
L.	I light up a cigarette without realizing I still have one burning in the ashtray.	5	4	3	2	1
M.	I smoke cigarettes to give me a "lift."	5	4	3	2	1
N.	When I smoke a cigarette, part of the enjoyment is watching the smoke as I exhale it.	5	4	3	2	1

SELF-TEST

WHY DO YOU SMOKE? (continued)

O.	I want a cigarette most when I am comfortable and relaxed.	5	4	3	2	1
P.	When I feel "blue" or want to take my mind off cares and worries, I smoke cigarettes.	5	4	3	2	1
Q.	I get a real gnawing hunger for a cigarette when I haven't smoked for a while.	5	4	3	2	1
R.	I've found a cigarette in my mouth and didn't remember putting it there.	5	4	3	2	1

Scoring

1. Enter the number you have circled for each question in the spaces below, putting the number you have circled to Question A over line A, to Question B over line B, etc.
2. Add the 3 scores on each line to get your totals. For example, the sum of your scores over lines A, G, and M gives you your score on Stimulation, lines B, H, and N give the score on Handling, etc.

TOTALS

```
    +        +        =
___      ___      ___              _____
 A        G        M                STIMULATION
    +        +        =
___      ___      ___              _____
 B        H        N                HANDLING
    +        +        =
___      ___      ___              _____
 C        I        O                PLEASURABLE RELAXATION
    +        +        =
___      ___      ___              _____
 D        J        P                CRUTCH: TENSION REDUCTION
    +        +        =
___      ___      ___              _____
 E        K        Q                CRAVING: PSYCHOLOGICAL ADDICTION
    +        +        =
___      ___      ___              _____
 F        L        R                HABIT
```

Scores can vary from 3 to 15. A score of 11 and above is high; a score of 7 and below is low.

*Test written by Daniel H. Horn, National Clearinghouse for Smoking and Health. U.S. Department of Health and Human Services.

CAFFEINE

HISTORY

Coffee drinking in America is an extension of the European custom brought to this country centuries ago. In Europe, coffee houses were the common meeting places for conversation, political argument, and camaraderie. The drinking of coffee continues to be a custom that gives people an excuse to sit down to conversation or take "time out." The coffee break became a national institution partly because of the need for a rest from work, but also because of the stimulation this beverage offers.

CLASSIFICATION

Caffeine is the stimulant found in coffee, tea, and soft drinks labeled cola or pepper. It is a chemical that belongs to the xanthine group of drugs. Xanthines are powerful amphetamine-like stimulants that can increase metabolism and create a highly awake and active state. They also trigger release of the stress hormones that, among other factors, are capable of increasing heart rate, blood pressure, and oxygen demands on the heart.

HOW TAKEN INTO THE BODY

Coffee (from the *Coffea arabica* tree) is the most frequently consumed source of caffeine in America, with those over the age of 17 drinking six or more cups of coffee or tea a day. Other caffeine sources are chocolate, cola, other soft drinks containing the name "pepper," and anti-sleep preparations such as No-Doz. Caffeine may also be found in other over-the-counter drugs such as appetite suppressants and analgesics.

CHARACTERISTICS OF DEPENDENCE

People who drink more than one or two cups of coffee every day develop some tolerance, physical dependence, and most likely some psychological dependence on their coffee habit. Individuals who drink more than one or two cups of coffee a day often feel that they cannot get started in the morning without their coffee, and continually drink it throughout the day just to keep going. Withdrawal from caffeine occurs when the drug is abruptly discontinued by those who have become tolerant to it. Symptoms of withdrawal include headache, irritability, lethargy, mood changes, sleep disturbance, and mild physiological arousal (Greden, 1981).

PHARMACOLOGY

It appears that caffeine interferes with adenosine, a naturally occurring chemical that acts as a natural tranquilizer in the brain. It attaches to sites on neurons and makes them less sensitive to other neurotransmitters that would normally excite them. Caffeine also attaches to brain cells and blocks adenosine from acting on them, making the receptor cells more sensitive to chemical stimulation (Rinzler, 1982).

EFFECTS ON THE BODY

Caffeine consumption of more than 250 milligrams per day is considered by many to be excessive because it can have adverse effects on the body. (The average brewed 6-ounce cup of coffee contains about 110 milligrams of caffeine, as well as other xanthines, theobromine and theophylline.) In addition, Cheraskin and Ringsdorf (1978) reported that a significantly higher number of psychological complaints existed among persons drinking seven or more cups a day than among those whose intake was more moderate. A lethal dose of caffeine could be consumed in the form of twenty cups of coffee, if drunk all at once. Frequent side effects of excessive coffee intake are anxiety, irritability, diarrhea, arrhythmia (irregular heartbeat), and the inability to concentrate. Coffee may also stimulate the secretion of the digestive enzyme pepsin within the stomach. In an empty stomach, this enzyme, combined with the natural oils in coffee, can irritate the stomach lining, a reason why those who already have ulcers should cut out caffeine products.

Research is not clear as to whether fibrocystic (benign) breast disease in women is improved with the elimination of caffeine from the diet, but it does appear that such elimination is associated with less premenstrual breast tenderness (Rinzler, 1982). Researchers are also investigating a link between coffee and cancer.

Additional sources of the xanthine stimulants are tea (*Camilia theca*), cola beverages, chocolate, cocoa, some over-the-counter drugs such as aspirin and other analgesics, and preparations to keep you awake, such as No-Doz. It appears that tea does not contain the irritating oils found in coffee and will not counteract homeopathic remedies as coffee does. Table 4 lists examples of caffeine sources and their caffeine content.

TABLE 4
COMMON SOURCES OF CAFFEINE

Beverages	
Brewed coffee	80–150 mg per 5–6 oz cup
Instant coffee	85–100 mg per 5–6 oz cup
Decaffeinated coffee	2–4 mg per 5–6 oz cup
Tea (bag)	42–100 mg per 5–6 oz cup
Tea (leaf)	30–75 mg per 5–6 oz cup
Cocoa	5–50 mg per 5–6 oz cup
Cola drinks	25–60 mg per 8–12 oz
Chocolate bar	about 25 mg per oz
Nonprescription (OTC) drugs	
Analgesics	
Anacin, Cope, Darvon Compound, Empirin Compound, Midol, Vanquish	32 mg
Excedrin	60 mg
Stimulants	
No-Doz	100 mg
Vivarin	200 mg
Caffedrine	250 mg
Many cold preparations	32 mg

Source: Greden, 1981; Holbrook, 1983.

SPECIAL DANGERS

The following neurological effects are seen following caffeine toxicity.

1 Significant increase in norepinephrine secretion
2 Sensitizing of CNS postsynaptic receptors to catecholamines
3 Possible change in acetylcholine and serotonin activity
4 Changes in calcium metabolism

"Caffeinism" is a recent clinical term that characterizes the acute or chronic overuse of caffeine, with subsequent caffeine toxicity. The symptoms of the syndrome include anxiety, mood changes, sleep disturbances, and other psychological complaints. Symptoms are usually dose-related extensions of caffeine's usual effects. The *Diagnostic and Statistical Manual of Mental Disorders* of the American Psychological Association (APA, 1980) gives as the criterion for caffeine intoxication recent consumption of caffeine, usually in excess of 250 milligrams, and at least five of the following symptoms:

1 Restlessness
2 Nervousness
3 Excitement
4 Insomnia
5 Flushed face
6 Diuresis
7 Muscle twitching
8 Rambling flow of thought and speech
9 Cardiac arrhythmia
10 Periods of inexhaustibility
11 Psychomotor agitation
12 Gastrointestinal complaints

In order to be considered caffeine intoxication, these symptoms cannot be due to any other mental disorder (APA, 1980).

MEDICAL USE

Medical use includes treatment for drowsiness and fatigue and treatment for migraine and other vascular headaches in combination with ergot (Griffith, 1988).

REFERENCES

APA (1980). *Diagnostic and Statistical Manual of Mental Disorders,* 3d ed. (DSM-III). New York: American Psychological Association.

Cheraskin, E., and Ringsdorf, W. M., Jr. (1978). *Psychodietetics.* New York: Bantam Books.

Greden, J. F. (1981). Caffeinism and caffeine withdrawal. In J. H. Lowinson and P. Ruiz (Eds), *Substance Abuse: Clinical Problems and Perspectives.* Baltimore, Md.: Williams and Wilkins, pp. 167–184.

Griffith, H. W. (1988). *Complete Guide to Prescription and Non-prescription Drugs.* Los Angeles: The Body Press.

Holbrook, John M. (1983). CNS stimulants. In Gerald Bennett et al. (Eds.), *Substance Abuse: Pharmacological, Developmental, and Clinical Perspectives.* New York: Wiley.

Rinzler, C. A. (1982). The coffee war. *American Health,* September/October, pp. 44–47.

MARIJUANA

HISTORY

Alcohol became a symbol in a social class struggle in the nineteenth and early twentieth centuries culminating in a period known as Prohibition. With the increase in popularity of marijuana (*Cannabis sativa*) in the 1960s, many similarities were drawn between its prohibition and the prohibition of alcohol. However, marijuana represented a symbol of differences not between the working class immigrant and the aristocracy, but between the generations, in their lifestyles, values, and social and political philosophies.

During the 1930s, headlines told of crimes committed by normally law-abiding citizens who were under the influence of the "killer weed." One-sided congressional hearings were quickly convened, and the result was the Marijuana Tax Act. Compared to that of alcohol, the prohibition of marijuana was relatively quiet and unopposed. This was the atmosphere in which early attitudes toward marijuana developed. Little else was heard on the subject until the easy-going, pleasure-seeking "hippie" lifestyle of the 1960s engendered fear of social disorder and moral decay in the greater population. Marijuana soon became the symbol of a conflict between social and moral stability and individual freedom. Law enforcement agencies were caught in the middle, as legal enforcement of the prohibition of marijuana was found to be virtually impossible. The costs were staggering, not only in monies for police, lawyers, and judges, but also in the misery of those jailed for possession and use of what many regarded as a harmless drug.

In 1970, a presidential commission, the President's Commission on Marijuana and Drug Abuse, was established to separate fiction from fact and to recommend a uniform policy that would not only reflect the attitudes of the majority but also provide legally and morally for the freedoms of the individual

81

(National Commission on Marijuana and Drug Abuse, 1972). The commission's survey showed that dominant public opinion still opposed marijuana use, so it could not recommend legalization of marijuana or even a position of neutrality toward it. Instead, the commission recommended a social policy of discouragement, asking for increased efforts by schools, churches, and families to implement this policy. Such implementation would decrease the need for legal regulation.

The commission also recommended that the possession of marijuana for personal use no longer be a criminal offense but that marijuana possessed in public remain contraband, subject to seizure. It further recommended that states adopt a uniform statutory scheme similar to the proposed federal laws, whereby private possession would not be considered a criminal offense, possession of small amounts in public would be punishable by a fine, and sale would remain a serious offense with stringent penalties.

To help educate society and to make sure that lawmakers and politicians were kept abreast of the latest scientific information, the marijuana lobby (the National Organization for the Reform of Marijuana Laws, or NORML) was formed in 1970. NORML used a middle-class, pragmatic, time-honored lobbying style to get legislators to accept the recommendation of the President's Commission: the decriminalization of marijuana users (not legalization of marijuana). They continually emphasized that while scientists debate the question of the dangers of marijuana, thousands are being punished for using what might be found later to be a relatively harmless drug.

These historical events led to our current laws, which generally decriminalize possession of small amounts (usually 1 ounce) of marijuana while keeping strict enforcement regarding import and sales of the drug. Each state legislates its own marijuana laws.

Until 1977, Mexico supplied the largest amount of marijuana for the United States, but Mexican officials at that time launched an effective campaign against marijuana growing and smuggling. During this crackdown, marijuana fields were sprayed with paraquat, a herbicidal solution that was found to be associated with lung damage in smokers of marijuana coming from sprayed fields. As the trade in Mexican marijuana slowed down, Colombian marijuana began to fill the gap. In 1980, Colombia not only provided about two-thirds of the marijuana smoked in the United States, it was also considered the largest supplier of marijuana in the world. The Colombian marijuana crop provided more revenue to the local economy than did coffee or other field crops, with the approximately 250,000 acres of marijuana potentially yielding 6 billion pounds of marijuana per year. Each pound was worth $600 on the streets of the United States. Although the Colombian farmer saw only about 1 percent of that $600, at $6 per pound he still had a more profitable crop than corn or cotton (Willis, 1984).

Recently, high prices have elevated marijuana past corn as America's number one cash drop. It is estimated that marijuana growers collected around $13 billion in 1990 (Wiegand, 1991).

It is becoming evident that destruction of domestic crops and interdiction of foreign marijuana is making an impact on the American marijuana market. For instance, Operation Wipeout's eradication of marijuana plants in Hawaii, home of the famed Maui Wowee, destroyed 80 to 90 percent of the marketable crop in 1990, the first time in history that more marijuana was imported into the islands than was exported from them. Observers of the marijuana market say that there has been a marked shift in marijuana's acceptance as a "harmless" drug and that it has become desocialized in the present hard-to-get market. A NIDA survey done in the spring of 1990 reflected the downturn in availability and use; the number of Americans who said they smoked marijuana at least once a month dropped to 10.2 million in 1990 (down from 22.5 million in 1979) (NIDA, 1991).

CLASSIFICATION

Marijuana has the lowest potency among cannabis preparations; therefore, in its lower concentrations it must be considered a sedative-hypnotic, much like alcohol. Stronger THC preparations (see Pharmacology) such as high concentration marijuana, hashish, and hash oil may be considered psychedelic or hallucinatory.

HOW TAKEN INTO THE BODY

In the Western world, cannabis is usually smoked, and in this form it is considered more potent than when taken orally in drinks or food preparations, as is the practice in Eastern countries. Smoking allows more control over the use of cannabis, because the effects can be felt much more rapidly and intake can be altered accordingly. The effects of ingestion last longer, but nausea and vomiting may occur as an aftermath. As with most other drugs, the effects of marijuana are dose-dependent.

CHARACTERISTICS OF DEPENDENCE

Long-term administration of cannabis results in the development of tolerance to a wide variety of the short-term drug effects in both humans and experimental animals. Though scientific opinion is more divided on the question of dependence on cannabis, there is now substantial evidence that dependence (both psychological and physical), does occur and that these drug dependents have been "lost between the cracks" in treatment (McConnell, 1991). The National Institute on Drug Abuse reports that of the 10.2 million American marijuana users, slightly more than 1 million of them cannot control their use of the drug (NIDA, 1991).

PHARMACOLOGY

Nearly any student of drugs knows that marijuana is derived from the flowers and the top leaves of the female *Cannabis sativa* plant, a weed of the hemp family that flourishes without the need for special cultivation. The resin, a sticky yellow substance, is produced by the plant as a protective shield against the elements; marijuana plants grown in hotter, sunnier climates produce more resin in order to protect themselves from the sun's heat. The resin contains the active drug ingredients of the plant. Marijuana contains 421 chemicals from 18 chemical classes, but the most important active ingredient is thought to be tetrahydrocannabinol (THC)—specifically, delta-9-tetrahydrocannabinol— with possible synergistic effects from other cannabidiols and cannabinols (Turner, 1981). When THC enters the blood, it is quickly changed to the psychoactive compound 11-hydroxy THC in the liver. THC and its breakdown products may bind to proteins in the blood and remain for long periods of time in stored body fat. It has been found that THC in its active form may be retained in the body for as long as 45 days after its introduction into the body.

Breakthrough research in 1990 established the location in the brain of numerous binding sites (receptors) specific for THC, and in 1991 the gene that is responsible for the production of these receptor sites was isolated (Holloway, 1991). It appears that the cannabinoid receptor has an important physiological role in the nuclei in charge of sending messages out of the basal ganglia, and in the hippocampus, cerebral cortex, and cerebellum. These regions are associated with movement and with thought processes, including perception, knowledge, and memory. The scarcity of THC binding sites in the lower brainstem areas controlling heart and lung functions may explain why high concentrations of THC are not lethal (Herkenham et al., 1990).

Until recently the measurement of THC levels in the body was inadequate, but now through radioimmunoassay or gas–liquid chromatography along with mass spectroscopy, THC and other cannabinoids can be reliably measured. However, very few laboratories are equipped with the expensive equipment to carry out these measurements, and unless steps are taken against the danger of invalidation of the urine test, false negative readings will occur.

There are a number of strains of cannabis, the strength of each depending on the amount of active THC that it contains. In the United States, the weakest, and most widely used, preparation is derived from the tops of uncultivated flowering shoots and is simply called marijuana (or "pot," "grass," "weed," or other nicknames). Much of the marijuana used in the United States is grown here, and until the last few years it was a very weak variety (1 to 2 percent THC). The olive-green native *Cannabis sativa* has been hybridized with the potent Asian *Cannabis indica* and a rapid-growing *Cannabis ruderalis* from Russia to form a "superstrain" of marijuana. Cultivation techniques that include destruction of the male plant and removal of seeds from the female plant have produced the potent simsemilla strains. Foreign (or imported) marijuana is generally stronger than domestic, and some varieties are identified by color, such as Panama Red, Acapulco Gold, and the dark brown plants from Jamaica and Colombia.

Cannabis used in the preparation of bhang in India is of similar potency to American marijuana and appears to be widely used there as a mild intoxicant with no great health or social hazard. For a cannabis product of greater potency than bhang, the small red leaves and resinous material are treated in such a manner that one solid mass is formed. This preparation is called ganja by the

Indians. The most potent source of THC is the pure resin, which is carefully removed from the leaves of the plant. This gummy substance is called charas in India, but Americans are more likely to know it as hashish. Its potency is five to ten times that of marijuana, depending on growing conditions and its use. The resin hardens into a brown lump, a darker color signifying increased potency. Reports vary, but hashish usually has between 10 and 20 percent THC. Liquid hashish, called hash oil, may have concentrations of 30 to 40 percent. Concentrations as high as 43.8 percent have been recorded (Turner, 1981).

Contraband marijuana seized by law authorities is monitored for component chemicals and THC content at the NIDA laboratory at the University of Mississippi. Reports from this laboratory make it apparent that THC concentration in the marijuana available in the United States has been increasing since 1965 (Wiegand, 1991). In 1965 the THC concentration of street marijuana was between 0.1 and 0.2 percent, in 1983 it was between 2 and 4 percent, and in 1986 it averaged 4.13 percent. The sinsemilla variety averaged 6.9 percent THC, with some samples as high as 14 percent (DHHS, 1987).

EFFECTS ON THE BODY

Although many more "smoker-years" will be needed to confirm long-term effects of smoking marijuana, some of the effects of the drug are constant enough in the literature to merit comment. With a brief overview of the physical, phychological, and psychosocial effects that have been suggested to date, we offer a word of caution to those who study the research documents regarding marijuana. When perusing each document, determine the number of subjects used, the presence of control groups, the potency of the substance in terms of the THC content per kilogram of body weight, the mode of administration, the setting, and other aspects of valid experimental research. When comparing newer research with older research, remember that the THC content of marijuana is rising.

Short-Term Effects

Heart Rate and Blood Pressure The most verified effect of marijuana on humans is a dose-related temporary increase in heart rate. Blood pressure tends to drop if the person is standing but remains the same or even rises if the person is sitting or reclining. Health scientists at the National Academy of Sciences Institute of Medicine indicate that marijuana use may be a threat to those with hypertension, cerebrovascular disease, and coronary atherosclerosis. It appears, however, that there are minimal changes in the electrocardiograms of healthy young adults after smoking marijuana (Barnett et al., 1985).

Conjunctival Congestion With the smoking or ingestion of marijuana, there is a reddening of the eyes due to vasodilation of blood vessels.

Psychomotor Performance Research confirms early findings that marijuana use decreases hand steadiness and increases body sway while standing erect. When experiments demand uncomplicated responses to a simple stimulus, marijuana has little effect on reaction time, but when the task is complex, performance is impeded. What appears to be involved is the inability of the marijuana user to display continuous attention or to digest complex information processing. Tracking is an example of a task that requires continuous attention; it has special importance to marijuana smoking because it is a task involved in driving a car, piloting a plane, and operating machinery.

Subjects are also adversely affected by marijuana in experiments in which they are asked to detect and respond to light cues in their peripheral visual fields. These effects may also hinder driving and other machine-operating skills.

Driving Skills Simulator studies show that marijuana intoxication impairs driving skills. In situations that closely simulate actual driving conditions, there is a greater deficit in the ability to perform them while high. It has been found in simulator study that the greatest impairment due to marijuana occurs in the area of perceptual demands rather than car control, but when more realistic conditions were produced by a computer-controlled simulator, marijuana users were significantly less likely to be able to control car velocity and proper positioning in response to wind gusts and driving curves. Also affected are the ability to maintain proper distances and lane position and respond to route signs. The responses seen in simulator study would have resulted in accidents in actual driving situations (DHHS, 1987). It has also been shown that glare recovery time (after driving into headlights at night, for example) is lengthened in marijuana-intoxicated drivers.

It has been found that deficits in automobile driving performance due to marijuana may last several hours after smoking (Barnett et al., 1985), and, using the more complex task of piloting an airplane, Yesavage and colleagues (1985) determined that pilots are impaired for 24 hours following the smoking of one marijuana cigarette containing 19 milligrams of THC. The pilots in this study reported feeling alert and no longer under the influence of marijuana when the 24-hour test was done.

In 1985, fatal auto crashes involving marijuana and alcohol were studied by Williams et al. (1985). In a sample of 440 California male drivers between the ages of 15 and 34 slightly more than half were killed in single-vehicle accidents and 88 percent were considered responsible for the crash. Only 19 percent had no drugs present in the body; 81 percent had one or more drugs present. Alcohol was detected in 70 percent of the cases, cannabinoids in 37 percent, cocaine in 11 percent, diazepam and phencyclidine piperidine (PCP) in 4 percent, and other drugs in 3 percent or less. THC was found alone in 12 percent, in combination with alcohol in 81 percent, and with other drugs in 7 percent.

It was found by Hingston and Zuckerman (1982) that teenagers who drove more than six times per month after having smoked marijuana were nearly 2.5 times more likely to have been involved in traffic accidents than those who did not smoke and drive. Heavier users (fifteen or more times per month) were nearly three times more likely to have an accident. Studies such as these do indicate that marijuana increases the danger of driving under its influence.

Long-Term Physiological Effects

Respiratory Research suggests that marijuana smoke has many harmful effects on the respiratory system in much the same way as cigarette smoke has. When marijuana and tobacco cigarettes are consumed under similar conditions, marijuana produces 38 milligrams of tar compared to 15 milligrams of tar from a popular high tar cigarette brand. When marijuana is smoked as it usually is (deeply inhaled and unfiltered) and compared with a cigarette of equal weight smoked as tobacco typically is, the marijuana cigarette yields 3.8 times as much tar as the tobacco cigarette (DHHS, 1987). Because delta-9-THC localizes in body fat, particularly in the liver, lung, and testes, and disappears slowly, these tissues may be more susceptible to damage.

Extensive pulmonary macrophage infiltration of the lung has been documented in animals and by biopsy in humans. Morris (1985) reported moderate to severe infiltration of the pulmonary alveolar spaces with pigmented macrophages leading to a fibrous tissue response and ulceration. The pigmentation was due to deeply inhaled marijuana smoke. Smokers of marijuana show greater lung impairment than comparable tobacco smokers, at least partially due to the fact that they inhale very deeply, retain the smoke in their lungs for a longer period of time, smoke the joint clear down, and inhale unfiltered smoke. This suggests that chronic obstructive pulmonary disease is a definite possibility in heavy users.

Marijuana smokers display decreased lung diffusion capacity, specific airway conductance, and forced expiratory flow after 2 months of smoking an average of about five marijuana cigarettes daily (Tashkin et al., 1980).

Studies of hash smokers show that heavy use of that drug is related to occurrence of bronchitis, asthma, and sinusitis, and there is evidence that marijuana smoke and smoke residuals contain carcinogenic substances that are related to malignant cellular changes of lung tissue and exposed skin in experiment animals (Glantz, 1984). In fact, marijuana smoke contains 70 percent more carcinogens than cigarette smoke.

Reproduction Although there has been no conclusive statement regarding a possible long-term effect on sperm count in males, studies have shown that delta-9-THC lowers the concentration in blood serum of pituitary hormones (gonadotropins) that control reproductive functions. Chronic marijuana use can lower sperm counts in males and may affect menstrual cycles and ovulation in females. These effects appear to be reversible when use stops and, in females, when tolerance is established. Temporary sterility may sometimes result, however, when couples are marginally fertile. Despite earlier speculation and warnings of potential genetic damage, no evidence of chromosome damage to cells incubated with THC has been found in either animals or humans (Cook et al., 1990).

Regular marijuana use during at least two developmental phases can be detrimental: during adolescence and during fetal development. Endocrine development during puberty is strongly dependent upon a properly functioning hypothalamus and pituitary gland, areas where marijuana is known to adversely affect the production of gonadotropins. Marijuana consumption by adolescents or males with marginal fertility may pose a hazard.

It can now be said with certainty that maternal marijuana use poses a hazard to the fetus. Marijuana readily crosses the placenta, although transport is higher in early pregnancy than in the last trimester. The drug level in the bloodstream of the marijuana-smoking mother is generally greater than that of the fetus, ranging from 2.5 to 7 times higher (Cook et al., 1990). Marijuana increases carbon monoxide levels in the mother's blood, which can reduce the oxygen in the fetal blood.

Marijuana use by the mother is associated with lower infant birth weight and length compared to non-users. Hingston and colleagues (1984) reported that women who used marijuana fewer than three times a week delivered infants averaging 95 grams lighter, and those who used it more than three times a week delivered babies 139 grams lighter than those of non-using mothers. Other studies have failed to find consistent reductions in gestation, infant length, and birth weight, and so it is possible that variations in the composition of marijuana; other maternal factors such as health, socioeconomic background, and lifestyle; and other methodological issues may be involved.

It has been shown that the mother's use of marijuana during pregnancy is a predictor of symptoms of fetal alcohol syndrome (FAS) in the infant, and of all drugs that might be taken during pregnancy, marijuana is the most highly predictive of congenital malformations (Zuckerman et al., 1989). Hingston and colleagues (1982) found that pregnant women who used marijuana during pregnancy were five times as likely to deliver infants who showed features seen in FAS. A study in Brooklyn (Qazi et al., 1985) of five mothers who had smoked two to fourteen joints a day prior to and during pregnancy reported that all the infants had low birth weights, small head circumferences, tremors at birth, abnormal epicanthic folds, posteriorly rotated ears, long philtrums (the groove on the upper lip), high arched palates, and abnormal palm creases—all symptoms of FAS. These mothers denied any use of alcohol or other psychoactive drugs during this time.

Marijuana is rapidly transmitted into breast milk and remains there for a prolonged period. Thus nursing is not recommended for mothers who smoke marijuana and are unwilling or unable to give it up (Cook et al., 1990).

The effects of marijuana on prenatally exposed children appear to include slower visual responsiveness and diminished mental, motor, and language outcomes in the 1-to-4-year-olds studied to date. For many children, these effects may be too subtle to be measured in early childhood but may be manifested by school age.

Scientific evidence to date suggests that there are no mutagenic or cytogenic effects that occur from marijuana use, but investigation should not be considered complete until we experience many more smoker-years of marijuana use.

Immunity   Some studies of the immune system demonstrate marijuana's immunosuppressant effect. Cabral and colleagues (1985) noted that THC does decrease host resistance to herpes simplex in guinea pigs. It also appears to inhibit the production of both B- and T-lymphocytes, especially the former. Other preliminary reports suggest that THC modifies lymphocyte membranes and prostaglandin production in vitro (it should be noted that AIDS is caused by a destruction of T4 lymphocytes). The jury will remain out on the issue of marijuana and human immunosuppression until more time can be given to its study. The question is of some importance because THC is used to reduce the nausea associated with cancer chemotherapy. Since chemotherapy chemicals are themselves severely immunosuppressive, any additional suppression would not be desirable (DHHS, 1987). In vitro studies have shown that THC modifies lymphocyte membranes and prostaglandin production and inhibits macrophage spreading and phagocytosis. If confirmed in animals or humans, a further mechanism of immune inhibition might be established. Long-range, large-scale studies in this area have yet to be done, and most smokers are relatively young and still have a healthy degree of immunity.

Brain   Researchers at the National Center for Toxicological Research have provided the first quantitative evidence that chronic THC exposure damages and destroys nerve cells and causes other pathological changes in the hippo-campal area of the brain. The research showed not only a loss of neurons in the hippocampus, but also changes in glial (or supporting) cells like those typically seen following brain damage. The loss of cells appears to be identical to the loss seen with normal aging. Mild functional losses due to aging and those due to THC use could be additive, possibly placing long-term marijuana users at risk for serious or premature memory disorders as they age. Although these studies are preliminary and are being replicated, their results are currently the best available evidence indicating that long-term marijuana use has a toxic effect on the brain (Friedman, 1987).

Brain wave changes from cannabis generally consist of an increase and slowing of alpha waves. Although scalp EEG records show minimal altera-tions, electrodes implanted in deep brain structures like the septum (a center for emotionality) show marked changes in electrical activity. The findings from deep electrode study in septal areas are suggestive that long-term heavy use of marijuana or THC may produce microscopic changes. The possibility of mac-roscopic changes in the form of cerebral atrophy remains open (DHHS, 1987). Although there appears to be no permanent change in brain structure due to marijuana use, behavioral changes are apparent (Glantz, 1984).

Behavior   From the time of early popularization of marijuana, some users have reported negative experiences that range from mild anxiety to acute panic, and an acute brain syndrome that includes disorientation, confusion, and memory impairment was reported as early as 1969 (Talbott & Teague, 1969). These negative experiences usually occur in inexperienced users, those who encounter an unexpectedly high potency, or those who use higher doses than usual. A Swedish study reported a causal link between heavy hashish use and a schizophrenic-like state that included aggressiveness, confusion, and affective lability (Palsson et al., 1982). It is becoming clear in the United States that marijuana is capable of having adverse effects on both physical and mental health.

It is usually found that marijuana-related cognitive or behavioral difficulties are not attributed to the drug initially. Only later in psychological treatment do adolescent clients become aware of the role marijuana plays in their dysfunction. Older users are more likely to see a connection between their drug use and impairment of their various relationships or their inability to curtail the use of marijuana. Prompting the client to remain abstinent for several months may be especially helpful in therapy because he or she often notices an emergence from mildly confused thinking, apathy, and loss of energy, whereas the entry into the state was imperceptible.

It appears likely that long-term marijuana use is related to apathy, lack of goal pursuit, and general confusion in many young and older users alike. It is difficult to say which came first, this amotivational syndrome or the smoking of marijuana. There are strong indications that motivational effects are highly related to use and that normal motivation may return following cessation of use of the drug. More than half of the high school seniors who stopped using marijuana said they did so because of "loss of energy or ambition," and about 40 percent of the daily users thought that it interfered with their ability to think and contributed to their loss of interest in other activities (Barnett et al., 1985).

Of grave concern are the possible behavioral effects of marijuana on the social and psychological growth and development of child and adolescent users. Clinicians who treat children and adolescents who are heavy users are convinced that such use seriously interferes with normal functioning and development (Barnett et al., 1985). This interference can be reasonably assumed, as the drug experience is a temporary pleasure device, totally unreal and thus unrelated to ongoing life. Such experiences tempt the user to go back for a better feeling. Overemphasis on the "feeling" world of subjective experiences may lead the user to withdraw in order to search for triggers of such experiences, becoming self-absorbed and selfish, with diminished motivation to participate in growth experiences. Growth experiences are those for which the individual feels responsible; they are active and creative and are used as stepping stones toward additional growth, and they are activities that meet long-term psychological needs such as self-respect, self-esteem, and self-love. Growth experiences are often directed outward to others, helping the individuals to overcome feelings of separateness and fulfilling the need to belong. If drug use inhibits this process, especially in the adolescent years, social and psychological growth can be severely retarded.

Psychological and Psychosocial Effects

Several specific types of psychological performance are impaired by marijuana use. These include recent memory, transfer of information from immediate to long-term memory storage, digit/symbol substitution, digit span, serial subtraction, complex reaction time, reading comprehension, and estimation of time. All of these effects are dose-related. The more complex, unfamiliar, and demanding the task, the greater the impairment is apt to be. Because of these findings, it is apparent that marijuana use has disruptive effects on classroom abilities.

Marijuana use also alters perception of sight, sound, and touch; it affects mood and social interaction. For some, it is these effects that are sought in the marijuana high.

The psychological tests currently available for use cannot detect significant differences between moderate users and non-users of marijuana, but they show that long-term marijuana use seems to correlate with manifest psychopathology. Heavy users of marijuana (twenty to thirty times per month) appear to be psychologically similar to abusers of other drugs. Heavy marijuana users were discovered to be multiple drug users who exhibited some degree of psychological dependence, manifested by anxiety when supply is uncertain, and a self-perceived inability to relate to the world in general when not high. Heavy users were judged to have a poorer work adjustment and a self-reported inability to master new problems. In addition, heavy users expressed poor heterosexual adjustment and were found to be more depressed and hostile toward society and to have more anxieties than casual users. The average casual user (one to four times a month) was not unlike the average non-user in the above-mentioned categories.

Longitudinal and cross-sectional studies have shown that heavy marijuana use is associated with poor academic performance and motivation, various kinds of delinquent behavior, problems with authority, and lack of self-esteem (Glantz, 1984). These aspects of psychosocial behavior (see Table 5) have generally been found to precede the drug use, although individual case studies may show that the drug use precedes diminished motivation and performance.

Predictors may also include lower self-esteem and a greater degree of personal dissatisfaction and depression.

TABLE 5
PSYCHOSOCIAL DESCRIPTORS
OF MARIJUANA USERS

Rejection of parental and school authority (rebellion)
A dislike for school
A sense of alienation
Truancy
Valuing independence more than achievement
Being more peer-oriented than parent-oriented
Having a more positive attitude toward drug use in general
Theft and vandalism
Lying
Interpersonal aggression

Generally, young people who are highly peer-oriented are more likely to use drugs. Users are much more likely than non-users to have friends who are users also.

Another issue with marijuana use has continually arisen. This issue is the "stepping stone" theory—that the use of marijuana leads to the use of other illicit drugs. There is statistical certainty that marijuana use (especially heavy use) is associated with the use of other drugs, including alcohol and tobacco. Because of the relationship between the use of marijuana and that of licit drugs, prevention strategies are being broadened to include the licit drugs.

MEDICAL USE

Reports found in ancient Chinese and Indian texts of the medicinal use of cannabis show that it was recommended for hundreds of problems, including insomnia, pain, anxiety, and tension, and was used sporadically throughout history. By the early 1900s, however, Western medicine had nearly given it up, since the extract was of a varying potency and was considered to have a poor shelf life. Also, because of its poor water solubility, a physician had no way of knowing whether or not it was absorbed by the patient. The final death knell for the medicinal use of marijuana was sounded by the Marijuana Tax Act in 1937, when the drug was officially classified as a narcotic. Physicians found it easier and safer to prescribe other drugs.

In the 1970s, Pfizer Pharmaceutical Company manufactured a drug called levonantradol, based on THC, in the hope of using it as an analgesic. They found it to be effective as a painkiller, but the side effects of sedation, red eyes, dry mouth, dizziness, and dysphoria outweighed its clinical usefulness. The drug did not make it past clinical trials. Currently, there is one FDA-approved THC compound, dronabinol, which is used to prevent the nausea and vomiting that often accompany the taking of anticancer medication (Griffith, 1988). Dronabinol has been used with AIDS patients to help them regain their appetities, and preliminary studies have shown some success. Marijuana has also been found to have therapeutic effects on epilepsy, glaucoma, asthma, pain, and hypertension. With the discovery of THC receptor sites in the brain, new therapeutic applications of THC may expand to such disorders as tremors, spasticity, muscle tone problems, and others (Herkenham et al., 1990).

Because of the side effects of smoking marijuana (e.g., bronchial irritation), because of the difficult chemical properties of cannabis, and because cannabis cannot be patented by pharmaceutical companies, the cannabis products recognized in the United States are synthetic analogues of THC tailored to avoid some of the effects of the natural drug. The ideal agent would demonstrate stability and water solubility and would selectively cause vasodilation, sedation, or whatever effect is sought, with as few side effects as possible. In all cases of its use, there is the possibility of undesirable psychological side effects, which makes it necessary for the physician to administer this drug selectively.

REFERENCES

Barnett, G., Licko, V., and Thompson, T. (1985). Behavioral pharmacokinetics of marijuana. *Phychopharmacology,* 85:51–56.

Cabral, G. A., Miskin, E. M., and Holsapple, M. P. (1985). Delta nine THC decreases host resistance to herpes simplex virus type 2 vaginal infection in the guinea pig. In D. J. Harvey (Ed.), *Marijuana 84: Proceedings of the Oxford Symposium on Cannabis.* Oxford: IRL Press.

Cook, P. S., Petersen, R. C., and Moore, D. T. (1990). *Alcohol, Tobacco, and Other Drugs May Harm the Unborn.* Rockville, Md.: U.S. Department of Health and Human Services.

DHHS. (1987). *Second Triennial Report to Congress from the Secretary of Department of Health and Human Services.* Washington, D.C: U.S. Government Printing Office.

Friedman, David. (1987). Effects of marijuana on the brain. *NIDA Notes,* 2(1):6–7.

Glantz, Meyer D. (ed.). (1984). *Correlates and Consequences of Marijuana Use.* Washington, D.C.: U.S. Department of Health and Human Services.

Griffith, H. W. (1988). *Complete Guide to Prescription and Non-prescription Drugs.* Los Angeles: The Body Press.

Herkenham, M., Lynn, A. B., Little, M. D., et al. (1990). Cannabinoid receptor localization in the brain. *Proceedings of the National Academy of Sciences,* 87:1932–1936.

Hingston, R., and Zuckerman, B. (1982). Teenage driving after using marijuana or drinking and traffic accident involvement. *Journal of Safety Research,* 13(1):33–38.

Hingston, R., et al. (1982). Effects of maternal drinking and marijuana use on fetal growth and development. *Pediatrics,* 70(4):539–546.

Hingston, R., et al. (1984). Effects on fetal development of maternal marijuana use during pregnancy. In D. J. Harvey (Ed.), *Marijuana '84: Proceedings of the Oxford Symposium on Marijuana.* Oxford: IRL Press, pp. 323–332.

Holloway, Marguerite. (1991). Trends in pharmacology: Rx for addiction. *Scientific American,* March, pp. 95–103.

McConnell, H. (1991). Many marijuana users need help. *The Journal, Addiction Research Foundation,* February, p. 34.

Morris, R. R. (1985). Human pulmonary histopathological changes from marijuana smoking. *Journal of Forensic Sciences,* 30:345–349.

National Commission on Marijuana and Drug Abuse. (1972). *Marijuana: A Signal of Misunderstanding.* Washington, D.C.: U.S. Government Printing Office.

NIDA. (1991). Statistics from the national household survey on drug use. *NIDA Notes,* 6(1):31.

Palsson, A., Thulin, S. O., and Tunving, K. (1982). Cannabis psychoses in south Sweden. *Acta Psychiatrica Scandinavica,* 66:311–321.

Qazi, Q. H., et al. (1985). Abnormalities in offspring associated with prenatal marijuana exposure. *Developments in Pharamacoligical Therapy,* 9:141–148.

Schwartz, R. H., Hayden, G. F., and Riddle, M. (1985). Laboratory detection of marijuana use. *American Journal of Diseases of Children,* 139:1093–1096.

Talbott, J. A., and Teague, J. W. (1969). Marijuana psychosis: acute toxic psychosis associated with the use of cannabis derivatives. *JAMA,* 210:299–302.

Tashkin, D. P., et al. (1980). Respiratory status of seventy-four habitual marijuana smokers. *Chest,* 78:699–706.

Turner, C. E. (1981). *The Marijuana Controversy.* Rockville, Md.: American Council for Drug Education.

Wiegand, Steve. (1991). Marijuana of '90s more potent, less plentiful. *Fresno Bee*, pp. 3, 6.

Williams, A. F., Peat, M. A., and Crouch, D. S. (1985). Drugs in fatally injured young male drivers. *Pharmacological Chemistry Newsletter*, 14:1–11.

Willis, D. K. (1984). Global war on drugs. *Denver Post*, Feb. 19, p. 23.

Yesavage, J. A., et al. (1985). Carry-over effects of marijuana intoxication on aircraft pilot performance; a preliminary report. *American Journal of Psychiatry*, 142(11):1325–1329.

Zuckerman, B., et al. (1989). Effects of maternal marijuana and cocaine use on fetal growth. *New England Journal of Medicine*, 320(7):762–768.

COCAINE

HISTORY

Cocaine is a powerful central nervous system stimulant derived from the leaves of the shrub *Erythroxylon coca,* which is native to South America, especially Peru and Bolivia, where it thrives in the warm valleys around 5,000 feet above sea level. In favorable conditions the plant yields crops four or five times a year for about 40 years.

Cocaine is a drug with recorded use dating back hundreds of years. Coca's oldest use was in religious ceremonies as an inducer of meditative trance and as an aid for communicating with nature. The Incas reserved coca use for the nobility and priests, and those who were granted permission to use it were in extreme imperial favor. The leaves were offered in sacrifice to the gods, chewed during worship, and placed into the mouths of the dead to ensure a favorable welcome in the next life. For a while after the Spanish conquest of Peru, coca use was forbidden, until the Spanish discovered that the Indians could perform more work on less food while using the drug. A daily ration was then provided for the laborers. That practice became a habit that has never been relinquished. Even today Indians carry on their long, arduous journeys a wad of coca leaves and a wad of plant ash. The leaves dipped in a small amount of ash are made into a quid in the mouth and chewed for hours. When physical exertion is to be increased, so too is the amount of leaves to be chewed.

The coca plant from which cocaine is derived was introduced to Europe in the sixteenth century but went practically unnoticed until the late nineteenth century when scientific investigation into its potential was begun. In 1884 one of its most ardent supporters, Sigmund Freud, began a series of experiments and published numerous reports on its beneficial effects. Freud was an enthusiastic user of cocaine, which he called the "magical drug." He proclaimed that it possessed almost unbelievable curative power and could relieve a number of disorders, including morphine addiction, depression, and chronic fatigue. Although Freud never publicly retracted his broad endorsement of cocaine, he eventually acknowledged its dangers and conceded that it had failed as a cure for morphine addiction.

In America during that same era, cocaine was enjoying considerable popularity as a remedy for numerous ills and became a common ingredient in many medicinal tonics. The most famous of these was the original Coca-Cola, which included flavoring from imported coca leaves. The government soon became alarmed at the number of Americans with the "cocaine habit" and moved to ban its consumption. In 1906 the Pure Food and Drug Act legally classified cocaine as a narcotic, imposing the same penalties for illegal possession of cocaine as for heroin, opium, and morphine. This gave rise to the lingering misconception that cocaine is a narcotic, which, of course, it is not. The inclusion of cocaine in this act did not go unopposed because cocaine enjoyed wide popularity. It was argued that cocaine was the greatest of all drugs, curing melancholy and restoring vigor to men. Cocaine was said to bring on liveliness, creativity, energy, glamor, and even lust. And when consumed by people aware of its potential dangers, it would cause no harm. The one argument that proved an accurate prognostication was that prohibition would result in underground traffic and enormous profits for the dealers, who would seek out and entice new customers.

For the next 40 years, cocaine use seemed to reach an all-time low. But confiscation at border checkpoints and medical reports in the late 1970s signaled an increase in cocaine traffic and use; during the first half of the 1970s, cocaine became one of the most popular street drugs. The reasons for the sudden increase in popularity are still not known. Some experts hypothesize that publicity created a snowball effect in a culture increasingly enamored with drug consumption in general.

Today, cocaine is sold to street-drug buyers at a high price. Because it was scarce and expensive, cocaine became the "champagne of drugs," known in the drug subculture as the "rich man's drug." Its scarcity, its processing, and its elaborate distribution network all contributed to its high price. With increasing amounts of cocaine coming into the country, its use now appears regularly among the middle class, young and old alike, creating the need for educators to learn how to identify progressive cocaine abuse among adolescents. With more women leaving the traditional homemaker role, they constitute one-third to one-half of all substance abusers, including those linked to cocaine addiction. Cocaine has emerged as the illegal drug of choice among women, second only to marijuana (Greenleaf, 1990).

The coca plant is grown and harvested mainly in Bolivia and Peru, and the leaves are made into cocaine paste. This in turn is converted into cocaine base, and then into cocaine hydrochloride. Colombia is the major refiner and exporter of cocaine to the United States. It processes and distributes up to 70 percent of the cocaine entering this country, which is mainly through Florida. Once in the United States the drug is distributed through a hierarchical system similar to the heroin distribution system. The fact that cocaine's potency deteriorates over time creates the necessity of a precise network of distribution, which increases the risk and also the profits. Cocaine is almost always adulterated, being cut with synthetics such as Procaine, Benzocaine, and speed.

CLASSIFICATION

Cocaine is a powerful stimulant that produces an overwhelming sympathetic nervous system response.

HOW TAKEN INTO THE BODY

Cocaine comes in three basic forms: the rock form, the flake form considered by connoisseurs to be a delicacy, and the most common "street coke," the powder form, which is usually diluted. In its pure form, cocaine is a white crystalline powder that looks like sugar (hence the nickname "snow"). It is sniffed (snorted) in powder form, liquefied and injected, or made into "freebase" and smoked (Jeffcoat et al., 1989). Freebasing removes water-soluble adulterants in order to increase the drug's lipid solubility for better absorption and to produce a substance that is more suitable for smoking. Smoking freebase produces a shorter and more intense "high" because the drug enters the blood more rapidly than with oral or nasal administration (NIDA, 1986). Smoking freebase is also becoming increasingly popular as a method of taking cocaine into the body because sniffing cocaine leads to deteriorating of the lining of nasal passageways and, eventually, of the nasal septum.

Until about 1985 street market freebase was produced almost exclusively via the ether method. This process was relatively quick, but ether is quite volatile and explosive accidents were not uncommon. More recently the freebase distributed in the street has been produced using baking soda rather than ether. The product known as "crack" or "rock" appears as hard shavings similar to slivers of soap (but has the general texture of porcelain) and is sold in small vials, folding papers, or heavy aluminum foil. It is smoked in a pipe or mixed with marijuana and gives an instant cocaine high, which may last 5 to 10 minutes or up to half an hour. Crack is poorly soluble in water and cannot be injected or snuffed. It is easily prepared from cocaine hydrochloride powder, baking soda, and water. When crack is heated at 95 degrees Celsius or higher, it vaporizes. The vapors are inhaled deeply through a special glass pipe or a homemade apparatus made from an aluminum can. The vapors are immediately taken into the lung circulation and enter the brain in about 8 seconds (faster than intravenously administed cocaine).

Coca paste, the first extraction of the manufacturing process, is another form of cocaine that can be smoked. It is usually placed in a marijuana or tobacco cigarette. Coca-paste smoking, while very common in South America, is not popular in the United States.

Rock cocaine is pebble-sized, irregularly shaped crystalline chunks of cocaine hydrochloride, initially seen by its users as being free of any adulterants. Rock cocaine makes use of cocaine hydrochloride and a bonding agent, with the resulting compound pressed to a uniform size. Rock cocaine is typically white and has been described as being about the size of a pencil eraser, it is usually heated and inhaled.

CHARACTERISTICS OF DEPENDENCE

Cocaine is highly sought after for its euphoria-producing capability, and thus cocaine or "crack" users are highly susceptible to psychological dependence on the drug. Physical dependence and a formidable withdrawal also occur with cocaine.

Most heavy users (those who have smoked crack more than fifty times) report preoccupation with thoughts of crack, rapid loss of ability to modulate their use of the drug, and rapid development of pharmacologic tolerance. A majority of heavy users progress from first crack use to using it at least once a week in less than 3 months (Schwartz et al., 1991).

PHARMACOLOGY

Pharmacologically, cocaine exhibits two different and unrelated actions. First of all, it acts as a local anesthetic. After local application, cocaine will block the conduction of impulses in nerve fibers for about 20 to 40 minutes, owing to its ability to interfere with the movement of sodium ions through the nerve cell. Second, it is a powerful central nervous system stimulant.

It appears that cocaine diminishes the ability of central nervous system cells (specifically in regions such as the nucleus accumbens and the frontal cortex) to break down dopamine and take it back into the nerve cells. This allows the excitatory neurohormone dopamine to continue to stimulate other cells that, in this case, mediate reinforcement or self-administration behavior (Goldstein, 1989; Reith, 1988).

Unlike most natural reward systems (e.g., food, water, sex), which have an upper boundary of self-administration, cocaine does not turn itself off. Intravenous or inhaled cocaine eludes this inhibitory defense mechanism, and laboratory animals will self-administer intravenous stimulants until they kill themselves unless they have to work too hard or it becomes too painful to obtain the reward (Herrnstein, 1990).

EFFECTS ON THE BODY

Cocaine can be absorbed through any mucous membrane and is carried by the blood to the heart, lungs, and the rest of the body. Inhaled intranasally, it reaches the brain and neurons of the sympathetic nervous system in 3 minutes; injected, in 15 seconds; smoked, in 7 seconds.

Cocaine affects two major areas of the brain—the cerebral cortex (which governs higher mental activity, such as memory and reasoning) and the meso-limbic system (an inner brain region governing emotion and such drives as appetite, body temperature, sleep, and thirst) (Holloway, 1991). The brain chemical responsible for cocaine's euphoria (dopamine) may also cause the intense craving addicts experience when they stop taking the drug (Medical Post, 1990).

Upon introduction into the body, the chemical is metabolized rapidly by the blood and liver. Its actions on the sympathetic nervous system mimic the body's fight-or-flight response. Cocaine is a vasoconstrictor, narrowing peripheral blood vessels. The heart rate and respiration are quickened, blood pressure increases, and the body's metabolism is stepped up. Cocaine's effects are similar to those of amphetamine. In fact, subjects in research studies could not distinguish between the effects of the two at lower doses, except that amphetamine's actions are longer-lasting.

Exhilarating euphoria (ecstasy), feelings of omnipotence, affability, and invincible self-confidence are experienced for about 20 minutes after crack use, followed by a period of about an hour of hypomanic behavior. After that, a period of anhedonia (the inability to experience pleasure) and, in many cases, deep depression (perhaps caused by depletion of neurochemical transmitters of the dopaminergic type) often persist for several hours if the system is not exposed to more cocaine (Schwartz et al., 1991).

The intense high from smoking freebase strikes almost immediately, producing an overwhelming rush similar to that experienced by intravenous users. This rush lasts a few seconds and is replaced by a euphoric excitation that lasts for several minutes. A 5-to-20-minute period of less pleasurable hyperexcitability follows.

The extreme euphoria associated with cocaine tapers off—gradually when used intranasally, more quickly when injected—and the physiological and psychological depression that follows is characterized by a "letdown" feeling of dullness, tenseness, and edginess. The ultimate high degenerates into an ultimate low.

Throughout history coca has been used as a physical energizer. The ability of coca to reduce hunger and fatigue and to stimulate muscular activity has been widely published. Even if this metabolic action does occur, the effect on the user still depends on numerous factors. As with any drug, the effects of a minimal dose in particular varies with the mental state and physical well-being of the individual user. The stimulation is much more profound if the user is physically below par, feeling fatigued or hungry. The effects are minimal if the normal euphoria associated with good health is present. Cocaine has been shown to have a positive effect on muscle activity in general and, more specifically, on reaction time and muscular strength. Researchers have not been able to demonstrate any direct effect of cocaine on motor nerves or muscle groups; thus they have concluded that its effect is probably indirect, acting to increase the general sense of well-being and preparedness for work.

The action on the central nervous system, creating euphoria and a feeling of excitement, represents the prime motivator for the use of cocaine. Cocaine reinforces the highest aspirations of initiative and achievement by providing the user with greater energy and optimism.

Because cocaine is short-acting, it may be used repeatedly, and excessive amounts (10 grams or more) may be taken within a single day. A lethal dose is approximately 1.2 grams for most individuals if the entire amount is taken at one time. When applied to mucous membranes, cocaine can cause death with a dose as low as 30 milligrams. Death in this case is due to respiratory failure, although this occurrence is rare. Large doses or long-term use may lead to anxiety, hallucinations, impotence, and insomnia. Large doses create a feeling of muscular and mental strength as well as visual, auditory, and tactile hallucinations. Paranoid delusions, combined with the excessive sense of personal power, can make a person who is consuming large doses, especially by injection, very antisocial and dangerous. Quick changes in perception occur frequently; judgment is impaired; there is a release of inhibitions; and aggression, panic reactions, and eventual agitated depression are characteristic of the cocaine abuser.

SPECIAL DANGERS

The dangers inherent in cocaine use, discovered during the drug's first wave of popularity a century ago, were largely forgotten or disregarded when the drug resurfaced in the late 1960s. As recently as the mid-1970s, cocaine was commonly regarded as harmless and benign and was viewed by many as the ideal "recreational" drug. Since that time the risks associated with cocaine use have become increasingly clear, currently making it a prime target of the war on drugs. The violence that often follows abuse of this drug is continually in the media, and the first wave of "crack babies" have recently entered the public school systems throughout the United States (Hanzlick & Gowitt, 1991; Rist, 1990).

One of the most severe dangers of cocaine is that regular use can create a dependence as intense as that associated with any other drug. A true withdrawal syndrome following long-term use is also now believed to occur. Such symptoms as depression, social withdrawal, drug craving, tremor, muscle pain, eating disturbance, and sleep and EEG changes, which are powerful motivators to resume use, are now believed to have a physiological, and not simply a psychological, basis (Weddington et al., 1990). Those who become habitual users see their physical and mental health begin to erode, their financial resources are drained, they lose their families and friends, and their careers are left in shambles. The elation and excitement created by the drug wear off, leaving the user exhausted and depressed. If more of the drug is available, the temptation is strong to "self-medicate" by taking more. This can lead to binges that can last for several days. Binges are followed by "crashes," periods of intense dysphoria, irritability, restlessness, lethargy, and the inability to feel emotions. This "post-cocaine" state persists for days and provides a powerful incentive for the user to procure even more of the drug. "Crashes" are less common and less severe among those who use cocaine intranasally, but the more serious one becomes about cocaine use, the more likely one is to begin freebasing or shooting it. Because these routes of use produce a far more intense high, those who smoke or inject it are rarely content to return to snorting.

Daily or binge users characteristically undergo profound personality changes. They become confused, anxious, and depressed. They are short-tempered and grow suspicious of friends, loved ones, and coworkers. Their thinking is impaired, and they have difficulty concentrating. They experience weakness and lassitude, and other responsibilities fall into neglect. Some become aggressive; some experience panic attacks.

Over time, cocaine begins to exact a toll on the body as well as the mind. Those who sniff the drug regularly experience a running nose, burns and sores on the nasal membranes (sometimes to the point of perforating the septum), sore throats and hoarseness. Long-term use may damage the liver. Although there has been insufficient study to determine whether cocaine causes neural damage, the common properties it shares with the drugs that do would lead one to believe that neural damage due to cocaine is highly likely. Cocaine has been shown to injure cerebral arteries. The acute hypertension sometimes brought on by cocaine use has been known to burst weakened blood vessels. Studies suggest that cocaine can bring on acute high blood pressure that can cause a blood vessel in the brain to rupture, causing a stroke.

Some medical complications of crack use are chronic fatigue, insomnia, anorexia, weight loss, chronic cough, fainting spells, and brain seizures. For further discussion of cocaine-related conditions, refer to Section 3 of this book.

Overdose and Death

The most common causes of death from cocaine abuse are respiratory paralysis, heart rhythm disturbances, and repeated convulsions, usually from massive overdoses or at the end of a binge. Death from cocaine overdose comes swiftly. Typically, individuals with no apparent symptoms lapse suddenly into grand mal convulsions, followed in a minute or so by respiratory collapse and death. Users sometimes die from smaller doses than those they have taken previously with no obvious effects. Murder is not uncommon in the high stakes world of cocaine dealing (Prevention Networks, 1986).

MEDICAL USE

Therapeutic or medical use of cocaine as a local anesthetic is becoming very limited. It is sometimes used in cosmetic surgery.

REFERENCES

Goldstein, A. (Ed.). (1989). *Molecular and Cellular Aspects of the Drug Addictions.* New York: Springer-Verlag.

Greenleaf, V. D. (1990). Women and cocaine. *New Realities,* May/June, pp. 21–27.

Hanzlick, R., and Gowitt, G. T. (1991). Cocaine metabolite detection in homicide victims. *JAMA,* 265(6):760–761.

Herrnstein, R. J. (1990). Addictions and other pathological choices. *American Psychology,* 45(3):356.

Holloway, M. (1991). Trends in pharmacology: Rx for addiction. *Scientific American,* March, pp. 95–103.

Jeffcoat, A. R., et al. (1989). Cocaine disposition in humans after intravenous injection, nasal insufflation (snorting), or smoking. *Drug Metabolism and Disposition,* 17:153–158.

Medical Post. (1990). Cocaine cravings in addicts linked to dopamine function. *Medical Post,* June 5, p. 19.

NIDA. (1986). *Cocaine Use in America.* Washington, D.C.: U.S. Department of Health and Human Services.

Reith, M. E. A. (1988). Mechanisms of cocaine abuse and toxicity. In D. Clouet, K. Asghar, and R. Brown (Eds.), *Mechanisms of Cocaine Abuse and Toxicity.* NIDA Research Monograph 88.Washington, D.C.: U.S. Government Printing Office.

Rist, Marilee. (1990). The shadow children: preparing for the arrival of crack babies in school. *Research Bulletin of Phi Delta Kappa,* July, No. 9; pp. 1–6.

Schwartz, R. H., Luxenberg, M. G., and Hoffmann, N. G. (1991). "Crack" use by American middle-class adolescent polydrug abusers. *Journal of Pediatrics,* 118(1): 150–155.

Weddington, W. W., et al. (1990). Changes in mood, craving, and sleep during short-term abstinence reported by male cocaine addicts. *Archives of General Psychiatry,* 47:861–868.

AMPHETAMINES

HISTORY

Amphetamines (*alpha-methylphenethylamines*) have been used as stimulant drugs for a number of years. In 1927, Alles (1927) synthesized an amphetamine (Benzedrine) and learned of its stimulatory nature, which mimicked the action of the sympathetic nervous system. One of the first uses of Benzedrine was as a vasoconstrictor for nasal passageways—the Benzedrine inhaler was introduced in 1932 by Smith, Kline and French Laboratories of Philadelphia. Later, this inhaler was removed from the market because of its frequent abuse.

Further study indicated that there was an amphetamine closely related to Benzedrine (this was called Dexedrine) and led to the discovery of methamphetamine ("speed"). Dexedrine is of greater potency than Benzedrine, with the effects of methamphetamine somewhere in between. Of the three, Dexedrine is probably of greatest medical use because, even though its stimulatory effects on the central nervous system are greater than those of the other two, it offers fewer side effects. This is one of the main reasons Dexedrine is the amphetamine most frequently used in diet pills today.

The Drug Abuse Warning Network system reported a 200 percent increase in methamphetamine abuse between 1985 and 1987, with an additional 100 percent increase in 1988 (NIDA, 1990a). The "typical" abuser is characterized as 20 to 35 years old, white, with a high school education. Approximately one-third of all methamphetamine abusers are women of childbearing age (Burchfield et al., 1991).

The use of Ice (also known as L.A. Glass and crank), a synthetic smokable form of methamphetamine, has been low and limited to several Western cities on the U.S. mainland but has reached epidemic proportions in Hawaii. Ice (*d*-methamphetamine hydrochloride) is a highly pure crystal that produces an intense euphoria when smoked. The effects of Ice last from 4 to 14 hours. Some fear that Ice will replace crack as the U.S. epidemic drug of the 1990s because of its availability, affordability, and prolonged high (NIDA, 1990b).

CLASSIFICATION

The effects of the amphetamines are typically those of an activated sympathetic nervous system. These combined reactions of alertness, wakefulness, and attentiveness are characteristics of the stress reaction, or the "fight-or-flight" syndrome. The following physiological reactions occur:

1 Constriction of blood vessels
2 Increased heart rate and stronger myocardial contractions
3 Rise in blood pressure
4 Dilation of the bronchi
5 Relaxation of intestinal muscle
6 Mydriasis (dilation of the pupil)
7 Increased blood sugar levels
8 Shorter blood coagulation time
9 Increased muscle tension
10 Stimulation of the adrenal glands

HOW TAKEN INTO THE BODY

Pharmaceutical company amphetamines come in pills and capsules and thus are taken orally in most instances. Methamphetamine ("speed," "meth," "crystal meth") is commonly injected intravenously, making it a doubly dangerous drug if the syringe is contaminated. These drugs may also be smoked (inhaled). About 62 percent of abusers report intravenous administration, 13 percent oral administration, and 7 percent smoking methamphetamine (Hall et al., 1988).

CHARACTERISTICS OF DEPENDENCE

Tolerance and psychological dependence occur with continued use of amphetamines. When amphetamine administration ceases after long-term abuse, withdrawal occurs.

PHARMACOLOGY

The mechanism of the stimulants appears to be that of mimicking the action of, increasing the release of, or decreasing the reuptake of, one or both of the neurotransmitters dopamine and norepinephrine in specific brain areas such as the cortex and reticular activating system (Holbrook, 1983). Amphetamines also block the enzyme monoamine oxidase (MAO), which normally inactivates the neurotransmitter. Collectively, these mechanisms cause more endogenous neurotransmitter substance to interact with its receptor. Analysis of both the physiological and behavioral effects suggests that the site of amphetamine action is in the brainstem, closely related to the reticular activating system, which accounts for the effect of alertness, and in the hypothalamus, which explains behavioral reactions such as the elevation of mood and loss of hunger. However, the observed behavioral effects of amphetamine are dependent upon which area of the brain is most affected (McMillen, 1983).

EFFECTS ON THE BODY

Amphetamines are quickly absorbed from the alimentary tract and also from other sites of administration. A relatively large proportion of an amphetamine taken into the body is excreted unchanged through the kidney; thus amphetamine is found in the urine soon after ingestion. Since metabolism of amphetamines is slow, the drug is found in the urine for several subsequent days.

Subjective effects of amphetamines include a feeling of euphoria, a sense of well-being, a reduced hunger for food (anorexia), loquaciousness, hyperactivity, and a feeling of increased mental and physical power. A single dose (5 to 15 milligrams) of amphetamine can produce these symptoms, and it has been found useful to administer the drug in emergencies when a person must keep awake and alert over a longer than usual period of time (for instance, in the case of the astronauts, upon reentry into the earth's atmosphere). If wakefulness is prolonged more than 1½ to 2 days, there is a high possibility that irritability, anxiety, and other undesirable effects will develop.

The extreme physical effects of amphetamine (speed) are the primary reason for its popularity. Within seconds after inhalation or feeding the drug into the vein, the user experiences an intense tingling sensation analogous to an electric shock; some appropriately refer to it as a "buzz." This is followed by more intense tingling sensations, some muscle contraction, and an immediate sense of extreme pleasure. It has been hypothesized that this feeling may be the result of rapid release of norepinephrine and its subsequent replacement by a breakdown product of the amphetamine. Numerous reports of orgasms, near-orgasms, and a vibrating feeling of the brain and spinal cord are indicative of intense stimulation of the sympathetic nervous system.

As tolerance develops, initial users progress from doses of around 10 to 40 milligrams several times a day to many times that amount as they become habitual users. These amounts are sufficient to activate the thalamus, hypothalamus, and reticular activating system to produce prolonged euphoria accompanied by feelings of extreme alertness, increased energy, and clever, insightful, and profound loquaciousness (Chait et al., 1985). Users in the group setting profess an ability to relate to the others in frank honesty and with extreme confidence. The excessive conversation is spurred by the belief that what one is saying is profound and that the others desire to listen rather than talk themselves (Smith & Byrd, 1985).

Amphetamine involvement with the limbic system and the hypothalamus seems to be responsible for many of the effects of speed, including the lack of appetite, insomnia, thirst, and hypersexuality (Holbrook, 1983). One who is high on speed exhibits extreme optimism as well as an overextended feeling of love; prolonged body contact is common, but afterward, in most cases, expression of love is either forgotten or regretted. This hypersexuality may result, at least in part, from accelerated tactile, auditory, olfactory, and visual impulses.

Because of amphetamine action on the hypothalamus, extreme anorexia occurs. A large weight loss is not uncommon with long-term abuse. Despite the knowledge that large amounts of vitamins, liquids, and nutritional supplements are necessary, symptoms of malnutrition such as abscesses, ulcers, and brittle fingernails are often observed in speed users. Extreme pain in muscles and joints, accompanied by muscle tremors, often occurs after several days of prolonged use. Serious overdoses are uncommon, but high doses may result in unconsciousness, chest pain, heart throbbing, and a feeling of paralysis (Griffith, 1988).

The longer the continued use, the more the situation changes from one of pleasant optimism and euphoria to one of hyperactive aggressiveness. This is not hard to understand, in light of the action of methamphetamine on the limbic and reticular activating systems. Accelerated and intermixed sensory impulses are combined with the extreme fatigue caused by sleep deprivation. Unknown tactile, visual, and auditory stimuli appearing in the periphery trigger fear and aggressive responses. This effect is not necessarily inherent in the amphetamine reaction alone but is a result of group interaction in a situation in which five or six people, hypersensitive to external stimuli, are all moving and talking at once. Psychotic-like characteristics begin to appear. Objects are observed in detail, and the individual becomes overly concerned with attaching significance to even inanimate objects, such as cracks in the wall or specks of dirt. These are often mistaken for micro animals and snakes, and adverse emotional reactions may occur. Also common to amphetamine psychosis is an inability to recognize faces in an acute psychotic reaction (Morgan, 1981).

Historically, the use of amphetamines and other stimulants has been associated with aggressive behavior (Cherek et al., 1986). In laboratory procedures measuring aggressive behavior, amphetamine in doses of 5 to 10 milligrams per 70 kilograms produced dose-related increases in aggressive behavior. Further, a higher degree of provocation produced more aggressive behavior. These changes in aggressive behavior were accompanied by increases in nonaggressive behavior, even at the highest amphetamine dose. Previous studies using this same procedure found that other stimulants such as nicotine and caffeine failed to increase aggressive behavior (Cherek et al., 1986). Ethanol did, however, increase aggressive behavior (Cherek et al., 1985). The biphasic nature of amphetamine effects indicates that amphetamine's effects on aggressive behavior cannot be attributed to its stimulant or depressant effect. Results of these studies indicate that the level of aggressive displays parallels the degree of provocation. The fact that the subjects continued their nonaggressive response after the highest amphetamine dose demonstrates that they are capable of pursuing goal-directed behaviors. While much has been written on the aggressiveness and violence associated with the stimulants, it appears that this violence is the result of long-term use and is highly dependent on the environment, which can easily trigger potential hostility.

SPECIAL DANGERS

The term "abuse" is usually reserved for a pattern of drug use that produces antisocial behavior or is detrimental to the health of the user. Various patterns of amphetamine use have emerged and reemerged over the last 20 years, many of which can be labeled abuse.

One such pattern is long-term extension or exaggeration of the misuse patterns seen with prescription amphetamines. Low-dose oral amphetamines are taken compulsively on a daily basis in a desperate attempt to maintain a stimulated pace of life, to chemically reinforce an outgoing personality, to keep the mood elevated, and to hold back the inevitable depression that sets in as the body rebounds from the repeated stimulation. A common pattern usually emerges—uppers in the morning and afternoon, downers such as alcohol and barbiturates at night. In an attempt to reduce some of the nervous side effects of amphetamine stimulation, some commercial brands add sedatives, usually barbiturates, to the amphetamines, resulting in an unintentional barbiturate dependence.

A pattern of amphetamine abuse lies in the intravenous use of high-dose methamphetamine. Unlike the long-term oral abuse, the use of injected speed is usually cyclical. Each episode or run may last from several hours to a few days, and users are almost always motivated by the extreme euphoric effects (Senay, 1983).

Paranoia and Violence

Intravenous, high-dose amphetamine use inevitably leads to some degree of paranoia, but the user can prepare for it. However, as was described in the preceding section, long and intense runs usually result in a loss of rationality, and as time goes on, the hypersensitivity, visual and tactile illusions, and fatigue state may cause paranoia. Once the user experiences extreme paranoia, a return to the same level of consciousness often triggers a similar experience. Extreme hyperactivity, fatigue, paranoia, and the social conditions are all responsible for the increased violence associated with high-dose amphetamine use. The user changes moods rapidly and is irrational in the evaluation of a situation; thus coping behavior is overreactive and aggressive (Cherek et al., 1986).

Overdose and Death

Amphetamine overdoses are uncommon and not fatal. A user can develop a tolerance to the awakening effects of the drug, which often leads to the use of amounts hundreds of times the clinical dose. Symptoms such as extreme chest pain, unconsciousness, aphasia, mental and/or physical paralysis, and erratically racing thought patterns often lead to shooting up again and hence an exaggeration of the problem that may require hospitalization.

Death is more often caused by chronic toxicity of amphetamines or by social conditions surrounding the user. Diseases such as AIDS and viral hepatitis are not uncommonly associated with those who share unsterilized hypodermic equipment. Hepatic damage as a direct toxic effect of amphetamines has also been suggested. If not properly cared for, infection from skin lesions and endocarditis may also cause death in extreme cases.

Perinatal Problems

The effects of abuse of amphetamines during pregnancy are similar to those of smoking and cocaine. Fetal development is compromised due to vasoconstriction, and negative birth outcomes include low birth weight and retarded growth (Oro and Dixon, 1987).

MEDICAL USE

There are currently only three medically acceptable uses for amphetamines in the United States. These are narcolepsy, adolescent attention deficit disorder (ADD), and obesity. Amphetamines are prescribed to counteract narcolepsy (attacks of uncontrollable sleepiness) and hyperactivity. They may also be found in antianxiety drugs such as Dexamyl, which is a combination of amobarbital and amphetamine. There is little doubt that the use of amphetamines in the first two disorders is warranted. The sudden attacks of sleepiness, loss of muscle tone, and paralysis associated with narcolepsy are reduced by amphetamine. However, tolerance does develop, weakening its beneficial effects and necessitating an increase in the dose or occasional periods of abstinence. Children with attention deficit disorder, or hyperkinetic syndrome, respond quite well to amphetamines or methylphenidate hydrochloride (Ritalin), which paradoxically produce a calming effect. Tolerance rarely develops, allowing the children to be treated for long periods of time, and the children are not at greater risk of becoming substance abusers. The use of amphetamines to treat obesity remains controversial. Amphetamines appear to be moderately helpful in some patients as short-term adjuncts to a behavioral treatment program including dieting, but the long-term benefits are no better than with diet alone.

REFERENCES

Alles, G. A. (1927). The comparative physiological action of phenylethanolamine. *Journal of Pharmacology and Experimental Therapy*, 32:121–133.

Burchfield, D. J., et al. (1991). Disposition and pharmacodynamics of methamphetamine in pregnant sheep. *JAMA*, 265(15):1968–1973.

Chait, L. D., et al. (1985). The discriminative stimulus and subjective effects of *d*-amphetamine in humans. *Psychopharmacology*, 86:307–312.

Cherek, D. R., Steinberg, J. L., Kelly, T. H., and Robinson, D. E. (1986). Effects of *d*-amphetamine on human aggressive behavior. *Psychopharmacology,* 88:381–386.

Cherek, D. R., Steinberg, J. L., and Manno, B. R. (1985). Effects of alcohol on human aggressive behavior. *Journal of Studies on Alcohol,* 46(4):321–328.

Griffith, H. W. (1988). *Complete Guide to Prescription and Non-prescription Drugs.* Los Angeles: The Body Press.

Hall, J. N., Uchman, R. S., and Dominguez, R. (1988). *Trends and Patterns of Methamphetamine Abuse in the United States.* Bethesda, Md.: National Institute on Drug Abuse.

Holbrook, John M. (1983). CNS stimulants. In Gerald Bennett et al. (Eds.), *Substance Abuse: Pharmacological, Developmental, and Clinical Perspectives.* New York: Wiley, pp. 312–334.

McMillen, B. A. (1983). CNS stimulants: two distinct mechanisms of action for amphetamine-like drugs. *Trends in Pharmacological Science.* 4(10):429–432.

Morgan, J. P. (1981). Amphetamines. In J. H. Lowinson and J. P. Ruiz (Eds.), *Substance Abuse: Clinical Problems and Perspectives.* Baltimore, Md.: Williams and Wilkins, pp. 86–105.

NIDA. (1990a). *NIDA Capsules,* January, C-89-06:1–3.

NIDA. (1990b). NIDA monitors Hawaiian "Ice" epidemic. *NIDA Notes,* 5(2):22.

Oro, A. S., and Dixon, S. D. (1987). Perinatal cocaine and methamphetamine exposure: maternal and neonatal correlates. *Journal of Pediatrics,* 111(4):571–578.

Senay, E. C. (1983). *Substance Abuse Disorders.* Boston: John Wright.

Smith, E. O., and Byrd, L. D. (1985). *d*-Amphetamine-induced changes in social interaction patterns. *Pharmacology, Biochemistry, and Behavior,* 22:135–139.

THE OPIATES

HISTORY

Opioids are natural and synthetic drugs that act on the central nervous system. Classified as narcotics, this group of drugs includes the illicit substance heroin, as well as such well-known therapeutic medications as morphine, codeine, meperidine (Demerol), oxycodone (Percodan), hydromorphone hydrochloride (Dilaudid), pentazocine hydrochloride (Talwin), and methadone (used in the treatment of heroin and other opioid dependence) (Cook et al., 1990).

The family of opiates derive from the parent plant *Papaver somniferum* and its raw exudate, opium. For centuries poppy fields were planted in the fall or early spring throughout the belt that reaches from Turkey's Anatolian plateau through Pakistan and northern India to the Golden Triangle of Burma, Laos, and Thailand. After the petals drop from the plant, the poppy pod is exposed. It is at this precise time (before the seed pod matures) that laborers score the pod in a manner prescribed by centuries of ancestral experience. White milky sap oozes out of the pod and is scraped off patiently by workers of the poppy field within the next 24 hours. It is estimated that one person spends a full 40-hour work week to collect 1 pound of opium.

After opium is collected from the field it is air-dried and may be used by the local population. In this raw form it is brown, possesses a strong odor, and may be smoked, sniffed, or eaten. The next step in processing is to cook out the rest of the water so that the morphine content per unit weight rises to about 10 percent. By soaking and filtering opium with the addition of slaked lime and ammonium chloride, organic impurities are removed and morphine content rises to 50 to 70 percent. This is an intermediate product and not easily absorbed by the body; thus it is converted into morphine salt compounds or into heroin. The former is the form in which morphine is used for medical purposes—morphine hydrochloride, morphine sulfate, and morphine acetate.

Diacetylmorphine is simply the morphine base that has been treated with acetic anhydride (or acetyl chloride, but since the former is less hazardous, it is the compound most often used) and passed through a process of heating and filtering that involves other chemicals such as acetone, alcohol, and tartaric acid. The resultant substance is called crude heroin and may be the same as No. 2 heroin in the heroin number code of southeast Asia.

The natives of southeast Asia use crude heroin to manufacture purple or No. 3 heroin, which is smoked. The process is one of heating, crushing, and drying plus the addition of strychnine, caffeine, and barbitone (which offsets extreme intoxication), to the extent that heroin content is lowered to around 15 percent. It is tan to gray in appearance and granular or coarse in composition.

Crude heroin is also precipitated, dried, and crushed to form white or No. 4 heroin, the injectable drug seen in the United States. It resembles talc or flour in consistency and may have a heroin content of 95 percent or more before it is adulterated. The color varies from white to creamy yellow unless it comes from Mexico, in which case it is brown due to a chemical process differing from that used in Europe and Asia. About 50 percent of the heroin sold and used in New York City is from southeast Asia, about 37 percent from southwest Asia, and the remainder from Mexico (DeStefano, 1990).

A so-called designer opiate, China White (3-methylfentanyl), has recently caused an outbreak of drug overdose deaths in the United States. This drug, a homologue of a legal opiate named fentanyl, is approximately 1000 times as potent as morphine. Fentanyl (and its designer homologues) are administered intravenously, reach peak effectiveness within 4 minutes, and can cause death by blocking respiratory drive (Hibbs et al., 1991). China White has caused more than 100 deaths in California and is suspected of that many more overdose deaths in Pennsylvania.

Other designer opiates being found in New York City include Tango and Cash (which substitutes fentanyl for some of the heroin), Good Fella, Blue Thunder, and Godfather.

Another worry to officials is the arrival of pure, inexpensive heroin on the American market. It can be smoked or snorted with the same effectiveness as the older heroin compounds that had to be taken intravenously. With the use of needles and the accompanying fear of AIDS no longer such a heroin issue, health authorities suspect that heroin will once again become a popular street drug of choice (DeStefano, 1990). Another reason that heroin use may re-emerge is the prediction that the crack and cocaine decade is over and that drug abusers are looking for a more "mellow" drug. The amount of heroin seized by customs inspectors at Port of New York airports and seaports went up from about 300 pounds per year in 1987 to 882 pounds in 1990.

CLASSIFICATION

Heroin and the other opiates are narcotic sedatives that exert their effects by depressing the central nervous system, especially areas of the thalamus, cerebral cortex, and medulla. This depressant action works to relieve pain and, in large doses, to induce sleep. Overdose causes death because of the narcotic's selective depressant action on the respiratory center in the medulla.

HOW TAKEN INTO THE BODY

The heroin user's preferred form of administration of the opiates is intravenous because of the immediate rush that is felt. With the influx of more potent heroin into the street market, more and more users are snorting it.

Experienced opiate addicts can discern heroin from morphine because its acetylated form assists its entry into the central nervous system. Other forms of administration include snorting (sniffing), intramuscular injection (skin-popping or joy-popping, or as used in a hospital setting), and smoking. Many of the American GIs who experienced heroin use in Vietnam smoked it in tobacco cigarettes. The heroin available there was much more potent than American street heroin because it was sold in almost pure form, but when smoked it was rapidly reduced in potency because the high burning temperature of the cigarette (around 850 degrees Centigrade) destroys about 80 percent of the effect of the heroin. Thus, a milder dependence would develop from smoking almost pure heroin than from other modes of administration.

CHARACTERISTICS OF DEPENDENCE

According to one school of thought, there are three major factors that create dependence: life situation, personality, and pharmacology of the drug. It has often been said that people start to use drugs for one reason but often continue using them for very different reasons. This is particularly true in the case of the heroin user. This is because opiates can "create" a personality complete with specific drives, needs, and values that may be entirely different from those possessed by the individual when not addicted. Recent research has added credence to this long-held hypothesis.

A definition of dependence includes several criteria such as physical dependence, behavioral dependence, the negatively reinforcing abstinence syndrome, and the positively reinforcing conditioning factors. The complex interaction of personality, environment, and drug effects can be understood best as a continuum along which these different factors contribute in varying degrees to the dependence behavior.

Opiate dependence represents a classical model of conditioning. A specified antecedent condition elicits a response that becomes reinforced. The opiate becomes an effective positive reinforcer, and the environmental context in which the drug is self-administered becomes one of the antecedent conditions in addition to being a conditioned secondary reinforcing stimulus.

Long-term use of opiates, natural and synthetic, causes physical dependence and is associated with the classic withdrawal syndrome when the opiate is abruptly withheld. With most opiate use, psychological dependence is a motivating factor to take the drug.

PHARMACOLOGY

The discovery of endogenous opiatelike neuropeptides and their natural receptor sites on nerve tissue in the brain has led to the identification of an endocrine system within the CNS (DHHS, 1987). ACTH neuropeptides are active in the processes of motivation and attention; β-endorphin neuropeptides are involved with pain perception, pathological pain, and psychopathological disorders; and vasopressin is active in memory processes. These findings suggest that because of the opiates' ability to mimic and displace natural brain endocrines, they can influence pain and reward responses and subsequently are self-reinforcing (Holloway, 1991). Thus, opiates have the ability to "control" behavior, which leads to their continued use.

Heroin's pharmacological action is that of morphine because it is converted back into morphine in the body. Thus, both drugs are eliminated through the urine as morphine, which becomes the basis of urinalysis. Heroin is also eliminated in the breast milk of a lactating mother, and in sweat and saliva. Because it easily crosses the placental barrier, infants born of heroin abusers come into the world as narcotic addicts too.

EFFECTS ON THE BODY

Heroin has a rapid onset of action and proceeds with its analgesic effect. The results are a flush of euphoria, elevation of mood, and a feeling of peace, contentment, and safety as the drug offers relief from the environment, both internal and external. This is one of the most significant reasons for heroin's having the highest addiction potential of all the illicit drugs. Its analgesic effect is about three times that of morphine—2 to 5 milligrams of heroin via intramuscular injection has about the same effect as 8 to 16 milligrams of morphine administered in the same manner or 300 to 600 milligrams of opium given orally. Heroin is still used in Britain as a medicine and is an efficient tranquilizer, cough suppressant, and short-acting pain reliever. It also counteracts diarrhea and has been used in the treatment of cancer patients.

TABLE 6
OPIATE DRUGS: THEIR ORIGIN AND POTENCY

Drug	Origin	Potency
Laudanum	Alcohol solution of 10% opium	0.10 × opium
Paregoric	4% tincture of opium	0.04 × opium
Morphine	Natural alkaloid	10 × opium
Codeine	Natural alkaloid	0.50 × opium
Heroin	Semisynthetic	3 × morphine
Dilaudid	Semisynthetic	3–4 × morphine
Meperidine	Semisynthetic	0.1 × morphine
Methadone	Synthetic	Equals morphine

Common effects of the opiates (see Table 6) are respiratory depression (both rate and depth), constipation, pupillary constriction, postural hypotension, libido suppression, and release of histamine (which causes the itching that may accompany heroin use). Nausea and vomiting also often accompany heroin use, especially in the neophyte. Contrary to common belief, high-dose users of the opiates can function quite adequately, and aside from the danger of unsterile needles and other catastrophes inherent in the lifestyle of the heroin user, the addict does not suffer the physical deterioration resulting from long-term use of other drugs such as alcohol. Diseases such as hepatitis, septicemia, and endocarditis can result from the use of unsterile needles, and abscesses are common among heroin addicts also. Another cause of fatality in heroin addicts is cardiovascular collapse due to allergic reaction to the injected substance.

As the effects of an injection of heroin wear off, addicts generally have 4 to 6 hours in which to find their next supply. If a strong depressant is not taken within this time, withdrawal symptoms begin to appear—runny nose, dilation of pupils, stomach cramps, chills, and the other symptoms of the classic abstinence syndrome. Barbiturates, nonbarbiturate sedative-hypnotics, cough syrup with codeine, or other such depressant may be used by the addict to postpone withdrawal if heroin or the money to purchase it is not available.

In case of overdose, addicts are given narcotic antagonists such as levallorphan tartrate, nalorphine, or naloxone hydrochloride that will reverse the acute, life-threatening respiratory depression. Such antagonists counteract the pharmacological action of narcotics and, in essence, induce "cold turkey" withdrawal. The severity of withdrawal symptoms differs with the user and is dependent on numerous factors. In a study of heroin users who ranked withdrawal symptoms by severity, it was found that the most severe were insomnia, aching bones and joints, anxiety, irritability, excessive sweating, muscle cramps, lack of energy, and restlessness (Cohen et al., 1983).

SPECIAL DANGERS

Dependence and the Dependency Lifestyle

In an examination of past histories of heroin users, an underdeveloped personality emerges, one that is retarded in development by pathological social conditions. This may account for the high incidence of drug experimentation in economically depressed areas. It is difficult to pinpoint the initial factor, but the poor sections of large cities are places of high anxiety and frustration, with little development of competence to handle these problems. Broken homes are commonplace, and children and parents both suffer from the disadvantages that result from them. Even in two-parent homes, fatigue and preoccupation with life struggles allow little time for gaining insight into the child. Expectation as well as discipline are sporadic, based on mood. Goals are often unrealistic dreams. Inexperienced teachers often see the children who come from this impoverished preschool environment as unteachable and incorrigible misfits.

On the street, an aimless delinquent subculture develops as the only sympathetic diversion from a hostile home and school environment.

Superficially, there is nothing mysterious or obscure about the conflicts that develop in these situations, but researchers have been a bit overzealous in reasoning that these conflicts are responsible for a lifelong desire to withdraw. More realistically, these may be powerful motivators for initial experimentation, for few examples of consistent psychopathological personality have been observed when the drug cycle has been blockaded in programs such as methadone maintenance (Dole & Nyswander, 1983).

Since the late 1950s and early 1960s, the heroin scene in the United States has changed somewhat, not by the elimination of the underprivileged user but by the addition of more users from the middle and upper socioeconomic classes. Even though these individuals are more privileged, they possess some of the same developmental problems as their less fortunate counterparts. In this light, the heroin user is regarded as being abnormally high in externalization and abnormally low in ego development. The result is a particular susceptibility to social and environmental reinforcers and influences. In the case of dependence, drugs as well as many other environmental influences become powerful determinants of behavior. Current psychological literature is saturated with research results suggesting a trend toward the increased externalization of society in general. Certainly an abuser of anything, be it TV, food, smoking, or drugs, has surrendered some of his or her inner power to the external object or substance or, in many cases, to another person. The heroin-dependent individual, however, has relinquished his or her power to a more destructive force, a potent drug that can reduce anxiety, relieve pain, and bring the external world more "in line" with the inner world (Roberts, 1986).

There is no universal agreement as to the cause of dependence. Consequently, there has been no agreement on the most effective methods of rehabilitation. The life of chemical dependence becomes a total lifestyle. Heroin is not just a chemical taken at intervals; it is a social life, a psychological life, a physical life—in fact, the addict's life is totally centered on that necessary chemical. This totality contributes to the difficulty of rehabilitation. To the heroin-dependent person, only money and heroin count. In the process of rehabilitation, something must be substituted for heroin, and the first step in this substitution is that of filling up time. The ex-user has all the time in the world—time formerly spent in the cycle of hustling and shooting up. Now that time must be filled with non-drug-oriented behavior, and in the absence of supportive aid, this sick, disoriented person, who continually has the feeling that "something is missing," will go back to the old drug life for lack of anything better to do.

Because of this need for multidimensional reorientation, only a small percentage of heroin addicts up to this time have been "cured." Treatment and rehabilitation attempts must strive for this goal, and the closer they come, the higher the cure rate will be.

Immune System

The immune systems of heroin addicts become depressed when they are on the drug, making the addict more prone to various diseases such as hepatitis and HIV (Carr & Blalock, 1989; NIDA, 1990). In one study, researchers determined that heroin addicts displayed decreased numbers of T-lymphocyte cells, those cells that tell other cells about the presence of infectious agents and combat viral infection in cancer (Novick et al., 1989).

Perinatal Problems

Opiates taken by the mother cross the placenta and enter fetal blood, and babies suffer withdrawal symptoms if their mothers are habitual heroin users. A pregnant woman's use of narcotics may reduce the oxygen supply to the fetus, and because heroin and other narcotics suppress maternal appetite, the fetus may also suffer from malnutrition.

Animal studies have found reductions in the number of brain cells, alterations in brain ribonucleic acid (RNA) and protein content, reductions in the thickness of the cerebral cortex, retarded development of biochemical systems that carry nerve impulses, and retarded growth of cells affected by withdrawal of opiates.

The prenatal human brain contains opioid-like chemicals, and one theory suggests that prenatal exposure to opioid drugs retards fetal development by interfering with the growth of brain cells that are sensitive to opioids, both those produced naturally (endorphins and enkephalins) and those taken as drugs (Silverman, 1989).

Pregnancy complications for heroin addicts include increased risk of early separation of the placenta, eclampsia (a serious, sometimes fatal, toxic condition with high blood pressure, swelling, seizures, or coma), placental insufficiency, breech presentations, premature labor and ruptured membranes, and caesarean sections. Ten to fiften percent of heroin addicts develop toxemia during pregnancy that may lead to eclampsia.

Heroin use during pregnancy increases the risk of stillbirths and fetal distress and of aspiration pneumonia in the newborn. Nearly one-half of heroin-dependent women who receive no prenatal care deliver prematurely, often because of infections (Cook et al., 1990).

A well-confirmed risk to newborns of heroin-addicted mothers is intra-uterine growth retardation. In addition, about 80 percent of babies born to heroin-addicted mothers have such serious medical problems as hyaline membrane disease of the lungs, brain hemorrhages, and respiratory distress syndrome. The majority of these are the result of prematurity.

These newborns are also at risk for perinatally transmitted HIV infection (later developing into AIDS), and higher death rates among these infants are attributed to sudden infant death syndrome (SIDS) and infections.

Dramatic withdrawal symptoms are the most frequently observed consequence to newborns from prenatal narcotic exposure. Restlessness, tremulousness, disturbed sleep and feeding, stuffy nose, vomiting, diarrhea, a high-pitched cry, fever, irregular breathing, or seizures usually start within 48 to 72 hours. The heroin-exposed infant also sneezes, twitches, hiccups, and weeps. This irritability, resulting from overarousal of the CNS, usually ends after a month but can persist for 3 months or more (Cook et al., 1990).

Heroin, methadone, and other narcotics are transmitted in breast milk, so nursing by the opiate-dependent mother is contraindicated. However, breast-feeding by motivated mothers in well-supervised methadone treatment programs should not automatically be ruled out, particularly during the first 6 to 8 weeks when the greatest immunological and bonding benefits are likely to result.

MEDICAL USE

Morphine and other narcotic analgesics are prescribed to relieve pain and as cough suppressants.

REFERENCES

Carr, D. J. J., and Blalock, J. E. (1989). Neuroendocrine characteristics of the immune system. *EOS Journal of Immunology and Immunopharmacology,* 9(4):1–5.

Cohen, A. J., Klett, C. J., and Ling, W. (1983). Patient perspectives on opiate withdrawal. *Drug and Alcohol Dependence,* 12:167–172.

Cook, P. S., Petersen, R. C., and Moore, D. T. (1990). *Alcohol, Tobacco, and Other Drugs May Harm the Unborn.* Rockville, Md.: U.S. Department of Health and Human Services.

DeStefano, A. M. (1990). Cheaper, high-test heroin snorting up yuppie market. *Newsday,* Dec. 9, pp. 20–22.

DHHS. (1987). *The Second Triennial Report to Congress from the Secretary of the Department of Health and Human Services.* Washington, D.C.: U.S. Department of Health and Human Services.

Dole, Vincent, and Nyswander, Marie E. (1983). Behavioral pharmacology and treatment of human drug abuse—methadone maintenance of narcotic addicts. In J. E. Smith and J. D. Lane (eds.), *The Neurobiology of Opiate Reward Processes.* Amsterdam: Elsevier Biomedical Press, pp. 294–317.

Hibbs, J., Perper, J., and Winek, C. L. (1991). An outbreak of designer drug-related deaths in Pennsylvania. *JAMA,* 265(8):1011–1013.

Holloway, Marguerite. (1991). Trends in pharmacology: Rx for addiction. *Scientific American,* March, pp. 95–103.

NIDA. (1990). *Drugs of Abuse: Chemistry, Pharmacology, Immunology, and AIDS.* Washington, D.C.: U.S. Department of Health and Human Services.

Novick, D. M., et al. (1989). Natural killer cell activity and lymphocyte subsets in parenteral heroin abusers and long-term methadone maintenance patients. *Journal of Pharmacology and Experimental Therapeutics,* 250:1–5.

Roberts, W. J. (1986). An hypothesis on the physiological basis for causalgia and related pains. *Pain,* 24:297–311.

Silverman, S. (1989). Scope, specifics of maternal drug use, and effects on fetus are beginning to emerge from studies. *JAMA,* 261(2):1688–1689.

SEDATIVE/ANTIANXIETY DRUGS

This chapter discusses two particular classifications of depressants, both of which in the popular pill form are commonly misused and abused. These sedative/antianxiety drugs are among the most widely prescribed of all compounds and are used in treating anxiety, insomnia, muscle spasticity, and convulsions. The first group is represented by the barbituates, such as secobarbital and pentobarbital, and the nonbarbiturates, such as methaqualone and glutethimide. These drugs are of different chemical formulations, but all produce similar effects and problems. The second group are commonly called psychotherapeutic or antianxiety drugs and are better known as tranquilizers or benzodiazepines. The benzodiazepine compounds have largely replaced barbiturate and nonbarbiturate anxiolytics/sedatives in medicine.

Barbiturate and Nonbarbiturate Sedative-Hypnotics

HISTORY

At the turn of the century, bromides were being used to combat sleeplessness, anxiety, and minor pain, but with the discovery of barbituric acid in the late 1800s, bromides were gradually replaced with the barbiturates. In 1903, the first barbiturate, Veronal, was placed on the market, and it was soon followed by Luminal. Since that time, nonbarbiturates such as glutethimide and methaqualone have also flooded the prescription market.

Because of the antianxiety and antitension qualities of the sedative-hypnotics, their illegal use increased dramatically, and with their misuse and abuse, the dangers inherent in these drugs became apparent. The dependence-producing nature of these drugs and their potential for respiratory depression stimulated medical research for safer substances. The drugs that emerged from this research were the tranquilizers, most of which possess potential dangers identical to those of the barbiturates and nonbarbiturates—tolerance, dependence, and overdose. Benzodiazepines (e.g., Librium, Valium), which are among the safest, most effective, and widely prescribed psychotropic compounds, have largely replaced barbiturates as anxiolytics (antianxiety drugs), sedatives, and hypnotics over the last two decades. Their prescriptive use steadily increased through 1975 to a peak level of about 100 million prescriptions annually. A declining rate, down to 65 million prescriptions by 1981, then occurred, and the number leveled off. The recent trend of decreasing prescriptions is probably attributable to a decreased rate in refilling prescriptions, with little change in prescription size or proportion of the population receiving prescriptions each year. This tendency toward more conservative use is probably due to the substantial recent increase in negative attitudes of patients toward use (DHHS, 1987). The nonmedical use of barbiturates has also decreased over the past few years.

CLASSIFICATION

These are classic depressant drugs. They depress the central nervous system, making it necessary to increase doses in order to obtain the same effects if the drugs are administered often. Physical dependence occurs when tolerance builds, and the withdrawal from this physical dependence is life-threatening. Because these drugs are used to relieve tension, anxiety, and insomnia, they often become psychologically habit-forming.

HOW TAKEN INTO THE BODY

Sedative-hynotics are most commonly taken orally in pill, tablet, and capsule form.

CHARACTERISTICS OF DEPENDENCE

These drugs create tolerance (and cross-tolerance to other depressant drugs) and psychic and physical dependence (Okamoto, 1984). Abrupt withdrawal after long-term abuse brings on an abstinence syndrome more severe than that caused by any other drug, mainly because of the life-threatening convulsions that accompany withdrawal.

PHARMACOLOGY

The barbiturates and nonbarbiturates produce their depressant effect by inhibiting the arousal systems of the central nervous system; that is, they depress the reticular formation by interfering with oxygen consumption and energy-producing mechanisms (Stimmel, 1983). The depression here reduces the nerve signals that reach the cortex, thus promoting sleep. A sedative dose makes the user only slightly drowsy but damps out enough incoming stimuli to reduce anxiety and tension.

The body eliminates these sedatives via the kidneys at varying rates, and it is mainly this rate of elimination that determines the duration of the effects of any one drug. There is an exception here in that short- and ultrashort-acting barbiturates rapidly redistribute themselves in adipose tissue, thus diminishing their levels and effects in the brain. The intermediate- and long-acting drugs are metabolized more slowly and may produce some residual sedation (hangover) because they have not been thoroughly metabolized.

EFFECTS ON THE BODY

An interesting paradox with these drugs is that abusive levels in habitual users or normal doses in susceptible patients, especially the elderly, can produce excitation before the customary depressant action sets in. Another interesting effect of barbiturates is that when taken in the presence of psychological stress or extreme pain, they may cause delirium and other side effects such as nausea, nervousness, rash, and diarrhea (Goodman & Gilman, 1990). Another adverse effect of barbiturates, glutethimide, and other drugs of this classification is that they decrease the potency of certain other drugs, as shown in Table 7.

Barbiturates radically change sleeping patterns by decreasing REM (rapid eye movement) sleep, and then cause sleeping problems when the drug is no longer used. Barbiturates also stimulate hepatic (liver) enzyme production, which in turn causes other substances (such as anticoagulents or antibiotics; see Table 7) to be broken down more quickly than expected, thus diminishing their effectiveness. Finally, because the barbiturates depress the respiratory center, they pose a danger to those with respiratory problems.

Although the nonbarbiturates and the antianxiety substances may not possess all of the inherent dangers seen in the barbiturates, all of them share the dangers of dependence, tolerance, withdrawal, and abuse potential, and some of them may possess all of the dangers cited for barbiturates.

TABLE 7
INTERACTION OF BARBITURATES WITH OTHER DRUGS

Drug	Effect
Alcohol (acute intoxication)	Increased CNS depression
Alcohol (chronic intake)	Decreased sedation
Anticoagulant	Decreased anticoagulant effect
Corticosteroid	Decreased steroid effect
Digitoxin	Decreased cardiac effect
Phenothiazine	Decreased tranquilizing effect
Phenytoin	Decreased anticonvulsant effect
Tetracycline	Decreased antibiotic effect
Tricyclic antidepressant	Decreased antidepressant effect

An important drawback to prescribing sedative-hypnotics for relief of insomnia is that many of these drugs reduce REM sleep time. These include chloral hydrate, barbiturates (especially pentobarbital, secobarbital, and amobarbital), glutethimide, and methaqualone. It appears that REM sleep is necessary, for if individuals are deprived of this period of sleep in which dreams occur, they grow irritable, anxious, and even neurotic. In a normal night's sleep, five or six periods of orthodox sleep occur broken up by short periods of REM sleep, with the first period occurring about an hour to an hour and a half after onset of sleep and lasting varying lengths of time. Normally, REM sleep makes up 20 to 25 percent of one's total sleep time (Holbrook, 1983).

Insomnia is a common condition and can arise from numerous underlying causes:

1 Situational (e.g., jet lag, being in unfamiliar surroundings)
2 Medical (e.g., pain)
3 Psychological (e.g., anxiety, feelings of inadequacy, neurosis)
4 Drug intake or withdrawal (e.g., alcohol, caffeine)

The sedative-hypnotics have been used as sleeping aids for various difficulties in sleeping—inability to fall asleep, early morning awakenings, inability to stay asleep, and combinations of these. For whatever purpose the sleeping aid is taken, it is important to know that the sleep that it produces is not "normal" sleep.

Unfortunately, the use of a barbiturate as a sleeping aid creates an initial reduction of REM sleep, which occurs during the first week of nighttime hypnosis. Subsequent nightly use of barbiturates for as little as 2 weeks brings about some tolerance—it takes longer to fall asleep, and total sleep time is shorter—but REM sleep time rises to normal levels again. Even though one regains a normal level of REM sleep, a serious situation has arisen with the REM sleep that was lost initially. There is a large increase in REM sleep after one discontinues using sleeping pills, and when this increase occurs, patients experience nightmares, restlessness, and nighttime awakenings. They feel they do not get a full night's sleep and become anxious about their poor sleeping behavior. This situation is likely to induce them to return to barbiturates to "cure" the problem. Study has shown that it takes a month or more to repay this REM sleep debt, but if the patient can withstand the transition period, he or she can escape the barbiturate-induced sleep routine.

Diazepam and antihistamines have been suggested as substitute drugs for barbiturates in cases of insomnia and other neurotic symptoms because these drugs appear to have fewer adverse effects (Griffith, 1988).

SPECIAL DANGERS

Policy makers of federal drug abuse organizations have called for a reevaluation of barbiturate use. The very fast acting barbiturate anesthetics and the slow-acting phenobarbital have escaped this evaluation, however, because of their low abuse potential. The major reason for reevaluation is the misuse and abuse potential of the other barbiturates, such as secobarbital and pentobarbital. It is apparent that there is a group of patients complaining about the symptoms for which these drugs are prescribed who demonstrate a considerable degree of psychopathology. In addition, a large population of users, the elderly, may be more vulnerable to life crises, making them a high-risk group for misusing these drugs.

Some of the problems seen with these drugs (along with nonbarbiturate sedatives such as methaqualone) include the following:

1 Barbiturates are used more frequently as the means of suicide than any other drug. However, 5-year emergency room data for a period ending in 1985 showed a decreasing number of emergency room mentions for barbiturates/nonbarbiturates and tranquilizers (except for lorazepam). In many cases of barbiturate-related death, it is difficult to determine whether death was accidental or planned, because the effects of drug poisoning occur gradually. Termination of life is not instantaneous. Thus, insomniacs who take one or two sleeping pills and find that that dose doesn't work immediately may take more. If the second dose added to the first exceeds the lethal dose for the individual, death will occur.

2 Another way in which suicide or accidental death occurs is through self-administration of sedative-hypnotics or tranquilizers after ingesting a large amount of alcohol. The lethal dose of these depressants is markedly reduced in such a case because alcohol has already depressed vital cell action. Similar effects occur with any multiple drug use that is a combination of depressant drugs, such as barbiturates and opiates, methaqualone and alcohol, or alcohol and methadone.

3 The abuse of barbiturates and nonbarbiturate sedatives has been linked with death by overdose, violent behavior, and accidents due to motor clumsiness. The benzodiazepines show a considerable margin of safety between their therapeutic dose and the dose required to produce serious overdose or death, but the barbiturates, nonbarbiturates, and nonbenzodiazepine sedative-hypnotics demonstrate a much narrower margin of safety than do the benzodiazepines such as Valium and Librium (Greenblatt et al., 1983). Due to its high lipid solubility and anticholinergic action, glutethimide presents special difficulty in the treatment of overdose, as does methaqualone.

Barbiturates and similar drugs cause a type of intoxication that is much like alcohol intoxication. The individual initially experiences a relaxed feeling and release of social inhibitions, just as in the first stages of alcohol intoxication. Further use of the drug brings on sluggishness, lack of motor coordination, slurred speech, and eventually sleep. However, large doses of these drugs in the stomach do not trigger the vomiting mechanism as large amounts of alcohol do (rescuing the drunk from death); thus, large doses of barbiturates, for example, are more dangerous than alcohol. Operating machinery, especially an automobile, while under the influence of sedative drugs is particularly dangerous.

4 Withdrawal from barbiturate dependence is a serious medical consideration and is life-endangering to the dependent individual.

5 Long-acting barbiturates (e.g., phenobarbital) taken as antiseizure medications have been associated with congenital birth defects resembling FAS. Short-acting barbiturates (e.g., Seconal) have also been associated with increases in birth defects and are not considered to be safe to take during pregnancy.

Chronic use of barbiturates during the last few months of pregnancy has been associated with infant withdrawal symptoms. These symptoms typically include high-pitched crying, irritability, tremulousness, and sleep disturbances that may persist for months and can interfere with mother–infant bonding (Cook et al., 1990).

MEDICAL USE

Although their use is diminishing, the barbiturates and nonbarbiturates are still prescribed. Tables 8 and 9 list the barbiturates and nonbarbiturates, respectively. These drugs are mainly used as follows:

1 Daytime, low-dose sedative therapy is used to treat normal and neurotic patients by reducing tension and anxiety. This is done without inducing leth-

TABLE 8
BARBITURATE CLASSIFICATION

Drug	Action	Trade Name
Hexobarbital	Very short	Sombulex
Methohexital	Very short	Brevital
Thiamylal	Very short	Nonformulary
Thiopental	Very short	Pentothal
Amobarbital	Short/intermediate	Amytal
Aprobarbital		Alurate
Butabarbital		Butisol
		Butazem
		Buticaps, Butal
		Sarisol
Pentobarbital		Nembutal
		Nebralin
Secobarbital		Seconal
Phenobarbital	Long	Pheno-Squar
		Solfoton
		Luminal
		Eskabarb
Mephobarbital		Mebaral
Metharbital		Nonformulary

Note: The short- and intermediate-acting barbiturates listed here are the characteristic barbiturates of abuse, especially Seconal, Nembutal, and Amytal.

Very short-acting = under 3 hours; short/intermediate = 3–6 hours; long-acting = 6 or more hours.

TABLE 9
COMMONLY USED AND ABUSED NONBARBITURATE,
NONBENZODIAZEPINE SEDATIVE-HYPNOTICS

Chloral derivatives	Carbamates	Bromides	Piperidinediones	Quinazolones
Chloral hydrate (Somnos)	Meprobamate* (Miltown, Equanil)	Sedamyl	Glutethimide (Doriden)	Methaqualone (Quaalude, Sopor)
Chloral betaine (Beta Chlor)			Methyprylon (Noludar)	Methaqualone HCl (Parost, Somnifac)
Triclofos sodium (Triclos)				
Ethchlorvynol (Placidyl)				

* Classified as a minor tranquilizer.

argy that in turn could lower mental alertness to potentially dangerous levels or decrease reactivity to the environment.

2 Moderate-dose or hypnotic therapy is used at bedtime to counteract insomnia. With the use of a barbiturate, onset of sleep occurs sooner, and a dreamless night's sleep ensues.

These drugs are not analgesics, but they often aid in reducing the psychological component involved in cardiovascular, gastrointestinal, respiratory, or other diseases and reduce anxiety that the patient may experience from the somatic symptoms of these diseases.

Tranquilizers

HISTORY

The tranquilizers are divided into antipsychotic and antianxiety substances (Tables 10 and 11, respectively). The difference between these two groups of tranquilizers is of significance when we speak of drug abuse, because the antipsychotics present no hazard of physical dependence and are not abused as street drugs. The antipsychotics are mentioned here merely to complete the tranquilizer picture.

The phenothiazines (aliphatic or Thorazine-type drugs, piperidine or Mellaril-type drugs, and piperazine or Stellazine-type drugs) are the standard antipsychotic agents (Table 10). It appears that all drugs in this category are equally effective but should be chosen on the basis of which will get the best results and cause the fewest side effects in the individual patient.

Like the barbiturates and nonbarbiturates, the antianxiety substances (Table 11) are common drugs of misuse and abuse. The rise in consumption of

TABLE 10
ANTIPSYCHOTIC AGENTS (PHENOTHIAZINES)

Generic name	Brand name	Single adult dose	Duration
Chlorpromazine	Thorazine	10–25 mg	4–6 hr
Prochlorperazine	Compazine	10 mg	4–6 hr
Trifluoperazine	Stellazine	2 mg	4–6 hr
Rauwolfia	Reserpine	1 mg	4–6 hr

Note: These drugs are used for treatment of alcoholism, neurosis, psychosis, psychosomatic disorders, and vomiting. Their potential for psychological dependence is minimal, and they hold no potential for physical dependence, thus making their overall potential for abuse minimal. Usual short-term effects are CNS depression, relaxation, relief of anxiety, and improved functioning, while long-term effects may be drowsiness, dryness of mouth, blurred vision, skin rash, tremor, and, occasionally, jaundice.

tranquilizers began in the 1960s with Miltown and Equanil (generic name, meprobamate) as the prototypes, and these were later replaced by Librium and Valium. In 1968, 40 million prescriptions were written for the latter two drugs. Five years later the number was 80 million and in 1976 the figure had increased to 91 million, comprising about 8 percent of all prescriptions written by physicians in the United States. More prescriptions are written for tranquilizers than for any other type of psychoactive drug. In 1983 Dalmane (flurazepam) was reported to be the most commonly prescribed sleeping pill, accounting for more than one-half of all sedative-hypnotics prescribed (Parker, 1983). The implications here are that many Americans are trying to solve their problems through the use of psychotropic drugs, and that American physicians feel that tranquilizers are the most efficient manner in which to deal with their anxiety-ridden patients. The all-out prescribing of tranquilizers has its impact on the street-drug scene in two ways—directly, by supplying legitimate drugs (via theft) to the black market system, and indirectly, through parental example of attitudes toward drugs. Use of illicit drugs by teenagers has been shown to parallel their parents' use of tranquilizers, with children being especially influenced by their mothers' use of these drugs.

TABLE 11
COMMONLY USED BENZODIAZEPINES
(ANTIANXIETY AGENTS)

Generic name	Trade name
Chlordiazepoxide	Librium
Clorazepate	Tranxene, Azene, Tranzene SD
Diazepam	Valium
Flurazepam	Dalmane
Lorazepam	Ativan
Oxazepam	Serax
Prazepam	Verstran, Centrax
Ketazolam	Halcion
Temazepam	Restoril

The more recent trend of decreasing numbers of anxiolytic prescriptions is probably due to a decreased rate in refilling prescriptions, with little change in prescription size or proportion of the population receiving prescriptions each year (DHHS, 1987). There is increasing clinical consensus that long-term use is undesirable and that patients so maintained should be regularly evaluated for possible termination of the medication (Hollister, 1985).

CLASSIFICATION

The tranquilizers are classified as anxiolytic (antianxiety) drugs that selectively depress the central nervous system.

HOW TAKEN INTO THE BODY

These drugs come in pill, tablet, and capsule form. Thus they are taken orally in most instances.

CHARACTERISTICS OF DEPENDENCE

The drugs that appear in Table 11 have been selected because of their incidence of abuse. If taken in excessive doses over a long period of time, all of the drugs listed will create tolerance and physical and psychological dependence (Griffiths et al., 1985).

PHARMACOLOGY

The action of the benzodiazepines on the central nervous system is quite dissimilar to that of the barbiturates and nonbarbiturates. Rather than suppress activity of the reticular activating system, the tranquilizers appear to act on brain tissue at special benzodiazepine binding sites. The receptors are widespread throughout the brain, accounting for the multiple levels of benzodiazepine action. The benzodiazepines appear to affect all of the known neurotransmitters, but their greatest interaction appears to be with γ-amino butyric acid (GABA), a major inhibitory neurotransmitter whose effects are increased by these tranquilizers. It is thought that these drugs alter the post-synaptic GABA response. In general, these drugs affect the limbic system, the part of the brain that governs emotion. Every effective antipsychotic blocks dopamine receptor sites, which counteracts the excessive firing of dopaminergic neurons in the limbic system.

EFFECTS ON THE BODY

Tranquilizers diminish one's response to the environment so that situations that previously would have triggered negative responses no longer do so or the response is diminished. Individuals may react to the drugs with clumsiness, drowsiness, dizziness, headache, insomnia, dry mouth or unpleasant taste, constipation, fatigue, or weakness. A "sweet tooth" may also be a side effect.

More serious complications of the tranquilizers include hallucinations, confusion, depression, irritability, rash, itch, vision changes, jaundice, blurred vision, and eye pain. Some individuals may also experience diarrhea, nausea, vomiting, difficulty in urination, and indigestion. Mouth and throat ulcers and fever are rare reactions but occur in some patients (Griffith, 1988).

SPECIAL DANGERS

Operation of Machinery

The operation of machinery may become hazardous, especially before the individual knows how the drug affects him or her. Patients are cautioned to not drive or pilot aircraft, climb ladders, work around dangerous machinery, or work in high places. It is important to know that alcohol potentiates the effects of the tranquilizers and they should not be taken together. Heavy perspiring may reduce the excretion of these drugs from the body, thus heightening and prolonging their effects.

Perinatal Problems

All the benzodiazepines have been associated with increased reproductive risks. They may complicate delivery and leave newborns lethargic, with breathing difficulties, episodes of not breathing, poor muscle tone, and decreased sucking ability.

Diazepam (Valium) taken during the first 3 months of pregnancy has been linked to a fourfold increase in cleft palate, lip anomaly, and other malformations of the heart, arteries, and joints. Chlordiazepoxide (Librium) use during the first 6 weeks of pregnancy has been linked to CNS abnormalities in infants.

Diazepam and meprobamate (Equanil, Miltown) should not be used by nursing mothers because these drugs accumulate in breast-fed infants (Cook et al., 1990).

Withdrawal Risks

Studies in laboratory animals and humans have shown that abrupt termination of high dose long-term use of benzodiazepines can produce a severe withdrawal syndrome, sometimes including delirium and grand mal convulsions (DHHS, 1987).

It is clear that benzodiazepines can produce a withdrawal syndrome after prolonged treatment with normal therapeutic doses. Such withdrawal occurs in significant proportion of long-term benzodiazepine users (Rosenberg & Chiu, 1985). There is some evidence that lorazepam produces more withdrawal problems than other anxiolytic benzodiazepines.

MEDICAL USE

These drugs are used to treat nervousness and tension, muscle spasm, and convulsive disorders and to relieve (not cure) depression (Griffith, 1988).

REFERENCES

Cook, P. S., Petersen, R. C., and Moore, D. T. (1990). *Alcohol, Tobacco, and Other Drugs May Harm the Unborn*. Rockville, Md.: U.S. Department of Health and Human Services.

DHHS. (1987). *Second Triennial Report to Congress from the Secretary of the Department of Health and Human Services*. Washington, D.C.: U.S. Government Printing Office.

Goodman, L. A., and Gilman, A. (1990). *The Pharmacological Basis of Therapeutics*. New York: Macmillan.

Greenblatt, D. J., Shader, R. I., and Abernathy, D. R. (1983). Current status of benzodiazepines. *The New England Journal of Medicine*, 309:410–416.

Griffith, H. W. (1988). *Complete Guide to Prescription and Non-prescription Drugs*. Los Angeles: The Body Press.

Griffiths, R. R., et al. (1985). Relative abuse liability of triazolam: experimental assessment in animals and humans. *Neuroscience and Biobehavior Review*, 9:133–151.

Holbrook, John M. (1983). The autonomic and central nervous systems. In G. Bennet et al. (Eds.), *Substance Abuse*. New York: Wiley.

Hollister, L. E. (1985). Principles of therapeutic applications of benzodiazepines. In D. E. Smith and D. R. Wesson (Eds.), *The Benzodiazepines: Current Standards for Medical Practice*. Lancaster, England: MTP Press.

Okamoto, M. (1984). Barbiturate tolerance and physical dependence: contribution of pharmacological factors. In C. W. Sharp (Ed.), *Mechanisms of Tolerance and Dependence*. Washington, D.C.: U.S. Department of Health and Human Services.

Parker, J. M. (1983). *Valium, Librium and the Benzodiazepine Blues*. Phoenix, Ariz.: D.I.N. Publications.

Rosenberg, H., and Chiu, T. H. (1985). Time course for development of benzodiazepine tolerance and physical dependence. *Neuroscience and Biobehavior Review*, 9:123–131.

Stimmel, Barry. (1983). *Pain, Analgesia, and Addiction: The Pharmacological Treatment of Pain*. New York: Raven Press.

HALLUCINOGENS

General Introduction

The hallucinogenic drugs are also called "psychotomimetic" drugs because their action in the body mimics psychotic states in whole or in part. They are classified as to chemical structure into:

1 The indolealkylamines such as tryptamine, dimethyltryptamine (DMT), psilocin.

2 Lysergic acid amides such as LSD.

3 Some of the phenethylamines such as mescaline, dimethoxymethylamphetamine (DOM), and MDA. In addition to the phenethylamines, there are other chemically related drugs that have hallucinogenic effects, such as methylenedioxymethamphetamine (MDMA), which is closely related to MDA (DHHS, 1987).

4 M-cholinergic antagonists such as atropine and QNB. These drugs are found in plants such as jimsonweed and may occasionally be abused.

5 Arylcyclohexylamines such as phencyclidine piperidine (PCP). It has been discovered that drugs chemically unrelated to PCP have PCP-like effects, but these are not considered drugs of abuse.

6 Cannabinoids can produce hallucinogenic effects at high THC doses. Marijuana was considered at length in Chapter 2.4

The compounds in the six groups above can be considered to represent three groups of drugs having similar effects. The first group comprises the indole and phenethylamine hallucinogens. They generally produce a similar type of intoxication. They differ in the amount of sympathetic nervous system arousal they produce. For instance, MDA and MDMA have more amphetamine-like effects than the indoles (see Table 12). The second group, the anticholinergics, represents a class of drugs with more severe acute toxicity. The third group, phencyclidine and related drugs, have very little in common with the indole and

TABLE 12
HALLUCINOGENS CONTAINING AN INDOLE NUCLEUS

Indole amines or substituted indole alkylamines:
    Lysergic acid diethylamide (LSD)
    Psilocin
    Psilocybin
    Dimethyltryptamine (DMT)
    Diethyltryptamine (DET)

phenethylamine hallucinogens and appeal to a different type of drug user. All three of these groups are more different than similar to cannabinoids.

There is no simple unifying theory as to how hallucinogenic drugs act on the body. It appears, however, that the major neurochemicals in the brain (norepinephrine, dopamine, serotonin, acetylcholine) and several excitatory amino acids such as glutamate and *N*-methylaspartate are involved in their action.

LSD, the Prototype

HISTORY

A century of research into the chemistry of ergot alkaloids preceded the first written account of the synthesis of LSD by Stoll and Hofmann in 1943. Ergot is derived from the fungus *Claviceps purpurea*, which parasitizes rye and wheat kernels, and from some varieties of morning glory plants containing lysergic acid, the precursor of LSD.

Four years after Stoll and Hofmann's report, Stoll reported the accidental and experimental psychedelic experiences of Hofmann (1947). Since that time we have witnessed the ebb and subsequent flow of the hippie culture: the classification of LSD and other psychedelic drugs as illegal, the diminution of interest in LSD as a front-page story, the overall decrease in the use of hallucinogens but with sporadic surges of popularity of new drugs such as MDMA—the "ecstasy drug" in 1985. Research in this area has not kept pace with studies of drugs of greater abuse and health hazard. Much of what we know about LSD comes from classical research done during the 1950s and 1960s.

The use of psychedelics in American subculture had roots deep in American society of the 1940s and 1950s. At that time, the country had emerged from a depression and entered a postwar boom. Parents strove to obtain the possessions they lacked in the days of the depression, and vowed that their children would not have to experience that same kind of poverty and fear. The "war babies" (children of soldiers of World War II) knew a greater security than many of their parents had known, allowing them to experience a new kind of freedom. Out of this very freedom and security grew their disdain for material wealth and the superficial life that often accompanied it. Established practices were challenged by increasing numbers with increasing vigor, and a new movement was under way with an ethic of love, individual freedom, and personal honesty.

During this time, Timothy Leary, a Harvard professor, was discovering the religious wonders of psychedelic drugs and began making a case for their inclusion in religious ceremony. He wanted everyone to have religious experiences whereby they might learn the answers to four basic spiritual questions:

1 What is the power that moves the universe?
2 What is life?
3 What is the human role on this earth?
4 What is my own personal role? (Leary, 1970).

These questions were being asked by the youthful revolutionaries who were turning away from organized religion to a religion of their own. LSD and marijuana became the drugs of choice, as both were linked to a passive, introspective lifestyle.

In 1966, even before the great hippie upsurge, Huston Smith, an MIT professor, predicted that the psychedelic or "hippie" movement would not have a religious impact because it did not have an established, stable community or church, it had no guidelines for behavior, it failed to formulate an integrated social philosophy demonstrating how the psychedelic experience influenced ongoing life, and it failed to convince the established society that what it was experiencing was meaningful (Smith, 1970). Smith did prophesy the demise of the large hippie communities, such as the Haight-Ashbury community of 1967–1968, but current vestiges of the early psychedelic movement are the parapsychology search and research being conducted all over the world, and the resurgence of the Eastern philosophies of Taoism and Zen with their inherently holistic lifestyles.

CLASSIFICATION

The drugs discussed here are classified as hallucinogens, but few truly cause hallucinations when taken at usual doses. Most of the drugs in this classification more often cause illusions—sights and sounds that are based upon physical objects and real sounds. Hallucinations are entirely made up in the mind. Perhaps a more encompassing description for most of these drugs, especially LSD and the other synthetic analogues, is "psychedelic." This term connotes other-than-normal sights, colors, sounds, movement, and so on. It is also important here to note that too much of any substance or condition (such as sensory deprivation) may cause illusions or hallucinations. Some of the drugs described in this chapter are combinations of psychedelic substance and amphetamine or some other substance. Regardless of their chemical basis, hallucinogens are discussed here because of their street use, danger, or abuse.

HOW TAKEN INTO THE BODY

Although sniffing or injecting LSD produces more rapid results, the oral route is the more common one. Oral ingestion offers the longest latency period (time lapse between taking the drug and feeling its effects), while intrathecal injection (under the membranes covering the spinal cord) causes an almost immediate onset of effects. In early LSD research, Cohen (1968) reported an average latency period of 45 minutes for an oral dose of 2 micrograms per kilogram of body weight (that is, 140 micrograms in the 70-kilogram male). The latency period depends on the amount taken and the mode of administration.

CHARACTERISTICS OF DEPENDENCE

Physical dependence is not known to develop with LSD, but as a powerful mind-altering drug it can become habit-forming, and psychological dependence can develop. Tolerance to LSD develops quite rapidly. Abramson (1960) found that there was a noticeable decrease in subjective symptoms when the same moderate dose was given daily for several days. Hence, those who take LSD must either space their use or take ever-increasing doses if they use it daily.

A standard dose of pure LSD for the average person is considered to be 30 to 50 micrograms, while an average dose of "street acid" may be around 100 micrograms. Doses as high as 1500 micrograms have been reported in supervised medical treatment, and occasionally a habitual user will report taking doses as high as 10,000 micrograms. In addition to dosage, effects depend also on the frame of mind of the user and his or her personality and environment. To date, no deaths have been reported from overdoses of LSD in humans, but some connection was made in the 1960s between the taking of LSD and suicide.

PHARMACOLOGY

Ingredients used in the synthesis of LSD are lysergic acid, diethylamine, and trifluoroacetic acid. Lysergic acid is controlled by the Federal Drug Administration, but illicit manufacturers produce it in clandestine labs using *Claviceps purpurea* and mannitol. About 1 kilogram of lysergic acid will make ½ kilogram of LSD. When legal authorities look for signs of illicit LSD manufacture, they look for these basic ingredients in the laboratory and for an ice-cream freezer, because the temperature of the mixture must be lowered to approximately 20 degrees Fahrenheit in order to complete synthesis.

LSD-25 binds to 5-HT (5-hydroxytryptamine, or serotinin) receptor sites in the brain (Abood, 1988). There are two kinds of 5-HT receptors in the brain (5-HT1 and 5-HT2), and almost all of the three classes of hallucinogens seem to interact more on 5-HT2 sites. However, LSD interacts with both kinds (Peroutka & Snyder, 1983; Jacobs, 1984).

LSD is absorbed into the blood very rapidly, and upon absorption from the gastrointestinal mucosa (through oral administration), it is quickly distributed throughout the body, with the highest concentrations appearing in the liver, kidney, and adrenals. A high proportion of the ingested LSD is found in the bile, as this is the preferred route of excretion.

Although LSD apparently crosses the blood–brain barrier with ease, as little as 1 percent of the ingested dose has been found to actually concentrate in the brain. Upon examining levels of LSD in various parts of the monkey brain, Snyder and Reivich (1966) found the highest concentrations in the pituitary gland and pineal gland, but high levels were also found in the hypothalamus, the limbic system, and the auditory and visual reflex areas. Surprisingly low concentrations were found in the cortex, the cerebellum, and the brainstem. This information helps to explain the electrical storms found (via depth electrodes) in areas within the limbic system in LSD subjects, while electroencephalogram records of other brain areas show no change.

The neurochemical action of LSD, the prototype of psychedelic drugs, and the action of other psychedelics (see Table 12) occur mainly in the midbrain. All of the drugs listed in Table 12 contain an indole nucleus, a chemical configuration that is also basic to the neurotransmitter serotonin. The mechanism of action of these hallucinogens is believed to be related to their interference with the neurons that use serotonin as their transmitter substance. The serotonin-mediated neurons of note here are found in the reticular area of the brainstem, the hypothalamus, and the limbic system. LSD apparently stimulates the same cells that are stimulated by amphetamines in the reticular formation and also alters the function of fiber tracts that use serotonin. The stimulant effects of LSD increase sensory information delivery to the cortex, while serotonin pathway interruption results in a decreased ability to selectively damp out sensory input (Holbrook, 1983). Since LSD is the prototype of the psychedelic drugs, its actions and the drug taker's reaction to it are detailed fully in this chapter. The other substances in the hallucinogen category are described in less detail at the end of the chapter.

EFFECTS ON THE BODY

If LSD is ingested, a number of physiological effects become increasingly apparent as the latency period comes to an end. Among these are a tingling in the hands and feet, a feeling of numbness, nausea (and sometimes vomiting), anorexia (lack of appetite), a flushed appearance, sensations of chilliness, and dilation of the pupils (mydriasis). Mydriasis, along with increased heart rate, body temperature, blood pressure, and blood sugar level, persists throughout the experience, but the other physiological effects subside after their initial occurrence. LSD does not impair intellectual processes; the user cannot or will not perform given tasks, has difficulty concentrating, and shows an overall air of confusion.

In a supportive setting, the LSD user usually first shows signs of being affected by the drug by becoming extremely emotional. A minor remark or incident may set off an intense laughing or crying episode. Of all the senses, tactile sensitivity is most universally affected, and the most dramatic effects are those of hallucinations, although they are unusual.

As the drug begins to take effect, one of its first visual manifestations is that of ever-changing colors and shapes of objects in the room, and the appearance of rainbowlike halos around lights. The senses are further affected, and synesthesia, a crossing of sense responses (hearing colors and seeing sounds), may occur. All this time may be spent in awe of the deepness of colors, the beauty of one object, the pureness of sound; but while LSD changes visual and auditory perception (Kornetsky et al., 1990), it also works on other central nervous system centers. Time and space perception are quite lost, and because of its stimulatory nature, LSD permits many extra stimuli to enter thought processes. Sounds and sights may flash on and off, tripping thought processes that have been long forgotten.

If a large enough dose is taken, the drug taker will begin to lose touch with the outside "concrete" world and begin to feel part of some greater living cosmos in which ego boundaries have been erased. The ineffable nature of this feeling seems to parallel Maslow's "peak experience"—that of being one with all things, an ecstasy of spirit (Maslow, 1968). Especially in a supportive setting, LSD takers report seeing divine figures, enchanting places, and other images of religiosity.

In the area of creativity, LSD subjects have expressed the feeling of being more creative during the LSD experience, but the activities of drawing and painting during a trip are hindered by the motor effects of LSD, and the products of creative effort under the influence of LSD largely prove to be inferior to those produced prior to the drug experience. Paintings done in LSD-creativity studies have been reminiscent of schizophrenic art.

Harman et al. (1966) found that a very light dose of mescaline (a derivative of the peyote cactus) equivalent to 50 micrograms of LSD proved helpful to a select group of engineers, scientists, and administrators who had specific problems that they could not solve before the drug experience. A majority of these subjects developed solutions to their problems after the drug experience. Whether or not they could have arrived at a similar solution in a brainstorming session or some other nondrug experience is impossible to say. However, these were highly select, competent subjects who apparently possessed a certain degree of creativity before the drug experience.

McGlothlin et al. (1970) tested twenty-four college students and found, through the use of creativity, attitude, and anxiety tests, that three LSD sessions (200-microgram doses) had no objective effect of enhanced creativity 6 months later. However, many of the subjects said that they felt they were more creative. This paradox is noted in many areas of LSD study—subjects feel that they have more insights, are more creative, and have more answers to life's questions, but they do not demonstrate these feelings objectively. Their overt behavior is not modified, and these new insights are short-lived unless they are reinforced by modified behavior.

In general, it has been found that LSD subjects report a greater interest in art and music after an LSD experience, and this greater awareness of the arts may give rise to some of the subjective feelings of creativity that have been reported.

The literature reveals that noted drug researchers, such as Hoffer and Osmond (1967) and Cohen (1968), felt that LSD did not enhance creativity in a noncreative mind. The drug may alter electrical patterns so that sensations are different and thus evoke a new idea from existing knowledge. A person who does not know music will not become a pianist by taking LSD; however, he or she may become more interested in music.

SPECIAL DANGERS

Although there has been an atmosphere of adventure surrounding the psyche-delics, they are not without drawbacks. Two dangers involved in psychedelic use are the potential for acute panic reactions and for more long-term changes in personality (Bowers & Swigar, 1983). These phenomena are related in that both probably involve the memory process and other intricacies of the central nervous system. Cohen (1968) estimated that about 0.1 percent of normal individuals who take LSD under favorable laboratory conditions suffer serious reactions. However, most of the psychedelic drug use in America today is not done under laboratory supervision. Two other possible dangers that deserve mention are the teratogenic effects of the hallucinogens and the deceit that is often practiced in the street market.

Chronic Psychosis

A psychological danger of hallucinogen use is that of prolonged psychosis or neurosis. This is not a flashback but is a continuing problem after the LSD experience. Paranoiac and schizophreniform psychoses have been seen to occur as a result of LSD, and the conditions have continued after the intoxication has worn off (Gallagher, 1990). Severe depression accompanying these psychoses has been thought to be the cause of homicidal and suicidal actions that followed.

Acute Panic Reactions

The bad drug experience, or "freakout" as it once was called, can be triggered by various stimuli. The panic that might result from loss of time–space perception; the acute physiological reactions of heart palpitation, chilliness, and nausea; or mere confusion from the experience could initiate a bad experience. Users might get so involved in their pseudohallucinations (true hallucinations occur only with high dosages and/or a very supportive setting) that they can no longer extricate themselves from their environment. If they panic, lose self-control and judgment, and perhaps become incoherent or violent, they and those around them are in a potentially dangerous situation. Since LSD wears off gradually over a period of 10 to 16 hours, the user cannot come out immediately except with the use of an anti-LSD drug such as chlorpromazine. However, the use of such a drug should be weighed against the possible harmful effects of subsequent psychological problems and a higher probability of flashbacks. In many, if not most, cases, a person having a bad experience can be talked back into a calm state; force and restraint should be used only as a last measure. One should never tell users in this condition that they have lost their minds or damaged them permanently, because they are already in a frightened, irrational state and are unable to think calmly or to use logical reasoning.

The bad experience can occur from an unexpected upsurge of memories that are normally repressed. It is not wise for a person with an unstable personality to take LSD, because the problems he or she has during an undrugged state may be amplified by LSD. It is not known exactly how LSD works, but it appears that normal selective damping of incoming stimuli no longer takes place and electrical storms occur in various parts of the brain.

A danger to many initial users is an intense expectation that doors will open, truth will be seen, and the soul will truly be enlightened. Expectations may be so great that anything short of an extremely moving experience may induce depression, and a bad trip may ensue.

Another acute psychological danger is that ego boundaries may disappear; for example, the floor may seem to become part of the body, and to step on the floor may evoke bodily pain. Ego may be inflated to heights beyond compare— to pure omnipotence—or to extreme lows, where suicide may seem to be the only way out.

Thinking loses its logic. There is a danger that users will begin to be fanatically set on illogical "truths" that occur to them during an LSD experience. They may believe they can read minds, transmit ESP messages, or will themselves to do anything, or they may even believe beyond a doubt that others are trying to kill them or are fiendishly plotting against them. Because of this inability to separate idea from reality during the drugged state, a striking number of LSD users strongly believe in magic.

It appears that mental stability, a supportive environment, and a good frame of mind upon going into an LSD experience are essential. Taking LSD in an angry or apprehensive mood has been shown to increase the likelihood of a bad experience; hence, a person should never be given LSD when he or she is unwilling to take the drug. Above all, LSD should never be given to individuals who are unaware that they are taking it, for they will not be prepared for the effects, which sometimes even habitual users cannot handle.

Flashbacks

The flashback may be a reaction to the LSD experience, and although this phenomenon does not occur to everyone who takes LSD, it is impossible to predict who will experience it. It seems to occur most often in cases when the user has had a bad LSD experience. Feelings of paranoia, unreality, and estrangement are often experienced in the flashback along with distorted visual perceptions and anesthesias or paresthesias (prickly or tingling sensations) creeping over the body. It has been shown that the body rids itself of LSD quite completely in about 48 hours; it is not known how the body can react as if under the influence of LSD after that time has elapsed. Fischer (1971) attributed the flashback experience to a "stateboundness" initiated by a stimulus identical to one previously experienced. An example of this is the sudden reflection or reliving of an experience of a departed parent upon smelling her perfume or his pipe tobacco. Experienced drug users can sometimes cause a flashback by setting the environment that surrounded them in a previous experience; this is called a "free trip," for it occurs without the use of a drug. Those who do not use drugs experience the same free trip when they have a moving memory of a happy experience.

Flashbacks have been known to last from a few minutes to several hours, to occur once a month or several times a day, up to 18 months after LSD use, and to happen in many different settings. It has been found that other drugs may trigger a flashback, and flashbacks frequently occur while one is driving or going to sleep; thus it would seem that they occur during a time when the reticular formation is not forwarding a large number of stimuli into the cortex. This may permit random thoughts or an overriding influence of any one thought or stimulus to trigger a state-bound experience. Flashbacks can be set off by stressful situations but may occur at nonstressful times as well.

There appear to be three kinds of flashbacks: perceptual (seeing colors, hearing sounds of the original experience), somatic (experiencing tingling sensations, heart palpitations, etc.), and emotional (reliving of depressive, anxious, or otherwise emotional thoughts that may have been triggered by the initial trip). The first two usually elicit reactions of panic, fear, and hysteria in those who do not understand their nature, but the third type may be the most dangerous: The persistent feeling of fear, remorse, loneliness, or other emotions may lead to extreme depression or suicide.

Chromosome Damage

Numerous studies from the 1960s to the present report LSD's potential for causing chromosomal breaks, and although the significance of such breaks has not been definitely established, they have been found to occur in animal and human white blood cells. Researchers have found meiotic chromosome change in mice directly exposed to high doses of LSD, and have indicated that LSD may have serious effects on size of litters, congenital malformations, and frequency of leukemia and other neoplastic diseases (diseases involving the growth of nonfunctional tissue).

The complexity of the chromosome issue and the sophistication of the research tends to be somewhat confusing to the lay reader. Caution should be exercised in reading, analyzing, and comparing studies. Pitfalls such as method of analyzing breaks, subject selection (possibility of other drug contamination), type of experimental animal, weight of animal, purity of LSD used (pure chemical, dry LSD mixed with saline, street mixtures), time of examination after exposure to LSD, and, probably most important, amount of LSD per kilogram of body weight must be considered. Further consideration must be given to the type of teratogenic or cytogenic effect being studied. Chromosome breakage is of doubtful importance unless the germ cells are affected. Dishotsky et al. (1971) pointed out, however, that many reports of chromosome damage come from studies in which subjects have ingested illicit (not pure) LSD, and therefore the harmful effects observed may have stemmed from adulterating substances rather than from the LSD. Most researchers, who have no control over interpretations of their work by news reporters and the public, caution their readers against extending their findings to situations not covered by physical and/or statistical controls. The research papers on the potential dangers of LSD are too numerous and too well-executed to ignore, however, and women who are contemplating pregnancy or are in early pregnancy are warned against taking any unprescribed drug, especially in the first trimester.

Deceit by Dealers

Surveys show that many street users who think they are purchasing mescaline, peyote, psilocybin, or other organics are actually buying acid, PCP, or some other more easily manufactured hallucinogen. This deceit could be a hazard to those who expect one kind of drug reaction but find themselves in an entirely different experience. Because the intensity and length of the trip depend at least in part upon the drug and the dosage, the street buyer must exercise caution.

MEDICAL USE

LSD has been used with limited success in psychotherapy. It must be understood that, where found successful, the drug has been only a tool, just as a scalpel is a tool. In the hands of a competent surgeon, the scalpel can be used to benefit the patient, but in the hands of others, it can be a dangerous object. Therapeutic use of LSD has not increased greatly over the years because of its limited success, the legal implications, the difficulty in procuring the drug, the possibility of adverse reactions to the drug (even in a controlled environment, bad trips can and do occur), and the problem of rapid tolerance buildup in the patient.

LSD therapy has been tried by psychotherapists to help resolve various problems of their patients. It has had limited use in cases of alcoholism, autism, paranoia, and schizophrenia and various other mental and emotional disorders. Results of these uses have ranged from "no improvement" to "complete cure," but the largest percentage lies in the "slightly improved" category (Gallagher, 1990). LSD does not work for every therapist or every patient. When the drug does contribute to the improvement of a patient, it is the combination of patient, therapist, and drug, all working together, that effects a cure.

When the beneficial effects of therapy are presented as a rationale for using the drug in a nonmedical setting, one must realize that (1) the argument is based on therapy with limited use and limited success and (2) the question is one of psychedelic therapy as opposed to psycholytic therapy. Psycholytic therapy, the use of LSD in a medical setting, calls for a low dose (50 to 70 micrograms) administered repeatedly over a long period of time. This low dosage appears to facilitate recall, catharsis, abreaction, and other patient reactions that may aid in psychoanalysis. As one can see, this is not the nontherapeutic LSD experience, where a larger dose is taken and stronger reactions occur. Therefore, in rationalizing the nontherapeutic use of LSD, one cannot cite the beneficial effects of psycholytic therapy, because this use is quite different from street use in dosage and in effects.

Psychedelic therapy, which is used on occasion, is a specialized form of intensive therapy on a "one-shot" basis. A dose of 200 micrograms or more is used to create a typical LSD experience, in which it is hoped that the patient will "find himself." This type of therapy is used with patients who have a basic loss of self-respect, self-esteem, and self-image, in the hope that the drug experience will allow them to accept themselves once again. This experience must be preceded by extensive therapeutic preparation for several weeks prior to the therapy session. The setting must be extremely supportive—special music, lighting, pictures, etc., are used—and, most important, a trained therapist must be with the patient constantly during the 10-to-12-hour trip, shaping, directing, and guiding the trip. The therapist provides reassurance, averts anxiety, and is responsible for the success of the experience. The session is followed up with supportive therapy to help redirect the patient.

Not all sessions of psychedelic therapy produce effective results, and bad trips are known to occur in therapy as well as in street use. In the last several years, the drug MDMA has been used by therapists to help clients break down communications barriers, trust themselves and others, deal with jealousy in a positive manner, and solve other personal growth issues. Adler et al. (1985) reported that Lester Grinspoon and Norman Zinberg (both of Harvard Medical School and both longstanding experts in drug study) found MDMA to be a helpful therapeutic tool.

Other Hallucinogens

All hallucinogens produce similar reactions in the human body, but the intensity of the reaction varies among the different drugs. The preceding discussion of the psychotherapeutic use of LSD gives an idea of the difference between the less intense reactions produced by a 50-microgram dose and the typical LSD experience caused by a dose of 200 micrograms or more. The difference in intensity of other hallucinogens parallels this type of continuum. It is found that an oral dose of 0.1 milligram (100 micrograms) of LSD produces psychedelic effects comparable to those produced by 5 milligrams of psilocybin or PCP, 30 milligrams of inhaled DMT, or 300 to 500 milligrams of mescaline (Holbrook, 1983; Senay, 1983).

Other drugs in this classification that have seen high abuse, other than LSD, are mescaline, psilocybin, DMT and diethyltryptamine (DET, a street nickname), STP, and PCP. The more recent appearance of MDMA as a street drug also warrants attention. There are so many hallucinogens of minor popularity, such as nutmeg, certain morning glory seeds, jimsonweed, ibogaine (obtained from a plant grown in equatorial Africa), and countless others, that time and space will not allow a complete description of each. However, the effects of these are very similar to those described for LSD or one of the other hallucinogens described here if they are taken in large enough doses.

There is the ever-present danger to users of the more popular hallucinogens that street supplies of these drugs are regularly mislabeled and misrepresented. It appears that PCP is involved in most of the street drug misrepresentation.

FIGURE 17
The peyote cactus.

LSD has been described in detail in this chapter; the remainder of the chapter is devoted to brief descriptions of other drugs that are commonly placed in this classification, even though they may also have amphetamine-like or anesthetic qualities.

MESCALINE/PEYOTE

Mescaline is one of the principal alkaloids found in the peyote cactus (*Lophophora williamsii,* Figure 17) and is apparently responsible for the visual hallucinations that occur when one eats peyote.

Peyote intoxication differs somewhat from mescaline intoxication because peyote also contains alkaloids other than mescaline. A dose of 300 to 600 milligrams of mescaline can produce hallucinations and other psychedelic effects, whereas more than 50 times that amount of peyote must be ingested to produce similar reactions. Duration of effects for mescaline is 5 to 12 hours, but longer periods have been reported.

Mescaline may be marketed as a powder, as a gelatin capsule, or in liquid form, thus making it possible to sniff, ingest, or inject the substance. However, it is reported that most mescaline is taken orally. Peyote is taken orally in the form of mescal buttons, the brown, dried crowns of the cactus. These buttons are either chewed or sucked to extract the hallucinogenic substances within.

Peyote intoxication first brings on a feeling of contentment and hypersensitivity, then one of nervous calm during which visual hallucinations are apt to occur. Brilliant flashes of color, defying description, are seen prior to the visual hallucinations. It appears that visual hallucinations occurring from peyote ingestion follow a pattern. First, geometric figures appear, then familiar scenes and faces, followed by unfamiliar scenes and objects. It is this visual phenomenon that made peyote revered by peyotists—this was their way of communicating with their spirits.

Until 1990 peyote was the only drug of its kind that was legal in the United States. Its legality was based on the argument that it was part of the ritual ceremony performed by the members of the Native American Church of North America, a religious group preaching brotherly love, high morality, and abstention from alcohol. The taking of peyote in this church was limited to members who were at least one-quarter Native American blood and were registered by the state as such. In addition, all peyote used had to be secured from legal sources and registered. In 1990 the Supreme Court ruled that it is not a Constitutional right to take peyote for religious purposes.

The peyote ceremony usually consists of an all-night gathering inside the ceremonial meeting place, where the worshippers sit in a circle around a fire. Peyote is taken and works its effects as the worshippers are led in prayer, chanting, and meditation by a "road man." The meeting ends in the morning with a communal meal (Widener, 1985).

If this drug and its derivative, mescaline, were used only as religious objects, they would be of little concern. However, the use of these hallucinogens has entered the pleasure-seeking world, and if they are taken in sufficient dosage, their use and the problems they cause become similar to those described for LSD. As with LSD, no physical dependence on these drugs has been observed, but the need for further psychological gratification may provide the impetus for repeated use. Tolerance to mescaline develops, as does cross-tolerance between mescaline, LSD, and psilocybin.

PSILOCYBIN

In 1958, A. Hofmann (who discovered the hallucinogenic effects of LSD) isolated psilocybin, the hallucinogenic agent in *Psilocybe mexicana,* a small mushroom that grows in marshy places (Figure 18). This mushroom has been used for centuries in religious ceremonies. The Aztecs used it as a sacrament and to produce visions and hallucinations.

This drug (along with another *Psilocybe mexicana* derivative, psilocin) also has fallen into street use as a psychedelic. It is available in powder or liquid

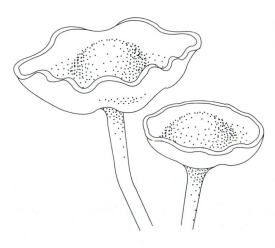

FIGURE 18
The mushroom *Psilocybe mexicana,*
from which psilocybin is produced.

form, and a dose of 4 to 8 milligrams will produce effects similar to those of mescaline, including initial nausea, coldness of the extremities, and mydriasis, followed by abrupt mood changes and visual hallucinations. The intoxication, lasting about 8 hours, is followed by mental and physical depression, lassitude, and distortion of one's sense of time and space.

Psilocybin use has been shown to cause development of tolerance. No physical dependence has been observed, but psychological dependence is a danger.

DMT AND DET

DMT (dimethyltryptamine) has been labeled the "businessman's trip" because a 70-milligram injected dose will cause an onset of hallucinatory effects within 2 to 5 minutes, with the condition subsiding within half an hour to an hour. Neither of these drugs is orally active, and therefore they must be smoked or injected.

DMT was originally obtained from seeds of *Piptadenia peregrina* and *Piptadenia macrocarpa*, legumes that are found in the Caribbean islands and in South America. The natives of these areas pulverized the seeds and then inhaled the substance as snuff through a tube.

DMT sold on the street is a semisynthetic that is easily produced from common materials and is thus inexpensive to buy. It is very similar in chemical structure to psilocin, the substance into which psilocybin is converted in the body and which subsequently causes the psychedelic experience to occur. It is usually smoked in a mixture of parsley, marijuana, tobacco, or tea.

DMT and its close chemical variant DET (diethyltryptamine) have not been found to cause physical dependence, but tolerance does develop, as may an intense desire to continually repeat the experience. In addition, no cross-tolerance develops between DMT and LSD, mescaline, or psilocybin (Jacobs, 1984).

STP (DOM)

Psychotomimetic amphetamines are a group of amphetamines that produce hallucinogenic effects along with the typical amphetamine reactions (discussed in detail in Chapter 2.6). This group of psychoactive drugs is exemplified by DOM (dimethoxymethylamphetamine), also known as STP. The nickname STP seems to have been derived from the motor oil additive "scientifically treated petroleum" or from the words "serenity, tranquility, and peace."

As has been mentioned, STP is capable of producing typical LSD-type reactions or amphetamine action, or both. As with most other drugs, the reaction depends on the dose. In clinical studies, reactions have been observed with doses varying from 2 to 14 milligrams, while street doses appear to be around 10 milligrams.

Ingested doses of fewer than 3 milligrams produce heart rate increases, pupillary dilation, increase in systolic blood pressure, and increase in oral temperature. The experience at this dosage has been described as a mild euphoria. The duration of reaction at low doses is from 8 to 12 hours, with peak reactions occurring between the third and fifth hours (Jacobs, 1984).

With higher doses, reactions may last from 16 to 24 hours. This duration may be responsible for the high incidence of acute panic reactions associated with this drug. In the extreme hyperactive condition, the even larger increases in heart rate, blood pressure, and body temperature, along with pupillary dilation, an extremely dry mouth, nausea, and profuse sweating, all seem to be endless. These effects are accompanied by LSD-type alterations in perception (such as enhancement of details), visual and auditory hallucinations (including blurred multiple images, distorted shapes, and vibration of objects), and a sense of slowed passage of time. The mind becomes flooded with a variety of irrelevant and incoherent thoughts, then becomes absolutely blank, exacerbating the feeling that one is going crazy. Also, as is the case with LSD, flashbacks or recurrent reactions have been reported to occur, but no mechanism for this phenomenon has been substantiated (Holbrook, 1983).

The significance of these hallucinogenic breaks with reality is that they allow for gross misinterpretation of the amphetamine-like somatic effects over an extended period of time. This combination of hallucinogenic and amphetamine-like effects appears to be the primary danger of psychotomimetic amphetamine compounds like STP. The pharmacological effects have not been widely investigated, but the limbic system, the thalamus, and the hypothalamus seem to be affected. These are the hypothesized sites of action because they are the sites of the greatest accumulation of STP in the brains of experimental animals.

MDMA

In the past decade MDMA (methylenedioxymethamphetamine), street name Ecstasy, became popular on campuses and on the street because it appears to relax inhibitions and enhance communication. Used since the 1970s as a tool in psychotherapy because of its ability to help people feel good about themselves, MDMA is now undergoing legal classification as a Schedule I drug (drugs with abuse potential but no medical use). Therapists are seeking to continue its legal use, however.

This drug has been touted as being "all that LSD was supposed to be, but was not." However, it is not a true hallucinogen, and unlike LSD it does not diminish the drug taker's ability to distinguish between fantasy and reality (Adler et al., 1985). The drug is related to amphetamines, mescaline, and MDA (a potent stimulant).

Adler et al. (1985) reported that the Haight-Ashbury Free Medical Clinic in San Francisco had seen patients in their detoxification unit who had taken ten to fifteen 100-milligram doses of MDMA in one day.

PCP

Phencyclidine piperidine HCl (PCP) is a street drug that has been used by more than 7 million people in the United States. It has stimulant, depressant, hallucinogenic, and analgesic properties, which make it difficult to classify, but it has been proposed that it be put in the class "dissociative anesthetic." We include it here because of its frequent misrepresentation as other psychedelic drugs. The drug is used legally as an animal-immobilizing agent, but it was originally developed as a human anesthetic. In 1965 its manufacturer, Parke, Davis & Company, requested that the use of PCP with human subjects be discontinued because of frequent postoperative side effects ranging from mild disorientation to delirium.

It appears that PCP (like the opiates and marijuana) has specific receptors in the brain. These PCP sites may mediate effects of certain psychotomimetic opioid agonists and other PCP-like drugs (Contreras et al., 1986). That there are specific PCP receptors in the brain raises the question of its normal physiological function in the body. Perhaps the most important new development in the mechanism of PCP action is the discovery of its effects on the excitatory amino acid neurotransmitters (DHHS, 1987). It has been reported that several substances with PCP-like behavioral effects inhibit the release of acetylcholine and dopamine, giving scientists a greater clue to the specific mechanisms of this drug (Piercey & Hoffmann, 1990).

PCP first appeared on the street in 1965 on the West Coast. Because of its dangerous side effects, it quickly gained a bad reputation and its use diminished. In 1977 this drug was associated with at least 100 deaths and more than 4,000 emergency room visits—signs that PCP use was increasing. It seems that the ease with which PCP can be synthesized and the change in mood of use from oral ingestion to smoking to snorting, which enables the user to control its effects better, have caused an increase in its abuse. For instance, in one year (1976–1977), the number who had used PCP nearly doubled for the 12-to-17-year-old group.

PCP is sprinkled on marijuana or parsley and smoked, with the amount in a joint varying between 1 and 100 milligrams. If swallowed, the effects last longer and are less controlled than if inhaled. The effects of 1 to 10 milligrams of orally ingested PCP last up to 12 hours, and a prolonged comedown period follows.

If sold in granular powder form, PCP is usually 50 to 100 percent pure, but it may run only 5 to 30 percent pure if sold in other forms, especially when sprinkled on leaves. When misrepresented in street sales, PCP is most commonly sold as THC, but it is also sold as cannabinol, LSD, mescaline, psysilocybin, or even amphetamine or cocaine. PCP has been used in combination with heroin, cocaine, methaqualone, LSD, barbiturates, procaine, and other drugs. Because of the many nicknames for PCP, the street misrepresentation of the drug, and its use in combination with other drugs, it is difficult to get an accurate picture of the use of PCP in the United States.

The acute effects of PCP are so unpleasant for most users that one wonders how the drug can survive on the street market. The most frequently reported effect at moderate doses is one of depersonalization, with the user sensing distance and estrangement from the surroundings. Sensory impulses in distorted form do reach the neocortex, but body movement diminishes, time appears to slow down, impulses are dulled, coordination fails, speech becomes senseless, and numbness sets in. Somatic effects include increases in heart rate and blood pressure. At higher doses auditory hallucinations may occur, as may convulsions. Feelings of impending doom or death are common, and bizarre behavior, such as nudity in public, has also been reported. Users of PCP may also feel a sense of invulnerability and power that may lead to acts of violence.

Habitual users report memory problems and speech difficulty that persist over time; after long-term daily use these effects may last for as long as a year. Mood disorders such as depression and anxiety occur, especially after a 2-to-3-day run. With long-term chronic abuse, the PCP user may become paranoid and violent. (Violence appears to be a recurrent side effect of this drug.) Because PCP produces schizophrenia-like symptoms, it is being used to study that mental disorder (Health Editor, 1990).

Continuing popularity of PCP is puzzling when one considers that even users acknowledge the persistent negative aspects of the drug. But some aspects such as heightened sensitivity, stimulation, mood elevation, and relaxation or tranquilization are positive motives given by users on at least some occasions. Continued use of PCP may also represent a desire for a prolonged altered state of consciousness, the risk taking that is inherent in this drug, or the fact that it helps in attaining new perspectives not found with other drugs such as marijuana or LSD. It has been found that more than half of the patients hospitalized with drug disorders (other than alcohol) were found to have a diagnosable mental disorder also (Regier et al., 1990).

A patient suffering from PCP overdose (doses of 0.5 gram or more in adults can be life-threatening) would exhibit some of the following symptoms: coma or stupor, vomiting, pupils in midposition and reactive, repetitive motor movements, shivering, muscle rigidity on stimulation, fever, flushing, and/or decreased peripheral sensations. These symptoms can be expected to occur with doses of 5 to 10 milligrams. At still higher levels (more than 10 milligrams) the symptoms may be prolonged coma (from 12 hours to many days), hypertension, convulsions, decreased to absent gag and corneal reflexes, hypersalivation, and decerebrate positioning.

In life-threatening situations, intensive medical management is called for initially, followed by isolation to reduce sensory stimulation. Often patients are so violent and unmanageable that restraints are necessary during this period. Constant vigilance is also required to monitor vital signs.

Some patients experience a psychotic phase that lasts from several days to several weeks. The initial phase is one of violent psychotic behavior, followed by more controlled restlessness and lessening of delusional activity and then a final stage of rapid improvement of thought disorders and paranoia (Clouet, 1986). Often, during this phase, PCP abuse is misdiagnosed because the symptoms so closely resemble an acute schizophrenic episode.

Low doses (7 milligrams orally) of PCP have effects that are similar to those of barbiturate intoxication, whereas larger amounts (12 to 15 milligrams) produce the psychedelic reactions generally seen with high doses of LSD. At the high-dose end of the scale (15 milligrams and up) hallucinations and paranoid psychosis occur, and there are reports of self-destructive behavior during intoxication at these amounts. Dramatic withdrawal signs occur in monkeys (that have been taught PCP self-administration) when PCP access is terminated after long-term use. Similar behavioral signs have been reported in humans, but such instances appear to be relatively rare because few use it in such a long-term manner (Balster, 1990).

Diazepam can be used medically to counteract severe psychoneurotic reactions or when there is risk of convulsions. Death from PCP overdose occurs due to convulsions and/or depression of the respiratory centers.

INHALANTS

In the early months of 1991, when the U.S. government was proud to announce new evidence that marijuana, cocaine, and other illicit substance use was declining, little notice was given to the increase in inhalant use. Thousands of youths in the United States use butane, gasoline, typewriter correction fluid, and other inhalants in search of a high (NIDA, 1990). Medical writers in England also report fatal use of inhalants by young people in that country (Anderson et al., 1985).

Inhalants can be classified into at least four categories:

Volatile organic solvents (e.g., gasoline, glue, lighter fluids, paint thinners)
Aerosols (e.g., hair sprays, deodorants, spray paint)
General anesthetic agents [e.g., nitrous oxide, tricholoroethylene (found in correction fluid)]
Volatile nitrites (e.g., amyl nitrite, butyl nitrite)

A large number of common substances (such as acetone, benzene, toluene, dichloro- and trichlorofluoromethanes, ketones, and petroleum products) found in the first two categories listed above have known toxicity and may cause toxic neuropathies and liver, renal, and bone marrow damage (DHHS, 1987). Especially important with the current AIDS epidemic is that the volatile nitrites reportedly diminish the capacity of the immune system. Other adverse effects of nitrite inhalation include contact dermatitis, irritation of the tracheobronchial tree and eyes, dizziness, pounding of the heart, and blurred vision (Schwartz & Peary, 1986).

All inhalants in high enough concentrations bring about the effects of intoxication and, in some cases, sudden death (Siegel & Wason, 1990). Some work as general anesthetics, others reduce oxygen to the brain or cause the blood pressure to fall. This state of intoxication is interpreted as euphoria, which may include an adrenaline-like release.

There is increasing evidence that exposure to abused solvents during pregnancy may have unfortunate consequences for the offspring (Cook et al., 1990).

REFERENCES

Abood, L. (1988). Receptor-transductive mechanisms for drugs of abuse. In L. S. Harris (Ed.), *Problems of Drug Dependence*. Rockville, Md.: U.S. Department of Health and Human Services.

Abramson, H. A. (1960). *The use of LSD in Psychotherapy*. New York: J. Macy, Jr. Foundation.

Adler, J., et al. (1985). Getting high on "Ecstasy." *Newsweek,* Apr. 15, p. 96.

Anderson, H. R., Macnair, R. S., and Ramsey, J. D. (1985). Deaths from abuse of volatile substances: a national epidemiological study. *British Medical Journal,* 290:304–307.

Balster, R. L. (1990). Behavioral pharmacology of PCP, NMDA and sigma receptors. In L. S. Harris (Ed.), *Problems of Drug Dependence 1989*. DHHS Pub. (ADM) 90–1663. Washington, D.C.: U.S. Government Printing Office.

Bowers, M. B., Jr., and Swigar, M. E. (1983). Vulnerability to psychosis associated with hallucinogen use. *Psychiatry Research,* 9:91–97.

Clouet, D. H. (Ed.). (1986). *Phencyclidine: An Update*. NIDA Research Monograph Series 64. DHHS Pub. (ADM) 86–1443. Washington, D.C.: U.S. Government Printing Office.

Cohen, Sidney. (1968). A quarter century of research with LSD. In J. T. Ungreleider (Ed.), *The Problems and Prospects of LSD*. Springfield, Ill.: Charles C Thomas.

Contreras, P. C., et al. (1986). Stereotyped behavior correlates better than ataxia with phencyclidine–receptor interactions. *European Journal of Pharmacology,* 121:9–18.

Cook, P. S., Petersen, R. C., and Moore, D. T. (1990). *Alcohol, Tobacco, and Other Drugs May Harm the Unborn*. Rockville, Md.: U.S. Department of Health and Human Services.

DHHS. (1987). *Second Triennial Report to Congress from the Secretary of the Department of Health and Human Services*. Washington, D.C.: U.S. Government Printing Office.

Dishotsky, N., et al. (1971). LSD and genetic damage. *Science,* 172:431–440.

Fischer, R. (1971). The flashback: arousal-statebound recall of experience. *Journal of Psychedelic Drugs,* 3(2):31–39.

Gallagher, W. (1990). LSD. *American Health,* December, pp. 61–67.

Harman, W. W., et al. (1966). Psychedelic agents in creative problem solving: a pilot study. *Psychological Review,* 19:211.

Health Editor. (1990). Researchers study relationship between PCP use and schizophrenia. *Canadian Doctor,* 33:428.

Hoffer, A., and Osmond, H. (1967). *The Hallucinogens*. Orlando, Fla.: Academic.

Holbrook, J. M. (1983). Hallucinogens. In G. Bennett et al. (Eds.), *Substance Abuse: Pharmacological, Developmental, and Clinical Perspectives*. New York: Wiley, pp. 86–101.

Jacobs, B. L. (1984). *Hallucinogens: Neurochemical, Behavioral and Clinical Perspectives*. New York: Raven Press.

Kornetsky, C., Williams, J. E. G., and Bird, Michael. (1990). Attentional and motivational effects of psychoactive drugs. In Lynda Erinoff (Ed.), *Neurobiology of Drug Abuse: Learning and Memory*. Rockville, Md.: U.S. Department of Health and Human Services.

Leary, Tim. (1970). The religious experience: its production and interpretation. *Journal of Psychedelic Drugs,* 3:76–86.

Maslow, A. H. (1968). *Toward a Psychology of Being*. New York: Van Nostrand Reinhold.

McGlothlin, W. H., Cohen, S., and McGlothlin, M. S. (1970). Long lasting effects of LSD on normals. *Journal of Psychedelic Drugs,* 3(1):20–36.

NIDA. (1990). Monitoring the future: statistics from the high school survey. *NIDA Notes,* Spring, p. 27.

Peroutka, S. J., and Snyder, S. H. (1983). Multiple serotonin receptors and their physiological significance. *Federation Proceedings,* 42:213–217.

Piercey, M. F., and Hoffmann, W. E. (1990). Cerebral pathways activated by PCP-like compounds: relevance to neurotransmitters and their receptors. In L. S. Harris (Ed.), *Problems of Drug Dependence 1989.* DHHS Pub. (ADM) 90–1663. Washington, D.C.: U.S. Government Printing Office.

Regier, D. A., et al. (1990). Comorbidity of mental disorders with alcohol and other drug abuse. *JAMA,* 264:2511–2518.

Schwartz, R. H., and Peary, P. (1986). Abuse of isobutyl nitrite inhalation (Rush) by adolescents. *Clinical Pediatrics (Philadelphia),* 25(6):308–310.

Senay, E. C. (1983). *Substance Abuse Disorders.* Boston: John Wright.

Siegel, E., and Wason, S. (1990). Sudden death caused by inhalation of butane and propane. *New England Journal of Medicine,* Dec. 5, p. 1638.

Smith, H. (1970). Psychedelic theophanies and the religious life. *Journal of Psychedelic Drugs,* 3(1):87–91.

Snyder, S. H., and Reivich, M. (1966). Regional location of lysergic acid diethylamide in monkey brain. *Nature,* 209:1093.

Stoll, A. (1947). Lysergsaure-diathy-amid, ein Phantasticum aus der Mutterkorngruppe. *Schweizer Archiv für Neurologie und Psychiatrie,* 60:279.

Widener, Sandra. (1985). The peyote path to God. *The Denver Post Magazine,* June 16, pp. 14–23.

NONPRESCRIPTION DRUGS

Americans are basically independent and like to take care of themselves, and professional medical care is rapidly pricing itself out of the reach of the majority of our population. The persuasive television announcer outlines symptoms and assures us that we are not alone, that millions have insomnia or simple nervous tension, and either can be easily remedied by simply, inexpensively, taking brand X or Y or Z. Thus the foundation is laid for a rapid proliferation of nonprescription (or over-the-counter) drugs. It is not that Americans have that many ailments, but hundreds of millions of dollars in advertisements have convinced us we do. We are encouraged to self-diagnose and self-medicate for everything from falling hair and fallen arches to the condition of our breath, stomach, or bowels. We are so convinced of the need for self-medication that in the average American household thirty different drugs can be found, twenty-four of which are nonprescription.

Although the average American does not buy over-the-counter (OTC) drugs in the pursuit of pleasure, he or she does seek and expect the drug to relieve some of life's painful reality. It is often said that we are a drug-using society, but, more important, we are a drug-misusing society. If you define *misuse* as the taking of a substance for an effect other than that which the substance was intended to produce or can produce, then you must add the multitudinous proprietary medicines to the list of America's misused drugs.

Antacids

HISTORY

The stomach is equipped with cells that make and secrete hydrochloric acid (HCl) so that a proper pH can be established for digesting food, especially proteins. The stomach also has cells that produce mucus so that the stomach lining is protected from its own acids and enzymes. The ingestion of food becomes a stimulus for secretion of HCl into the stomach; certain foods especially stimulate this production (for instance, coffee and spicy foods). Nervousness can also cause hypersecretion of HCl. Gulping air while eating may also cause the heartburn or sour stomach that calls for an antacid. All of these problems then can singly, or in combination, result in acid indigestion.

Americans spend well over $100 million annually on antacid preparations. There are over 300 different brands of tablets, pills, gums, and lozenges, about 150 liquids, and over 100 different powders. Antacids are usually considered effective if used properly; however, overuse can cause problems.

The first Food and Drug Administration (FDA) panel to meet was the antacid review panel, and some of the pertinent guidelines brought out in this review process in 1974 were the following (FDA, 1974):

1 Antacid manufacturers could make only three therapeutic claims on their labels—that their product was safe and effective for the symptomatic relief of "heartburn," "acid indigestion," and/or "sour stomach." The label was also to include warnings of side effects that could be expected to occur in 5 percent or more of the consumers taking the product. Virtually all antacid labels one sees in the drugstore now comply with these early rulings.

2 The panel determined that there were only thirteen acceptable ingredients or groups of ingredients for antacids (these are listed in Table 13). Manufacturers who did not comply with this ruling could continue to market a product if the ingredients were changed to comply with the panel's standards.

3 Maximum safe and minimum effective dosage levels were established for each of the active ingredients.

CLASSIFICATION

Drugs that comply with the relevant FDA guidelines are classified as antacids (see Table 13).

TABLE 13
FDA-ACCEPTABLE ACTIVE INGREDIENTS IN ANTACIDS

Aluminum-containing ingredients	Citrate-containing ingredients
Bicarbonate-containing ingredients	Magnesium-containing ingredients
Bismuth-containing ingredients	Phosphate-containing ingredients
Calcium-containing ingredients	Potassium-containing ingredients
Sodium-containing ingredients	Tartrate-containing ingredients
Sodium bicarbonate	Glycine (aminoacetic acid)
Dried milk solids	

HOW TAKEN INTO THE BODY

Antacids are available in every conceivable size, shape, and form to fit the needs and convenience of the users. Nearly all of them are oral preparations that are swallowed, chewed, or taken in liquid form.

CHARACTERISTICS OF DEPENDENCE

The taking of antacids is not physiologically habit-forming (Griffith, 1988).

PHARMACOLOGY

Active ingredients in the nonabsorbable antacids are usually combinations of magnesium hydroxide and aluminum hydroxide, but a wide variety of ingredients may be encountered. In the stomach, they neutralize some of the hydrochloric acid and reduce the action of the digestive enzyme pepsin. They also stimulate the muscles in the lower bowel walls.

EFFECTS ON THE BODY

The ingredients in aluminum, calcium, and magnesium antacids help to neutralize hyperacidity in the upper gastrointestinal tract, especially the stomach and esophagus; they bind with excess phosphate in the intestine, and some may give constipation relief. Common side effects of antacid use include headache, irregular heartbeat in patients with heart disease, abdominal pain, belching, distended stomach, and loss of appetite. Infrequently, side effects such as bone pain, dizziness, muscle weakness or pain, and nausea occur.

SPECIAL DANGERS

Many of these preparations use aspirin, and individuals suffering from gastric ulcers, gastritis, and other stomach disorders should limit their intake of any product containing aspirin. Even for those without stomach disorders, antacids containing aspirin are not recommended for upset stomach, for aspirin is the single most ingested gastric irritant. In fact, the most often cited reasons for the use of antacids (that is, heartburn, upset stomach, and acid indigestion) represent situations in which aspirin should have no place in the treatment. Also, alcohol and unbuffered aspirin exert a synergistic effect in promoting augmented blood loss from gastric mucosa.

Antacids are used by sufferers of gastritis and ulcers to keep acidity levels from doing further damage to the stomach or intestinal lining, but because of the "overshoot" phenomenon (when stomach pH is reduced by an antacid, the stomach's reply is to produce more acid), popping Tums or Rolaids may be as much a cause of the problem as it is a cure. Antacids are usually safe and effective when taken as directed; however, the stomach empties rapidly, and the neutralizing effect is lost within 30 minutes. If the condition persists, additional antacids must be consumed. Food, especially protein from lean meat or milk (skim milk is as good as whole) provides good natural neutralization of the gastric environment and produces less constipation than do antacids.

Laxatives

HISTORY

It has been suggested that laxatives are the most overused and misused over-the-counter products in America. Hundreds of different laxatives are on the market, and Americans spend several million dollars yearly on them.

CLASSIFICATION

There are bulk-forming laxatives, saline (salt-containing) and other hyper-osmotic laxatives, intestinal stimulation laxatives, and lubricant-type laxatives.

HOW TAKEN INTO THE BODY

Laxatives are usually taken orally.

CHARACTERISTICS OF DEPENDENCE

Most nonprescription laxatives are not habit-forming, but laxatives that stimulate the gut must carry a label warning about possible dependence. Psychological dependence on laxatives is seen in some individuals suffering from anorexia nervosa and bulemia.

PHARMACOLOGY

See Effects on the Body for discussion on how the different types of laxatives work in the body.

EFFECTS ON THE BODY

The bulk-forming laxatives may contain cellulose derivatives, polycarbophil, or dietary bran. These create bulk so that water will be absorbed into the intestines, thus easing the passage of fecal material. The FDA panel stated that bulk-forming laxatives are among the safest because they work naturally. These laxatives require the ingestion of 8 ounces of water with each dose to ensure that obstruction does not occur in the digestive tract. Dietary bran was given top billing by the panel: 6 to 14 grams per day plus liquid is considered safe and effective. Bran-rich breakfast cereals and whole wheat bread are good sources of wheat bran: 100 grams of bran flakes contains between 2.7 and

6.5 grams of crude fiber; one slice of whole wheat bread contains 1 to 2 grams. Bran tablets were not given safe and effective status by the panel.

The saline (salt-containing) and other hyperosmotic agents were once believed to act by drawing water into the gut by osmotic attraction to the salt or other osmotic agent, but the mechanism of action appears now to be a complex series of exchanges in the GI (gastrointestinal) tract. The saline laxatives should be restricted to occasional use only, as serious electrolyte imbalances have been reported with long-term or daily use. Examples of these laxatives are products with magnesium and phosphate salts. Sodium warnings must appear on the labels of these products, as must warning against prolonged use or use by those with kidney disease or other ailments.

Laxatives that stimulate the gut (e.g., Ex-Lax and castor oil) should be used only occasionally, and the label on such a laxative must read "Prolonged or continual use of this product can lead to laxative dependency and loss of normal bowel function. Serious side effects from prolonged use or overdose may occur" (DHEW, 1975a). The mechanism of action of these laxatives is to move intestinal components through the tract more quickly by stimulating peristalsis in the gut.

Lubricant laxatives (mineral oil, for instance) are designated as safe and effective in amounts usually administered orally. These laxatives are to be taken at bedtime only. The drawbacks to the use of mineral oil are that fat-soluble vitamin absorption is impaired, prothrombin levels may be lowered, and regular use in pregnancy may predispose to hemorrhagic disease in the newborn. Also, with chronic use (particularly with excess dosage), anal leakage and skin reactions may occur (DHEW, 1975a).

SPECIAL DANGERS

Since constipation is of such concern to Americans, greater knowledge concerning its cause should be sought. Definition is generally given as "difficult or infrequent evacuation of the large bowel," but many people have their own definition of "infrequent." The panel recognized as normal, three bowel movements a week to three bowel movements a day. Information indicating that the low fiber content in refined foods common in the American diet may contribute to the high prevalence of diverticular disease, irritable bowel syndrome, appendicitis, and cancer of the colon suggests that regular emptying of the bowels is important to good health.

However, when the causes of constipation are reviewed, we can deduce that laxatives are not the answer to the problem. Constipation is caused by (1) inadequate water intake, (2) inadequate bulk in the diet, (3) inadequate physical activity, and/or (4) not listening to Mother Nature when she calls.

Therefore, it follows that to avoid constipation, one should first of all drink plenty of water. Some authorities suggest ⅓ ounce of water per pound of body weight: In other words, a 120-pound person would drink 40 ounces (five 8-ounce glasses) of water a day. Also, fiber content in the diet—raw fruits, vegetables, nuts, and whole grains—should be increased. Besides the fiber content, these foods are full of vitamins and minerals beneficial to the body. Exercise, even walking, is another curative element that has fringe benefits here: Not only does it help to tone the smooth muscle of the gut, but it also can increase endurance, strength, agility, flexibility, and skill—not to mention the relief from mental stress that may accompany, or may even be a causative agent of, constipation. And finally, keep in mind that it's not healthy to fool with Mother Nature—when she calls, answer. Try to establish a time of day when you will not be hurried out of the bathroom, and develop a habit. Generally, the entire GI tract is stimulated by food, so become aware of the gut and its signals after a meal.

It is healthier and safer to treat your body naturally to prevent constipation, but if circumstances cause this problem, a natural laxative (bulk-forming or lubricant) is better for one's health than a stimulant or hyperosmotic laxative.

Nighttime Sleep Aids and Daytime Sedatives

HISTORY

Until the FDA panel reported on the safety and effectiveness of sleep aids and daytime sedatives, most of the OTC sleep aids contained antihistamines, scopolamine compounds, bromides, and/or miscellaneous compounds such as aspirin. The action of most of these substances was derived primarily from their anticholinergic properties; that is, they blocked acetylcholine at nerve synapses. The effects of the anticholinergic agents were variable and unpredictable, and often a bizarre combination of excitation and depression of the central nervous system occurred in users. Most brands contained some combinations of several substances, and this often compounded the confusing symptomatology. Prior to 1979, OTC sedatives containing scopolamine posed a potential problem known as "atropinic psychosis." Users of these sedatives frequently developed CNS toxicity (Moore, 1983).

The outcome of the FDA panel's review of OTC sedatives was that the ingredients mentioned above (bromides, scopolamine compounds, and antihistamines) were not generally recognized as safe and effective as nighttime sleep aids or daytime sedatives (DHEW, 1975b). The bromides were considered unsafe in therapeutic doses as OTC nighttime sleep aids or daytime sedatives because of toxicity and possible teratogenic effects. Similarly, the scopolamine products were pronounced unsafe at doses high enough to be possibly effective. The panel concluded that antihistamines were "probably safe and may be effective" but could not be considered safe and effective because additional data were required before the marketing of sleep aids with these ingredients could be sanctioned.

Presently, the main OTC sedatives sold in the United States rely on de-phenhydramine HCl and diphenhydramine monocitrate (see Table 14). Drugs of similar chemical configuration are sold as antihistamines, which are commonly used to treat allergies and symptoms of the common cold. (As the name implies, antihistamines block the vasodilation action that histamine exerts on

TABLE 14
DIPHENHYDRAMINE NAME BRAND PRODUCTS

Allerdryl	Bena-D
Benadryl products	Benahist
Bendylate	Benoject-10
Benylin Cough Syrup	Caladryl
Compo	Hiahist
Dihydrex	Diphen
Diphenacen	Diphenadril
Eldadryl	Fenythist
Fynex	Hydramine
Hydril	Hyrexin-50
Insomnal	Noradryl
Nervine Nighttime Sleep Aid	Nordryl
Nytol products	Phen-Amin
Robalyn	SK-Diphenhydramine
Sleep-Eze products	Sominex products
SominiFere	Tusstat
Twilite	Valdrene

the capillaries, thus decreasing fluid loss and congestion in the nasal cavity.) The drowsiness or hypnotic side effects were, in the past, considered undesirable; today, it is the side effect that is being marketed in sedatives.

At recommended doses of the two antihistamines mentioned here, most people will develop some sedation. Common side effects of antihistamines include dizziness, ringing in the ears, fatigue, lassitude, blurred vision, double vision, mood changes, and even delirium. Other side effects that may occur are nausea, vomiting, loss of appetite, constipation or diarrhea, dry mouth, heart palpitations or other heart irregularities, skin rash, and changes in urination. Convulsions, coma, and even death may be side effects (Zimmerman, 1991).

The problem with antihistamines is that the drug must be strong enough to deliver the kind of sedation desired, yet not so strong as to cause toxic effects.

CLASSIFICATION

The main active ingredient in sleep aids is an antihistamine.

HOW TAKEN INTO THE BODY

These drugs are most often taken orally in the form of tablets, pills, or capsules.

CHARACTERISTICS OF DEPENDENCE

These substances do not cause physical dependence, but psychological dependence may occur. A prescription is needed for high-strength products, but not for low-strength products such as Nervine (25 milligrams of diphenhydramine hydrochloride), Compoz (50 milligrams), Nytol (25 milligrams), or Sominex (25 milligrams). Other substances that may be present in sleep aids and sedatives include lactose anhydride, microcrystalline cellulose, stearic acid, and FD&C Blue No. 1 coloring.

PHARMACOLOGY

Diphenhydramine hydrochloride and diphenhydramine monocitrate are antihistamines that block the action of histamine. Histamine is a natural substance in the body that causes vasodilation and is part of the inflammatory process.

EFFECTS ON THE BODY

In addition to the reduction of allergic symptoms, symptoms of motion sickness, and the stiffness and tremors of Parkinson's disease, antihistamines induce sleep.

After studying the effects of an over-the-counter tranquilizer (Compoz), prescription tranquilizers (Librium), and a sugar pill placebo on patients showing mild to moderate symptoms of anxiety and tension, Rickels and Hesbacher (1973) concluded that in terms of clinical efficiency, Compoz did not differ from the placebo. The prescription tranquilizers proved most effective.

It is becoming increasingly apparent that sleep requirements differ from one individual to the next and that as we age we need fewer hours of nightly sleep. However, many people hold the old concept that everyone must have 8 hours of undisturbed sleep. No hypnotic drug can produce a natural, normal night's sleep, as all drugs change sleep patterns, and few drugs continue their original sedative effect for more than a few nights in a row.

SPECIAL DANGERS

One problem inherent in the ineffectiveness of the OTC sleep aids is that when they do not give the desired results, users tend to overmedicate themselves. Two or three times the recommended dose may produce disorientation and hallucinations. The toxicity of these newer formulations is not expected to be of the degree seen in the past with combinations that included scopolamine, but as they have anticholinergic properties, large doses could produce confusion and impairment of memory. In acute toxicity, there may be fever, excitement, fixed and dilated pupils, and hallucinations (Griffith, 1988).

Americans have become aware of and, to some extent, preoccupied with the detrimental effects of arousal caused by the stress and tension of modern society. It has been estimated that as many as one-half of the patients crowded into physicians' waiting rooms have ailments that are either entirely emotional or have significant emotional overtones. Consequently, it can be seen why tranquilizers rank just behind antibiotics as the most-often-prescribed drugs.

While recognizing that the experience of occasional sleep problems is a valid indication for OTC medication, the FDA panel warned that people with severe or chronic insomnia are not candidates for self-medication. If insomnia is serious enough to interfere regularly with a person's normal waking activities, the need for clinical treatment and/or prescription is indicated. Insomnia is not a disease, it is the symptom of a problem (worry about something or someone), so the only conclusive way to cure insomnia is to go to the heart of the problem and deal with it. Professional therapeutic help in the form of psychological counseling may be indicated.

Analgesics

HISTORY

It should come as no surprise that the most common analgesic in the world is aspirin (acetylsalicyclic acid). Although this acid was not synthesized as aspirin until the nineteenth century, natural sources of its active ingredients have been used for thousands of years. Thanks to the stress and strain of our modern society (or to effective advertising), the "ailing" U.S. population's daily ingestion of aspirin tablets is rapidly approaching 50 million. There are hundreds of products that have acetylsalicylic acid as their primary ingredient. Pharmaceutical manufacturers have buffered it, colored it, sugar-coated it; they have made it fizz, given it a round or oblong shape, and put it in time-released capsules. As the packaging changes, so does its use. One shape is advertised for use on the good old-fashioned headache, another for nervous tension. Of course, the ones for nervous tension caused by screaming children are different from the ones for nervous tension caused by missing a bus! If it is pretty enough and has a feminine-sounding name, women can use it for menstrual pain; and if it is candy-coated, children will enjoy it. Symptoms such as headache, upset stomach, and nausea constitute to millions of Americans a signal for the ingestion of aspirin. If one is looking for an example of drug misuse, aspirin consumption in the United States today is as good an example as any.

Although aspirin is still the leading OTC analgesic, two other drugs are gaining on the market. These drugs are acetaminophen (Tylenol, Panadol) and ibuprofen (Advil, Nuprin, Motrin).

CLASSIFICATION

Aspirin is an analgesic, antipyretic, and anti-inflammatory. Acetaminophen is reported to have analgesic and antipyretic action but seems to be less toxic to the gastrointestinal system than aspirin, resulting in less gastric blood loss, and does not seem to affect blood coagulation. However, it does not have the anti-inflammatory properties of aspirin. Ibuprofen is used for treatment of inflammation and is also an analgesic. Aspirin is highly effective (and inexpensive, especially the generic brand) for pain, fever, and inflammation for those people who can take it safely.

Acetaminophen was introduced before aspirin (in 1893), and milligram for milligram it is about as effective as aspirin—except for inflammation, such as is seen in arthritis. It is a safe, effective pain reliever when taken as recommended. In recommended doses it is relatively free of adverse effects in most age groups. It does not cause gastrointestinal bleeding and does not interfere with drugs used to treat gout. It may affect blood clotting, and some people are allergic to it.

Ibuprofen is an anti-inflammatory (nonsteroidal) over-the-counter drug that is used to treat joint pain, stiffness, inflammation, and swelling of arthritis and gout. It is a pain reliever, and it is used to treat dysmenorrhea. Ibuprofen is contraindicated for those who are allergic to aspirin or any nonsteroidal anti-inflammatory drug, for people who have gastritis, peptic ulcer, enteritis, ileitis, ulcerative colitis, asthma, heart failure, high blood pressure, or bleeding problems; and for patients younger than 15 (Griffith, 1988).

HOW TAKEN INTO THE BODY

These drugs are usually administered orally. There are analgesic gels, however, that are applied topically.

CHARACTERISTICS OF DEPENDENCE

Analgesics are not habit forming.

PHARMACOLOGY

Aspirin, acetaminophen, and ibuprofen work by inhibiting or reducing tissue concentration of the prostaglandins (natural hormonelike substances in the body) that trigger fever, inflammation, and pain. It appears that aspirin works to inhibit the prostaglandins that set off these three responses in the body, while acetaminophen inhibits only the prostaglandins that cause pain and fever. Ibuprofen works against an array of prostaglandins, especially those in the uterus, making this drug effective in relieving menstrual cramps (*UCB Wellness Letter*, 1984).

There is still some controversy as to the site of the analgesic action of aspirin. Some researchers believe it is central in the hypothalamus, while others believe the action is peripheral. Still others believe the action to be purely psychological (the placebo effect).

The rapid absorption of aspirin from the GI tract is one of its most attractive features. Fifty percent of the normal dose of 650 milligrams (usually two 325-milligram tablets) is absorbed within 30 minutes. The convenience of analgesia over an 8-hour period has prompted many pharmaceutical houses to develop time-release capsules. However, the convenience of the time-release capsule may be overshadowed by decreased effectiveness.

EFFECTS ON THE BODY

Analgesic Action

Empirical evidence would seem to indicate that acetylsalicylic acid is effective in the relief of pain. The evidence is still empirical, for researchers have not developed quantitative measures of pain or pain relief. Such measures as pricking the skin, applying heat to the skin and teeth, sending electric current through metal dental fillings, etc., have produced varying levels of pain in different people. Some studies have shown aspirin to be more effective than morphine and codeine in relieving pain, while others show aspirin as being no more effective than a placebo.

It bears mentioning that even though the advertisements insinuate that aspirin will relieve the pain of a headache, they do not state this fact directly, for there is no evidence to support such a claim. Although headache is the most "popular" ailment in the United States, not a great deal is known about its causes and cures. It would stand to reason that the most common type of headache, the tension headache, thought to be caused by the referral of pain of tense muscles of the head and neck to subcutaneous pain receptors around the head, would be predominant in fast-paced technological societies. Not all headaches are psychological; many are psychosomatic, that is, the pain is as real as that caused by muscle tension. These headaches perhaps result from psychological stress and worry for which aspirin may offer some relief by dulling the perception of the pain. In Africa, Asia, and the Antarctic, headache is almost completely unknown. In industrialized South America and Europe, headaches are a minor nuisance of life and are not a topic of conversation, a convenient excuse, or an indication that the individual is important enough to have something to worry about. In the United States, however, advertising has elevated the headache to a national institution. Symptoms are outlined, throbbing pain is vividly described, and, most important, the social situations that might cause a headache are mentioned continually. An artificial ailment can usually be cured by a substance that is perceived as being effective. It is little wonder that 40 cents of each dollar spent on such products is allotted to advertising.

It is important that headache sufferers know that hypertensive and migraine headaches should not be treated with nonprescription analgesics. However, headaches from fever, hangover, and caffeine withdrawal can be successfully treated with over-the-counter analgesics (Zimmerman, 1991).

Antipyretic (Antifever) Action

Infectious disease often causes the body to produce and retain increased amounts of heat. Body heat is elevated by increasing body metabolism and through muscular activity, usually shivering. The delicate temperature regulator, or thermostat, in the hypothalamus, although functional, becomes set at a higher level. Body temperature in relation to the thermostat is cool; thus, shivering is initiated while heat dissipation processes are decreased.

Although the exact pharmacological mechanism is not well understood, aspirin seems to lower the thermostat and allow for dissipation of heat through normal processes such as the dilation of cutaneous vessels. Aspirin is effective in the treatment of fever, but it will not lower temperature in individuals with normal body temperature.

Anti-inflammatory Action

Acetylsalicylic acid has become one of the most used therapeutic agents in the treatment of rheumatoid arthritis. Neither the pharmacology nor the mechanism of action is known, but aspirin seems to be effective in reducing the inflammation by decreasing the leakage of fluid from capillaries in the inflamed sac directly, or indirectly by action on the anti-inflammatory hormones produced by the adrenal cortex. Aspirin has also been shown to reduce fever associated with rheumatoid arthritis and to raise the pain threshold by interfering with the brain's interpretation of the pain or through interference with peripheral transmission. Ibuprofen is also an effective anti-inflammatory.

SPECIAL DANGERS

Acetylsalicylic acid is truly a wonder drug. Its adverse effects are minimal compared to its beneficial pharmacological action. Still, aspirin follows only barbiturates, alcohol, and carbon monoxide in the number of fatal poisonings attributed to it annually. Excess use of aspirin has also been linked with certain kinds of kidney disease. Approximately 2 out of every 1,000 persons are hypersensitive to aspirin, and approximately 16 percent of asthmatic patients are allergic to it. Young children whose systems cannot withstand the dehydration and acid–base change are most affected. It should come as no surprise that flavored children's aspirin compounds are responsible for 62 percent of the salicylate poisonings (Dipalma, 1981). Also, since two aspirins can have an adverse effect on blood-clotting time for up to 2 weeks, women who use them immediately before or during their menstrual periods may increase the blood volume lost, thus adding to their menstrual problems. Likewise, aspirin should not be taken before surgery or by a blood donor before giving blood. One of the more publicized dangers of aspirin, especially nonbuffered aspirin, is possible gastrointestinal bleeding.

Too much acetaminophen can damage the liver and kidneys, and ibuprofen has been shown to cause kidney failure in people with mild kidney disease (Lauerman, 1990). Ibuprofen causes fewer side effects and allergic reactions than aspirin, but it does have some drawbacks (as shown in Table 15). Table 15 compares the indicated use, allergic reactions and other side effects, and contraindications of aspirin, acetaminophen, and ibuprofen.

When aspirin is taken, stomach lining irritation and bleeding are decreased if the tablets are crushed and mixed with juice, milk, or water before swallowing. All of these analgesics should be taken as directed. If greater doses are needed over a prolonged period (more than 10 days in a row), seek medical aid. Last of all, protect small children by using safety-cap containers stored out of their reach.

TABLE 15   A COMPARISON OF ASPIRIN, ACETAMINOPHEN, AND IBUPROFEN

	Aspirin	Acetaminophen	Ibuprofen
Indicated use	Pain, fever, inflammation	Pain, fever	Pain, fever, inflammation
Allergic reactions, side effects	Allergic reactions of itching, rash, choking. Common side effects of upset stomach, ringing of ears. About 40% have some gastral bleeding. Can lead to ulcers or anemia.	Fewer than aspirin. Rare cases of skin rash and painful urination. High dose over long time may damage liver or kidneys.	Fewer than aspirin. Can cause skin rash, itching, GI upset, stomach distress, dizziness. May interfere with antihypertensive and diuretic drugs.
Contraindication	Pregnant women in last trimester; children under 16 with chicken pox or flu (risk of Reye's syndrome); those known to be allergic to aspirin; those with ulcers, gout, or stomach bleeding.	Alcoholics; people with liver or kidney disease or kidney infection.	People with gout, ulcers, or aspirin allergy; children under 14; pregnant women in last trimester.
Used in treating:	Sprains, simple headaches, arthritis, broken bones, rheumatism, rheumatic fever. May help prevent heart attack.	Reduce pain, fever in those who react poorly to aspirin. Does not affect blood clotting, so is safe after oral surgery.	Relief of joint pain, fever, inflammation of arthritis, toothaches, aches, and fever of cold. Excellent for menstrual cramps. Reduces blood clotting.

161

Cough and Cold Products

HISTORY

If you have experienced the sneeze that is followed by a chill through your body and then shortly thereafter a sore throat, runny nose, drippy eyes, and a cough, be assured that you have something in common with virtually everyone else: the common cold. The common cold is caused by a virus that changes strains as fast as some folks change their minds, and therefore it has been impossible to develop a vaccine to cure the cold. The best that can be done is to treat the symptoms. The common cold will run its course in a week if you don't treat it with medicines, and it lasts about seven days if you do! What medicines will do—on the positive side—is allow you to feel less uncomfortable during your waking hours and perhaps to sleep better at night. What they will not do is cure the cold. And on the negative side, cold and cough medicines depress natural reflexes like coughing and sneezing, thus allowing mucus buildup in the air passageways, especially those of the lungs, that may become an ideal breeding ground for bacteria. This may help to explain the chest cold that sometimes follows a head cold.

CLASSIFICATION

Commercial cough and cold remedies can be listed in a number of different categories: the cough suppressants; the antihistamines that dry up the runny nose and water eyes; the anticholinergics, which also dry up eyes and nose; the nasal decongestants that open nasal passageways; the bronchial muscle relaxants (bronchodilators); and the expectorants, which encourage removal of mucus from air passageways of the lungs and throat. Each of these categories is represented by a variety of over-the-counter products. There is also a large "miscellaneous" category of nonprescription drugs that are used for colds, coughs, and allergies.

HOW TAKEN INTO THE BODY

These drugs are most often taken orally in pill, tablet, capsule or liquid form. Nasal decongestants/bronchial dilators may come as a spray.

CHARACTERISTICS OF DEPENDENCE

Generally, these drugs are considered to be non-habit-forming (Griffith, 1988), but psychological dependence and/or tolerance may occur.

PHARMACOLOGY

The action of cough suppressants is to inhibit the reaction of the cough reflex in the medulla. The narcotic codeine and dextromethorphan (a strong nonnarcotic) both act in this manner.

The antihistamines block the action of histamine after an allergic response triggers histamine release in sensitive cells. The effect is to dry out the tissues involved.

The anticholinergics block nerve impulses at parasympathetic nerve endings, preventing muscle contractions and gland secretions in the organs involved. They affect the tissues by blocking the mechanisms that allow eye and nose glands to secrete tears and mucus.

The main action of the decongestants is to block histamine action in sensitized tissues. Bronchodilators dilate constricted bronchial tubes, improving air flow. Expectorants work to loosen mucus in the bronchial tubes to make mucus easier to cough up.

EFFECTS ON THE BODY

Cough suppressants exist mainly in the form of cough syrup, often in combination with an expectorant and decongestant (Table 16). The FDA panel reviewing these drugs warned that combination products are a waste of money if a cough is not accompanied by other symptoms.

Cough preparations with codeine were found to be safe and effective, as were preparations with dextromethorphan. The narcotic cough suppressants may become habit-forming; history shows that before strict laws on the marketing of codeine were passed, heroin or morphine addicts unable to get their drug of choice would resort to taking cough syrup with codeine.

Taking a cough suppressant may prolong a cold because the natural mechanism for clearing the throat and lungs is depressed, but if the cough is a dry, hacking one, a product that soothes the throat may be helpful. It is particularly dangerous to disregard a sore throat because streptococcal infection can result in rheumatic fever or other autoimmune disease.

Antihistamines affect the body by relieving allergic reactions caused by the release of histamine, which attaches itself to secretary cells of the nose, eyes, lungs, and skin. This action of histamine enhances the fluid-making activity of these cells, so antihistamines have a drying effect on these tissues. The main side effect of antihistamines is drowsiness (as was discussed in the nighttime sleep aid section).

Anticholinergics act as drying agents for runny nose and rheumy eyes. Drying agents such as these work on bronchial secretions, reducing their volume and making them stickier. This may block the passageways and allow fertile ground for infection. Anticholinergics are potent drugs and must be used with caution. Atropine sulfate and belladonnna alkaloids (excluding those that are inhaled) are used as drying agents and are safe if used as recommended.

Nasal decongestants work by reducing the swelling of nasal tissues and the volume of serum lost from those tissues. Most decongestants in cold remedies are not effective at the doses recommended. Decongestants applied directly to the nasal passageway (usually by spray) are generally more effective than those taken orally, but the rebound effect here endangers the cold victim, and he or she may actually become dependent on nose drops or nasal inhalants. This

TABLE 16   COUGH AND COLD PREPARATIONS

Action	Mechanism	Active ingredient	Brand name (examples)	Drawbacks
Suppressant (antitussive)	Inhibits cough reflex in medulla	Dextromethorphan, codeine, or diphen-hydramine	Benylin, Congesperin, Pertussin 8 hour, Romilar 8 hour, St. Joseph's Children's	Can suppress productive cough, leads to risk of infection of lungs due to mucus buildup.
Expectorant	Helps loosen and thin mucus and other secretions	Usually guaifenesin	Anti-Tuss, Robitussin Expectorant	Question about effectiveness, still under FDA review.
Combination	Clear or prevent runny nose and sinus congestion; loosen mucus and other secretions; inhibit coughing	Dextromethorphan or codeine (suppressant); guaifenesin (expectorant); phenylephrine HCl, ephedrine, or phenylpropanolamine (decongestant); doxylamine, chlorpheniramine maleate (antihistamine); acetaminophen (pain reliever); alcohol; other	Cheracol, Cheracol D, Coricidin, Dristan Cough Formula, Consotuss, Anti-Tuss DM, Halls Cough Syrup, Quiet-Nite Liquid, NyQuil Liquid, Romilar III, Robitussin DM and PE, Sudafed Cough Syrup, Triaminic DM, Vicks 44, 44D, and 44M, Robitussin CF	As a group, these combinations are not endorsed by the FDA. May contain less than effective doses of ingredients; combinations may be counterproductive and/or unsafe.

Source: UCB Wellness Letter, 1985; Moore, 1983.

occurs because even though there is an initial shrinkage of tissue, once the medication is taken there is an engorgement of the tissue that surpasses the original stuffiness—hence more decongestant is needed. Labeling should indicate that one should not use the product for more than 3 days in a row. These products must also warn that persons with diabetes, heart disease, hypertension, or thyroid disease should not use the decongestant.

Approved active ingredients include topical ephedrine preparations, naphazoline hydrochloride (topical), oxymetazoline hydrochloride (topical), phenylephrine hydrochloride (topical or oral), and phenylpropanolamine preparations taken orally.

Bronchodilators help relax muscle spasms of the bronchial tubes. They help open up the airways for clearer breathing. They are also used by asthmatics. These drugs are potent and can be dangerous. An overdose may present symptoms such as restlessness, irritability, confusion, delirium, convulsions, rapid pulse, and coma.

Expectorants promote the removal of secretions (phlegm, mucus, or sputum) from the bronchial tubes. They are useful in relieving nonproductive coughs. These drugs have a fairly good safety record over the years but do not have a research background proving them effective.

SPECIAL DANGERS

Whenever a cough or cold product is purchased, the consumer should be aware that (1) the preparation will not cure a cold; (2) it may have adverse effects, especially if it has a combination of ingredients; (3) it should be taken only as directed; and (4) the product should not be taken at all by some persons (Zimmerman, 1991).

Weight Loss Preparations

HISTORY

Weight loss preparations carve out a large portion of the dollars spent on the nonprescription drug market. Even though armed with the knowledge that long-term weight reduction is the product of eating sensibly and getting enough physical activity, millions of Americans seek prescription and nonprescription drugs to do the job for them. Prescription appetite suppressant preparations containing various amphetamines, although pharmacologically effective in curbing appetite, are not effective in long-term weight control. One can hardly expect nonprescription commercial preparations to be more effective. The "active" ingredients of these drugs range from caffeine and methylcellulose to various combinations of natural plants.

CLASSIFICATION

Antiobesity preparations can be divided into five categories: (1) bulk preparations, (2) low-calorie foods and artificial sweeteners, (3) benzocaine preparations, (4) glucose preparations, and (5) appetite suppressants that work on the central nervous system.

PHARMACOLOGY

Most OTC appetite suppressants contain phenylpropamine and caffeine as active ingredients (Table 17). Phenylpropanolamine is a CNS stimulant, and in high doses its stimulating effect can be significant enough to contribute to appetite suppression. High doses can elevate mood and increase confidence, but they can also cause headaches, anxiety, irritability, apprehension, insomnia, agitation, and psychosis. Caffeine toxicity may also occur with high doses, especially when it is taken in combination with phenylpropanolamine. Many people respond to amounts of caffeine in excess of 1,000 milligrams per day with behavioral symptoms that mimic anxiety neurosis.

Benzocaine, another active ingredient in some appetite suppressants, is used to temporarily deaden the taste receptors in the mouth, dulling the pleasure of taste, especially sweetness.

EFFECTS ON THE BODY

Bulk preparations add bulk to the gastrointestinal tract for the purpose of producing a sensation of being full. The active ingredient is usually methylcellulose, a nonabsorbable cellulose that is supposed to swell in the stomach. Popular examples of this type of preparation are Melozets, which contains methylcellulose, flour, and sugar; Metamucil, which contains dextrose, psyllium, and muccilloid; and Reducets, with methylcellulose.

Low-calorie foods and artificial sweeteners are sold as drugs in drugstores and as food in supermarkets but should probably best be classified as a food. A popular example from the past is Metrecal, which contains dry milk, soy flour, sugar, starch, dried yeast, corn oil, coconut oil, and vitamins. A similar product on market shelves today is Sego.

Benzocaine preparations are substances that act as local anesthetics to diminish response and sensitivity of the mouth and stomach. Examples of this type are Shape Up, which contains benzocaine and sodium carboxymethyl-

TABLE 17
EXAMPLES OF OTC APPETITE SUPPRESSANTS

Brand name	Caffeine	Phenylpropanolamine
Anorexin	100 mg	25 mg
Appedrine	100 mg	25 mg
Dex-A-Diet II	200 mg	75 mg
Dexatrim	200 mg	50 mg
Pro-Dax		75 mg
Prolamine	140 mg	35 mg

cellulose; and Slim Mint, which contains benzocaine, methylcellulose, and dextrose.

Glucose preparations use glucose to stimulate the satiety centers of the hypothalamus, thus reducing physiological hunger. Examples here are Ayds, which contain corn syrup, vegetable oil, vitamins, and sweetened condensed whole milk; and Proslim, which contains soy isolate, sucrose, dextrose, and powdered milk.

Most appetite suppressants that work on the central nervous system have as an active ingredient caffeine (a derivative of xanthine), which is indigenous to coffee, tea, and many soft drinks (especially the colas), or phenylpropanolamine (see Table 17). Caffeine does produce some stimulation of the CNS and in most individuals results in slight wakefulness, restlessness, and mild excitement. The diuretic action of caffeine may promote dehydration.

SPECIAL DANGERS

Phenylpropanolamine toxicity may become more evident in the United States due to its CNS stimulating effect, which has been "black-marketed" as various street drugs. It has appeared at drug paraphernalia shops and on the street as Coco Snow, Pseudocaine, and capsules that look like popular amphetamines. As discussed in the chapter on hallucinogens, the dangers of street drug lookalikes have been apparent since the 1950s and 1960s.

REFERENCES

DHEW, Food and Drug Administration. (1975a). Over-the-counter drugs. *Federal Register* 40(56):12902–12944.

DHEW, Food and Drug Administration. (1975b). Over-the-counter sleep aid drug products. *Federal Register,* 40(236):57292–57329.

Dipalma, J. R. (Ed.) (1981). *Drills Pharmacology in Medicine.* New York: McGraw-Hill.

FDA (Food and Drug Administration). (1974). A new standard for antacids, *FDA Consumers,* July/October, 5.

Griffith, H. W. (1988). *Complete Guide to Prescription and Non-Prescription Drugs.* Los Angeles, CA: The Body Press.

Lauerman, Connie. (1990). Playing doctor. *Good Health,* October, p. 26.

Moore, D. F. (1983). Over-the-counter drugs. In G. Bennett et al. (Eds.), *Substance Abuse: Pharmacologic, Developmental, and Clinical Perspectives.* New York: Wiley, pp. 208–214.

Rickels, K., and Hesbacher, P. (1973). OTC daytime sedatives. *JAMA,* 223:29–33.

UCB Wellness Letter. (1984). Buying guide: pain relievers. *University of California, Berkeley Wellness Letter, 1(2):3.*

UCB Wellness Letter. (1985). Buying guide: over-the-counter cough syrups. *University of California, Berkeley Wellness Letter,* 1(4):3.

Zimmerman, D. R. (1991). *The Essential Guide to Nonprescription Drugs.* New York: HarperCollins.

ANABOLIC STEROIDS

HISTORY

Weight lifters and shotputters began to use anabolic androgenic steroids more than 30 years ago in an attempt to enhance their performance. Until only recently, physicians dismissed the muscle-making power of steroids as myth, thus seriously deterring efforts to outlaw steroid use by athletes.

During the 1950s the Russians administered testosterone to their athletes, who seemed to be aided in building muscle. An American doctor who felt that the Russians were thus given undue advantage in competitive sports developed a form of anabolic steroid that was supposed to mimic the muscle-building effects of testosterone while minimizing the masculinizing effects of that hormone. When American weight lifters found that the recommended dosage did help build muscle, they mistakenly assumed that increased dosage would add even more muscle. It is not uncommon to find muscle builders today taking 20 times the recommended dose. It is this abuse of steroids that has uncovered their detrimental side effects.

Steroids are made by U.S. pharmaceutical companies and veterinary drug houses, and some are produced in other countries and then smuggled into the United States. Many are made in clandestine laboratories. Since the demand for steroids has created a black market in the production and distribution of these drugs, they often turn out to be counterfeits with fake labels to make them look legitimate. Federal agencies estimate that Americans spent between $300 million and $400 million for black market steroids in 1989, a three- to four-fold increase over the previous year (Franklin, 1990). Black market steroids may be distributed through mail-order houses and magazine promotional advertisements to targeted audiences, or, paradoxically, they may even be sold at fitness centers and health clubs. The ease with which athletes can obtain steroids promotes the probability of their use without medical approval or supervision.

Drug testing programs in athletics have uncovered steroid use in many sports, and well-known athletes have lost or had serious setbacks in their careers following the discovery of steroid presence during competition.

A 1989 survey of 17,000 high school boys indicated that nearly 1 in 20 admitted they had used steroids to build muscles or to "improve appearance" (Franklin, 1990). It is estimated that some 262,000 adolescents are using or have used steroids, with 5 to 11 percent of teenage boys and 0.5 to 2.5 percent of girls in grades 7 through 12 implicated (Cowart, 1990). More than half of those estimated to have taken steroids began using them by age 16, and nearly one-third have been using them for 5 years or more. Nearly all use injectable steroids and take doses many times that of normal therapeutic levels (Fuerst, 1990). Unfortunately, the use of steroids in the 10-to-14-year-old age group is not accompanied by knowledge of the dangers of their use. One survey of this age population found that 78 percent had heard of anabolic steroids but only 49 percent had had someone explain the adverse effects of using them. Of this group, 45 percent believed that using steroids would increase their performance, 68 percent said that Olympic athletes use steroids, 55 percent believed that steroid usage alone would increase muscle size and strength, and 43 percent said that steroids would not harm a user who is careful (Cowart, 1990). A particular danger of steroids for this age group is the risk of premature closure of the epiphyses (where bone growth occurs) and possible alteration of the normal development of sex hormones.

There is increasing evidence that anabolic steroid users are turning to legitimate veterinary drugs because (1) black-market steroids are smuggled into the United States, and many counterfeits are produced in crude, unsanitary labs, and (2) veterinary steroids are alleged to be cheaper and more effective, and users seem to believe they are legitimate pharmaceuticals (McConnell, 1991).

Anabolic steroids are now on the U.S. list of controlled substances. The Anabolic Steroid Control Act of 1990 reclassified these drugs, making them a Schedule III controlled substance, increasing penalties for illegal distribution, and making possession without a prescription a federal crime. This legislation transferred jurisdiction in these matters from the Food and Drug Administration to the Drug Enforcement Administration. Under the new law, the maximum penalty for trafficking in steroids is 5 years in prison and a $250,000 fine, which may be doubled for a second offense. Possession of steroids carries up to 1 year in prison and at least a $1,000 fine (Hiskey, 1991).

CLASSIFICATION

Anabolic steroids mimic the natural hormone testosterone, the hormone that controls the development of masculine characteristics in adult males. Small amounts of testosterone are also manufactured by females and are the primary steroid source for the production of estrogens after menopause.

HOW TAKEN INTO THE BODY

Most steroids are taken by injection or in pill form. The doses and patterns of administration of steroids by athletes differ markedly from the pattern and dosage for legitimate medical purposes. Doses commonly taken are 10, 100, or even 1000 times larger than those prescribed for medical conditions, and not only do athletes take higher than medically indicated doses, they also commonly use several of the drugs concurrently (known as "stacking") or cycle the drug dosage up and down to fit the competition schedule (Schuckit, 1988).

CHARACTERISTICS OF DEPENDENCE

In the last several years an increasing number of psychiatrists, psychologists, and counselors have identified the classic chemical dependency syndrome in individuals abusing steroids. Scientists agree that only a small percentage of steroid users become dependent on these drugs, but those who do can be clinically identified as addicted users. According to the American Psychological Association (APA) diagnostic handbook (APA, 1987), anyone who exhibits three or more of nine categories of symptoms is considered chemically dependent; these categories include taking drugs longer than intended, not being able to cut back or stop, having to take more of the substance to achieve the same results, and having withdrawal symptoms upon cessation of drug administration. Withdrawal symptoms may include headaches, fatigue, and depression. In one survey of 45 professed male steroid users, more than 50 percent reported three or more symptoms of chemical dependency. Almost all of them reported at least one symptom linked to withdrawal—usually fatigue or depression (Franklin, 1990).

PHARMACOLOGY

Androgenic steroids stimulate cells that produce male sex characteristics, stimulate red blood cell production, and suppress production of estrogen (Griffith, 1988). Ingestion of anabolic steroids may overload the body with testosterone, thus triggering the hypothalamus to shut down further hormone production. This shutdown may continue when steroids are discontinued, causing an imbalance in male and female hormones in the body. This could result in characteristics such as enlarged breasts in males. In female users of steroids, the body often responds by developing the masculine characteristics of lowered voice, male pattern baldness, reduced breast size, and facial hair growth, all of which may not be reversed when steroid use is stopped.

Recommended dosages for legitimate purposes may be as little as 1 milligram administered by injection every 3 to 6 weeks. In an attempt to build muscle quickly, steroid abusers may often ingest massive quantities daily.

Brain wave activity during steroid use is similar to that seen in stimulant and antidepressant use.

EFFECTS ON THE BODY

The effects of taking androgenic steroids appear to be dose- and duration-dependent. The reason for which they are taken is to build muscle. It has been found that bodybuilders using steroids for 10 weeks put on an average of 8.9 pounds of lean muscle. Many may be able to duplicate that gain in every such 10-week cycle, putting on as much as 40 pounds of muscle in one year (Franklin, 1990). John Norris, Deputy Commissioner of the U.S. Food and Drug Administration, cautioned that steroids increase muscle mass and strength only in those who are weight-trained and continue intensive training while maintaining high protein, high calorie diets (Norris, 1987).

The dangerous side effects of these drugs include both physical and psychological aspects. The term "roid rage" has been applied to a set of psychological/behavioral symptoms that include aggression, violence, recklessness, increased irritability, confusion, sleep difficulties, and delusions. It has been suggested that violence such as spouse abuse and date rape may be related to steroid abuse (Clinical Observations, 1990). Up to one-third of one steroid-using population reported symptoms characteristic of psychosis, mania, or major depression, and another one-third reported uncharacteristic episodes of aggression to such an extent that their jobs and social lives suffered (Pope & Katz, 1988). All of the subjects who reported psychiatric problems during steroid abuse also reported that their symptoms eventually disappeared when they stopped taking steroids.

Some physical side effects of steroids include rapid weight gain over several months, unusually heavy, bulky muscles, extensive upper body acne, sore mouth, heightened sex drive, frequent erections, sterility, beginning hair loss, aggressive behavior, and sexual dysfunction. Additional signs are testicle size reduction, breast growth, high blood pressure, and high cholesterol and liver enzyme levels.

Steroid users increase their risk of liver and kidney cancer, incidence of kidney stones, cardiovascular problems, and reduction of sperm count and volume of semen. As mentioned earlier, adolescent growth may be stunted. In addition, steroids may cause enlarged prostate and urinary retention in those over 60, and for pregnant mothers the risk to the unborn child outweighs drug benefits.

Some of the most serious side effects associated with steroid use, such as liver tumors and cardiovascular problems (including precursors such as elevated circulating concentrations of low-density lipoproteins and reductions in high-density lipoprotein cholesterol concentrations), may not develop for a decade or two, making it difficult to use the knowledge of these side effects as a deterrent to the use of steroids in young athletes.

Another recent danger is possible HIV infection that may be associated with injections of anabolic steroids (Scott, 1989).

SUMMARY OF STEROID SIDE EFFECTS

Liver	Reproductive	Psychological	Cardiovascular
Cancer	Genital atrophy	Depression	Cholesterol modification
Jaundice	Genital swelling	Listlessness	Heart disease
Tumors	Sexual dysfunction	Aggressiveness	Anaphylactic shock
Hepatitis	Sterility (reversible)	Combative behavior	Death
	Impotence		High blood pressure
			Septic shock

OTHER SIDE EFFECTS OF STEROID USE

Acne	Edema	Hairiness in women (irreversible)
Oily skin	Stunted growth	Male pattern baldness (irreversible in women)
Bone pain	Abdominal/stomach pain	Changes in bowel and urinary habits
Chills	Diarrhea	Gall stones
Hives	Headache (continuing)	Excessive calcium
Insomnia	Kidney stones	Kidney disease
Rash	Nausea or vomiting	Purple or red spots on body, inside mouth/nose
Weight gain	Muscle cramps	Unpleasant breath odor (continuing)
Weight loss	Unusual bleeding	

MEDICAL USE

Early in the 1930s steroids were used to build tissue and prevent its breakdown in some diseases. The FDA did not approve the use of steroids for this purpose but did approve them for treatment of certain kinds of anemia, for some breast cancers, and for a rare disease called hereditary angioedema (periodic swelling of some parts of the body) (JAMA Council Report, 1990).

More recently, steroids have been effectively used in cases of asthma, particularly if the asthmatic is over 50 (Health Editor, 1990). Medical research has attributed the onset of asthma attacks to a special kind of inflammation of the airways that leads to contraction of the smooth muscle of the airways. The first line of treatment is to suppress the inflammatory response, and the best drugs for this purpose are inhaled steroids. It is now recognized by the medical profession that oral steroids, except in very small doses, produce a wide array of undesirable side effects. Few side effects have been reported from the use of inhaled steroids because the doses can be kept very low (Health Editor, 1990).

Currently androgenic steroids are used to correct male hormone deficiencies, reduce ''male menopause'' symptoms (loss of sex drive, depression, anxiety), decrease the calcium loss seen in osteoporosis, block growth of breast cancer cells in females, correct undescended testicles in male children, reduce breast pain and fullness following childbirth, augment treatment of aplastic anemia, stimulate weight gain after illness of injury or for chronically underweight persons, and stimulate growth in treatment of dwarfism (Griffith, 1988).

Medical use accounts for fewer than 3 million prescriptions per year in the United States (Bennett, 1990).

REFERENCES

APA. (1987). *Diagnostic and Statistical Manual of Mental Disorders,* rev. ed. (DSM-III-R). Washington, D.C.: American Psychological Association.

Bennett, D. B. (1990). Androgens and anabolic steroids. In *Drug Evaluations Subscription.* Chicago, Ill.: American Medical Association, pp. 1–10.

Clinical Observations. (1990). Study of athletes shows aggression and other psychiatric side effects from steroid use. *NIDA Notes,* 5(1):14–16.

Cowart, V. S. (1990). Blunting "steroid epidemic" requires alternatives, innovative education. *JAMA,* 264(13): 1641.

Franklin, D. (1990). Drugs. *In Health,* May/June, p. 22.

Fuerst, M. L. (1990). Teens' use of steroids increases. *Medical Tribune,* Oct. 4, p. 19.

Griffith, H. W. (1988). *Complete Guide to Prescription and Non-prescription Drugs.* Los Angeles: The Body Press.

Health Editor. (1990). Inhaled steroids grow in favor as asthma treatment. *Johns Hopkins Medical Letter,* July, p. 1.

Hiskey, M. (1991). New federal steroid law in effect. *Sports and Law,* February, p. 6.

JAMA Council Report. (1990). Medical and nonmedical uses of anabolic-androgenic steroids. *JAMA,* 264(22):2923–2927.

McConnell, Harvey. (1991). Steroid users turn to veterinary drugs for supplies. *The Journal, Addiction Research Foundation,* 20(3):39.

Norris, John. (1987). FDA warns: steroids may be hazardous to your health. *Challenge,* 2(2): 5–8.

Pope, H. G., and Katz, D. L. (1988). Affective and psychotic symptoms associated with anabolic steroid use. *American Journal of Psychiatry,* 145(4): 487–490.

Schuckit, M. A. (1988). The abuse of anabolic steroids. *Drug Abuse and Alcoholism Newsletter,* 17:1–4.

Scott, M. J. (1989). HIV infection associated with injections of anabolic steroids. *JAMA,* 262:207–208.

Thompson, P. D., et al. (1989). Contrasting effects of testosterone and stanozolol on serum lipoprotein levels. *JAMA,* 261:1165–1168.

U.S. Department of Education. (1987). *The Challenge.* Special Issue, 2(2): 1–20.

DRUG-RELATED DISEASES AND CONDITIONS

INTRODUCTION

Every drug of abuse poses serious physical, mental, and emotional hazards. This section describes the major diseases and conditions that are related to drug abuse. These diseases and conditions are accompanied by higher death rates and/or are extremely lethal (e.g., AIDS), and the associated medical and other social costs have a large-scale negative impact on the country. The greatest incidence of disease is related to the drugs of highest consumption, alcohol and tobacco.

AIDS is discussed in Chapter 3.4 (Intravenous Drug Use: AIDS) rather than in connection with any specific drug, as various drugs may be involved.

As the issue of drug dependence was discussed in the chapters on specific drugs, it will not be dealt with in this section. Also, the individual chapters on specific drugs contain information about special hazards such as drinking and driving that are not considered to be a disease or condition.

ALCOHOL-RELATED DISEASES AND CONDITIONS

Alcoholism
Cancer
Cardiovascular disorders
Cirrhosis of the liver
Endocrine disorders

Fetal alcohol syndrome and
 fetal alcohol effects
Gastrointestinal disorders
Neurological impairment

ALCOHOLISM

"Alcoholism" is a general term for a set of physical, psychological, and sociological conditions, yet it is specific enough to be used as a synonym for "drinking disease." The majority of Americans who consume alcohol do so without problems. A second group can be identified as problem drinkers or alcohol abusers who experience negative consequences of their drinking— accidental injury or death; loss of spouse, children, employment, etc.—but are not dependent on alcohol. For these individuals, health, social, and economic consequences develop secondary to alcohol abuse because of their poor judgment, failure to understand the risks, or lack of concern about the damage to themselves or others. A third group, however, have the disease called alcoholism and are dependent on the drug alcohol. They become ill when drinking is interrupted (i.e., they experience the withdrawal syndrome); they are tolerant to large amounts of alcohol; they miss alcohol intensely or "crave" it at times when they are abstinent; and they frequently display lack of control over their drinking. Unlike normal drinkers who seem to have an internal signal that says "enough," alcoholics generally cannot control the amount of alcohol they drink on any occasion. They drink compulsively despite the obvious damage their drinking causes (Gordis, 1989).

Alcoholism in the following discussion will be regarded mainly as a medical and psychological problem, in other words, drinking that has become pathological, habitual, and progressive, with true addictive aspects of tolerance and physical dependence. Alcohol *tolerance* is the ability of the brain to adapt to the presence of alcohol such that greater and greater quantities of alcohol become necessary to produce the same effects. This increases the likelihood that the individual drinking for some desired effect or feeling will increase his or her alcohol consumption. *Dependence* is the adaptation in structure and function of the nervous system as a consequence of long-term alcohol use, which makes it necessary for the drinker to continue consuming alcohol in order to prevent the unpleasant withdrawal reaction (Gordis, 1989).

Approximately 75 percent of American adults of drinking age and approximately 80 percent of high school students have consumed alcohol. Surveys indicate that one-half of the teenagers who drink do so at least once a month, but no accurate breakdown into specific frequency categories has been made for this age group. In the adult drinking groups, approximately 9 percent are classified as heavy drinkers, 18 percent as moderate, 31 percent as light, and 42 percent as either abstainers or infrequent drinkers. As has been discovered about other drugs, consumption of alcohol is slightly higher on the East Coast and the West Coast and lowest in the southern states.

The Stages Leading to Alcoholism

Using a disease orientation, E. M. Jellinek conducted a classic study in 1952 that describes the process of alcoholism. Jellinek interviewed over 2,000 alcoholics and found a characteristic pattern that constituted the "road to alcoholism." With a knowledge of this characteristic pattern, problem drinkers may recognize their problem earlier and control their drinking habit before the habit controls their lives.

The phases that most alcoholics follow appear to go from controlled social drinking to complete alcohol addiction. The relationship between these phases and the drinker's tolerance level is illustrated in Figure 19.

FIGURE 19
Tolerance to alcohol during characteristic phases of alcoholism. (Modified from Jellinek, 1952, p. 67.)

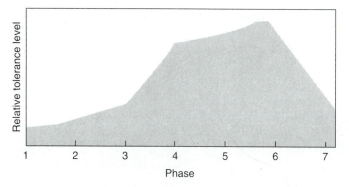

Prealcoholic Stage

Phase 1 The first phase is that of controlled social or cultural drinking. It is said that some drinkers become alcoholics with their first drink, but complete loss of control to alcohol progresses over a period of 10 to 20 years or longer.

Phase 2 Just as social drinkers do not become alcoholics overnight, they also have no warning that their drinking has gone beyond that of social or cultural drinking and has progressed to purposeful drinking—to escape from tensions.

Phase 3 The third phase is entered as innocently as was the second. As drinkers find that they can temporarily escape the tensions and frustrations of their everyday lives through the use of alcohol, they begin to turn to this escape from real life more often.

During these first three stages, the drinker's tolerance to alcohol steadily increases, but in Phase 3 alcohol tolerance takes a sharp upswing and the drinkers must consume more liquor to achieve the same depressant effect that was previously experienced (see Figure 19).

Early Alcoholic Stage

Phase 4 Continued drinking takes the escape drinker into the fourth phase, which is associated with the occurrence of the first blackout. A blackout is not merely passing out from drinking too much; it is more like temporary amnesia. One may carry on a conversation, move about, even drive a car—but remember none of these actions later. It has been hypothesized that this phenomenon is due to the drinker's will to remain in control in order to prove his or her ability to handle the liquor, but the drug effect still overtakes part of the brain so that memory patterns are not established. Tolerance continues to develop slowly during this phase and will continue through Phase 5, where it reaches its peak.

The actions of problem drinkers during this phase may be characterized as a progressive preoccupation with alcohol. When social functions are announced, they are more interested in whether drinks are to be served than in who will be attending the function. Before attending social functions, they fortify themselves with alcohol, and at parties they are in continual pursuit of an alcohol supply. These drinkers are past the social drinking stage. They may begin to drink alone, gulping down the first few drinks to obtain an immediate effect, and their behavior may begin to be embarrassing to others, especially their spouses. Also, during this phase, problem drinkers may develop conscious or unconscious guilt feelings about their drinking and offer "good excuses" for taking a drink. No longer do they brag about their alcohol consumption, but rather they tend to underestimate the number of drinks they have consumed. They begin to avoid conversation concerning alcohol.

At this time, changed drinking patterns (drinking at a different time of day, switching to a new alcoholic beverage, using a different mix, etc.) may be used as a means of controlling one's drinking habits, and there may even be periods of total abstinence to prove that alcohol is still on a "take-it-or-leave-it" basis.

True Alcoholic Stage

Phase 5 Again, let it be emphasized that these phases are not definite periods of time made obvious by calendar dates or road signs. Over a period of time, habitual drinkers move from the early alcoholic stage to the true alcoholic stage, in which everything in their being revolves around alcohol. Appearance, home, job, and possessions are neglected, and relationships begin to deteriorate. Family members change their habits to avoid confrontations with the alcoholic, and as a result of this, deep resentment and self-pity are manifested by the alcoholic. He or she may go through extended periods of constant drinking for consolation.

It is during this phase that the drinker loses the ability to stop after one drink. It has been suggested that perhaps by this time the alcoholic's first drink of the day or evening affects those cortical cells that control drinking judgment, and thus he or she cannot stop after one drink.

Phase 6 The sixth phase is ushered in by regular morning drinking, drinking that usually continues throughout the day. The alcoholic is now in danger of withdrawal symptoms if alcohol is not kept in his or her system at all times. This phase is often represented by the person who hides bottles all over the house and office. At this point the alcoholic is a tragic figure who neglects proper nutrition and whose family life deteriorates to the point of complete disruption. Alcohol is the alcoholic's purpose for living—he or she has become totally addicted to the drug.

Phase 7 The last phase of alcoholism is one in which social, medical, and psychological help must be given to the alcoholic to prevent death. By this time, he or she may have severe liver damage and possible brain tissue damage.

In this or the previous stage, the alcoholic is most likely to experience the DTs (delirium tremens). This reaction is characterized by delirium, muscle tremors, confusion, and hallucinations or delusions (mainly visual, such as moving animals, but tactile hallucinations may occur—a feeling that small animals or bugs are crawling on the skin). DTs do not generally occur until the alcoholic has been in the Phases 5 and 6 for several years, and at the onset of DTs the alcoholic may hallucinate only occasionally, but the symptoms gradually increase in duration and intensity. The psychotic episode lasts from 2 days to 2 weeks, frequently terminating in a long, deep sleep. In about 10 percent of the cases, death occurs, mainly due to pneumonia, complete renal shutdown, or cardiac arrest (NCADI, 1989a).

During any one of these phases, alcoholics may change their drinking pattern to one of partial or complete abstinence. It is believed that once habitual drinkers can no longer control their drinking—that is, they can no longer stop at one or two drinks—they cannot return to a social drinking status but must become totally abstinent. Alcoholics Anonymous calls for this complete abstinence, and it has been the most effective agency in the nation in helping alcoholics to recover.

The Causes of Alcoholism

Genetic factors, environmental factors, and the interplay between them have all been implicated in the etiology of alcoholism (Gordis, 1989). It has been known for many years that some families have more than their share of alcoholic members, leading to the hypothesis that alcoholism runs in families. Research in this area has provided evidence of a genetic component in defining the risk for alcoholism in a significant subset of the population (Blum et al., 1990). More refined knowledge about the genetics–environment interaction as well as the genetic determinants of alcoholism is being sought through research with twins and adoptees.

Under study as possible psychosocial behavioral predictors of later problem drinking are childhood antisocial behavior, parental drinking, cognitive functioning, attitudes, expectations, personality, environmental stress and coping, ethnicity, and cultural and socioeconomic factors.

It is clear that predisposing genetic factors may remain dormant in the absence of environmental cues and that alcoholism may develop in the absence of genetic predisposition. Some authorities on alcoholism and its treatment feel that it is mainly individuals with serious personality maladjustments who become chronic alcoholics. Various studies on alcoholism have shown that alcoholics tend to be insecure, anxiety-ridden, oversensitive, and dissatisfied with themselves and their lives. Without alcohol they feel inferior to others and find it difficult to socialize or feel at ease in most social situations.

Alcoholics have been compared to psychiatric patients in personality profile, which has led many researchers to conclude that alcoholism is only a symptom of deeper, more profound psychiatric disturbances. Many alcoholics have been found to exhibit such personality characteristics as dependence, low self-esteem, compulsivity, confusion of sex roles, immaturity, and low frustration tolerance, which can be identified as "addiction-promoting" traits (Schuckit, 1989). Other variations of the psychological model of alcoholism lean more toward learned behavior. In these models, alcohol consumption is considered to be a learned coping device that aids the drinker in dealing with stress. The more severe and frequent the stress, the more alcohol is used to solve the problem, thus completing the reinforcement loop. The more personality deficiencies one has, the more chance there is of interpreting life as being stressful (Girdano et al., 1990).

Although personality maladjustment may be a basic characteristic of the alcoholic, it is not the only hypothesized "cause" of alcoholism. A second proposal or theory is that alcoholism is the result of a biochemical defect, a lack of certain body chemicals, perhaps enzymes or hormones (Hoff, 1968). This theory contends that, owing to a genetic deficiency, certain normal enzyme systems are not produced in the body. This creates a biological state or balance that can be maintained only by the intake of alcohol. Animal studies have been conducted showing that rats with a vitamin B_1 deficiency prefer a mixture of water and alcohol to water alone (NIAAA, 1990).

Studies among family members, between twins, and between adoptees and their adoptive and biological parents have provided persuasive data linking hereditary factors with alcohol-related behaviors. This evidence in no way diminishes the importance of environmental influences; it only serves to illustrate the impact of both nature (biology) and nurture (environment). It is impossible to study the genetic influence of some physiological factors on human subjects. However, studies with rats and mice have demonstrated a genetic influence on ethanol consumption, central nervous sensitivity, acquired tolerance, and withdrawal symptoms. The evidence suggests that alcohol consumption, as well as some of the physiological actions of alcohol, may be influenced by differences in heredity, metabolism, and some brain amines (Schuckit, 1986).

Another basic causative factor that has been proposed is that of cultural readiness, which depends on the following conditions.

1 The degree to which the society brings about a need for escape—how much the society causes inner tensions in its members. In search of society-set goals, individuals may become so pressured that they must find an escape, and alcohol provides that escape (Crosby, 1975).

2 The kind of attitudes toward drinking that the society engenders in its members. Because drinking has become a sign of being grown-up and is often regarded as socially acceptable behavior, typical American youths may actually be pressured into drinking alcohol. Adult drinkers set the trend for the younger members of society. When alcohol is used in the home without fanfare or is used for religious purposes, it is less likely that members of those homes will use alcohol unwisely (Jessor & Jessor, 1975).

3 The number of suitable substitute means of satisfaction that the society provides. When a society offers a variety of desirable outlets for its members to occupy their thoughts and release tensions, self-destructive habits such as habitual drinking or drug taking will be less prevalent than in societies offering no socially acceptable escapes. For instance, some societies may offer religion as a form of escape. Also, a habit as simple as eating food may become a substitute escape mechanism.

Another theory is moral in substance. Even though this theory has strong historical and religious roots, it seems to be losing support in all but the most fundamental moralist circles. To the moralists, alcohol is an evil substance that has the power to accentuate human moral weaknesses. If one knows the power of alcohol, then drunkenness and alcoholism must be willful. The alcoholic is regarded as a sinner who freely chooses to drink, and drinking is considered a sign of moral weakness. As extreme as this position may sound, do not be too quick to dismiss its influence in the list of causes of alcoholism. If the drinker's family and friends judge the alcoholic as weak, or even as a sinner, that judgment can lead to the drinker having feelings of guilt, self-hate, and alienation, which further intensify the problem. The vicious circle is well known:

increasingly bitter family quarrels, mounting debt, job difficulties, punishing remorse, self-condemnation, hate of others, and, even worse, self-hate.

The moral issue is more often associated with the discussion of female alcoholics. The force of public condemnation is more pronounced in the case of a woman because of the remnants of the double standard, which brands alcohol abuse in a wife and mother as more shocking and "unnatural" than in a husband and father. The increased shame and guilt are only one special problem faced by women drinkers. The others create a constellation of causes and consequences special enough to examine in a separate section.

The Woman Alcoholic

Until recently, the drinking problems of women were largely ignored in our society, because alcoholism was considered a man's illness. Trapped by society's mythical image of the alcoholic female as a "fallen woman," a woman suffered doubly by being considered not only sick, but immoral as well. It is no wonder women alcoholics and their families labored to conceal, disguise, and deny the problem. Today women account for more than one-third of those who abuse alcohol in America—about 6 million women.

Until recently, it was assumed that women were just smaller versions of male alcoholic beverage drinkers, but we now know that sex difference plays an important role in the consequences of alcohol abuse. Research evidence suggests that the associated morbidity and mortality (completed suicide, accidental death, and death resulting from cirrhosis of the liver) due to alcoholism and alcohol-related problems is greater among women than men. For example, studies completed in a number of countries now demonstrate that the alcoholic woman is more susceptible to developing cirrhosis of the liver in association with a lower level of daily alcohol consumption and following a shorter history of heavy drinking than her male counterpart. In addition, she may become alcoholic in a shorter period of time. A major biologic basis of the difference in mortality and morbidity between women and men lies in the fact that men have more gastric alcohol dehydrogenase, an enzyme that breaks down alcohol in the stomach, so less alcohol gets into the rest of their system (Roine et al., 1990). When men and women drink the same amount relative to their weight, about 30 percent more alcohol enters the woman's bloodstream. This puts her brain, liver, reproductive organs, pancreas, and all other parts of her body in contact with relatively greater amounts of alcohol than a man's. Another sex difference that may affect the incidence of cirrhosis in female habitual drinkers is that estrogen may impair the functioning of the liver, making it even harder for that organ to break down alcohol. Female alcohol abusers have more problems with their menstrual periods, sexual performance, and getting pregnant than non-alcohol-abusing women, and they also have more miscarriages, more hysterectomies, more babies with birth defects, and earlier menopause than the latter group. In addition, the suicide rate of heavy-drinking women is 16 times that of nondrinking women. There is consensus that most female alcoholics suffer from common problems of low self-esteem, poor self-concept, anxiety, and depression, although it remains unclear as to whether such traits are the cause or the result of problem drinking.

Although more women than ever are seeking help for their drinking problems, the medical system is often reluctant to diagnose the problem as alcoholism and instead prescribes tranquilizers or other antidepressant drugs for depression or "nervous conditions." These women may develop yet another addiction, an addiction to the prescribed drugs (Wilsnack, 1984).

Because of the comparatively minor efforts to study women drinkers, evidence is lacking regarding etiological factors. For example, although it has been demonstrated through studies of individuals raised by adoptive parents that genetic factors play an important role in the development of alcoholism in men, the evidence is inconclusive regarding alcoholism in women (Wilsnack, 1984).

Studies comparing male and female alcoholics in treatment indicate that the alcoholic syndrome is much the same for both sexes in advanced alcoholism, but important differences exist between the life experiences and social problems encountered by each group. General population surveys show that among drinkers men have a higher prevalence of problems than women, but when frequency of intoxication is held constant (which is almost never done) most of these differences disappear (NIAAA, 1990). Prevalence of clinical depression is higher among female alcoholics, whereas prevalence of sociopathy is higher among males. Marriages of alcoholic women show a much higher frequency of disturbances than those of men. The prevalence of alcoholic husbands in these marriages is especially striking and deserves exploration. Many studies have addressed the question of sex role conflict in women as an influence on drunkenness and alcoholism.

As a group, women suffer a great deal of stress, and some of the stresses are very different from those faced by men. Since the traditional roles that society has defined for women and men produce quite different behavior, goals, self-images, and life experiences, women face certain problems that are not relevant to men (Finkelstein et al., 1990). Barriers to entry into treatment for many women include lack of funds, child care problems, the stigma of going into treatment, and the lack of interpersonal support (about one-fourth experience family opposition). Barriers to staying in treatment include family duties, too much responsibility for taking care of others, lack of a comprehensive plan for continued abstinence, and an inadequate sensitivity to gender issues within the treatment plan (Beckman & Amaro, 1986). Some of these barriers carry over into the reasons women do not stay sober after treatment. These include lack of a support group, lack of employment, lack of assertiveness skills, lack of autonomy skills, psychiatric disorders, and being in a relationship where the partner uses/abuses alcohol.

From childhood, females are taught that as the "second sex" they can expect to derive their sense of self-worth primarily through their relationships with men rather than through their own achievements and activities. Until recently, women were rarely encouraged to develop as independent persons with strong, secure identities. This is not to say that women's drinking problems stem entirely from their role in society, but regardless of what women do

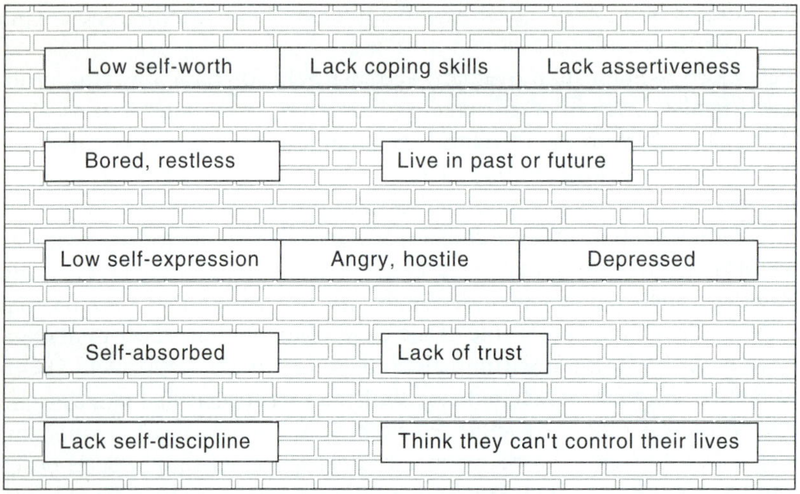

| Low self-worth | Lack coping skills | Lack assertiveness |

| Bored, restless | | Live in past or future |

| Low self-expression | Angry, hostile | Depressed |

| Self-absorbed | | Lack of trust |

| Lack self-discipline | | Think they can't control their lives |

FIGURE 20
Common psychosocial characteristics identified as risks.

with their lives, they cannot escape the judgment that, on some very basic level, they are inadequate because they are women. Studies repeatedly show that women drink primarily to relieve loneliness, inferiority feelings, and conflicts about their sex roles, regardless of their lifestyles.

The psychosocial characteristics of female substance abusers of all types include those shown in Figure 20 (NCADI, 1985; Chatham, 1990).

The Pregnant Woman   About 60 percent of adult American women drink alcohol. An estimated 6 percent of these women have been classified as problem drinkers. During the peak reproductive age range of 18 to 34, an estimated 5 percent of American women consume an average of two or more drinks per day, or 14 or more drinks per week. Estimates of the proportion of women who drink at least this amount during pregnancy vary widely, ranging from 0.5 percent to 16 percent, with a median of 2 percent across the United States (NIAAA, 1986).

Pregnancy is a natural crisis that is amplified by alcohol. The crisis that a pregnant woman faces includes a change in role, appearance, physiological functioning, and other changes that may make pregnancy a particularly trying time. Add problem drinking or alcoholism to that, and we see the following profile of the alcohol-abusing pregnant woman. According to Kronstadt (1989) and others, these women

Have a history of physical, sexual, or emotional abuse
Feel greater personal distress than comparison women
Have lower self-esteem
Have fewer social supports

Possess fewer personal resources and skills for coping with distress or with practical problems

Believe that people look down on them, and feel guilt and responsibility for their plight

Rate themselves low on masculine traits associated with ego strength, effectiveness, and self-esteem

Rate themselves low on feminine expression

Do not recall their childhood as bleak in either material or social resources but report having fun away from home more often and at an earlier age

Report heavier use of alcohol in their families

Remember themselves as having been reasonably good, skilled, and accepted by peers in childhood

Had problems during high school, became bored and restless, experimented with drugs, and had trouble with authorities

Are more likely to have become pregnant during adolescence and quit high school before finishing.

Women who drink alcohol during their pregnancy (or immediately before pregnancy) risk not only their own health but also the health of their babies. The National Institute on Alcohol Abuse and Alcoholism (NIAAA, 1990) recommends that pregnant mothers and those contemplating becoming pregnant abstain from drinking alcohol because as little as one alcoholic drink within 2 hours after conception could cause problems with the pregnancy.

Medical complications that may occur with alcoholic mothers include (1) the likelihood of no prenatal care, as pregnant abusers of alcohol tend not to come to the medical system for prenatal care for fear of detection and reprisals; (2) premature delivery (about 30 percent of all women who use alcohol during pregnancy deliver prematurely); (3) small-birth-weight babies, which therefore have increased health risks; (4) babies with physical abnormalities, especially fetal alcohol syndrome or fetal alcohol effects; and (5) babies with neurological problems (Kronstadt, 1989).

The Women at Home   Many women derive great satisfaction from a full-time career as a mother and homemaker. Yet this role drives other women to drink. Not every woman is interested in being a housewife, but may women abandon outside career goals for a home-centered life because of pressure to fulfill their feminine role. Feeling trapped in a lifestyle at odds with their real interests and goals, many women become increasingly frustrated and angry as the years go by. At the same time, they may fight enormous guilt feelings for wanting a life beyond the home. Caught in a paralyzing conflict, and finding that a couple of drinks have a way of dissolving feelings of anxiety, they begin to depend more and more on alcohol to shield them from their feelings. Before they realize it, they are relying on liquor simply to get through the day. Without acknowledging it, they have become alcoholics.

Another often-described situation involving the housewife is the empty-nest syndrome. The children grow up and leave home, a fatal illness strikes in the family, an unexpected divorce occurs. For many women, the center of their lives, the home and family, is suddenly gone. They have few resources, no job, few close friends, no real outside interests. Anxiety and loneliness set in. For these women, drinking often relieves the pain.

The Working Woman Even when a woman decides to work outside the home, she often finds that she is labeled as inferior and must work twice as hard as a man to prove that she is competent. The pressure not to fail can become overwhelming; as with the housewife, the working woman may find that alcohol seems to reduce the pain and anxiety, that the three-martini lunches and 5 o'clock pick-me-ups are the best part of the day. As the pain and pressure increase, so do the visits to the bar and the amount drunk during each visit.

A special case with regard to the working woman exists when she is also head of the household. Over 9 million American women are faced with this situation. While most seem to make it, many find the situation unbearable and seek relief from harsh reality through alcohol. The stresses involved in these circumstances are obvious. Few of these women are in jobs that pay well enough to allow for household help. Although busy with work and household chores, the woman in this situation is often alone because there is little time for socializing. When a few drinks temporarily reduce the pain, anxiety, and pressure, the motivation to take another drink to prolong the high is almost irresistible (Beckman & Amaro, 1986).

An examination of the problem encountered by the woman alcoholic drives home the point that there is no one cause for alcoholism but probably a combination of factors. At the present stage of our knowledge we can only say that this disorder is due to some complex combination of an individual's biological and psychological makeup, reacting to another complex combination of external factors that precipitate the dependency on alcohol (see Figure 21).

Adolescent Alcoholics

Studies show that alcohol is the most commonly used drug of adolescents between the ages of 12 and 17. These studies also reveal that problem drinking increases sharply with age and that adolescent problem drinkers are more likely than nondrinkers to use other illicit drugs. Adolescent drinking problems are related to other delinquency and social problems and as expected, to poor performance in school.

The factors associated with prevalence of alcohol use are varied and include both parental and peer influence. Attitudes about drinking as well as actual drinking behavior influence the adolescent. Other factors are academic achievement and religious affiliation and commitment. It is clear from the research that adolescent drinkers share a variety of personality and psychosocial characteristics. It is important to remember that programs designed to

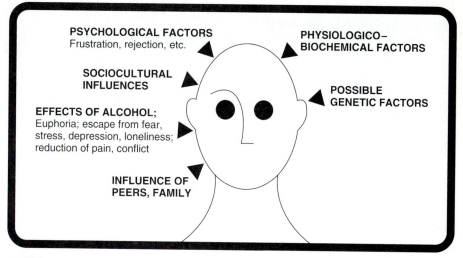

PSYCHOLOGICAL FACTORS
Frustration, rejection, etc.

**PHYSIOLOGICO–
BIOCHEMICAL FACTORS**

**SOCIOCULTURAL
INFLUENCES**

**POSSIBLE
GENETIC FACTORS**

EFFECTS OF ALCOHOL;
Euphoria; escape from fear,
stress, depression, loneliness;
reduction of pain, conflict

**INFLUENCE OF
PEERS, FAMILY**

FIGURE 21
Causative factors in alcoholism.

prevent adolescent drinking problems must also vary in their approach and techniques (NCADI, 1989b).

CANCER

Alcohol, as a cocarcinogen, enhances the effects of other carcinogens in the body, making smoking and drinking a potent pair of health risks. Chronic alcoholics have a higher risk of cancers of the mouth, pharynx, larynx, esophagus, liver, and upper respiratory and upper gastrointestinal systems. Heavy drinkers are five to six times as likely as nondrinkers to develop cancer of the mouth and throat, and those who also smoke increase that risk 15-fold.

CARDIOVASCULAR DISORDERS

Alcohol plays a number of roles in the etiology of cardiovascular disorders. Most cardiologists now recognize the existence of a condition known as alcoholic heart disease, which is caused by the direct toxic effects of alcohol on the heart muscle tissue. A cofactor in this condition seems to be malnutrition, especially thiamine deficiency. Hypertension is another cardiovascular disorder with varied etiology that has also been linked to excessive alcohol consumption (three or more drinks per day). The mechanism for this relationship has not been established. Some studies have shown that moderate drinkers are less at risk than nondrinkers for major coronary problems. A possible mechanism is that moderate amounts of alcohol increase high-density lipoprotein

(HDL), which has been found to be inversely related to coronary athero-sclerotic disease (NIAAA, 1990).

CIRRHOSIS OF THE LIVER

Laennic's cirrhosis is a chronic disease in which there is a progressive spread of connective tissue between portal spaces where there was once functional tissue. It is believed to develop by a process of fat accumulation followed by dysfunction and finally by fibrosis of the liver. It is also theorized that hepatitis may be a step in this disease process.

About 75 percent of all alcoholics show impaired liver function, and approximately 8 percent of all alcoholics eventually develop cirrhosis, a rate of incidence that is about six times that of the nonalcoholic population. Cirrhosis has become the fourth leading cause of death for persons between the ages of 25 and 45 in large urban areas.

Alcoholics have a greater chance of developing cirrhosis of the liver because (1) alcoholics tend to be malnourished, and the lack of nutritive elements allows the cirrhotic process to occur; and (2) alcohol itself (in the presence of adequate nutrition) causes cirrhosis.

The basis of the malnutrition theory of cirrhosis causation is that dietary deficiencies, especially a deficiency of proteins, result in a low level of lipotropic substances (e.g., choline, folic acid, and cynanocobalamin or vitamin B_{12}), which are necessary for normal removal of fat from the liver. In experimental animals, when these lipotropic substances are withheld from their diet, fatty liver results, and in most species cirrhosis follows. High-protein diets, especially those that include choline, may aid in the arrest of the cirrhotic process (Martin et al., 1991).

Fatty liver is a logical forerunner of a fibrotic condition because

1 Excess fat interferes with normal metabolism in hepatic cells, thus causing death of the cells.

2 Fat-filled cells next to each other tend to merge, creating a larger, non-working complex that ruptures.

3 Excess fat causes a diminution of reproductive activity in hepatic cells, and as a result, worn-out cells are not replaced as quickly as they would be normally.

4 Fat obstructs normal blood flow in the liver cells, resulting in anoxia (oxygen deficiency) and death of the cells. Once liver cells die, the fibrotic process begins, and it will continue as more cells die. This is not a reversible process.

It has also been shown that high alcohol consumption has a direct deleterious effect on the liver. When the liver is forced to metabolize very large amounts of alcohol, there is an excess buildup of metabolites there that inhibits the production of energy from dietary fats. That is, the liver preferentially produces energy from alcohol rather than from other foods. This leads to deposition of fat in hepatic cells and holds much the same potential for liver damage as fat deposition caused by dietary deficiency. Cirrhosis has been produced in animals even when there was no dietary deficiency; experimental animals developed cirrhosis even though their diets were more than adequate.

ENDOCRINE DISORDERS

A review of recent literature has clearly shown that alcohol depresses testosterone levels in both the short and long term. In addition, this depression may be somehow related to the metabolic tolerance a person develops with long-term alcohol abuse. Alcohol has been found by most investigators to increase the output of adrenal hormones, but it is not clear at this time whether this is a direct result of the alcohol or of stress. Several other endocrine hormones have been found to be altered with long-term alcohol abuse, and this is thought to be one of the primary mechanisms involved with both tolerance and physical dependence (NIAAA, 1990).

FETAL ALCOHOL SYNDROME AND FETAL ALCOHOL EFFECTS

Fetal alcohol syndrome (FAS) is an abnormal pattern of growth and development that occurs in some children born to alcoholic women. FAS is a well-defined clinical entity comprising physical, mental, and behavioral abnormalities: low birth weight, abnormally small head, specific facial abnormalities, heart defects, joint and limb malformation, and frontal retardation. (See Figure 22.) The exact number of children affected by maternal alcoholism is unknown. Abel and Sokol (1987) surveyed nineteen worldwide studies on FAS frequency and calculated the incidence to be 1.9 cases per 1,000 live births. Retrospective studies yield higher rates than prospective studies, and reported rates are higher in North America than in Europe and other countries. The populations that have been studied causes variance in the reported prevalence of FAS. For example, if only the population of heavy-drinking, alcohol-dependent women is considered, the incidence rate may be as high as 25 per 1,000 live births (NIAAA, 1990).

Studies of moderate- and heavy-drinking women, compared with abstainers and light-drinking women, indicate that alcohol may negatively affect the developing fetus—even when the mother is not alcoholic. These children lack the full fetal alcohol syndrome; they may have some but not all of the features of FAS, or they may be less severely affected. These problems, when attributable to alcohol, are called fetal alcohol effects (FAE) and include low birth weight, irritability and hyperactivity after birth, short attention span, learning disabilities, and behavioral disabilities.

Alcohol is fat-soluble and easily passes through the umbilicus to the embryo or fetus (at 12 weeks the embryo is referred to as a fetus). The pregnant mother, by virtue of her adult status, has the ability to detoxify her body by breaking

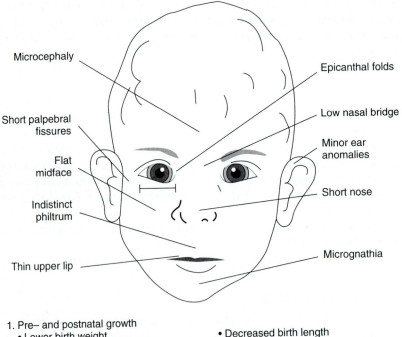

FIGURE 22

Fetal Alcohol Syndrome. This syndrome is a pattern of physical and mental defects that is a direct result of the mother's drinking alcohol during pregnancy. Listed below are specific disorders that may be present in varying degrees. If only some of these are present, a diagnosis of Fetal Alcohol Effects may be made.

1. Pre– and postnatal growth
   - Lower birth weight
   - Smaller head circumference
   - Decreased birth length

2. Facial abnormalities
   - Small head circumference
   - Flattened area above upper lip
   - Underdevelopment of midface region
   - Narrow eye slits
   - Thin upper lip (no cupid's bow)

3. Central nervous system involvement
   - Neurologic abnormality
   - Intellectual impairment
   - Developmental delay

down foreign substances, but the unborn fetus has a number of handicaps that leave it much more vulnerable to a toxic drug.

1 The fetus has the anatomical disadvantage of an enormous surface area of placenta, which permits easy transfer of a substance such as alcohol from the mother's blood to the blood of the fetus.

2 Its gastrointestinal mucous membrane has a high degree of permeability.

3 The fetus is deficient in functional kidney structures (glomeruli) that help excrete unwanted substances from the body.

4 Fetus enzyme systems are insufficiently developed to effectively break down or metabolize foreign substances.

Thus, until the fetus leaves its uterine environment (and for some time there-after), its ability to metabolize or detoxify toxic substances is hampered.

The results of alcohol exposure on outcome of pregnancy are related to dosage, timing and extent of exposure, and the genotype of the embryo and the mother. During the first 2 weeks of pregnancy, exposure to alcohol is more likely to result in miscarriage than in embryonic malformations. After the first 2 weeks and up to 11 weeks, the organs are being formed, and exposure to alcohol could result in serious organ malformation. This is the time period in which most major birth defects originate. From 11 weeks to term there is rapid growth of the fetus. Exposure to alcohol at this time may result in a functional or behavioral abnormality (such as significant learning disability) rather than a major birth defect. Some infants (even in their embryonic stage) are more susceptible to the insult of alcohol and other substances and will have poorer outcomes than others.

An average of one to two reported drinks daily by the mother is linked to decreased birth weight, growth abnormalities, and behavioral problems in the newborn and infant. Increased risk of spontaneous abortion has been found at an even lower dose: one to two drinks twice weekly (Little & Irvin, 1985). In addition, not all women who drink in excess during pregnancy deliver babies with FAS or even FAE, making it important to look at other variables that may contribute to FAS and FAE. These may include such variables as race, genet-ics, nutrition, the taking of other drugs (both licit and illicit) during pregnancy, and behavioral and attitudinal patterns. There are many scientific limitations to investigations of human pregnancies. This means that precise cause-and-effect relationships can seldom be demonstrated and that the amount of alcohol that is "safe" to consume during pregnancy cannot be established. The need for long-term assessment of children whose mothers drink different amounts of alcohol, in different patterns (such as daily drinking versus binge episodes), is essential to a better understanding of the association between drinking during pregnancy and children's well-being. In the meantime the National Council on Alcoholism and Drug Dependence (NCADD, 1990) "perceives any alcohol consumption during pregnancy as high-risk drinking and supports a clear no-alcohol-use message as the only responsible public health message."

It is known that the probability of having a child with FAS or FAE increases with the amount of alcohol consumed and frequency of consumption and that when a pregnant woman stops drinking she reduces the risks of FAE and the consequences of alcohol exposure. FAS is the number one cause of mental retardation in the United States and is totally preventable.

GASTROINTESTINAL DISORDERS

Disorders of the food breakdown and metabolism systems of chronic heavy drinkers include ulcers of the stomach, gastritis, pancreatitis, cancer, and colitis (-*itis* means inflammation, usually of the lining of the organ). In relation to all these disorders, nutritional deficiencies are quite common among heavy drinkers.

Alcohol's presence in the stomach causes the secretion of gastric acids that irritate the stomach lining. Over a period of time the irritation of the lining may cause lesions, which in turn become ulcers. Alcohol is thought to be a cocarcinogen (an agent that, in the presence of a carcinogen, helps cause cancer). A chronic drinker continually exposes the mouth, esophagus, stomach, intestines, and other organs of digestion and metabolism to alcohol.

NEUROLOGICAL IMPAIRMENT

Alcohol impairs the brain's ability to utilize oxygen, thus disrupting the neurological flow of information. It also kills brain cells, which impairs memory, learning ability, and cognition. Alcoholics in treatment centers have been found to exhibit both brain abnormalities and cognitive impairment. Even when not drunk, alcoholics may exhibit the poor motor performance and loss of memory that is related to brain damage. Computerized axial tomography (CAT) scan studies show that the brains of alcoholics have shrunk. A condition called alcoholic peripheral neuropathy causes numbness, burning sensations, and muscle weakness (NIAAA, 1990).

The evidence on cognitive impairment suggests that the effects of drinking alcohol vary with consumption. There is very little impairment in a light drinker, whereas there is sometimes severe impairment in alcoholics. In some respects, alcoholics manifest characteristics of premature aging, while in others, they do not (NIAAA, 1990).

Wernicke–Korsakoff Syndrome

The Wernicke-Korsakoff syndrome is a neurological syndrome that can occur in chronic alcoholics. The syndrome has two distinct phases. The acute phase is characterized by mental confusion, paralysis of the eye muscles, temporary nerve dysfunction, memory loss, loss of balance, confusion, and hallucinations. The chronic or long-term effect is primarily memory loss. This condition develops over years of alcohol abuse and is due to both the direct effect of the alcohol and the interaction of the toxic effects of alcohol and malnutrition.

REFERENCES

Abel, E. L., and Sokol, R. J. (1987). Incidence of alcohol syndrome and economic impact of FAS-related anomalies. *Drug and Alcohol Dependence*, 19:51–70.

Beckman, L., and Amaro, H. (1986). Personal and social differences faced by females and males entering alcoholism treatment. *Journal of Studies on Alcohol*, 45: 135–145.

Blum, L, Noble, E. P., and Sheridan, P. J. (1990). Allelic association of human dopamine D_2 receptor gene in alcoholism. *JAMA*, 263:2055–2060.

Chatham, Louis. (1990). Understanding the issues: an overview. In Ruth Engs (Ed.), *Women, Alcohol and Other Drugs*. Washington, D.C.: Alcohol Drug Problems Association.

Crosby, W. H. (1975). Those two martinis before dinner every night. *JAMA*, 231(5):509.

Finkelstein, N., Duncan, S., Derman, L., and Smeltz, J. (1990). *Getting Sober, Getting*

Well: A Treatment Guide for Caregivers Who Work with Women. Cambridge, Mass.: The Women's Alcoholism Program of CASPAR, Inc.

Girdano, D. A., Everly, G., and Dusek, D. E. (1990). *Controlling Stress and Tension: A Holistic Approach,* 3d ed. Englewood Cliffs, N.J.: Simon and Schuster.

Gordis, Enoch. (1989). Major initiatives in alcoholism research. In L. S. Harris (Ed.), *Problems of Drug Dependence 1989.* Washington, D.C.: U.S. Department of Health and Human Services.

Hoff, C. E. (1968). Pharmacologic and metabolic adjuncts. In R. J. Catanzaro (Ed.), *Alcoholism.* Springfield, Ill.: Charles C Thomas.

Jellinek, E. M. (1952). Phases of alcohol addiction. *Quarterly Journal of Studies on Alcohol,* 13:672.

Jessor, R., and Jessor, S. L. (1975). Adolescent development and the onset of drinking: a longitudinal study. *Journal of Studies on Alcohol,* 36(1):27–51.

Kronstadt, Diana. (1989). *Substance Abuse During Pregnancy—Impact on Mothers and Children: A Guide to Resources.* Washington, D.C.: Office of Substance Abuse Prevention.

Little, R., and Ervin, C. (1985). Alcohol use and reproduction. In S. Wilsnack and L. Beckman (Eds.), *Alcohol Problems in Woman.* New York: Guilford Press.

Martin, D. W., et al. (1991). *Harper's Review of Biochemistry.* Los Altos, Calif.: Lange Medical Publications.

NCADD. (1990). *National Council on Alcohol and Drug Dependence Policy Statement: Women, Alcohol, Other Drugs and Pregnancy.* Washington, D.C.: National Council on Alcohol and Drug Dependence.

NCADI (National Clearinghouse for Alcohol and Drug Information). (1985). *Prenatal Drug Exposure: Kinetics and Dynamics.* NIDA Research Monograph 60. Washington, D.C.: U.S. Department of Health and Human Services.

NCADI (National Clearinghouse for Alcohol and Drug Information). (1989a). *Alcohol Alert: Alcohol Withdrawal Syndrome.* Washington, D.C.: U.S. Department of Health and Human Services.

NCADI (National Clearinghouse for Alcohol and Drug Information). (1989b). *Treatment for Adolescent Substance Abusers.* Washington, D.C.: U.S. Department of Health and Human Services.

NIAAA (National Institute on Alcohol Abuse and Alcoholism) (1986). *Program Strategies for Preventing Fetal Alcohol Syndrome and Alcohol-Related Birth Defects.* Washington, D.C.: U.S. Department of Health and Human Services.

NIAAA (National Institute on Alcohol Abuse and Alcoholism) (1990). *Seventh Special Report to the U.S. Congress on Alcohol and Health.* Washington, D.C.: National Clearinghouse for Alcohol and Drug Information.

Roine, Risto, et al. (1990). Aspirin increases blood alcohol concentrations in humans after ingestion of ethanol. *JAMA,* 264(18):2406–2408.

Schuckit, M. (1989). *Drug and Alcohol Abuse: A Clinical Guide to Diagnosis and Treatment.* New York: Plenum.

Schuckit, M. A. (1986). Genetic and clinical implications of alcoholism and affective disorder. *American Journal of Psychiatry,* 143:140–147.

Wilsnack, Sharon. (1984). *Alcohol Problems in Women.* New York: Guilford Press.

AMPHETAMINE- AND COCAINE-RELATED CONDITIONS

Amphetamine psychosis
Bowel ischemia
Cardiovascular problems
Pregnancy complications and outcomes

Psychosis
Seizures
Sudden death

AMPHETAMINE PSYCHOSIS

Most psychoactive drugs have the ability to trigger a psychotic episode in psychosis-prone individuals; however, study of amphetamine users suggests that psychosis is not idiosyncratic, but rather an inevitable consequence of long-term high-dose amphetamine abuse (Holbrook, 1983). Acute psychotic episodes can be precipitated by an exaggeration of many of the conditions normally found in the amphetamine experience—lack of sleep, visual and tactile illusions, visual and auditory hallucinations, lack of food, extreme anxiety, paranoid delusions, aggressiveness, and irritability. Psychosis related to amphetamine abuse is acute and may recur with additional use, but it usually is not chronic and does not carry over into the nondrug state unless the individual is psychosis-prone.

BOWEL ISCHEMIA

Owing to impairment of blood flow to the bowels, cocaine-induced ulcerations of the bowel and severe colitis may develop in cocaine users. These conditions require surgical treatment and have been known to result in death of the patient (Nalbandian et al., 1985).

196

CARDIOVASCULAR PROBLEMS

The nature of cocaine is to stimulate the sympathetic nervous system to the extreme (see Section 2.5). When this occurs, the heart must also respond to the increased demand for oxygenated blood from all the other systems of the body. The cardiovascular response is a faster and more forceful pumping of the heart. If the heart cannot obtain enough oxygenated blood fast enough, myocardial infarction (death of heart muscle tissue) occurs. If the vascular system is compromised in some way (e.g., weakened vessel walls), blood vessels leading from the heart may rupture because of increased blood pressure. Rupture of the aorta (the large blood vessel leaving the heart) is a medical complication that is linked with cocaine use, as is cardiac arrhythmia (including life-threatening ventricular arrhythmias) and acute myocardial infarction, both with and without underlying coronary artery disease (Cregler & Mark, 1988).

PREGNANCY COMPLICATIONS AND OUTCOMES

Cocaine use during pregnancy can be a major perinatal risk factor (ACOG, 1990). Women who use cocaine during pregnancy increase their risk of spontaneous abortion, abruptio placentae, premature labor and delivery, intrauterine growth retardation, sudden infant death syndrome (SIDS; the normal rate is 1 or 2 per 1,000, whereas in cocaine-exposed infants it is 33 to 170 per 1,000), and neurobehavioral deficiencies of the child, as well as other documented medical problems and long-term developmental abnormalities (Chasnoff & Griffith, 1989; Sobrian et all, 1989). The risk of preterm birth is up to 25 percent, and for small-for-gestational-age infants it is up to 20 percent among cocaine users.

The consequences of cocaine use for the embryo or fetus may be caused by the effect of the drug on the placenta (causing severe vasoconstriction so that the transport of oxygen and other nutrients is seriously reduced) or the direct effect on the developing child. Possible malformations or abnormalities caused by in utero cocaine exposure include genitourinary malformations such as malformation of the kidney, ureter, bladder, or genitalia; heart abnormalities such as septal defects or enlarged heart; and central nervous system abnormalities such as atrophy or infarctions. It is possible that the unborn child may experience stroke due to the fluctuation in the mother's blood pressure. When cocaine or crack babies are born, they may experience painful withdrawal and are likely to show a number of the following neurodevelopmental effects:

Irritability	Poor feeding
Increased tremulousness	Poor visual attention
Poor sucking	Failure to thrive
Difficult to soothe	

A survey of urban hospitals in 1989 showed that 10 to 25 percent of pregnancies demonstrated positive urine toxicology for cocaine metabolites (Chasnoff & Griffith, 1989). Pregnant addicts often forget their own health, increasing even further the risk to the unborn child. The health of pregnant women addicted to cocaine is especially at risk because of the anorectic effect of the drug, leading to under- or malnutrition.

Although some of these infants are abandoned in hospitals by their addicted mothers, from 50 to 75 percent of them go home with their mother or a relative. If the mother is drug-dependent, the infant often enters a life characterized by poverty and abuse. These mothers tend to have little talent, knowledge, or desire to learn bonding skills, and so an already handicapped child is placed in further jeopardy. The ''crack babies'' that were born after crack cocaine became popular in the mid-1980s have now entered the public school system, and educators are wary of how the influx of this population will affect the resources of the system.

PSYCHOSIS

In cases where consumption is high and/or frequent, users may suffer a partial or total break with reality. The ''cocaine psychotic'' has delusions, may become paranoid, and may commit violence against anyone he imagines is pursuing him. Many have visual, auditory, or tactile hallucinations (one of the most common is ''coke bugs'' or formication, the sensation of insects crawling under the skin). This condition might continue for days, weeks, or months. Hospitalization and the use of antipsychotics are necessary in some cases.

SEIZURES

Cocaine-induced seizures can cause a general diminution of alertness and mental functioning. Cocaine can also induce epilepsy, even in those with no previous signs of it.

SUDDEN DEATH

Most sudden deaths from overdose of cocaine are due to respiratory paralysis, heart rhythm disturbances, and repeated convulsions, usually from massive overdoses or at the end of a binge. Some users suffocate in the deep stupor that follows an extended period of use; some drown in their own secretions. Still others succumb to allergic reactions to the adulterants in the drug. Death from overdose comes swiftly. A user with no apparent symptoms may suddenly go into grand mal convulsions, followed rapidly by respiratory collapse and death.

REFERENCES

ACOG. (1990). *Cocaine Abuse: Implications for Pregnancy*. Washington, D.C.: The American College of Obstetricians and Gynecologists.

Chasnoff, I. J., and Griffith, D. R. (1989). Cocaine: clinical studies of pregnancy and the newborn. *Annals of the New York Academy of Sciences*, 565:260–266.

Cregler, L. L., and Mark, H. (1988). Medical complications of cocaine abuse. *New England Journal of Medicine*, 315(23):1495–1500.

Holbrook, John. (1983). CNS stimulants. In G. Bennett (Ed.) *Substance Abuse: Pharmacological, Developmental, and Clinical Perspectives*. New York: Wiley.

Nalbandian, H., et al. (1985). Intestinal ischemia caused by cocaine ingestion. *Surgery*, 97(3):374–376.

Sobrian, S. K., et al. (1989). Neurobehavioral effects of prenatal exposure to cocaine. *Annals of the New York Academy of Sciences*, 562:383–386.

INTRAVENOUS
DRUG USE: AIDS

AIDS

The use of any drug that is injected may be related to acquired immune deficiency syndrome (AIDS), because a high percentage of nonsexual transmission of the human immunodeficiency virus (HIV) is due to sharing contaminated needles. Theoretically, alcohol, marijuana, cocaine, and the opiates may be linked to the occurrence of AIDS in that they are suspected to cause immunosuppression in the body. Taking the correlation another step, any drug that diminishes the ability to think clearly and behave in a socially responsible way may contribute to the transmission of HIV due to unsafe sexual practices.

The Disease Process

The AIDS virus is transmitted by direct contact with infected blood, semen, vaginal secretions, or breast milk. It is NOT transmitted by casual contact (hugging, shaking hands), coughing, sneezing, food, shared utensils, dry kissing, sharing office or classroom space, or mosquito or other insect bites. Specifically, the virus is transmitted by the following mechanisms:

Sexual intercourse with an infected partner
Sharing of needles or equipment by IVDUs
Transmission from mother to infant during pregnancy or delivery
Transfusion with contaminated blood
Occupational exposure to infected blood
Breast feeding from infected mother
Transmission from infants with oral lesions to mother with cracked nipples

The risk of transmission by oral sex or French kissing is unknown but theoretically possible (Rosenberg & Fauci, 1989).

From the time of exposure, the average incubation period for AIDS is 8 years, but it varies with the age of the patient. The time from exposure to seroconversion (making its presence known in the body) can be from as little as 2 weeks up to 6 months. It is generally agreed that if a person has had a single potential exposure to HIV and has not seroconverted from negative to positive in 6 months, the exposure did not result in infection. The Centers for Disease Control (CDC) recommends that testing laboratories not report positive results until a screening test has been repeatedly reactive on the same specimen and a supplemental, more specific test is done. Nearly all HIV testing programs screen specimens with an ELISA (enzyme-linked immunosorbent assay). If the ELISA is reactive, it is repeated, usually twice. A repeatedly reactive specimen is then tested with a supplementary test—usually the Western Blot. This combination has an extremely high predictive value (Schuckit, 1989). An example of a consent form that is used in HIV testing programs is illustrated in the box on page 202.

Infection Time Line

Infection occurs when HIV becomes permanently incorporated into the host cell DNA, and the person is infectious from this time on, even though tests may not be positive for several weeks or months. About 20 percent of HIV-infected persons will experience seroconversion illness within a period of time varying from 5 days to 3 months after exposure. This illness has such symptoms as fever, sweats, general malaise, muscle and joint pain, headaches, diarrhea, and rash. Asymptomatic HIV infection may last for several years. The disease then progresses to the stage of persistent generalized lymphadenopathy (PGL), characterized by two or more enlarged lymph nodes that persist for 3 months or more. This may last up to 3 years. Then AIDS-related complex (ARC) symptoms begin to occur. These indicate advanced HIV disease, with symptoms of fatigue, night sweats, fever, and diarrhea. AIDS is the end stage of HIV infection. Major defects in the immune system allow the development of opportunistic diseases such as *Pneumocystis carnii* pneumonia. The nervous system is often affected during this time also (Sande & Volberding, 1990).

Before the development of AZT (a drug that inhibits the virus from reproducing), half of those diagnosed with AIDS died within 10 months. Average survival time has increased to about 2 years (Volberding & Lagakos, 1990).

Demographics of AIDS

Over 140,000 cases of AIDS have been reported in the United States since 1981, when the virus was isolated and AIDS was given a name. There were just over 33,000 new cases reported in 1989. Ninety percent of these patients have been males, with 60 percent of these being bisexual or homosexual, 28 percent

EXAMPLE OF A CONSENT FORM FOR HIV TESTING

I, _____, understand that a blood test is to be performed to determine whether I have been exposed to the Human Immunodeficiency Virus (HIV) believed to cause Acquired Immune Deficiency Syndrome (AIDS).

I understand that a small amount of blood will be drawn for laboratory testing. This will be done by venipuncture, which is the standard method of drawing blood by placing a needle in my vein.

I understand that my blood will be tested to determine whether it contains antibody to HIV. A positive test result indicates that I have been exposed to HIV.

Test results may be inaccurate: I understand that there is a possibility that a "false positive" or "false negative" result may be obtained due to the fact that the available tests used to determine whether I have been exposed to HIV are not completely accurate or reliable.

(This paragraph applies only to states in which reporting of HIV testing results is required:

Reporting Required: I understand that my physicians, the hospital, or the testing laboratory, or all of them, are required to report all positive test results and may make other reports to the Department of Health or the local health department. If my blood tests positive for HIV the following information will be initially reported to these agencies: my name and address, date of birth, sex, and risk category.)

If an initial positive test result (ELISA) is obtained, my blood will be submitted for further (Western Blot) testing to confirm the results of the initial test.

I further understand that if my blood test indicates that I have been exposed to HIV, the medical staff taking care of me may be informed of this result if I give my consent. I also understand that the medical records maintained by the notified medical staff will show that I have been tested and will also show the test results.

Insurance: I further understand that if I make a claim to another health carrier for the cost of the HIV test, I may be required to release medical information to that insurance carrier (including Medicare or Medicaid), including the HIV test results.

I have read and understand the information on this form. I have had the opportunity to ask questions about any matter which I did not understand and I have received satisfactory explanations. By my signature below, I consent to having a blood sample taken from me for testing for exposure to HIV.

_____ Patient's initials indicate that further information has been requested by the patient and has been provided by the physician.

_____   _____
Patient   Witness

_____
Date of Birth

_____   _____
Date   Date

being intravenous drug users (IVDUs), 5 percent heterosexual contact with an HIV-positive person, 2 percent from transfusions, 1 percent hemophiliacs, and 3 percent undetermined. The proportion of AIDS cases among heterosexuals is increasing (CDC, 1988).

Blacks and Hispanics have a greater percentage of AIDS than their proportion in the population. Blacks make up 11 percent of the U.S. population, but they constitute 28 percent of all AIDS patients and 52 percent of all pediatric AIDS cases. Hispanics make up 7 percent of the U.S. population, but 16 percent of all AIDS patients and 26 percent of all pediatric AIDS cases. Black and Hispanic women have an 11 percent greater chance of infection than white women, and black and Hispanic men have a 10 percent greater chance of infection than white men (CDC, 1988).

Intravenous drug use is a primary risk for women: 49 percent of HIV-positive women got the virus from their own drug use and 21 percent from sexual contact with men who used drugs. HIV-infected women create the link to a new generation of AIDS patients—83 percent of children with HIV acquired it prior to or at birth from an infected mother (10 percent get the virus through transfusions, and 5 percent by receipt of clotting factors). It is estimated that 30 to 50 percent of infants born to HIV-infected women will be infected (CDC, 1988). Approximately 83 percent of the U.S. children with AIDS are known to have a mother who either has HIV or is at risk of the infection. HIV can be transmitted to the child in utero through maternal circulation or during labor and delivery by contact with or ingestion of infective fluids or blood. Russia has reported a case of infant infection through breast feeding.

AIDS AND INTRAVENOUS DRUG USE (IVDU)

The obvious linkage between substance abuse and AIDS is that HIV is transmitted by sharing contaminated needles. Intravenous drug use is resonsible for most HIV infections of heterosexual men and women, and there is the added danger for multidrug users that alcohol, cocaine, marijuana, and amphetamines may cause immunosuppression. Chemical use also decreases critical thinking and behavior, leading drug users into unsafe sexual practices.

HIV seroprevalence among IVDUs varies with geographic location: 60 percent in New York City, 26 percent in Baltimore, 5 percent in Denver, and 2 percent in San Antonio. Black IVDUs have 14 times more HIV seroprevalence than white IVDUs in New York City. Needle sharing is common— IVDUs share needles perhaps 70 to 90 percent of the time. Needle sharing is reported to occur 77 percent of the time with relatives and close friends (Becker & Joseph, 1988).

A common misconception about AIDS among IVDUs is that only homosexuals get AIDS. There is additional complacency in that there may be a long latency period between HIV infection and the signs and symptoms of the disease. Many times IVDUs do not connect AIDS illnesses with death, because IVDUs often have many AIDS-like symptoms such as weight loss, fevers, diarrhea, and night sweats that are drug-related rather than AIDS-related.

It is difficult to conduct AIDS prevention and risk reduction programs among the IVDU population because these people characteristically mistrust institutions and authority, and the outreach and education strategies that work with the general population are often ineffective with them. Other barriers that prevent successful risk reduction in the IVDU population may include fees, paperwork, and waiting time. Existing drug and alcohol treatment centers may be the most effective interface for risk assessment, counseling, and referral (Newmeyer, 1989). Counseling and prevention of AIDS for IVDUs includes the following advice:

Don't start using drugs,
If you use drugs, get treatment,
If you continue to use drugs,
    Don't share needles,
    Clean your needles,
    Clean your skin before injecting,
    Avoid shooting galleries.

REFERENCES

Becker, N. H., and Joseph J. G. (1988). AIDS and behavioral change to reduce risk. *American Journal of Public Health*, 78:394–410.

CDC. (1988). Human immunodeficiency virus infection in the U.S. *Morbidity and Mortality Weekly Report*, 38(S-4): 1–38.

Newmeyer, J. (1989). The epidemiology of HIV among intravenous drug users. In J. W. Dilley, C. Pies, and Mitlelquist (Eds.), *Face to Face: A Guide to AIDS Counseling*. San Francisco: University of California AIDS Health Project.

Rosenberg, Z. F., and Fauci, A. S. (1989). The immunopathogenesis of HIV infection. *Advances in Immunology*, 47:377–431.

Sande, M. A., and Volberding, P. A. (Eds.). (1990). *Medical Management of AIDS*. Philadelphia: W. B. Saunders.

Schuckit, M. A. (1989). *Drug and Alcohol Abuse: A Guide to Diagnosis and Treatment*. New York: Plenum.

Volberding, P. A., and Lagakos, S. W. (1990). Zidovudine in asymptomatic human immunodeficiency virus infection. *New England Journal of Medicine*, 322:941–949.

SMOKING-RELATED CONDITIONS

Heart disease	Chronic bronchitis
Lung cancer	Smoking and pregnancy
Emphysema	Peptic ulcer

HEART DISEASE

Most of the excess deaths among smokers (deaths beyond the number encountered among nonsmokers) are due to the drug effects of nicotine on the circulatory system, which lead to heart disease. Coronary artery disease accounts for about 45 percent of the total excess deaths related to smoking. Then, if one adds the excess deaths from other heart diseases, general arteriosclerosis, and hypertensive heart disease, the total of preventable deaths associated with heart disease accounts for more than 50 percent of all excess deaths in smokers.

Nicotine is a stimulant that affects the human system in a manner similar to that of the amphetamines. It increases heart rate and blood pressure, and other changes occur that are normally attributed to the sympathetic nervous system. However, nicotine works in a twofold manner to stimulate the system. First, it directly affects cholinergic nerve synapses by mimicking acetylcholine. This not only elicits great excitability but also blocks out meaningful impulses that would normally be directed by acetylcholine. After initially exciting these nerve fibers, nicotine "overloads" the ability of the nerve cells to respond, creating a blocking effect at the synapse (DHHS, 1987).

The second way in which nicotine affects the nervous system is through its action on the adrenal glands. It causes these endocrines to release adrenal hormones, which circulate in the blood, causing excitation of the sympathetic nervous system. In addition to exciting the adrenals, nicotine releases the same hormones from other sites as well, thus completing its sympathomimetic action.

When a smoker takes nicotine into the lungs, the substance is quickly taken up by the blood and carried to all parts of the body. Then all the excitatory effects caused by nicotine combine to overwork the heart. If a smoker's heart is exposed to these events ten, twenty, or more times a day (often in rapid succession), it will almost certainly be adversely affected.

Nicotine is also thought to be responsible for the elevated levels of free fatty acids found in the plasma of smokers. The exact physiological mechanism has not been determined, but stimulation of the sympathetic nervous system and adrenocortex is known to be activated by nicotine and must play an important role in the release of fatty acids from adipose deposits.

The carbon monoxide in the gaseous phase of cigarette smoke is thought to significantly decrease cardiac work capacity. Hemoglobin picks up the carbon monoxide from the lungs, forming carboxyhemoglobin, which alters myocardial metabolism, interferes with oxygen delivery, and results in myocardial hypoxia. The carboxyhemoglobin is a result of the incomplete combustion of the organic material in the cigarette. The carbon is oxidized to carbon monoxide gas and inhaled. The affinity of hemoglobin for carbon monoxide is more than 200 times greater than its affinity for oxygen. Thus, carbon monoxide readily displaces oxygen from hemoglobin, which can harm cardiac tissue in several ways. Hemoglobin tied up with carbon monoxide cannot carry oxygen, so less oxygen will be delivered to the heart. Numerous studies have shown that this decreased oxygenation results in decreased work capacity. It should be noted that to the normal healthy heart this decrease in oxygenation is of minor consequence, unless the heart is functioning near capacity, as during exercise. However, the smoker's heart is not likely to be normal and healthy, and carbon monoxide has much to do with that cardiac deterioration as it significantly accelerates the atherosclerotic process. Carbon monoxide increases the permeability of the endothelial (inner lining) layer of the cardiovascular system. As a result, plasma leaks into the tissue, causing edema, which widens the gap between endothelial cells. The edema sets in motion a buildup of mucopolysaccharides, which facilitates precipitation of lipoproteins and the eventual accumulation of lipids in arterial plaques.

Carbon monoxide may be of more significance than nicotine in the development of cardiovascular disease among smokers. It is also one of the dangerous elements of polluted air in our cities, which affects smokers and nonsmokers alike. It is of interest to note that the trend toward low-nicotine cigarettes is in reality not of much value in the prevention of cardiovascular disease, because it is impossible to reduce the carbon monoxide content of the smoke.

In summary, we can say that cigarette smoking is related to cardiovascular disease in the following areas:

1 Increased heart rate
2 Increased peripheral vasoconstriction, which in turn causes increased blood pressure

3 Release of fatty acids from adipose stores, thus elevating the level of circulating fats, which are known precursors of atherosclerotic plaques

4 Reduction of blood clotting time

5 Reduction of the amount of oxygen delivered to the tissues due to the carbon monoxide content of smoke

6 Increases in edema, cell separation, and deposit of lipids in arterial plaque

LUNG CANCER

Serious chronic health problems other than heart disease that are releated to cigarette smoking are due mainly to the particulate and gaseous contents of smoke rather than to the sympathomimetic action of nicotine.

The second major cause of excess deaths due to smoking is cancer, most of that being lung cancer. Lung cancer started to become increasingly apparent in the 1920s and 1930s and has grown into a full-blown epidemic since that time. This outbreak of lung cancer not so curiously followed the sharp rise in cigarette use in the United States during World War I, and it followed it by approximately 20 years, the average time involved in producing cancer. To support this temporal theory of lung cancer, it was found that Iceland produced the same pattern, with a sharp rise in cigarette consumption during World War II followed by a lung cancer "epidemic" about 20 years later. In 1974, approximately 40,000 people died of lung cancer in the United States, and for middle-aged men cancer represents the second leading cause of death.

As is well documented now, cigarette tars or particulate matter (the particles that enable us to see smoke) that come into constant contact with the respiratory tract cause a slow change in the cells of that system. In time, this change may cause a cell to reproduce as cells that are modified versions of the original, productive one. New cells that serve no productive function in the body are cancer cells—they multiply rapidly and compete with normal cells for nutrients, slowly killing off and replacing normal cells, and the normal function of the system is affected.

Carcinoma of the bronchi accounts for approximatley 95 percent of the malignant tumors found in the lung. Both lungs have an equal chance of being affected. About 65 percent of bronchial tumors arise from the mainstream or first bronchi division, the section that is the first to be exposed as the smoke enters the lungs. At this point the smoke is at its greatest concentration, but particles smaller than 0.4 micrometer ($1 \ \mu m = 10^{-6}$ m) will settle out and become deposited, especially on ridges and bifurcations, just as the sediment in a river forms a delta.

Lung cancer begins with the inhalation of carcinogenic material. The paralyzed cilia cannot function to remove particles; thus tar is deposited on the respiratory passageways, and the tar and mucus that build up begin to attack the underlying epithelial tissues. Smoking alters the epithelium of the tracheobronchial tubes. Lesions consist of basal cell hyperplasia, with the normal epithelial cells being changed into more atypical cells that are sometimes indistinguishable from cancer cells. These atypical epithelial cells may be the site of cellular penetration of the constituents of smoke. Such lesions have been experimentally produced in smoking dogs, and some have ultimately developed into cancer.

This entire process takes time, usually 20 to 30 years. Early symptoms are a change in a chronic cough that the smoker may have had for years, fever, chills, an increase in sputum production, spitting of blood, or a wheeze. A worsening of these symptoms indicates that the bronchiole obstruction has increased and there is a loss of lung volume. Symptoms in the advanced stage include weight loss, anorexia, nausea, vomiting, and a generalized weakness. The longer the duration of symptoms, the more likely that the lesion is not surgically removable; survival time in these cases varies from 5 to 14 months after diagnosis. Thirty to fifty percent prove to be treatable; of those treated, about 20 percent survive for 5 years. In other words, if bronchogenic carcinoma is diagnosed in ten people, it is probable that six will die within 14 months, and two within 2 to 4 years, while the last two will most likely die during the fifth year.

It is becoming increasingly apparent that children who grow up in a home where both parents smoke are considerably more susceptible to lung cancer than children who grow up in smoke-free homes.

Cigar and pipe smokers also have a higher incidence of lung cancer than nonsmokers, but not as high as cigarette smokers. Pipe and cigar smoke is harder to inhale, but those who learn to tolerate it run the same risk as cigarette smokers. The pipe or cigar smoker is not immune to cancer, however, for this person's chance of developing oral cancer is similar to that of the cigarette smoker. If the tissues are exposed to the carcinogen, the same probabilities for the development of cancer arise. Death rates from cancer of the oral cavity, larnyx, pharnyx, and esophagus are approximately equal in users of pipes, cigars, and cigarettes. There is also an increase in cancer of the pancreas and urinary bladder among smokers. Pancreatic cancer in particular has increased markedly over the last 25 years.

EMPHYSEMA

Another lung ailment not well known at the turn of the century, but rapidly making its presence felt as a smoking-related disease, is emphysema. Emphysema is characterized by the rupture of alveolar (air sac) walls; this reduces the surface area in which gas exchange can take place. Large pockets separated by scar tissue are formed, elasticity of the air sacs is lost, and the emphysema victim finds it very difficult to release the air taken into the lungs.

Here is the emphysematic process in more detail. In a healthy individual, when air is taken into the lungs, the bronchial passageways expand. Gas exchange (carbon dioxide from the tissues is exchanged for oxygen) then takes place in lung capillaries that perfuse the millions of tiny air sacs throughout the lungs. Then the state gases are exhaled with the help of pressure exerted on the lungs by the rib cage and diaphragm and also by virtue of the elastic rebound of the air sacs and air passageways that were stretched upon inhalation. This process is normally a simple, automatic one, but in individuals with an accumulation of cigarette tars (or other particulate matter such as coal dust) in their bronchial tubes, air is allowed in by the normal expansion of the passageways and then is trapped because of the artificial blocking agent—the tar that has accumulated over a period of time. Pressure builds up in the blocked-off structures, and tissues rupture, making large areas out of many small ones. Scar tissue then develops, decreasing the elasticity of that area, so that it becomes even more difficult for the individual to exhale. It is not uncommon that an emphysema patient cannot blow out a match held only an inch or two in front of his or her mouth. Emphysema victims become barrel-chested as a result of labored exhalation, but gradually their increasing inability to exchange gases makes the remainder of their lives an agonizing effort.

In 1970, Hammond ended any remaining doubts concerning the relationship between smoking and emphysema. Beagles were taught to smoke cigarettes and were exposed to various levels of tar and nicotine as they smoked every morning and afternoon for 875 days. The results clearly showed that fibrosis of the lung increased with exposure to higher tar and nicotine levels, as did the incidence and severity of emphysema. No emphysema was detected in the nonsmoking dogs. Another classic study was conducted by Auerbach (1972), but this was an investigation of human lung sections from autopsies. They found that 90 percent of nonsmokers had no emphysema, 47 percent of pipe and cigar smokers had no emphysema, 13 percent who smoked less than one pack per day had no emphysema, and 0.3 percent who smoked more than one pack per day had no emphysema.

CHRONIC BRONCHITIS

Chronic bronchitis frequently precedes or accompanies emphysema. It is characterized by excessive mucus production in the bronchi of the lungs. The inflammation and hypersecretion of bronchial cells results in increased sputum, and eventually a cough develops to remove the material that would normally be removed by ciliary action. Although chronic bronchitis has been found in persons exposed to extreme air pollution, coal dust, etc., the incidence in smokers is twenty times that in nonsmokers and is greater in smokers who leave their cigarettes dangling from the lips between puffs.

SMOKING AND PREGNANCY

From the preceding discussions on the relationship between smoking and physiological functions, it should be obvious that a developing fetus would also be affected. It has been estimated that approximately one-third of the women of childbearing age in the United States are smokers. Although not definitely known, it is estimated that only 5 to 10 percent of these women quit smoking during pregnancy. Women who smoke while pregnant have a higher percentage of perinatal problems than women who don't smoke. Maternal cigarette smoking is clearly linked with obstetrical complications such as toxemia, ectopic pregnancy, abruptio placenta (in which the placenta detaches prematurely from the uterus), premature labor and delivery, miscarriages, and stillbirths. Mothers who smoke are also more likely to have low-birth-weight babies. The Surgeon General reports that 20 to 40 percent of low-weight births in the United States are attributable to maternal smoking during pregnancy (U.S. Public Health Service, 1989). Low birth weight is a reflection of intrauterine growth retardation, posing a greater risk to the newborn. Low-birth-weight babies have increased rates of mortality and morbidity and are at greater risk for cerebral palsy, malformations, and developmental disabilities (Schroeder, 1991). Growth retardation caused by cigarette smoking is greatest following use during the last 3 months of pregnancy (Bankston, 1988).

Research also indicates a link between smoking during pregnancy and cleft palate, leukemia, and cancer. Also, children whose mothers smoked heavily during pregnancy are more likely to have learning disabilities and behavioral problems. In addition, a fetus who was regularly exposed to the products of tobacco smoke is twice as likely to die of sudden infant death syndrome (SIDS) (Schroeder, 1991).

The effects discussed here are directly related to the number of cigarettes smoked daily, so the fewer smoked, the better. For instance, it is known that the more the mother smokes, the less the child will weigh at birth. Changing to low-tar cigarettes will not correct smoking-related problems in pregnancy, because the greater harm comes from nicotine, cyanide, and carbon monoxide rather than the tars. If a woman quits smoking by the fourth month, her risk of delivering a low-birth-weight baby is similar to that of a nonsmoker (DPO, 1987).

When a pregnant woman smokes, nicotine, carbon monoxide, cyanide, and other chemicals from cigarette smoke cross the placenta and enter the fetal bloodstream. At the same time, the oxygen supply of the placenta is reduced because of the nicotine effect on that tissue. This causes the increase in premature labor and delivery, stillbirths, and miscarriages. Nicotine that enters the fetal bloodstream affects the unborn child in the same way it affects the mother. It is a sympathomimetic drug and therefore serves as a stressor to the child either directly or indirectly through the reaction of the mother. The carbon monoxide that enters the bloodstream of the mother decreases the amount of oxygen available to the fetus, thus limiting tissue respiration and growth.

A fetal tobacco syndrome has been demonstrated in children of heavily smoking mothers. This syndrome includes retardation in growth, development, and behavior patterns and is attributed to the nicotine and cyanide of cigarette smoke.

PEPTIC ULCER

Statistical relationships have been established between smoking and the incidence of peptic ulcers. It has also been shown that smokers have a higher mortality rate from peptic ulcers than do nonsmokers. Nicotine has been found to inhibit pancreatic bicarbonate secretion, and it is believed that this mechanism is responsible for the potentiation of acute duodenal ulcer formation (U.S. Public Health Service, 1989).

REFERENCES

Auerbach, O. (1972). Relation of smoking and age to emphysema: Whole-lung section study. *New England Journal of Medicine*, 286(16):653–657.

Bankston, Karen. (1988). *Great Expectations: Information About Drugs and the Unborn Child*. Madison, Wis.: The Wisconsin Clearinghouse.

DHHS. (1987). *The Second Triennial Report to Congress*. Washington, D.C.: U.S. Department of Health and Human Services.

DPO (1987). *Drugs and Pregnancy: A Guide for Women*. Santa Barbara, Calif.: The Drug Program Office.

Hammond, E. C. (1970). Effects of cigarette smoking on dogs. *Archives of Environmental Health*. 21:740–753.

Schroeder, Cheryl. (1991). *Teratogens and the Teratogenic Effects of Substance Abuse in Pregnancy*. Laramie, Wyo.: Wyoming Perinatal Substance Abuse Prevention Program. [An Office of Substance Abuse Prevention (OSAP) grant.]

U.S. Public Health Service. (1989). *Annual Report from the Surgeon General on the Health Consequences of Smoking*. Bethesda, Md.: Department of Health and Human Services.

PERSPECTIVES ON PREVENTION

INTRODUCTION AND OVERVIEW

The War on Drugs requires an emphasis on prevention.

The history of drug use in the United States shows periods of high activity followed by periods of lower activity, somewhat like the ebb and flow of the ocean waves. The ocean is always there. The waves become smaller and larger depending upon many atmospheric factors. The decade of the 1980s has been described as a "tidal wave" of illicit drugs that flooded across the United States, Western Europe, and much of the third world. According to government officials, this wave of drug traffic and drug taking added up to the worst drug crisis the world has ever faced, felt even more forcefully than the drug crisis of the 1960s. While the decade of the 1990s has started out with some encouraging downturns in casual use among some segments of the population, others are continuing to use drugs at an accelerated pace, and the incidence of drug dependence has essentially remained the same. Parents are particularly concerned about the incidence of drug use that appears to be starting at younger and younger ages, dipping into the junior high and elementary schools of the nation. In addition, the drug problem has come home to many of the drug-exporting nations, and they are finding that they do not have the experience or expertise to deal with their new problem. For these reasons and many others, a counter action has been launched by private groups and government officials to try to stem the rising tide of drug abuse in this country and throughout the world.

GOVERNMENT INITIATIVES

The government has embarked on an aggressive campaign to reduce the availability of illicit drugs through diplomatic initiatives, vigorous law enforcement, measures to enhance prevention, education, and aid to research and treatment activities. The initiatives, entitled *A Federal Strategy for Prevention of Drug Abuse and Drug Trafficking* (White House, 1982) and *National Drug Control Strategy* (White House, 1989) set the tone and direction for the government's overall effort to reduce drug abuse during the 1980s. These initiatives remain in place for the 1990s, albeit somewhat changed to reflect a changing philosophy based on the knowledge gained from successes and failures of the 1980s. It remains to be seen whether the increased reliance on law enforcement will remain the primary focus of activity. There are some indications that the government initiatives are shifting more toward prevention strategies.

Prevention includes a wide range of programs that attempt to reduce both the supply of and the demand for alcohol and other drugs. Prevention focuses on nonusers, casual users, and to a somewhat lesser extent, alcoholics and drug-dependent individuals. Prevention programs may be directed at the individual and/or group level considering the particular susceptibilities to alcohol and other drug-related problems and the knowledge and attitudes that influence drug-using behavior. Prevention programs may also attend to the environment or the setting in which the drug-using behavior occurs and the specific institutions and systems, such as schools, religious institutions, or the community at large, that influence use and abstinence. Prevention programs use social policy approaches at the community, state, or national level that are aimed at reducing supply and demand. More important, prevention efforts are aimed at reducing the demand for alcohol and other drugs by focusing on the individuals who use these substances for any number of complex biological, environmental, or psychosocial reasons.

Prevention strategies must help individuals develop and maintain healthy lifestyles, behaviors, and attitudes and improve their knowledge of possible consequences of drug use. More specifically, these efforts must help individuals improve their self-perceptions by teaching them that they are competent, that they are an important part of something larger than themselves, and that their actions affect the direction and events of their lives. Efforts targeting individuals must also assist individuals in developing skills such as self-responsibility, judgment and decision making, communications, and self-discipline. In order to achieve maximum effectiveness, prevention strategies must cultivate these skills and self-perceptions in relation to the specific behaviors and consequences that they are trying to prevent, such as alcohol or other drug use, delinquency, and unwanted pregnancy. By developing these personal resources, individuals can improve their chances of living personally satisfying and enriching lives as they constructively confront complex, stressful life conditions. As a result, their perceived need for alcohol and other drugs can be reduced or eliminated.

Demand reduction strategies must also go beyond the individual and extend into the environment. Alcohol and other drug use within any society is influenced by many environmental factors. Prevention efforts focusing on the environment must enhance each community's capacity to mobilize organizational and legislative efforts to change these environmental factors when they impact negatively on the individual. Through advocating appropriate actions, policies, and procedures, prevention practitioners and public policy makers can shape the norms and systems of a culture in a way that is supportive of and conducive to healthier lifestyles.

Prevention must be understood in the context of a prevention-intervention–treatment continuum. Prevention, the initial phase of this continuum, targets both users and non-users through both supply and demand reduction strategies directed at the general public and more specific populations and high-risk groups and must address needs from the prenatal stage of life until death. Early intervention efforts work among persons identified through the school system, the family, the workplace, and the criminal justice or other social systems who may be experiencing problems with alcohol and other drugs. Early intervention strategies assess the nature and extent of those problems and refer them to the appropriate services to prevent the development of more serious problems in the future.

The final phase of this continuum consists of treatment strategies that include aftercare and ongoing support for recovery. These strategies attempt to reverse the disabling effects resulting from the misuse of or addiction to alcohol and other drugs in order to avoid further problems or disability. Because a relatively small percentage of the population consumes a disproportionately large amount of alcohol and other drugs, effective treatment strategies provided to this small but significant consumer population can greatly reduce the overall demand for these substances.

All three components of this continuum of care are designed to identify and respond to critical points in an individual's, a group's, or a society's life when an investment of limited resources will have a high likelihood of promoting the practice of healthy lifestyles and of changing destructive lifestyles in a positive direction. This comprehensive approach acknowledges the equal importance of prevention, intervention, and treatment strategies designed to reduce the demand for these substances as well as their supply.

REFERENCES

NASADAD. (1989). *Prevention in Perspective: A Statement of the National Association of State Alcohol and Drug Abuse Directors and the National Prevention Network.* Washington, D.C.: National Association of State Alcohol and Drug Abuse Directors and National Prevention Network. January.

White House. (1982). *A Federal Strategy for Prevention of Drug Abuse and Drug Trafficking.* Washington, D.C.: U.S. Government Printing Office, Office of Policy Development.

White House. (1989). *National Drug Control Strategy.* Washington, D.C.: U.S. Government Printing Office.

LAW ENFORCEMENT

INTRODUCTION

This section discusses the various laws that have been passed in the United States to help cope with the abuse of drugs. The drug laws now in force are a combination of federal, state, and local laws that have accumulated since the passage of the Harrison Act of 1914.

Restriction of drug use seems to arise from two basic motives. One is moral, for society has deemed most drug use morally wrong and hopes that the drug laws will protect the user from his or her own "weakness." The second motive is the protection of society from potential harm inflicted by a drug-using population. Human welfare demands at least minimum order, and laws furnish guidelines for socially accepted conduct. Even in small, close-knit societies there exist standards of behavior thought to be in the best interest of all the members and negative sanctions that can be brought against those who deviate from these standards. Societies composed of one ethnic or religious group (as in many European, Asian, and African nations) can rely on general acceptance of long-standing tradition to ensure compliance with expected behavior, and minimum force is needed to maintain order. However, in countries like the United States with diverse social customs, beliefs, and moral values, the maintenance of order has emerged as an immense problem. That may be an understatement in describing the current legal crisis in the United States, which recently surpassed South Africa and Russia and now leads the world in percentage of citizens incarcerated.

The prison population is growing at a record pace. As of June 1990, there were 691,623 state prisoners and 63,902 federal prisoners in the United States. Add those being held in local jails, and the number jumps to more than 1 million. Florida's prisons now hold so many inmates that to avoid further

218

overcrowding the state is barred by court order from increasing its prison population. But 1,000 new convicts—most of them sentenced on drug-related charges—enter state prisons every week, so an equal number of prisoners must be released. California has almost 100,000 people behind bars, and the state corrections department has more employees than any other state agency. New York's prisons hold 55,000 inmates, and the system is operating at 126 percent of capacity even though it has doubled the number of prison beds in 9 years. The vast majority of new inmates were sentenced under a New York City program called TNT, designed to crack down on drug sellers. Texas has had to limit the number of new inmates admitted to its state prisons, so county jails are being choked. The state was ordered to pay 12 counties more than $100 million reimbursement (Debate, 1990).

To make room for new inmates, most states have resorted to early parole for those who have served some time even though they freely admit that rehabilitation is not complete. Many prisoners serve only one-third of their time. The parole end of the system is equally overburdened, so the supervision of the early released, unrehabilitated prisoners is severely limited. The overcrowding has the states pouring billions of dollars into building more prisons even though it is unlikely that the added space will ever catch up with the demand. One often-cited reason for the drain on law enforcement resources is the overconcern with the small-time criminal. The antidrug efforts have incarcerated a lot of first-time offenders with felony counts. About 70 percent of the new inmates have been convicted on drug charges or crimes in which drugs were a factor. The growth in number of drug offenders is equal to the growth in number of all other serious crimes combined, including burglary, robbery, auto theft, murder, and technical parole violations where no drugs were involved.

LAW AND ORDER

While no one can rationally argue against the need for basic law and order, the very nature of law requires a strong coercive force to ensure compliance. When the legal apparatus is overburdened and out of balance, equality is hard to maintain. If order and socially acceptable conduct can be maintained only by the negative reinforcement of legal threats, a police state will tend to evolve. The formulation of an effective drug policy to reduce drug use without endangering personal liberty poses a major challenge for government today. An often-asked question is, "If drug laws are not going to stop the abuse of drugs, why have them?" The answer to this question depends on whether you view the laws as a total deterrent to drug use or as a helper in an effort by the whole society. It is obvious that law enforcement used alone has been a failure. Drug abuse has steadily increased despite stronger laws and increasingly severe penalties.

All too often the long-term drug user with emotional difficulties does not operate within the confines of the established mores or laws. The person who becomes involved in murder, robbery, or the use of drugs is usually convinced that he or she will not be detected by the legal authorities. Laws do have their part, but only a part, in the total effort of society to protect its members. Overemphasis on the law and on punishment has not worked and will not work. This approach gives a false sense of security to those who see it as the answer to a problem that, in reality, can be solved only by effective education and resultant changes in societal behavior. Society has to denormalize drug use from the perspective of the individual. Drug demand must be reduced through lack of desire for drugs. Prevention efforts, especially in the minority communities, are concentrating on this approach (see Chapter 4.5). As for punishment, it must fit the crime. Imposing the same sentence on small-time drug criminals that is imposed on ax murderers doesn't make much sense and will bury the prison system (Tackett, 1990).

The United States is under seige from criminal behavior. It seems that everyone is either a victim or a criminal, and if you have not already been a victim of violent crime, you live in fear of becoming one. This atmosphere has motivated the current popular "Let's get tough on crime" attitude, especially with respect to drug crimes. However, our zeal is producing counterproductive solutions. This is not a unique situation. Currently we are in a conservative crime-and-punishment mode, and recently passed laws reflect this mood. But the history of drug legislation in our country shows the ebb and flow of concern with the drug problem. History also shows that it is the concerns and fears of the people that change; the drug problem stays. The history of drug legislation also accents the reasons behind the passage of laws and the social conditions and scientific knowledge that prevailed at different times.

THE HISTORICAL BASIS OF DRUG LAWS

In 1906 the Federal Pure Food and Drug Act was passed. Although this law was not particularly effective, it did symbolize the concern for drug use in the country at that time and was an experiment in government control over consumed products. The Harrison Act of 1914 was designed to control the distribution of narcotic drugs within the United States. It provided for registration of the sales, dispensing, and transfer of narcotic drugs. Its modus operandi was the imposition of a commodity tax placed on production and importation and an occupational tax placed on those who sold or dispensed the drug. The law restricted the use of narcotic drugs to physicians and dentists in cases where it was medically advised, and all other uses were made illegal.

The restrictions against opiate use were strengthened in 1922 with the passage of the Narcotic Drug Import and Export Act, which made it illegal to possess any form of heroin in the United States. Opium for smoking or for use in heroin was also illegal. Under the terms of the law, the Commissioner of Narcotics was given control over the amount of crude opium and coca leaves (from which cocaine is derived) that would be needed to supply medical and scientific needs.

The stimulus for passage of these laws—the Harrison Narcotics Act and the Narcotic Drug Import and Export Act—came from evidence that an ever-increasing number of persons were becoming addicted to opium and its derivatives. There was a growing awareness that many legal patent medicines contained narcotics. Some patent medicines containing morphine were advertised as cures for opium addiction. Still fresh in the minds of legislators of that day were stories of Civil War casualties becoming addicted to morphine, Chinese opium smoking, and the realization that narcotic drugs could be purchased or diverted from pharmacies and wholesalers with relative ease.

History is replete with accounts of the social conditions in 1920 that instigated passage of our most famous antidrug law, the Volstead Act, which prohibited all nonmedical usage of alcoholic beverages. After a decade of colorful disregard it was repealed in 1933.

The liberal use of drugs by the middle class in the 1960s produced a swing in drug legislation back toward the disease theory, and simple use, even addiction, was not a felony. In 1966 the Narcotic Addict Rehabilitation Act viewed narcotics addiction as being symptomatic of a treatable disease and not of a criminal condition. However, the horror over drug experimentation and lifestyle differences of the "hippies" of the 1960s generation led to the passage of one of the most comprehensive drug laws in the our history, aptly named the Comprehensive Drug Abuse Prevention and Control Act. With significant amendments made on July 1, 1971, this act replaced more than 50 separate laws previously enacted. This law, as amended, accomplished the following:

1 Enforcement authority was taken out of the hands of the Treasury Department and given to the Bureau of Narcotics and Dangerous Drugs (BNDD). This direct control of drugs replaced the confusing attempts at control through excise taxes. Subsequently, the new Drug Enforcement Administration (DEA) was created to uniformly enforce drug laws.

2 It simplified the classification problem by creating five categories (schedules based not on chemical nature but on the potential for abuse and the need for medical use of the substance).

Schedule I lists those substances that have no recognized medical use and that have a high potential for abuse. Some popular examples are heroin, marijuana, peyote mescaline, LSD, DET, DMT, and THC. Prescription provisions do not apply to these drugs because their only legal use is research, not for the practice of medicine.

Schedule II is made up of those drugs formerly known as "class A narcotics" plus amphetamines. These drugs have some medical use but possess a high potential for abuse. Some examples are codeine, opium, morphine, Dilaudid, Dolophine (methadone), Demerol, Benzedrine, Dexedrine, Dexamyl, Bamadex, Ambar, Methedrine, Desoxyn, and cocaine. More recently included in this group of drugs of high abuse potential are amobarbital, pentobarbital, secobarbital, methaqualone, and Tuinal. To obtain these drugs, a written prescription is required, and the prescription cannot be refilled.

Schedule III is made up of drugs formerly known as "class B narcotics" as well as some nonnarcotic depressants and some nonamphetamine stimulants. These drugs have a moderate to high potential for abuse and are used medically. Some popular examples are paregoric, Empirin with codeine, ASA with codeine, Doriden Preludin, and Ritalin. A prescription is needed and may be refilled up to five times in 6 months.

Schedule IV contains drugs that have low potential for abuse and are used in medicine. Some examples are phenobarbital, chloral hydrate, paraldehyde, Equanil, and Miltown. A prescription is needed and may be refilled up to five times in 6 months.

Schedule V contains drugs formerly known as "exempt narcotics" such as syrups containing codeine and some OTC narcotic preparations. Prescription requirements are the same as for Schedules III and IV.

3 It established more stringent penalties for pushers, dealers, and those involved in organized crime, and placed lesser penalties on the user.

4 It provided for liberal appropriations of funds for research and education.

5 It provided for appropriations for several hundred more agents to aid in enforcement of the act.

6 It established a commission to study marijuana.

In retrospect, the Comprehensive Drug Abuse Prevention and Control Act was a liberal law, as it placed lesser penalties on users, a significant portion of whom were still part of the white middle class. The drug scene in the 1980s still saw a lot of middle class users, but the addiction problem shifted to minorities, and the violent crime associated with cocaine and crack allowed lawmakers to take a harder line. As might be expected, the drug laws passed in the 1980s reflect the fear of crime and the frustration with the seemingly out-of-control nature of the problem. New laws heaped more jail time on offenders, and lawmakers scrambled to keep pace with the flow of new drugs appearing on the scene.

The Anti-Drug Abuse Acts of 1986 and 1988 prohibited the production, marketing, and possession of harmful psychoactive drugs. The new laws stressed user accountability through increased penalties, loss of federal benefits, and forfeiture provisions. They also placed a greater emphasis on prevention, education, and treatment through increased funding and the expansion of programs and activities. The act also created the Office of National Drug Control Policy, to be headed by the Director of National Drug Control Policy.

The 1990 Anabolic Steroid Control Act made anabolic steroids controlled substances and increased penalties for illegally manufacturing, distributing, importing, or possessing them.

SUMMARY OF PERTINENT DRUG ABUSE LEGISLATION

1906 Pure Food and Drug Act required patent medicine labels to list all "dangerous substances" contained.

1912 Hague Conference—An agreement was reached that production and trade of opiates and opium must be limited to amounts necessary for medical and scientific use.

1914 Harrison Act (a tax law)—Persons authorized to handle or manufacture drugs were required to register, pay a fee, and keep records of all narcotics in their possession.

1919–1924 Establishment of public outpatient narcotic clinics—these clinics were opened in hopes of rehabilitating the addict and preventing his or her involvement with criminal drug distributors. In general they were badly managed; by 1924 all were forced to close by a moralizing and crusading press and the Federal Bureau of Narcotics. Illicit narcotics then became the addict's only supply.

1920   Volstead Act—Nonmedical use of alcoholic beverages was prohibited.

1922   Behrman case—Prevented physicians from legally supplying drugs to addicts for self-administration. Implied that addicts must be isolated and hospitalized. Led eventually to the Public Health Service hospitals in Lexington, Kentucky (1935), and Fort Worth, Texas (1938).

1922   Jones-Miller Act (Narcotics Drug Import and Export Act)— Established firm penalties for violation of the Harrison Act.

1924   Prohibition of manufacture of heroin in the United States.

1925   The Supreme Court ruled that a physician may administer narcotics to allay withdrawal symptoms if done in good faith. The Federal Bureau of Narcotics ignored this ruling, punishing physicians who gave narcotics to addicts.

1933   Repeal of the prohibition of alcohol.

1937   Marijuana Tax Act—Brought marijuana under stern controls similar to those regulating the use of opiates.

1951   Boggs Act—Imposed graduated sentences with mandatory minimum sentences for narcotic drug offenses. Subsequent to the passage of the Boggs Act, many state legislatures enacted "little Boggs acts."

1956   Narcotic Drug Control Act—Even more punitive than the Boggs Act, it did, however, differentiate among drug possession, drug sale, and drug sale to minors. Medical use of heroin was prohibited.

1956   All existing heroin supplies in the United States were surrendered to the government.

1963   The Supreme Court (*Robinson v. California*) declared that addiction is a disease, not a crime. Legally an addict cannot be arrested for being "high" (internal possession) but can be arrested for external possession and sale.

1966   Narcotic Addict Rehabilitation Act—Viewed narcotics addiction as being symptomatic of a treatable disease and not of a criminal condition.

1966   Drug Abuse Control Amendments—Laws became effective whereby sedatives, stimulants, and tranquilizers came under tighter controls. Hallucinogens were specifically added to the laws in 1966. Enforcement became the responsibility of the Bureau of Drug Abuse Control of the Food and Drug Administration.

1968   The Bureau of Narcotics and Dangerous Drugs (Department of Justice) was given responsibility on a federal level for the entire drug problem. The Bureau of Narcotics was removed from the Department of the Treasury, and the Bureau of Drug Abuse Control was removed from the Food and Drug Administration; the two bureaus combined.

1969 Operation intercept—An attempt to block import of marijuana at the Mexican border, it coincided with the increased use of "harder" drugs throughout the country.

1969–1971 Controls were "tightened" at the federal level and foreign governments were urged to apply firmer restrictions with regard to manufacture and export of drugs.

1970 Comprehensive Drug Abuse Prevention and Control Act of 1970—Replaced previous acts for control of narcotics, marijuana, sedatives, and stimulants and placed their control under the Department of Justice. Drugs are classified in five schedules according to their potential for abuse and therapeutic usefulness. First-time illegitimate possession of any drug in the five schedules is considered a misdemeanor, and penalties are reduced. Provisions are made for rehabilitation, education, and research. House search ("no-knock" law) was legalized.

1972 Drug Abuse Office and Treatment Act—Brought about by the increasing drug use by U.S. troops in Vietnam and increased use in the United States, this law established the Special Action Office for Drug Abuse Prevention (SAODAP) to coordinate the nine federal agencies involved in drug abuse activities. With emphasis on treatment and rehabilitation programs, SAODAP develops federal strategies for all drug abuse efforts other than drug traffic prevention. Also detailed in the legislation was the establishment of the National Institute on Drug Abuse (NIDA), which took place in April 1974. NIDA will continue the programs established by SAODAP.

1986 The Anti-Drug Abuse Act prohibiting production, marketing, and possession of harmful psychoactive drugs covers virtually every aspect of the federal effort to combat the use of illegal drugs.

1988 The Anti-Drug Abuse Act—The new law, like its predecessor, the Anti-Drug Abuse Act of 1986, prohibited production, marketing, and possession of harmful psychoactive drugs. Key features of the 1988 act include greater emphasis on prevention, education, and treatment through increased funding and expansion of programs and activities, and user accountability through increased penalties such as loss of federal benefits and forfeiture provisions. The act created the Office of National Drug Control Policy, to be headed by the Director of National Drug Control Policy—the so-called drug czar.

1990 The Anabolic Steroid Control Act—Made anabolic steroids controlled substances and increased penalties for illegally manufacturing, distributing, importing, or possessing them. The maximum penalty for trafficking in steroids is 5 years in prison and a $250,000 fine, which may be doubled for a second offense. Doctors and pharmacists who illegally supply steroids face that punishment as well as the loss of their licenses to prescribe and dispense drugs. The law also authorizes federal agents to seize profits and assets from trafficking in steroids. Possession of steroids carries penalties of up to 1 year in prison and at least a $1,000 fine.

REFERENCES

Debate (1990). *USA Today*, Wednesday, Nov. 7, p. A8.
Tackett, M. (1990). *Chicago Tribune*, Friday, Nov. 9, p. A22.

PREVENTION STRATEGIES

PREVENTION AND PROMOTION

Effective prevention strategies include general promotion designed to attract people to prevention by showcasing its positive effects within the community and the respective target populations. Its basic strategy is to heighten public awareness, as a catalyst for increasing public support, commitment, and involvement. Effective prevention strategies are comprehensive, recognizing the interrelatedness of the use and misuse of all psychoactive substances—including alcohol, tobacco, over-the-counter medications, prescription medications, and inhalants, as well as all illicit drugs. Ideally, programming combines many strategies, including presentation of information, education, development of social competency skills, presentation of healthy alternatives, law enforcement community resource development, and social policy.

Effective prevention strategies target multiple populations, addressing all segments of the population, including all age groups and social classes. They also take into account the unique and special needs of the community by targeting special populations, such as the elderly, high-risk groups, and cultural, ethnic, and gender-specific groups. Within the community a collaborative effort involves religious institutions; schools; governmental bodies; public and private sectors; community groups; law enforcement agencies; the judicial system; business and industry; media, service, and social organizations; and health delivery systems, including alcohol and drug abuse agencies involved in providing referral, treatment, and aftercare services.

Prevention targets both users and non-users through strategies aimed at reducing both supply and demand. Its goals are

- To initiate a process among the general public that promotes overall health and wellness

• To deter the illegal use of alcohol and other drugs through enforcement and other appropriate sanctions
• To support abstinence as a legitimate choice
• To delay the age of onset of use of alcohol and other drugs
• To avoid the development of problems related to the use of alcohol and drugs

EDUCATIONAL INTERVENTION

The recent federal initiatives regarding the prevention of drug abuse have highlighted education as the primary vehicle for change, and, more than ever before, education must be directed toward behavioral change, especially with regard to decision making and assertiveness. Education is critical, for it gives people the ability to alter beliefs and attitudes on the basis of what they know. Knowledge about the effects of drugs, their mechanisms of action, and the influences of emotions on drug-taking behavior form the basis of drug education. However, just as important as knowledge about drugs is knowledge of self; self-concept and other personality factors can help students discover their resources and strengthen their decision-making skills. When students make their own decisions and practice them in the safety of a classroom environment, they are more likely to incorporate those skills into their everyday lives. Teachers enable individual learning and self-empowerment by offering experiences that are individually applied and processed.

The Role of Drug Education

Learning is an essential part of behavior. It is most critical in developing motivation for behavior, as humans have the ability to alter beliefs and attitudes on the basis of what they know. Knowledge about the benefits of health can increase a person's motivation to be healthy and drug-free. Knowledge about the mechanisms of action of drugs and the influence of one's emotions on the decision to try drugs can promote a greater understanding of the host–agent interaction. Knowledge of self, that is, self-concept, and other personality factors can help the client discover his or her own solutions to problems. Knowledge of behavior in general and progress in developing skills can allow students greater attainment of learning objectives.

Drug education enhances the development of healthy behavior by

1 Creating awareness
2 Changing attitudes
3 Promoting understanding
4 Aiding in the development of new skills (Blocher, 1982; Girdano & Dusek, 1988)

The primary emphasis of drug education is on drug misuse. Americans are a drug-misusing people—from the thousands of over-the-counter drugs used to treat real or imagined symptoms to the psychoactive drugs used in search of increased performance, sociability, coping ability, or pleasure. The most effective drug education strategy seems to be a combination of social influence and personal and social skills training approaches. These approaches to drug education are designed to

1 Supply information about a particular drug and what it can do and is unable to do. This information is designed to reduce students' motivation to use drugs through strategies to increase the perceived risks drugs pose to relationships, roles, or status (Hawkins et al., 1986).

2 Analyze motivations, separating underlying need fulfillment from socially acceptable excuses. There is evidence that students who began smoking in a social situation often knowingly entered the situation with that specific intention (Friedman et al., 1985). Having the skills to withstand social pressures is important, but not wanting to withstand them is more important.

3 Provide students with feedback concerning drug use by their peers, thus correcting the misperception that "everybody does it." Students are made aware of the social pressures to use drugs to which they are likely to be exposed, and are taught specific skills (e.g., refusal skills) with which to resist these pressures. Students often begin smoking, drinking, or other drug use after repeatedly observing parents, siblings, or other esteemed role models doing so or because of persuasive appeals by peers or advertisers.

4 Provide the stimulus for students to clarify their values with regard to health, risk-taking behavior, and drugs so that rational decision-making processes can be developed.

5 Teach coping skills. Using tobacco, alcohol, and other drugs may be a way of coping with tension and anxiety, particularly social anxiety. The personal and social skills prevention models combine training in the use of techniques to resist social influences to smoke, drink, or other drugs with intervention strategies designed to improve general life skills and focus indirectly on modifying psychological factors that may be conducive to substance abuse. These include increasing self-esteem, learning drug-free coping strategies for anxiety and frustration, reducing tension by using relaxation techniques, gaining cognitive coping skills, and enhancing interpersonal skills such as the ability to initiate social interactions, assertiveness, the ability to make requests, and the effective expression of feelings and opinions.

The extent to which individuals are susceptible to various influences may be related to their personal characteristics. Individuals with low self-esteem, low self-confidence, and a weak sense of personal autonomy appear most likely to succumb to social influences (Bandura, 1969; Rotter, 1972). Based on this hypothesis, some researchers (e.g., Botvin & Eng, 1982; Hawkins et al., 1985) have hypothesized that susceptibility to substance abuse may be decreased by using more broadly based intervention approaches that help develop personal characteristics opposite to those associated with that susceptibility.

REFERENCES

Bandura, A. (1969). *Principles of Behavior Modification*, New York: Holt, Rinehart and Winston, p. 677.

Blocher, Donald H. (1980). Some implications of recent research in social and developmental psychology for counseling practice. *The Personnel and Guidance Journal*, 58(5):334–336.

Botvin, G. J., and Eng, A. (1982). The efficacy of a multi-component approach to the prevention of cigarette smoking. *Preventive Medicine*, 11:199–211.

Friedman, L. S., Lichenstein, E., and Biglan, A. (1985). Smoking onset among teens. *Addictive Behaviors*, 10(1):1–14.

Girdano, D. A., and Dusek, D. E. (1988). *Changing Health Behavior*. Scottsdale, Ariz.: Gorsuch Scarisbrick.

Goleman, Daniel. (1984). Herbert Benson on the faith factor. *American Health*, 3(3):48–53.

Hawkins, J. D., Lishner, D. M., and Catalano, R. F., Jr. (1985). Childhood predictors and prevention of adolescent substance abuse. In C. L. Jones and R. J. Battjes (Eds.), *Etiology of Drug Abuse: Implications for Prevention*. NIDA Research Monograph No. 56. DHHS Pub. (ADM) 85-1335. Washington, D.C.: Superintendent of Documents, U.S. Government Printing Office, pp. 75–126.

Hawkins, J. D., Lishner, D. M., Catalano, R. F., Jr., and Howard, M. D. (1986). Childhood predictors of adolescent substance abuse: towards an empirically grounded theory. *Journal of Children in Contemporary Society*, 18(1/2):1–65.

Hay, Louise. (1984). *Heal Your Body*. Farmingdale, N.Y.: Coleman.

Houston, Jean. (1982). *The Possible Human*. Los Angeles: J. P. Tarcher.

Kriegel, Robert J., and Kriegel, Marilyn H. (1984). *C Zone: Peak Performance under Pressure*. New York: Doubleday.

Leventhal, H., and Cleary, P. (1981). Review of the research and theory in behavioral risk modification. *Psychology Bulletin*, 88:370–379.

McKay, M., Davis, M., and Fanning, P. (1981). *Thoughts and Feelings: The Art of Cognitive Stress Intervention*. Richmond, Calif.: New Harbinger.

Novaco, R. W. (1978). Anger and coping with stress. In J. Foreyt and D. Rathzen (Eds.), *Cognitive Behavior Therapy*. New York: Plenum.

Ostrander, Sheila, and Schroeder, Lynn (with Nancy Ostrander). (1978). *Superlearning*. New York: Delta.

Proghoff, Ira. (1980). *The Practice of Process Meditation*. New York: Dialogue House.

Ray, Sondra. (1982). *I Deserve Love*. Millbrae, Calif.: Les Femmes.

Rotter, J. B. (1972). Generalized expectancies for internal versus external control of reinforcement. In J. B. Rotter, J. E. Chance, and E. J. Phares (Eds.), *Applications of a Social Learning Theory of Personality*. New York: Holt, Rinehart, and Winston, pp. 260–295.

Shainess, Natalie. (1984). *Sweet Suffering: Woman as Victim*. New York: Bobbs-Merrill.

Simonton, O. Carl, Matthews-Simonton, S., and Creighton, James. (1978). *Getting Well Again*. Los Angeles: J. P. Tarcher.

Zdenek, Marilee. (1983). *The Right-Brain Experience*. New York: McGraw-Hill.

EARLY INTERVENTION

The key to controlling drug trafficking and drug abuse is to reduce the demand for the drug and to divert the interest and attention of young people from the "glamor" of the drug culture. One of the newest government initiatives is concentrating on denormalizing drug use so that it will no longer be the "thing to do."

Effective prevention strategies focus on early detection and remedial action among persons identified through the school system, the family, the workplace, and the criminal justice system or other social systems. These efforts are designed to identify those individuals or families who may be experiencing alcohol and other drug-related problems, to assess the nature and extent of those problems, and to refer them to the appropriate services to prevent the development of more severe problems in the future.

RISK FACTORS

The earlier an intervention is made, the less likely the individual will be to proceed toward drug abuse. If prevention of drug abuse is accepted as a goal of drug education programs, then the causative factors in abuse must be a target of the program. It has been well documented by Chein (1967), Smith and Gay (1972), and other respected sociologists, psychologists, and drug researchers that drug abusers do indeed share certain backgrounds and personality characteristics. These factors have been summarized by Hawkins et al. (1985). As with the risk factors for heart disease and other illness, these are characteristics that have been found to be associated with a greater than average chance of developing the problem. Individuals with one or more of these risk factors do not, of course, automatically become substance abusers. A brief review of the known risk factors, however, provides a useful backdrop for discussing the basis for prevention strategies.

A family history of drug use, especially alcoholism, is highly associated with substance abuse. Research has established a link between drinking problems in the family and the developing adolescent or young adult abusing alcohol and other drugs. Children from families in which other close family members have a criminal history are also more likely to abuse alcohol and other drugs. Problems of parental direction or discipline is another important factor. Unclear and/or inconsistent parental rules for behavior, inconsistent parental reactions to their children's behavior, unusual permissiveness, lax supervision of children's behavior or, conversely, excessively severe discipline, and constant criticism and an absence of parental praise or approval have all been found to be associated with higher rates of children's drug abuse. Parental drug use or parental attitudes approving use are also associated with children later becoming drug abusers. Parents serve as models for their children's behavior in many ways. Those children whose parents smoke, drink, or abuse drugs are more likely to do so than those whose parents do not.

Children whose friends (and/or brothers and sisters) use drugs are much more likely to use them than those whose peers do not. Having friends who are drug users is among the strongest predictors of drug use. Initiation into drug use is usually through friends.

Performance in school is also among the strongest predictors of drug use. Children who fail in school in their mid to late elementary school years are more likely to become adolescent drug abusers than those who do not. Further, adolescents who are not interested in school academic achievement are more likely to use drugs than those who are. Children who abuse drugs are generally children who feel alienated and strongly rebellious, are at odds with the dominant social values during early adolescence, misbehave in school, have a low sense of social responsibility, and fight or engage in other types of aggression. The earlier the child begins to drink or use other drugs, the greater the likelihood he or she will later develop a drug problem. The use of drugs before age 15 greatly increases the likelihood of later drug use.

The person who has little guidance in goal setting or decision making, has a poor self-concept and low self-esteem, and does not know how to cope is seen as being at high risk for chemical dependence. He or she is thus highly susceptible to external influence, especially that of peers. This person, like any other, has needs to be met—physiological, safety, belongingness, and self-esteem—but his or her ability to fulfill them is critically reduced. Such individuals resort to temporary fulfillment of these needs by submitting to (perhaps even happily accepting) peer group pressure in order to "buy" friendship or escaping from the situation rather than solving it. This behavior results in increased personal distress, fewer social supports, and even fewer personal resources and skills for coping with emotional distress or practical problem situations.

These individuals find it difficult to manage stress and often have drug dependencies or other behavior and health problems. Low self-concept may manifest itself as sensitivity to criticism, a tendency to blame others, over-responsiveness to flattery and attention, a hypercritical attitude, feelings of persecution, fear of competing with others, and timidity or shyness. The childhood environment that produces guilt, inferiority, learned helplessness, and self-consciousness blocks, or at least diminishes, the opportunity to attain an adequate feeling of self-worth. It is often found that a primary need of these children is enhancement of self-concept. The enhancement of self-concept contributes to the ability to cope in a healthy manner in all situations and the ability to change and grow.

INFLUENCES OF EARLY DEVELOPMENT

As people grow up they normally pass through the developmental pattern described by Erik Erickson: gaining basic trust (vs. mistrust) by age 1, autonomy (vs. shame) by ages 2 to 3, initiative (vs. guilt) by ages 4 to 5, industry (vs. inferiority) between 6 and 11, identity (vs. role confusion) between 12 and 18, intimacy (vs. isolation) between 16 and 25, generativity (vs. stagnation) between 20 and 40, and ego integrity (vs. despair) from 40 on. Those who do not succeed in learning the developmental pattern at any of these stages are blocked from the successful completion of the following stage(s).

As young people normally grow and develop, they form a concept of who they are, which has been termed the "real self." They also form a concept of what they should be, how they should behave, and what they want to be. This is termed the "ideal self." Their self-concept is constructed from the perceptions of how they are, how they would like to be, and how they ought to be. These beliefs evolve through personal observations and comparisons and by accepting and believing conclusions drawn by others. The judgment of and treatment by significant others determine, to a great extent (especially in childhood), how the individual sees herself or himself. If the real self is not congruent with the ideal self, anxiety and threat are experienced; when behavior is in opposition to how the ideal self would behave, guilt is evoked.

A healthy concept of self ensures confidence, worth, security, spontaneity, and other descriptors of Maslow's or Rogers' actualized person. Some use the terms "self-concept" and "self-esteem" interchangeably, but it would seem that total self-concept consists of many different components, each being necessary to complete the journey to ideal self. The components are like stepping stones on a path—if one is missing, the journey is more difficult. Three of these components—self-awareness, self-love, and self-worth—might be considered more "secondary" or inherent resources, while the others might be considered "earned" resources that are aptly applied to specific situation (Girdano & Dusek, 1988).

Self-awareness is accepting that you have an impact in this world, that your presence and actions can and do influence others and vice versa. This does not mean that you are *responsible* for the reactions of others—they may choose to feel enhanced or hurt by your presence, and that is their choice. There are some parts of the self-concept that are inborn, and *self-worth* is one of them. It was a basic tenet of the founders of the United States that we are all created equal. No one personal entity is worth more or less than any other human on this earth. We all have the basic rights to life, liberty, and the pursuit of happiness. This is an instance in which the written laws of the land parallel spiritual doctrine. We come into this world and travel through it with a worth that is equal to that of any other; nothing can make one person worth more than another—not wealth, or beauty, or charisma. Conversely, no horrible deed can reduce the basic human worth of a person. The only thing that reduces worth is the mind of the individual—the mind that assumes from life experiences that the person is worth less than the 100 percent he/she inherited at birth.

Just as with self-worth, there is an inborn capacity for *self-love*—it is not something one earns from others over a lifetime of struggle. Unfortunately, many people believe that they have to earn self-love through sacrifice and punishment of self to please others, which makes the process one of learning to love one's self again. Self-love is compassion for one's self in all situations, through all emotions and all actions. This compassion is relearned through letting go of judgments that one accepts from outside the self—judgments of self that are learned from parents, friends, teachers, society. Part of the relearning of self-love is self-forgiveness, which is based on the basic belief that everyone does the best they can with the skills they have at the time. This is not to say that one cannot learn more effective ways to behave, but it is an acceptance of "this is who I am, and this is the way I behaved in that situation. I'm learning to do it differently, but no matter how I do it and how it turns out, I love myself." This reflects the basic tenet that there is a positive intent to all behavior. In looking for the positive intent, the judgment regarding negative intent is stopped.

Self-esteem is probably the most familiar component of self-concept, and many people use the two terms interchangeably. However, self-esteem is a compassion for self that is *earned through one's actions* (unlike self-worth and self-love, which are inherent). Since self-esteem is an earned component, it comes from success. Many earn self-esteem through their academic accomplishments or through sports or doing their job well (whether their job is building computers or managing a household). Self-esteem that is rewarded internally is lasting, and it enhances the other self-concept components. Self-esteem that is earned from the outside can be taken away at any time, which can be devastating to the individual. If a child has earned esteem from the outside, the desire for the reward and attention from others that it brings becomes insatiable, and if that reward is removed or reversed (which happens from time to time within all relationships), there are feelings of powerlessness and anger due to being powerless. It again follows that internal resources are truer and more helpful for enhancement of self-concept than pats on the back from others.

Self-esteem is built on some basic components, beginning with *honesty*, especially with one's self—telling one's self the truth and seeking the highest truth for one's life. A second component is having the *integrity to be responsible for one's perception of what is real*, so that when something happens in that reality, the individual takes the responsibility of knowing that this is the way he/she perceives it. Life is truly a perceptual experience: how you see it is exactly how it is for you.

Self-confidence has been described as the earned or learned ability to cope with your perceptions of the world (your reality). Each individual sets up his or her perception of the world and then handles that perception in a confident or not-so-confident manner. Success in this particular component comes from seeing planned outcomes develop into real outcomes, using past resources, trust, hope, and courage. Self-confidence starts out in youth as a small spiral and continues as a larger and larger spiral upward with each success in one's world.

The final component of self-concept is *self-respect*. One definition of self-respect is the ability to honor, or appreciate, one's emotional nature; to express fear, happiness, anger, love, joy appropriately when it is felt. This does not mean "dumping" these emotions on someone else, but expressing them when the need is felt. Holding back from expressing an emotion not only blocks its energy, it also shows lack of self-respect. When you respect who you are, it follows that expressing your emotions is natural and appropriate. Low self-concept blocks energy and can lead to depression and/or anger. Both of these emotions are coping mechanisms that often lead to substance abuse. Depression is the coping mechanism used to defend one's self psychologically, as if by trying to deny the situation. Depression is a fear response—the mind blows the situation out of proportion, assigning it a life-or-death importance.

Perhaps the basic reason for anger is not getting what we expect or want—a violation of equity theory, which is the basis for our sense of justice. It is not the anger arousal itself that usually causes chronic tension, but rather the conflict over expressing the anger. Suppression of hostility is the bottled-up response in some situations to years of shaming, to holding certain disabling loyalties, or to boundary invasion. Unfortunately, shaming is an effective way to keep children in line, to make them behave in an other-centered manner. Children are shamed into being quiet, not talking back, not being messy, and so on, for the sake of the parents and others around them. Children need the approval of others and fear loss of self to such an extent that when they are shamed they may truly feel that they are so bad that no one could possibly love them. The need to please is fertile ground for forming unhealthy loyalties and allowing boundary invasion and other behaviors and conditions that feed the feelings of inferiority and low self-concept.

Research on children with the myriad of problems discussed in the previous section (risk factors) shows the same psychosocial characteristics exhibited by individuals in substance abuse treatment. Substance abuse problems develop when individuals with these psychosocial risk factors (lower self-esteem, higher levels of depression, anger, and anxiety) live in a sociocultural milieu where drugs are available and their use is sanctioned. These psychosocial risks need to be considered in early intervention. Substance abuse problems are expressions of emotions and unmet psychophysiological needs, or they may be just the opposite—"successful" coping mechanisms that turn out to be effectual coping attempts. Operating from the premise that many substance abuse problems are manifestations of emotional distress, maladaptive coping, or, at the very least, strongly reinforced habits leads us to take a different view of potential solutions.

Health behavior change theory and techniques are being developed in numerous disciplines, using prevention and treatment techniques. Successful programs are finding that the primary principles are

1 Individuals must be codesigners of their programs.

2 Individuals will work harder to achieve the positive and will move toward something they want more efficiently and effectively than they will eliminate that which is unwanted.

3 Individuals must be "ready" to change behavior. This readiness results from having the necessary resources and eliminating the blocks to success, which are usually the risk factors.

Techniques that focus only on negative characteristics and shortcomings may reinforce the individual's low self-esteem and depression. The programs that build on the strengths integrate educational and self-improvement programs that use education, behavioral intervention, and counseling worked into a general early intervention model that can be used in a variety of clinical and educational settings.

EARLY INTERVENTION AND EDUCATION

Drug abuse or dependence usually results in emotional difficulties that require supplemental treatment for the abuser and perhaps for the family of the abuser. Drug education can do little to directly help the individual who is already a

TABLE 18
TEENAGE DRUG AND ALCOHOL ABUSE IS A TREATABLE PROBLEM

You may never see your child drinking or using drugs; however, the following symptoms could mean your adolescent has an alcohol or drug problem.

☐ Problems getting along with family members.
☐ Moody, disrespectful, withdrawn.
☐ Very poor school performance, inability to concentrate, excessive truancy, or has dropped out.
☐ Suspension or expulsion from school for truancy or other reasons.
☐ Seriously disturbed sleeping or eating habits.
☐ Running away from home or school.
☐ Trouble with police or other authority figures.
☐ Frequently changing friends or hanging out with the "party crowd."
☐ Lying and other inappropriate behavior.
☐ Little or no family communication.

confirmed drug abuser, but good drug education can sensitize the general population to causative factors and the need for treatment. In addition, because teachers see students daily, they can be instrumental in identifying potential problems. Following the model established by the government in the ''troubled employee approach'' to early identification of those with drinking problems, teachers can identify those students who seem troubled. A teacher can take the following steps after a troubled student has been identified:

1 Identify whether any observable behaviors might be the result of drug involvement.

2 Request a conference with the parents.

3 Plan and schedule an intervention meeting at which the student, parents, and other concerned individuals are present.

4 State the specific change that is expected, refer the student for chemical evaluation or professional help, and provide support for change (or in the case of no change, state what further actions will be taken).

SUMMARY

Prevention strategies focus on early detection and appropriate intervention, including education. There is a set of common risk factors that help predict drug-related problems. These factors include social, environmental, and economic aspects as well as personal attitudes and behaviors. Children from dysfunctional families where discipline, expression of affection, supervision, and communication are poor and where alcohol and other drugs are abused by family members are especially vulnerable to drug problems. Low self-concept is one of the most basic risk factors here. It develops when a child is not given the necessary support for healthy growth and development. Children with low self-concept lead lives fraught with failure and are directed from a need to belong and conform. Education can help at-risk individuals by supporting their emotional growth, providing healthy living skills, and providing clear and truthful information on the risks of drug taking.

REFERENCES

Chein, I. (1967). *The Road to H: Narcotics, Delinquency and Social Policy*. New York: Basic Books.

Girdano, D. A., and Dusek, D. E. (1988). *Changing Health Behavior*. Scottsdale, Ariz.: Gorsuch and Scarisbrick.

Hawkins, J. D., Lishner, D. M., and Catalano, R. F., Jr. (1985). Childhood predictors of adolescent substance abuse. In C. L. Jones and R. J. Battjes (Eds.), *Etiology of Drug Abuse: Implications for Prevention*. NIDA Research Monograph No. 56. DHHS Pub. (ADM) 85-1335. Washington, D.C.: Superintendent of Documents, U.S. Government Printing Office, pp. 75–126.

Smith, D. E., and Gay, G. R. (1972). *It's So Good Don't Even Try It Once*. Englewood Cliffs, N.J.: Prentice-Hall.

4.5

MULTICULTURAL PREVENTION PROGRAMS

Drug abuse cuts across all boundaries of race.

Drug abuse is a national emergency that cuts across all boundaries of race. In order to develop culturally sensitive educational, prevention, and treatment programs, NIDA and other Department of Health and Human Services (DHHS) groups are exploring the incidence and prevalence of substance abuse among cultural minorities. Present knowledge of drug and alcohol use and abuse patterns among America's ethnic minority populations is sparse. Much of what we know is from limited studies among youth, and little is known about use and abuse patterns among ethnic minority adults, the elderly, refugees, the homeless, pregnant women, and families. However, what is known provides a portrait of a very serious and complex set of problems.

The United States is a multicultural society, which implies the need for more than one type of prevention program. Multicultural programs use prevention material that has "cultural relevance" for racial minority communities. Ideally "multicultural program" should refer to a design rather than to a program for one or more ethnic minority groups. However, for the present it denotes prevention activities specifically designed for a target minority group. Even with this difficulty, a great deal of progress in the area of prevention has been made in ethnic minority communities. Some very exciting and innovative programs have been developed and are currently being implemented. Yet it must be remembered that the situation confronting ethnic minority communities is fundamentally different from that found in white middle-class communities. Prevention programs, in addition to being sensitive to the community's culture and values, must also address basic survival needs, such as adequate housing, jobs, health care, and essential social services. Further, it must be remembered that there is great diversity within and among the ethnic minority groups and that one finds in each the full range of differences in customs and traditions, language usage, attitudes about assimilation into the mainstream, political activism, social assertiveness, and many other variables. Yet there is the overriding commonality of a sense of ethnic group-belonging, which is almost daily strengthened through contact with other group members (Harvey, 1985).

SUBSTANCE ABUSE PREVENTION FOR NATIVE AMERICANS

In the large body of literature about Native Americans and alcohol, there are many questions facing clinicians, educators, and community leaders regarding regulation, intervention, therapies, and outcomes. One that remains unresolved is the question concerning the genetic susceptibility of Native Americans to alcoholism that has long been postulated. Recent evidence suggests that a susceptibility to alcoholism may be transmitted genetically (Petrakis, 1985). This transmission is not racially linked but rather appears to be gender-linked within families. While the epidemiology of abuse among the Native Americans is clearly in excess of that of other races and the general population, genetic susceptibility is not the only issue. There are Native Americans who appear able to use alcohol safely. These social drinkers are able to handle alcohol and function normally, but there have been few studies to determine how it is that a majority of men and women in most American Indian communities manage not to abuse alcohol. Study of these social drinkers could yield important data on the impact that learning, behavior, perceptions, and values have on drinking behavior (Mail & Wright, 1989).

While abuse of other substances continues to increase among Native Americans, alcohol remains the substance of choice. By their ninth birthday, 12 percent of American Indian children regularly drink beer, wine, or distilled spirits; 97 percent use alcohol by the eleventh grade (Oetting & Goldstein, 1980). In any 2-month period, 35 percent of American Indian high school students have been drunk. This compares to 21 percent of non-Indian high school students (Oetting et al., 1980a). One important difference between the two cultures soon emerges, however. Among adults, the proportion who have gotten high or drunk during the last 2 months is 67 percent of Native American seniors and 45 percent of non-Native Americans. Only about one-fourth of the non-Native American seniors had been drunk enough to stagger, fall, or black out, whereas 46 percent of Native American seniors had been this drunk (Oetting et al., 1980a). Heavy drinking is the main reason that about one in two American Indian students never finishes high school (Royce, 1981).

In an extensive study on American Indian substance use and abuse, Oetting et al. (1980a, 1980b), found that alcohol was clearly the predominantly abused drug; marijuana, cigarettes, inhalants, stimulants, and cocaine ranked among the next most used drugs. Some of their more distinct findings in a comparative format show that 75 percent of American Indian youths beyond the sixth grade have tried marijuana, compared with 31 percent of non-Indian youths; 30 percent have tried inhalants, compared with 10 percent of non-Indians; 1 in 20 is exposed to heroin, compared with 1 in 200 for non-Indians; and American Indian youths may be exposed to stimulants, cocaine, sedatives, and tranquilizers at younger ages than non-Indians.

A poll of thousands of Native American teenagers shows that young people take drugs "to feel better" and "to get along with friends." Self-esteem and social skills are inversely correlated with drug use. Youths concurrently abusing several drugs had abysmal concepts of themselves and were socially dysfunctional (Oetting & Goldstein, 1980). As is true for any group, there are no universal and all-encompassing explanations for drug and alcohol abuse among Native Americans. Likewise, there is a significant lack of specific studies on alcohol and substance abuse prevention among Native American adolescents. Most experimental alcohol prevention programs targeted for young people focus on testing alcohol education modes. While some of the educational efforts are demonstrating effectiveness with non-Indian youths, there is little evidence that educational strategies are effective with young American Indians regardless of tribal affiliation or living status (Blane, 1976).

SUBSTANCE ABUSE PREVENTION FOR AFRICAN AMERICANS

Black teenagers are becoming models discouraging younger
brothers and sisters from using drugs.

In 1990 the Media-Advertising Partnership for a Drug-Free America, a coalition of communication businesses, created a series of ads aimed specifically at blacks. The campaign is part of the partnership's continuing program that uses high-impact advertising methods to "unsell" drugs. The group of ads directed to the African-American community is based on information about current drug abuse levels and what are thought to be blacks' attitudes toward drug use.

Analysis of current drug abuse levels, according to NIDA's 1988 *National Household Survey on Drug Abuse* (which is cited in Chapter 1.1), reveals that more than 13 percent of black Americans aged 12 and older had used illicit drugs in the year before they were surveyed. Almost 11 percent of blacks aged 12 and up had used marijuana in the past year, and more than 4 percent had used cocaine. Marijuana use by 12-to-17-year-olds in the preceding year was about 9 percent among blacks and 13 percent among whites.

While it seems that much is known about blacks and drug abuse in the United States, there appears to be a lack of knowledge about the determinants of the problem. Much of the epidemiological research that has been conducted concerning drug abuse among blacks has used a descriptive strategy comparing drug use among blacks with that among whites. Blacks are not usually investigated in terms of their own values, norms, or life conditions; their history and heritage; or their adaptive problems. Comparative research on blacks and whites is done within a normative framework, with the behavior of whites being the norm from which blacks deviate. The differences between races have been interpreted within a social pathology framework. Differences between blacks and whites in such things have been seen as stemming from economic and social oppression. The assumption has been that if we could only alleviate these condition blacks would become more like whites. Spread throughout the literature is evidence that in spite of many shared values, there are a number of very real cultural differences between blacks and whites (Miller & Dregner, 1973; Korchin, 1980). Using a cross-cultural approach that views the behaviors of black individuals in terms of their meanings within particular subcultures may lead to the development of more culturally relevant prevention programs. For now the aim of the campaign for reducing drug use among African-Americans is to foster intolerance for illegal drugs and make drug use intolerable. Research on attitudes indicates that although black parents are aware of the risks of drug use, they are more reluctant than white parents to voice disapproval to their children. Related messages therefore will help black parents learn to discourage their kids from using drugs and to keep children away from drug-using peers. Messages directed to older black teenagers are planned to convince them, as influencers, to actively discourage younger brothers and sisters from using drugs. Preteens will be the target of messages designed to deglamorize drug use and depict non-users as winners. Television, radio, and billboard ads for the new campaign were created and produced by black communication professionals. Print advertisements are also in production.

SUBSTANCE ABUSE PREVENTION FOR PACIFIC AND ASIAN AMERICANS

Asian and Pacific Americans—the "other" category of 32 ethnic groups.

"Pacific and Asian Americans" refers to a constellation of people from a number of ethnic and cultural backgrounds who in the past were designated simply as "other" (Yoshioka et al., 1981; Wong, 1982). Diversity among ethnic groups with vast within-group variation adds complexity to any drug abuse research effort. With the Asian and Pacific American population, these complexities are compounded by the unique phenomenon of the growth of a high-risk and vulnerable population. Between 1980 and 1990 this group increased by 108 percent, from 3.5 million to 7.3 million (Kim, 1981). This represents the largest proportional increase of any ethnic minority population in the United States during that period. With such diversity and complexities existing within the Asian and Pacific American population, any drug prevention research endeavor must take into consideration the particular subpopulations for which its findings have applicability. Clearly, findings from a Japanese American sample (with individuals who have lived in the United States for several generations) would be very different from those obtained from a sample of recently immigrated Korean Americans.

Nakagawa and Watanabe (1973) surveyed the Asian student population from Seattle, Washington, junior high schools and two high schools on personal use of hard drugs (excluding marijuana and alcohol). Among those surveyed, 12 percent of the males and 17 percent of the females were classified as "users." By ethnic group, 45 percent of Filipino, 29 percent of Japanese, 22 percent of Chinese, and 49 percent of "other Asians" had had some experience with hard drugs.

Survey studies of drug use among selected Asian and Pacific American populations do exist, but very few prevention programs specific to this population have been produced or evaluated. This is probably a result of an old stereotyped mind set that Asian and Pacific Americans do not have problems with drug abuse. This mind set has resulted in a general lack of evaluation of drug use and an underestimation of the problem. NIDA has not funded major research programs with an emphasis on Asian and Pacific Americans. Few sensitive, culturally aware, and skillful bicultural or bilingual prevention programs have been developed for Asian and Pacific Americans.

SUBSTANCE ABUSE PREVENTION FOR HISPANIC AMERICANS

Message to Hispanics: Drugs are uncool.

Drugs are uncool, they're unacceptable, and they can increase your risk of contracting AIDS. These are some of the messages being sent to Hispanic Americans by two separate, culturally sensitive ad campaigns, begun in 1990 by the Media-Advertising Partnership for a Drug-Free America. Most of the ads feature Hispanic Americans speaking Spanish and revolve around situations identified with Hispanic culture. To help change how Spanish-speaking Americans think about drugs, the partnership and NIDA are bombarding Hispanics with the antidrug ads, stressing that the costs of drug taking far outweigh any perceived benefit. The twenty different partnership ads previously mentioned are broadcast on both English and Spanish language television and radio stations and displayed in Spanish and general consumer publications. They primarily target non-users because research has shown that non-users are more responsive than users to antidrug messages. The ads also urge Hispanic parents, who are often unaware that their children are at risk for drug abuse, to warn their sons and daughters about the dangers of using illegal substances. Other ads engage parents in the drug prevention effort by telling them about the effects and prevalence of drug use even among preteens. Both ad campaign producers hope that, with a change in attitude, Hispanics will use fewer illegal drugs.

The Media-Advertising Partnership for a Drug-Free America's Hispanic ad campaign is designed particularly to "unsell" those drugs with high abuse rates—marijuana, cocaine, and crack. The idea is to change attitudes about drugs by portraying them as unattractive, unpopular, and unacceptable. Because Hispanic teens are half as likely as their non-Hispanic peers to fear the effects of drugs, some ads stress the many negative aspects of using drugs and correct users' misinformation about the drugs' effects.

Slightly more than 8.2 percent of Hispanic Americans compared to 7 percent of the general U.S. population over the age of 12 have taken illegal drugs within the last 30 days, according to NIDA's 1988 National Household Survey. Between 1985 and 1988 the number of Hispanic Americans aged 12 and over who had ever used illicit drugs increased from 3.7 million to more than 4.8 million. The percentage of Hispanics who had ever used cocaine rose from 7.3 percent in 1985 to 11 percent in 1988. In 1988, Hispanics accounted for about 10 percent of all drug-related emergency room visits.

With regard to the use and abuse of, or addiction to, controlled substances by Hispanics in the United States, Gomez (1976) found that the Hispanic addict does not differ from addicts of other ethnic backgrounds in terms of the psychogenic factors such as deficient character structure that might predispose them toward use. The difference between Hispanic addicts and non-Hispanic addicts rests primarily on sociocultural factors added to an acculturation, a forced change of cultural value, and mobility that impinges upon the quality of life and affects essential areas such as health, education, and housing. The resultant cumulative stress sometimes leads to escapism through the use and abuse of drugs. This profile can be seen in the life of the Mexican American drug user. In a series of studies by Guinn (1975, 1978; Guinn & Hurley, 1976), employing Mexican students enrolled in high schools in the lower Rio Grand Valley region of Texas, he reported that Mexican American adolescent drug users, compared to non-users, had poorer grades in school, reported higher rates of absenteeism, and participated in fewer school activities. In addition, users appeared to come from higher socioeconomic level families (as indexed by educational level and occupation of fathers). Adolescent users of marijuana also reported using a wide variety of other drugs, including stimulants, hallucinogens, barbituates, solvents, and opiates or cocaine. Non-users described users as mixed up, insecure, or emotionally disturbed, while drug users perceived themselves as "doing just what they wanted to do."

"Doing what they want to do" describes the life of the Chicano intravenous drug users who refer to themselves as *tecatos*. Tecatos stratify themselves into three groups: high-class, medium-class, and cucarachos. High-class individuals in this group are known as *tecatos buenos*, good tecatos. They provide for themselves; they have money, and they do not ask for credit. They go to the connection or drug source and buy what they need. If they do not have the money for the drug, they do without. If they are arrested and they have to "kick" (withdraw from the drug habit), they kick quietly and do not complain about the pain. Other characteristics of good tecatos are that they dress well and act and talk responsibly. It is also said that they are reliable. Moreover, they may be employed at a "regular" job, or they may have to hustle. In Spanish, medium-class drug users are called *medianos*. These individuals are also seen as good tecatos. They do not ask for credit or a handout, but they are different from tecatos buenos in that they usually steal to make connections. The *cucaracho* (cockroach) is an individual who hangs around the connection and is always asking for a handout. The cucaracho does not pay his own way; he depends on real tecatos. He just waits around to see who will give him a "taste" or provide him with the drug. Cucarachos get a taste of heroin by doing favors or little jobs for the user and the seller. The cucaracho may also get a taste by lending his works (drug equipment) to a user who does not have his own at the time of purchase (Remos, 1990).

A study of inhalant, marijuana, and alcohol abuse among a sample of Mexican American adolescents indicated that, compared to a national sample, Mexican American adolescents were at least 14 times more likely to be abusing inhalants. The prevalence rate of marijuana use was double the national rate, but the prevalence of alcohol use was equal to that found nationally (Padilla et al., 1979).

Researchers note that while Hispanics represent only 12 percent of the population of New York City, they account for approximately 20 percent of the estimated 125,000 addicts in the area. Puerto Ricans in New York consider drug abuse to be the most important health problem faced by their community. Alers (1982) notes that drug dependence during the period 1975–1980 was the second greatest cause of death (12 percent of all deaths among the Puerto Rican–born population of New York City, aged 15 to 44). More specifically, the annual death rate due to drugs was 37.9 per 100,000 compared to 23.2 per 100,000 for the total population.

Cuban American drug users are a complex population. Denial of the addiction and fear of loss of status make this population very difficult to reach and to maintain in treatment. As is usual among all Cuban American groups, the family is the first to identify the problem and mobilize for treatment. One important implication of these findings is that methodologies must be developed that more effectively help a concerned family member to persuade his or her entire family (or any relevant part thereof) to enter the therapy process. A major goal in prevention is to assist parents to counteract peer influence. The family is still the most significant and powerful force in the Cuban American adolescent's life, and this suggests that effective leadership on the part of the parents can negate negative peer influence. The family effectiveness training (FET) model of prevention has been hypothesized as being potentially useful in reducing drug abuse among Cuban Americans.

The efficacy of particular treatment and prevention strategies must be evaluated. Some strategies that have been described include: family effectiveness training, crisis intervention, bicultural education, youth intervention programs, and the Media-Advertising Partnership for a Drug-Free America campaign. The question of their efficacy remains with regard to the target populations. For example, how effective are educational programs with youths in various settings? What is the efficacy of peer-support groups in drug-free and drug-supplemented programs? To what extent are available prevention techniques differentially effective among different age groups? How do prevention programs differ with respect to age and generation of the target group? What treatment modalities (indigenous and traditional) are available to effectively deal with substance abuse and addictions (Timble et al., 1987)?

REFERENCES

Alers, J. O. (1982). *Puerto Ricans and Health*. New York: Hispanic Research Center, Fordham University.

Blane, H. (1976). Education and mass persuasion as prevention strategies. In R. Room and S. Sheffield (Eds.), *The Prevention of Alcohol Problems: Report of a Conference*. Sacramento: California Office of Alcoholism.

Brown, B. S. (1980). Assessing drug abuse in selected populations. Paper presented at World Health Organization Expert Committee on Drug Dependence meeting, 1980.

Gomez, A. (1976). Some considerations in structuring human services for the Spanish speaking population of the United States. *Journal of Mental Health*, 5:60.

Guinn, R. (1975). Characteristics of drug use among Mexican American students. *Journal of Drug Education*, 5(3):235–241.

Guinn, R. (1978). Attitudinal and behavioral aspects of Mexican American drug use: three year follow-up. *Journal of Drug Education*, 8(3):173–179.

Guinn, R., and Hurley, R. S. (1976). A comparison of drug use among Houston and lower Rio Grand Valley secondary students.

Harvey, W. M. (1985). *The Emergence of Multicultural Drug Abuse Prevention Programming*. NIDA Prevention Networks, DHHS Pub. ADM 85-1337. Washington, D.C.: U.S. Government Printing Office.

Kim, Y. K. (1981). Asian and Pacific Islander Population in the United States. Washington, D.C.: Bureau of the Census.

Korchin, S. J. (1980). Clinical psychology and minority problems. *American Psychologist*, 35:262–269.

Mail, P. D., and Wright, L. D. (1989). Point of view: Indian sobriety must come from Indian solutions. *Health Education*, 12:19–22.

Miller, K., and Dreger, R. (Eds.). (1973). *Comparative Study of Blacks and Whites in the United States*. New York: Seminar Press.

Nakagawa, B., and Watanabe, R. (1973). *A Study of the Use of Drugs Among Asian American Youths of Seattle*. Seattle: Demonstration Project for Asian Americans.

Oetting, E. R., and Goldstein, G. S. (1980). *Drug Abuse Among Indian Children*. Rockville, Md.: National Institute on Drug Abuse.

Oetting, E. R., et al. (1980a). Drug use among adolescents of five southwestern Native American tribes. *International Journal of the Addictions*, 15:439–445.

Oetting, E. R., et al. (1980b). Drug Use Among American Indian Youth, Fort Collins: Colorado State University, Western Behavioral Studies.

Padilla, E. R., et al. (1979). Inhalant, marijuana and alcohol abuse among barrio children and adolescents. *International Journal of the Addictions*, 14:943–964.

Petrakis, P. L. (1985). *Alcoholism: An Inherited Disease*. DHHS Pub. (ADM) 87-1519. Washington, D.C.: U.S. Government Printing Office.

Remos, Reyes. (1990). Chicano intravenous drug users. In *Collection and Interpretation of Data from Hidden Populations*. DHHS Pub. (ADM) 90-1678. Washington, D.C.: U.S. Government Printing Office.

Royce, J. E. (1981). *Alcohol Problems and Alcoholism*. New York: Free Press.

Timble, J. E., Padilla, A. M., and Bell, C. S. (1987). *Drug Abuse Among Ethnic Minorities*. DHHS Pub. (ADM) 87-1474. Washington, D.C.: U.S. Government Printing Office.

Wong, H. Z. (1982). Asian and Pacific Americans. In L. R. Snowden (Ed.), *Reaching the Underserved: Mental Health Needs of Neglected Populations*. Beverly Hills, Calif.: Sage, pp. 185–204.

Yoshioka, R. B., et al. (1981). *Mental Health Services for Pacific/Asian Americans* (2 vols.). San Francisco: Pacific Asian Mental Health Research Project.

DRUGS IN THE WORKPLACE

EXTENT OF THE PROBLEM

Government statistics document the pervasiveness of alcohol and other drugs that have become a fact of life in the United States. American adults currently consume approximately 33 gallons of beer, over 2.5 gallons of distilled spirits, and about 3 gallons of wine per year on a per capita basis. More than 3 billion doses of dangerous drugs are consumed each year for nonmedical reasons. The consumption of other illicit drugs is measured in metric tons. During each of the last few years, for example, around 6 tons of heroin, 50 to 75 tons of cocaine, and as much as 10,000 tons of marijuana have been consumed in the United States (Axel, 1986; U.S. Bureau of the Census, 1985).

Workers don't check their substance abuse problems at the door when they enter the workplace, and their problems become the company's problems. Corporations look at the costs of substance abuse in many ways. The effect on individual employees and their families is the most obvious. The resultant health consequences of chemical abusers include an average 12-year-shorter life span; cirrhosis of the liver; poor nutritional state; diseases of the nerves, digestive system, respiratory, and cardiovascular systems; parasitic diseases; musculoskeletal disorders; anemia, infections, convulsions, hypertension; stress; and emotional and personality disorders. The costs of substance abuse are also reflected in its effects on the working family members who are not themselves abusers. Approximately 10 million persons in the United States fit the clinical definition of alcoholism. For each of these, four or five other people are directly affected, raising the total to 60 million. The untreated adult children of alcoholics form still another category of approximately 20 million persons. This means that up to 80 million people—a third of the U.S. population—have had a profound, sometimes almost catastrophic, experience with alcohol. Moreover, clinical experience shows that rarely is a person involved with only one drug. Someone who uses heroin, cocaine, or marijuana is very often also a problem drinker (Wrich, 1986).

A second concern is the cost to the company and its shareholders, because substance abuse problems will inevitably affect the firm's bottom line. The overall cost of alcohol abuse in the United States is nearing $100 billion annually. The impact on industry is equally staggering, as it is estimated that 6 to 10 percent of the U.S. work force (5 to 10 million people) are alcoholics, and another 10 percent are problem drinkers (Goldbeck, 1980). Approximately 15 percent of all workers have emotional problems that significantly limit their job performance and require professional treatment. Troubled workers in general account for 40 to 70 percent of employee relations problems. Each troubled employee can cost a company $2,500 to $5,000 per year in direct costs and ten times that amount in indirect costs. Employees caught up in substance abuse tend to be absent from the job up to sixteen times as often, claim three times as many sickness benefits, and file five times as many workers' compensation claims as non-users. Costs are seen in reduced work performance and efficiency, lost productivity, absenteeism and turnover costs, increased health benefits utilization, accidents, and losses stemming from impaired judgment. It is difficult to put a price tag on low morale and impaired judgment in decision making at work caused by substance abuse. Nor is it easy for an organization to figure the costs of pilfering, high turnover, and recruitment training. There are also some less obvious implications, such as the cost of losing a customer because of low-quality products and the costs of overtime pay needed to meet production schedules because employees are not as productive as they could be on the job. No one knows how much is being lost in this way because of undetected or untreated substance abuse. All of these costs add significantly to the health care expenditures of a company and its medical facilities (Busch, 1981; Reinertsen, 1983; Wrich, 1981; Bensinger & Pilkington, 1983).

The National Institute on Drug Abuse estimates that between 10 and 23 percent of all U.S. workers use dangerous drugs on the job—one in every five workers aged 18 to 25 and one in every eight workers aged 26 to 34. The average drug user is not the old stereotypical alcoholic or drug abuser—a strung-out, deadbeat, skid row bum. The serious cocaine user, for example, is typically well-educated (14 years of education), employed (77 percent), well-paid (37 percent earn over $25,000 annually), and engaged in illegal activities to support the drug habit (56 percent).

Given these statistics and the fact that alcohol and drug problems are not obvious in early- or middle-stage users, individuals and organizations may wish to examine their workplace substance abuse problems. Because substance abuse tends to be a hidden problem, many organizations have decided to proceed on the assumption that there may be individuals in the workplace who have or are developing a problem with drugs or alcohol. Refusal to admit the possibility that alcohol or other drug use might occur at a work site could amount to a missed opportunity to help an employee get help. If there is a problem, ignoring it will not make it go away. Drug and alcohol problems do not usually get better if left alone—they get worse.

Beginning with education and prevention strategies and following up with rehabilitation provisions, a company or union can demonstrate a commitment to employee health and safety that encompasses a drug-free workplace. To determine whether an organization has a substance abuse problem or the potential for developing a problem, organizational indicators of substandard performance such as increases in the number of accidents, theft and property losses, security breaches, benefits utilization, absenteeism, training costs, and workers' compensation claims need to be identified. Representatives of key units within the organization such as occupational safety and health, security, employee benefits, personnel, employees, and the employee assistance program (EAP) need to work together to get a companywide sense of the problem. State or local statistics gathered by substance abuse agencies (health or law enforcement), medical or health societies, treatment facilities, chapters of the National Council on Alcoholism, business and industry, and trade organizations should be obtained. These statistics can be compared with workers' subjective views to get some idea of the substance abuse activity and the attitudes of the work force.

A considerable body of knowledge and experience has grown out of company efforts to deal with alcohol abuse. For many companies, particularly those with large hourly work forces, this experience has shown that the most effective corporate policies focus on job performance issues, are widely publicized, define specific codes of behavior, and spell out the penalties for failure to observe them. In these organizations, supervisors are trained to confront employees with alcohol problems on the basis of their poor performance record, not on their intemperate drinking habits. If a confrontation occurs, employees are advised that failure to improve performance or to seek counseling and treatment will result in disciplinary procedures or dismissal. Employees are encouraged to seek help on their own, with the promise that their problems will be kept confidential in these situations. However, research suggests that some aspects of this model do not work as well among professional and managerial workers. Such employees typically exercise more autonomy over their work assignments and schedules.

EDUCATION

Business has a responsibility to help minimize the impact of drug abuse on employees and on society. The support of top management is critical for achieving the goal of a drug-free workplace. Equally important to the success of the program is the support and inclusion of workers from all levels and sectors of the organization from the early stages of planning through implementation of the program. From an educational perspective, the key effort in dealing with drug abuse is a broad-based prevention program—using different approaches to confront different degrees of misuse and abuse.

PRIMARY PREVENTION

Primary prevention strategies are aimed at the general population, including those who have never abused drugs, and should involve both education and security measures. The first step consists of developing and publicizing a policy statement that lets the work force know that the commitment is strong and serious. The policy document should

- State the unacceptability of drug or alcohol use on the job.
- Define what constitutes an infraction of work policy and rules regarding substance abuse, and describe the consequences.
- Recognize that alcohol and drug problems are treatable.
- Spell out the availability of treatment and rehabilitation services.
- Integrate the ideas of corporate interest and employee well-being—state the company's concern for workers and dependents whose drug use could adversely affect job performance and the well-being of self, family, and co-workers.
- Identify the EAP or other health promotion program as the mechanism to help workers who have a problem.
- Make clear that participation in a program will not jeopardize future employment or advancement nor will it protect workers from disciplinary action for continued substandard job performance or rule infractions.
- Outline procedures for supervisory and union referrals, voluntary referrals, and peer referrals.
- Establish record-keeping procedures that ensure confidentiality.

This phase consists of educational activities designed to increase employees' knowledge about programs and about drinking in general. It is designed to increase awareness of the problem and to change attitudes toward substance abusers and others with serious personal problems. One goal of primary prevention programs is to promote voluntary use of helping services before the problem becomes serious.

SECONDARY PREVENTION

Secondary prevention efforts are primarily directed at people who are experimenting with drugs or using them recreationally, to help them to avoid more serious problems with drugs. At this level, business needs to develop structured drug education programs and should stress early identification. Through wellness and fitness programs, companies can also teach employees other, less dangerous forms of behavior modification that will help them deal with personal and job-related frustrations (Inaba, 1986).

Intervention techniques stress contructive confrontation with workers whose job performance is becoming substandard and unacceptable. Supervisors have a legitimate right to initiate a series of corrective actions with a worker whose performance begins to decline. Confronting a worker can be constructive when a caring but firm attitude on the part of the supervisor is coupled with an offer of assistance by referral to health and human services professionals if the performance problem is related to substance abuse. Workplace confrontation is one of the most effective ways known to help those with alcohol or drug problems admit to the problem and seek help. However, responsibility for monitoring job performance does not extend to identifying and resolving personal problems that are interfering with work performance.

Supervisors need to develop and communicate objective job performance standards so that deteriorating performance can be documented. They should talk with the worker about the need to improve performance that is unacceptable and determine whether workplace factors such as inadequate equipment or training are causing or contributing to the problem. Employee rights dictate that supervisors prepare a written memorandum documenting incidents and examples of performance problems, and that they hold a private meeting with the worker to discuss the performance or attendance problems and the needed improvements and set a time limit for improvement. They should also inform the employee of the availability of assistance for personal problems and should encourage the use of these resources.

When it appears that personal problems may be impacting performance, supervisors need to have an alternative for aiding the worker. Company policies usually dictate that supervisors emphasize that lack of improvement in job performance could lead to corrective action and possibly result in termination.

Intervention in substance abuse problems is not a matter of employer versus employee. The majority of employees do not want to work with drug-impaired coworkers and often can be instrumental in getting those individuals help. Many companies organize informal peer networks to inform workers about drugs, confront users with their unacceptable behavior, provide referral information, and support those who are becoming drug-free. In these programs workers can increase their knowledge about the effects of drugs, agree among themselves as to what constitutes unacceptable behaviors jeopardizing health, safety, and security at the work site, and confront employees who exhibit these behaviors. The informal network lets new employees know that a drug-free workplace is the norm. Reminders such as stickers, magazine articles on drug-related subjects, and small posters can also be used to get that message across (Girdano, 1986).

EMPLOYEE ASSISTANCE PROGRAMS

Corporations are increasingly using employee assistance programs (EAPs) to deal with employees' substance abuse problems. An EAP is a work-based strategy for early identification of employee difficulties that are adversely affecting job performance. Employee assistance programs have been shown to be effective in working with individuals who have already developed problems with drugs and in formulating intervention strategies that will get these individuals to enter and stay in treatment. They can also help to minimize the negative effects that substance abuse has on the morale, productivity, growth, and economic vitality of the organization. There are over 10,000 EAPs in operation across the country. All sizes and types of organizations have instituted EAPs.

Well-run EAPs have proved that they can improve employee morale, increase productivity, and enhance general employee well-being. Although figures on effectiveness vary widely, employers generally find that for every dollar they invest in an EAP, they save anywhere from $5 to $16. The average annual cost of an EAP ranges from $12 to $20 per employee.

Employee assistance programs originated as occupational alcoholism programs. However, years of experience have shown that the narrow focus on alcohol and drug problems limited the effectiveness of the program. Substance abuse, either by cause or effect, is usually one part of a larger constellation of social, emotional, physical, and job performance problems, and experience has shown that labeling workers as alcoholics by treating them in an alcohol abuse program tended to limit voluntary involvement. Another problematic element in the traditional alcohol abuse programs was the identification of a person as an alcoholic by a supervisor who was not trained to make such an evaluation. The broader concept of employee assistance requires that the supervisor only identify a worker who is not performing up to expected standards, an evaluation the supervisor is qualified to make. Research has shown that in more than half the cases where supervisors labeled drugs or alcohol as the problem, the basic problems were not related to either alcohol or drugs. With the EAP concept, diagnosis of the cause of the poor performance, whether it be alcoholism or some other personal or health problem, is left up to professionals (Jackson, 1983). The modern concept of employee assistance is to refer a troubled worker to the appropriate treatment or counseling service. The broadbrush concept of dealing with the wide range of employees' social, emotional, and personal problems is proving its effectiveness in both human and financial terms. Current trends seem to indicate that EAPs will place more emphasis on general health promotion and prevention (Otte & Groepper, 1984).

CONCLUSION

There are no simple solutions to the complex problem of drugs in the workplace. Everyone in the workplace must take an active part in fighting workplace substance abuse. The more people involved, the more successful the effort. Management, employee representatives, and employees must all take active and equal roles; this cannot be an employer-versus-employee issue. Everyone must take a firm position against workplace substance abuse and communicate that position. Everyone must learn about drugs and alcohol and how they affect individuals and those they work with, and they must make sure that this information is disseminated throughout the workplace. Without use of police-state tactics, everyone must be made aware of the signs and symptoms of possible substance abuse, especially when performance may be critical to the health and safety of coworkers and the general public. Finally, provisions should be made for employees who have a drug or an alcohol problem to get the help they need.

Assistance may take the form of a formalized employee assistance program or may constitute referral to available community resources. However, it is important to keep in mind that the purpose of business is to be productive and successful and to provide employees the opportunity to earn a creative living. It is not the purpose of business to be society's police officer or social worker. Business cannot take over the social, emotional, or moral support normally supplied by the family and society. If business is given that responsibility it will also take the authority or power, and basic human rights are likely to get trampled on in the process. Individuals must be ever-vigilant when human rights are concerned, as history has shown over and over again that the rights we give away today we will have to fight to get back tomorrow.

REFERENCES

Axel, H. (Ed.). (1986). *Corporate Strategies for Controlling Substance Abuse*. New York: The Conference Board, p. 1.

Bensinger, A., and Pilkington, C. F. (1983). An alternative method in the treatment of alcoholism. *Journal of Occupational Medicine*, 4:300–303.

Busch, E. J. (1981). Developing an employee assistance program. *Personnel Journal*, September, pp. 26–30.

Girdano, D. A. (1986). Employee assistance programs. In D. A. Girdano (Ed.), *Occupational Health Promotion*. New York: Macmillan, pp. 196–212.

Goldbeck, W. B. (1980). *Mental Wellness Programs for Employees*. New York: Springer-Verlag.

Inaba, D. (1986). The impact of substance on workers. In H. Axel (Ed.), *Corporate Strategies for Controlling Substance Abuse*. New York: The Conference Board, p. 20.

Jackson, G. U. (1983). "Prevention and alcoholism: The EAP in health care institutions," *Bulletin of the New York Academy of Medicine*, 59(2):249–253.

Otte, F., and Groepper, R. (1984). EAP and carrier development: indications for both. *EAP Digest*, May/June, pp. 46–47.

Reinertsen, J. (1983). Promoting health is good business. *Occupational Health and Safety*. June, pp. 18–22.

U.S. Bureau of the Census. (1985). *Statistical Abstract of the United States 1985*, 105th ed. Washington, D.C.: U.S. Government Printing Office.

Wrich, J. T. (1981). *Employee Assistance Programs—Updated for the 80's*. Minneapolis, Minn.: Hazeldon.

Wrich, J. T. (1986). The impact of substance abuse at the worksite. In H. Axel (Ed.), *Corporate Strategies for Controlling Substance Abuse*. New York: The Conference Board, p. 11.

DRUG TESTING

LEGAL ISSUES

The growing alarm about the drug problem has prompted a large number of employers to instigate what critics believe to be police-state tactics—the use of preemployment and on-the-job drug screening procedures that include the use of urinalysis, undercover agents, and drug-sniffing dogs. Newspapers report that a growing number of major organizations including IBM and Exxon, the military service, the Defense Department, many federally licensed utilities, and the transportation industries are drug testing prospective and, in some instances, current employees. While safety and national security are often used to justify such actions, the legality of drug testing and other hard-line procedures is currently being argued in the courts. Companies that are taking action to combat substance abuse problems among their employees are realizing the complexity of dealing with this issue and the fact that there is little law to guide them. Both employers and their lawyers are working on the basis of general legal principles developed for other issues.

Assuming that the existence of substance abuse within a company has been ascertained, the employer may decide to use a combination of methods for detection and prevention. These methods include traditional means of supervising employees such as observation by security personnel and searches of lunch boxes of entering employees, as well as newer technologies like urinalysis. Employees often object that some methods used to observe on-the-job behavior constitute a violation of their right to privacy. There are legal debates on the "right to privacy." One side holds that there are aspects of an individual's life that are private. What is a legally enforceable right to privacy is another issue. The legally enforceable right to privacy derives from state or federal laws or constitutions. While the U.S. Constitution recognizes no explicit right to privacy, the Supreme Court has implied such a right, in certain limited situations, by combining several provisions of the Constitution. The federal right to privacy protects individuals against actions by the government or its agents. Most employers act as private individuals in setting up substance abuse detection programs. There is normally no government action when a private business conducts drug screening through observation or other methods, so there is no violation of the federal right to privacy. The second restriction on the constitutional right to privacy is that it has been interpreted to be limited to certain restricted areas. That is, the government must interfere with some fundamental right before there is an invasion of privacy. These fundamental rights include such activities as marriage, procreation, and education. There are very few legally enforceable rights to privacy in the workplace. The courts have specifically stated that the use and/or possession of illegal drugs are not fundamental rights protected by the U.S. Constitution.

Within the past few years, new technologies—including urine, blood, and breath tests—have been shown to be useful in spotting drug use. Drug testing has become a big business. In January 1990, the American Management Association surveyed 1,021 companies concerning their policies on drug testing. More than half (51.5 percent) reported that they test for drugs, up substantially since 1987, when the figure was 21.5 percent.

ETHICAL ISSUES

A program for the detection of drug use should be considered in the context of an overall plan to reduce or prevent the negative impact of drug abuse on industry or organization. Experts advise the directors of workplace drug testing programs to proceed with a careful assessment of the group to be affected by the testing program by asking some directional questions.

- What personnel, if any, are affected by drug use?
- Which drugs pose the major problem?
- Can the organization shoulder the economic burden and the legal and emotional costs associated with such a program?

In some cases, it is obvious from incidents of known drug use or drug dealing with the organization that a problem exists. Or it may be only suspected, owing to higher than normal rates of absenteeism, decreases in productivity, or an increase in accidents or thefts in the workplace.

The presence and extent of a drug problem can be assessed by means of a survey based on anonymous questionnaires. Any assessment should include clarification of which substances are involved. Alcohol is the largest problem in most industries. The use of marijuana, cocaine, and, in some locations, phencyclidine (PCP) is also particularly high. These illicit drugs, along with opiates, amphetamines, or hallucinogenic compounds, have a significant presence in the workplace. A more complicated group of drugs to assess are the prescription drugs—tranquilizers, barbiturates (sleeping pills), and antidepressants. These are probably more prevalent in the workplace than illicit drugs and are potentially just as likely to impair job performance or to create health problems if used in excess of prescribed amounts or without adequate medical supervision.

When the "assessment" questions are resolved, an appropriate drug abuse deterrent program, tailored to the extent of the problem, should be established. If there is no clear indication of significant drug use at the work site or in the organization, a preventive educational effort may be the only type of program warranted. Evidence of heavy psychoactive drug use in job situations where safety is a sensitive issue should be dealt with more aggressively. The plan should give paramount consideration to the purpose of the program, the essence of which is usually the health and safety of employees as well as economic concerns. Another important element of the plan should be to guarantee the personal privacy and dignity of the employees as much as possible. Various alternatives may be considered. If the problem does not warrant a major program, it may be sufficient to maintain an awareness of drug abuse indicators, to define isolated problems regularly through the use of personnel data and supervisor reports, and to deal with identifiable drug users through an employee assistance program (Hawks, 1986).

URINALYSIS

Most of the urine samples being analyzed in industry today are associated with preemployment applications. While many of the rights usually accorded an applicant are not necessarily the same as those of an employee, the same rights of privacy and accuracy of analysis should be accorded the individuals. A preemployment screening plan may preclude the employment of individuals with positive urine test results, but such a plan should include some kind of counseling, not only to make the individual aware of why the job was denied but also to offer advice and direction in dealing with the drug problem. A more enlightened probationary policy might allow the hiring of such individual based on other merits, on the condition that counseling be obtained and drug use discontinued.

Philosophies and procedures differ among companies. Some use random testing, whereas others announce testing schedules. Preannounced tests can be effective even though drugs like cocaine can rarely be detected in the urine for more than a day or two. A cocaine-positive test therefore indicates recent and possibly dependent use, particularly if the individual was aware of the pending analysis and still could not abstain. A similar conclusion cannot be drawn from a single positive urine test for marijuana, for reasons that will be discussed later.

Effective programs for the detection of drugs of abuse in human urine specimens are best accomplished with sensitive testing procedures. Because of the numerous legally sensitive features of drug detection programs, the analytical results must be unquestionably reliable and able to withstand considerable scrutiny. Therefore, the testing laboratory must be experienced and capable in a number of important functions, including quality control documentation, chain of custody, technical expertise, and demonstrated proficiency over time in interpreting urinalysis results. Most important, the laboratory must produce data that are secure from false positives and defensible when challenged.

Many considerations are important in developing a sound drug program in an organization. It cannot be overemphasized that the documentation of well-thought-out policies, developed with input from all organizational elements, is at the top of the list. An effective program to discourage drug abuse in an organization must have clearly defined rationales, goals, and rules. The consequences of a positive urinalysis result must be clearly stated and not open to arbitrary responses by management. The rights and sensitivities of the individual should be protected as much as possible. Results of urine drug assays should be kept confidential (Hawks, 1986).

Labor unions typically have been against drug testing. In one instance the AFL-CIO complained that some testing labs have false positive error rates as high as 66 percent. Even if such drug tests were reliable, they would reveal only which individuals had taken a drug during a prior time, often encompassing off-duty hours. In reality, drug tests do not determine whether an individual is currently under the influence of a drug or unable to perform job functions because of drug use, which are the employer's only legitimate interest—judging an employee's ability to work. The union group urges members to bargain for programs that place appropriate limits and conditions for the use of tests focusing only on workers who exhibit symptoms of job-related impairment. They ask affiliated unions to resist participating in harsh and unjustifiable programs and to assist union members who are injured by such employer-imposed programs to invoke their rights under federal and state law (Frieden, 1990).

Specific Drug Assays

Drug testing, especially urinalysis, is one of the most significant and controversial issues of our time and has a significant impact on the basic rights of members of a free society. For that reason the following information on specific drug assays, although technical, is deemed essential for presentation in a drug education textbook. The material was assembled by Richard Hawks and C. Nora Chiang for publication by the U.S. Department of Health and Human Services (Hawks & Chiang, 1986).

Marijuana/Cannabinoids The concentrations of THC metabolites found in urine are influenced by the amount of THC (the dose) absorbed into the bloodstream, by frequency of prior use, by the timing of collection of the urine specimen with respect to the last exposure to marijuana, and by the rate of release of stored cannabinoids from adipose tissue. In addition, the quantity of liquids ingested prior to the time of sampling also affects cannabinoid concentrations in urine. For acute or occasional (less than twice a week) smoking, urine samples will generally be positive for 1 to 3 days. An individual who smokes regularly (daily or even as few as two or three times a week) will generally have marijuana-positive urine most of the time. A heavy (daily for at least months) smoker who stops smoking may continue to produce positive samples for longer than a month (depending on the assay cutoff) because of the amount of THC that accumulates in the body. It becomes difficult, therefore, to distinguish between the heavy smoker who may in fact have stopped smoking weeks before and the moderate smoker who has not.

The relative concentrations of THC and metabolites in blood samples are quite different following a dose taken orally and one taken by smoking. However, metabolic profiles in urine samples cannot generally differentiate between a dose taken orally and one taken by smoking. Marijuana smoke can be inhaled passively and result in detectable body fluid levels of THC and 9-carboxy-THC. However, the studies cited generally involve several smokers in a small room or car and one or more nonsmokers in the room for at least an hour without ventilation. The probability of this type of exposure leading to a positive urine test result is extremely small.

A positive urinalysis for THC metabolites indicates only that the individual consumed marijuana either within 1 hour or as much as several weeks before the sample was collected. It is generally accepted that total cannabinoid concentrations of less than 50 nanograms per milliliter by immunoassay in urine may be consistent with use beyond 36 hours, or with long-term excretion in the habitual user. Without other knowledge of the individual's habits, more specific interpretation than this is not usually feasible. Multiple sampling frequently helps make interpretations more specific. If the individual is an occasional or one-time user, the second or third sample should be negative. If the individual is a previously heavy long-term smoker who has stopped, samples may be positive for 3 or more weeks, but the concentrations show a generally decreasing trend, eventually becoming negative for an extended period (2 weeks). If, however, the individual continues to smoke, the sample will continue to be positive for several weeks with no particular indication of a decreasing concentration trend.

Cocaine Cocaine is rapidly absorbed, with the maximum plasma concentration occurring about 5 minutes after smoking. Plasma profiles after smoking are almost equivalent to those following an intravenous dose. There are significant differences in plasma cocaine between the intranasal route and the intravenous or smoking routes. Maximum cocaine concentrations are reached at around 30 to 40 minutes and persist longer after intranasal inhalation than after intravenous injection or smoking. The terminal half-life of cocaine is 1.5 hours regardless of the route of administration.

Cocaine is extensively metabolized by liver and plasma esterases, and only 1 percent of the dose is excreted in the urine unchanged. Approximately 70 percent of the dose can be recovered in the urine over a period of 3 days. Unchanged cocaine can sometimes be detected by chromatographic methods for up to 24 hours after a given dose, and metabolites can generally be detected by immunoassays for 24 to 48 hours. With this and other drugs that clear the body rapidly, the short detection times in urinalysis procedures mean that individuals using such drugs will be less likely to be detected than those using drugs that have longer detection times.

Amphetamine and Methamphetamine When methamphetamine is administered, some of the drug is metabolized into amphetamine, its major active metabolite, and both of these drugs will appear in the urine. Amphetamine is metabolized to deaminated and hydroxylated metabolites. Unchanged amphetamine has been detected in the urine up to 29 hours after a single oral dose of 5 milligrams. Unchanged methamphetamine also has been identified up to 23 hours following a single oral dose. After long-term intravenous administration, methamphetamine abusers have shown methamphetamine concentrations of 25 to 300 micrograms per milliliter and amphetamine concentrations of 1 to 90 micrograms per milliliter in urine. Several prescription drugs such as benzphetamine, fenfluramine, mephentermine, phenmetrazine, and phentermine can also produce positive immunoassay results. A positive amphetamine analysis indicates previous use of amphetamine or methamphetamine, generally within the previous 24 to 48 hours. However, several over-the-counter preparations used as decongestants and diet aids contain ephedrine and phenylpropanolamine, which are also capable of producing positive tests if present in the urine in significant concentrations.

Because of the high prevalence of phenylpropanolamine and ephedrine in dietary aid and cold remedies and the high probability of their cross-reactivity in immunoassays, it is important to perform careful confirmatory tests. A recent example points to the potential problems in a widely used federal drug testing procedure. A government-certified laboratory wrongly reported that workers had tested positive for illegal methamphetamine use when they in fact had been using over-the-counter cold or asthma medicines. The laboratory mistakenly identified a truck driver as a methamphetamine user. The driver, who was tested under the Department of Transportation's drug testing program, was removed from his job as a result of the test. He vehemently denied ever using the illegal drug and filed a labor grievance. The investigation discovered that the worker had actually been taking large quantities of ephedrine, a decongestant found in several over-the-counter cold and asthma medicines. NIDA officials and other drug testing experts said the case could have broad implications for the drug testing industry. Further review determined that four or six other positive methamphetamine tests reported by the same laboratory had been similarly misidentified (Isikoff, 1990).

Opiates Morphine is rapidly absorbed from an oral dose (peak plasma levels at 15 to 60 minutes) and from intramuscular and subcutaneous injection (peaks at 15 minutes). It is metabolized extensively, with only 2 to 12 percent excreted as unchanged morphine in the urine. Heroin is rapidly broken down, first to monoacetylmorphine, which is then metabolized to morphine in the body. Both heroin and monoacetylmorphine disappear rapidly from the blood (half-life is 3 minutes for heroin, and somewhat longer for monoacetylmorphine), while morphine levels persist longer and decline slowly. Codeine is rapidly absorbed from an oral dose; maximum concentrations occur 1 hour after ingestion.

A screening assay that is positive for opiates could be the result of several different circumstances of drug administration. Since immunoassays do not distinguish between codeine, morphine, and their glucuronide conjugate, a confirmation test that is specific for morphine and/or codeine is necessary. The presence of morphine alone or its conjugate can indicate either clinical morphine use or illicit morphine or heroin use within the previous 1 to 2 days. The presence of both morphine and codeine in urine is consistent with the ingestion of codeine alone. Prescribed use of codeine must be ruled out in this case. Generally the ingestion of a therapeutic dose of codeine (30 milligrams) will lead to detectable levels of the free morphine or codeine for only a few hours, although other metabolites may be detectable for 2 or 3 days. Street heroin also contains acetylcodeine, which metabolizes to codeine. Therefore, in cases of low morphine and codeine concentrations in the urine, it is not possible to determine whether the subject has taken heroin, codeine, or morphine. Although the presence of codeine in the urine may indicate illicit drug use, its presence in many antitussive or analgesic prescription preparations makes such a conclusion questionable.

PCP   Phencyclidine piperidine (PCP, or angel dust) is commonly taken orally, by inhalation (smoked), by insufflation, or intravenously. The drug can be added to parsley, mint, oregano, or other leaves and smoked in the form of a cigarette. In liquefied form, it can be swallowed, injected, or applied to smoking material. PCP is well absorbed following all routes of administration. Maximum plasma PCP concentrations are observed 5 to 15 minutes after smoking. Unchanged PCP is excreted in the urine in moderate amounts. PCP may be detectable in the urine for several days to several weeks.

A positive urine assay for PCP generally indicates drug use within the previous week. There have been reports that sufficient PCP can be absorbed through the skin to lead to a positive urinalysis. The use of saliva has been reported to correlate well with blood as a means of detection of recent PCP use. Hair analysis for the detection of PCP has also been reported. False positives in immunochemical assays for PCP have been reported with the administration of thioridazine (Mellaril), dextromethorphan, and chlorpromazine (Thorazine). This supports the need for specific confirmation of the screening analysis.

LSD   Following oral ingestion of lysergic acid diethylamide (LSD), the effects are perceived within 20 to 45 minutes and usually last for about 12 hours. Studies with laboratory animals showed that LSD is rapidly metabolized and only a small proportion of the dose is excreted in the urine as the parent drug. Because only small amounts of LSD are ingested, and because it is likely that the drug is rapidly metabolized, concentrations of the drug in the urine of a user are unlikely to exceed a few nanograms per milliliter. Two metabolites of LSD could be detected in urine specimens collected for up to 72 hours after administration.

Alcohol Alcohol is taken orally, and its concentration in the blood at any given time is influenced by such factors as the person's weight, the rate at which the individual drinks, whether food is consumed with the alcohol, and the drinker's tolerance. Blood alcohol concentrations (BACs) are usually expressed as percent (grams per deciliter) or as mg percent (milligrams per deciliter). Drinking 1.5 ounces of 86 proof alcohol in a short period of time will result in a BAC of approximately 0.03 percent in a 160-pound individual. The liver metabolizes 95 percent of the ingested alcohol at a relatively constant rate. A normal liver will metabolize alcohol at approximately 0.015 gram per deciliter per hour. This means it takes the body about 2 hours to metabolize 0.75 ounce of pure alcohol. This is equivalent to a 5-ounce glass of wine, a 12-ounce can of beer, or a 1.5-ounce glass of 86 proof liquor.

Unlike most of the other drugs discussed in this section, alcohol is a legal drug, and its presence in the urine does not indicate illicit activity. An alcohol analysis is always aimed at determining the BAC in order to relate this to a particular level of impairment or at least to a legal definition of impairment. In practice, evidence or suspicion of alcohol abuse is best confirmed by breath or blood analysis to determine the concentration present. If this concentration is more than, or close to, the legally accepted presumptive concentration for impairment (100 milligrams per deciliter or 0.1 percent in most states), grounds exist for an assumption of impairment.

Methaqualone Methaqualone (Quaalude) is a sedative-hypnotic drug taken orally in doses of 75 to 300 milligrams. Far higher doses may be taken in nontherapeutic abuse situations. Habitual use in tolerant individuals of over 3 grams per day has been reported. The absorption of methaqualone is rapid, with peak plasma concentration reached in 1.5 to 2 hours. The drug is extensively metabolized, with less than 1 percent of the dose being excreted as unchanged methaqualone in the urine. Approximately 30 percent of the dose is excreted in the urine within 24 hours. After the ingestion of a therapeutic dose (300 milligrams) of methaqualone, it is negligible (usually less than 1 nanogram per milliliter) in the urine, while metabolites may still be detected for more than a week by sensitive methods.

Barbiturates Barbiturates are central nervous system depressants and are used as hypnotic/sedatives. They are classified as ultrashort-, short-, intermediate-, and long-acting. The duration of action of barbiturates is quite variable, ranging from 15 minutes for ultrashort-acting drugs to a day or more for long-acting drugs. The most commonly abused barbiturates are short- and intermediate-acting agents such as pentobarbital (Nembutal), secobarbital (Seconal), and amobarbital (Amytal). Long-acting agents such as phenobarbital are rarely subject to abuse. Barbiturate derivatives are excreted in the urine in varying amounts as unchanged drug and metabolites. Long-acting barbiturates like phenobarbital are excreted with a higher percentage of unchanged drug in the urine, while short-acting barbiturates, secobarbital and amobarbital, are extensively metabolized and are excreted in the urine with a smaller percentage of unchanged drug. Phenobarbital-positive results have been noted for long-term users up to several weeks after cessation of use. With standard single doses of secobarbital, pentobarbital, or amobarbital, drug presence can be identified for up to 76 hours.

Benzodiazepines (Tranquilizers) The benzodiazepines are considered by many to be the most prescribed drugs in the United States. They are primarily used as antianxiety and sedative-hypnotic drugs and also have broad therapeutic use as anticonvulsants or muscle relaxants. These drugs are well absorbed when administered orally, the most common route of administration. Most benzodiazepines are extensively metabolized in the liver and are excreted in the urine as metabolites. Because of the long elimination time for the benzodiazepines, an individual who has been using one for months or years may maintain detectable urinary concentrations of the drug for weeks to months after discontinuation of its use. For more details about pharmacology, toxicology, and metabolism of drugs, several textbooks on these subjects are available (Baselt, 1982, 1984; Goodman & Gilman, 1985; Clarke, 1986).

HAIR ANALYSIS

Although most companies are using urinalysis to test for drugs, hair testing may also be an option. A test called radioimmunoassay of hair looks for a history of drug use in strands of hair. Hair grows at a rate of about 1 to 3 centimeters a month, so testers usually clip 60 strands, each about 3 or 4 centimeters long, to get a history of drug use during the previous 3 months. One standard screen uses gas chromatography/mass spectrometry to look for cocaine, meth-amphetamine, opiates, PCP, and marijuana. The cost is about $45 per test. One difference between hair testing and urinalysis is the period of time during which drugs are detectable. While some drugs are detectable in the urine for up to 72 hours after use, it takes 5 to 10 days for hair affected by drug use to grow above the scalp. On the other hand, hair gives a 3-month history, whereas urinalysis tells only what has been ingested recently. While urine and blood tests may be used in "for cause" cases, such as after an accident, hair analysis may be able to reveal the degree of drug use and might be used to determine which kind of rehabilitation program is necessary. In the best situations, hair testing could serve as a complement to urinalysis. However, the accuracy of hair testing is hotly debated. At present only the developers of the patented technique have reported its effectiveness. A panel formed by the Society of Forensic Tox-icologists concluded that the methods were unreliable. The toxicologists raised such questions as: What is the minimum dose needed to test positive? Could a non-user bank teller who handles money day after day test positive? Appar-ently, in some parts of the country bank tellers are constantly exposed to money that bears traces of cocaine—is that enough to show up in a hair test? After someone uses drugs, how long does it take to show up in the hair? Does the hair of one sex or race retain drugs better than the hair of others? Does cleaning the hair make a difference? The company maintains that its tests are accurate, and the debate goes on (Frieden, 1990).

COMPUTER TESTS

Inventors are perfecting new ways to detect whether people come to work stoned, exhausted, woozy from medication, hung over, emotionally stressed, or just generally impaired. The new technology is more a computer game than a drug test, and there are no urine bottles or searches. The test offers a potential alternative to drug testing and significant improvement for public safety. At a company in California, petrochemical truck drivers start off each work day sitting in front of a computer screen and testing their eye–hand coordination. In Arizona, commercial drivers wield the controls of a simulated truck cab while the highway patrol tests their psychomotor skills. Aside from spotting drug use, the tests can screen for other dangerous factors that limit performance. This may be the start of new, less invasive tests that target performance instead of behavior.

REFERENCES

Baselt, R. C. (1982). *Disposition of Toxic Drugs and Chemicals in Man*. Foster City, Calif.: Biomedical Publications.

Baselt, R. C. (Ed.). (1984). *Advances in Analytical Toxicology*, vol. 1. Foster City, Calif.: Biomedical Publications.

Clarke, E. C. (1986). *Clarke's Isolation and Identification of Drugs*. London: The Pharmaceutical Press.

Frieden, J. (1990). Corporate America's response to substance abuse. *Business and Health*, July, pp. 14–20.

Goodman, L. S., and Gilman, A. (1985). *The Pharmacologic Basis of Therapeutics*. London: MacMillan.

Hawks, R. L. (1986). Establishing a urinalysis program—prior considerations. In R. L. Hawks and N. C. Chiang (Eds.), *Urine Testing for Drugs of Abuse*. NIDA Research Monograph 73. Alcohol, Drug Abuse, and Mental Health Administration, DHHS Pub. (ADM) 87-1481. Washington, D.C.: U.S. Government Printing Office, pp. 1–5.

Hawks, R. L., and Chiang, N. C. (Eds.). (1986). *Examples of Specific Drug Assays in Urine Testing for Drugs of Abuse*. NIDA Research Monograph 73. Alcohol, Drug Abuse, and Mental Health Administration. DHHS Pub. (ADM) 87-1481, Washington, D.C.: U.S. Government Printing Office. p. 84–111.

Isikoff, M. (1990). Federal drug-test method probed for possible flaws. *The Washington Post*, Oct. 25, p. A4.

TREATMENT

INTRODUCTION

It is uncertain what the total cost of drug addiction is to the country, but there are estimates of $5 billion in tangible losses each year to victims of 9 million drug-related crimes and $30 billion in other annual costs of such crimes. The analysis of confidential, self-reported data from surveys of households, the homeless, and those in the criminal justice system estimates that there are 5 million Americans who need treatment for drug dependency—slightly more than 2 percent of the population. Treating them would require $2 billion a year more than the government now spends on treatment, plus $1 billion in initial one-time start-up expenditures.

Drug abuse and dependence involving illicit substances and alcohol is a chronic, relapsing disorder, involving drug-seeking behavior and a craving for drugs that are difficult but not impossible to extinguish once they have been established. Although complete abstinence from illicit drugs is always an underlying goal of treatment, more realistic goals, such as the ability to function in society and substantial reduction in the patient's consumption of illicit drugs, actually drive the day-to-day activities of treatment centers. Further goals may focus on reducing street crime, developing educational or vocational capabilities, restoring employment, averting fetal exposure to drugs, and improving general health, psychological functioning, and family life. These were some of the findings of a comprehensive report on drug treatment programs from the Institute of Medicine of the National Academy of Sciences. The report from the panel of medical and drug treatment experts, in general, urged (1) that treatment be more timely, indicating that on any given day 66,000 people are on waiting lists for public programs; (2) that caregivers be given better training; (3) that services be specifically tailored to pregnant woman, prison inmates, and those on parole and probation; and (4) that an increased effort be directed toward research effectiveness. The panel reported a disturbing trend in the expansion of unproven and very expensive private treatment for middle and upper class drug users covered by insurance and that these private treatment plans cost twice as much as public programs although there is no good evidence that the treatments are effective.

In the past, research on the treatment of substance abuse was concentrated on the management of opioid dependence. The recent rise in nonopioid problems, particularly those related to cocaine, has prompted a great deal of activity in new areas. The increased awareness of drug abuse in the workplace has also spurred the development of innovative programs for early detection and treatment of workers before drugs cause the loss of their jobs. The diversification of treatment approaches has led to increased attention to the complex interactions between drug use behavior and complicated problems in other areas such as social functioning, family problems, and occupational difficulties. Thus, the effectiveness of any treatment may be influenced by specific variables such as the availability of family support for the patient and more general factors such as the local economy and level of unemployment. There is increasing recognition that substance abuse is a multifaceted social-psychological syndrome rather than just a medical problem requiring medical treatment.

In recent years, there has been a cultural shift in attitudes toward substance use and abuse. For a while, drug use was the norm. However, more recently the tide has turned, and one of the primary objectives of antidrug efforts has become the denormalization of drug use. This has led to more people acknowledging their problem with substance abuse and seeking treatment. It has also allowed alcoholics and substance abusers to reduce their denial of their problem and refer themselves for treatment. The increase in the number of self-referrals and the number of individuals seeking treatment in the early stages of their problem improves the success rate. Much emphasis is now being placed on the early detection of drug problems.

Many barriers to early intervention remain. Likewise, there is no clear-cut evidence as to which treatment technique is most effective. The wide diversity of treatment methods reflects the present lack of precise knowledge about the nature of drug addiction and abuse. Uncertainty still exists regarding the causes, whether or not it is an illness, and the degree to which the condition is physical or psychological. Because no one method of treatment has proved to be the answer to the drug abuse problem, research and experimentation are being conducted on a wide variety of potential treatment methods. Some researchers are working with behavioral techniques such as aversion therapy, or negative conditioning, in which electric shocks or nausea-producing substances are administered simultaneously with narcotics. Others are using biofeedback techniques to train people to control internal states and body processes. Transcendental meditation has been investigated as a possible method of reducing soft drug use, particularly among college students.

Much attention is currently directed toward developing alternatives to drug abuse, which may include any meaningful activity or pursuits in which young people can become involved rather than resorting to drugs, and to working with the family of the patient to help break the cycle of abuse being passed down from parent to child. Policy makers continue to debate these issues, while research is attempting to increase our knowledge of this complex social problem. Meanwhile, even though treatment programs across the country are not "curing" some patients of their drug dependence, for the majority these programs are providing support and a marked degree of social rehabilitation for better functioning and a better life.

Substance abusers have been found to be a heterogeneous group who cannot be classified simply on the basis of their preferred drug. Therefore, this discussion of treatment is organized on the basis of type of program rather than type of drug abused.

DETOXIFICATION AND MAINTENANCE PROGRAMS

DETOXIFICATION

Most treatment programs begin with detoxification. This simply means withdrawing the drug upon which the person is dependent. The withdrawal symptoms usually consist of effects opposite to those produced by the drug. Cocaine, for example, produces euphoria and increased energy; cocaine-dependent persons usually feel tired and depressed during withdrawal. Detoxification from sedatives can be life-threatening because of seizures and cardiac effects, but medical treatment with prescribed sedatives in decreasing amounts is usually successful. Detoxification from opioids, while less dangerous, is still quite uncomfortable without medical help. Detoxification from short-acting opioids takes 7 to 10 days, but subtle symptoms can continue for months. Protracted withdrawal symptoms can be a significant problem, especially for those trying to withdraw from such a long-acting opioid as methadone. Senay et al. (1977) evaluated the utility of detoxification from maintenance on methadone in terms of the avowed goal of a maintenance treatment followed by detoxification and the achievement of a stable drug-free state. They found that those patients randomly assigned to a very slow detoxification over 84 days did significantly better than those assigned to more rapid detoxification in terms of both their comfort and their retention in drug-free treatment.

Drug detoxification is seldom effective in itself in producing recovery from dependence; it is generally seen as only the first step in a long-term treatment program. Detoxification programs provide a humane means of reducing drug dependency, an opportunity to break the cycle of addiction, and a chance to enter longer-term treatment. Detoxification episodes are often hospital-based, beginning with emergency admission for an overdose. Because of the narrow and short-term focus of detoxification programs and the high frequency of relapse, detoxification should not be viewed as a method of treatment; it is, however, an important gateway to treatment.

Most drug detoxification (at least 100,000 admissions a year) now takes place in hospital beds. It is doubtful that hospitalization (especially beyond 1 or 2 days) is needed in most cases, except for special problems—addicted newborns, heavy dependence on sedatives, concurrent medical or severe psychiatric problems. Detoxification can usually be undertaken safely on a residential, partial day care, or ambulatory basis. In contrast, the treatment for withdrawal from sedatives is one of intensive care and should be carried out in a hospital, where every medical advantage may be gained over the possibly fatal withdrawal symptoms. Many drug-dependent individuals who enter a hospital for treatment are addicted to heroin and sedatives. In such cases, withdrawal from the sedative drugs is the major focus, with heroin treatment following.

The antihypertensive drug clonidine has been used to treat the symptoms of opioid withdrawal (Gold et al., 1980). Clonidine is not an opiate-like drug, but it relieves many of the symptoms of opioid withdrawal, particularly those that involve physical symptoms of autonomic nervous system hyperactivity. Since clonidine is not an addicting drug, it can be given in medical settings where amelioration of withdrawal symptoms by a prescription opiate is not desirable. It is of interest to note that clonidine may relieve the symptoms of nicotine withdrawal in smokers attempting to quit (Glassman et al., 1984). This suggests that there may be a common neural pathway involved in the production of withdrawal symptoms among several classes of addicting drugs. An ultrarapid method of detoxification has been produced by combining the withdrawal precipitating effect of naltrexone with clonidine (Charney et al., 1982).

Methadone Withdrawal

The two major modalities that use methadone—detoxification and maintenance—are often confused. The methadone regulations issued by the FDA define detoxification treatment as the administering or dispensing of methadone as a substitute narcotic drug in decreasing doses to reach a drug-free state in a period not to exceed 21 days in order to withdraw an individual who is dependent on heroin or other morphinelike drugs from the use of these drugs. Methadone maintenance is discussed in detail later in this section.

Since the early 1950s various techniques using methadone for the detoxification of heroin users have evolved. Chambers and Brill (1973) grouped these techniques into two major categories: inpatient withdrawal and ambulatory (or outpatient) detoxification. Both of these techniques require certain basic adjustments to make the treatment appropriate to the patient, including modifications that take into consideration (1) the amount heroin habitually used; (2) the existence of multiple-drug dependency involving hypnotics, alcohol, or minor tranquilizers; and (3) the patient's overall physical and psychiatric condition.

Proponents of inpatient methadone withdrawal generally assert that users present themselves not only with a drug-dependency problem but with a multiplicity of psychosocial disorders as well. These external conditions are often regarded as the major underlying causes of the drug-dependency problem and figure importantly in the high relapse rates seen in patients following withdrawal. The goal of inpatient withdrawal is, therefore, to help an individual reach a drug-free state in a supportive and closely supervised environment that, for a limited time at least, protects him or her from the adverse pressures of the street. During this process it is hoped that the program will be able to provide adequate ancillary services (such as counseling and job placement) and that, once drug-free, the patient will be more likely to become a productive member of society.

The philosophy of ambulatory withdrawal programs shares many characteristics with that of the inpatient technique. The first major goal is to stabilize the addict on a low to moderate dose of methadone (20 to 40 milligrams per day) and then to gradually reduce the dose until the patient no longer requires the administration of a narcotic to allay withdrawal discomfort. During the treatment process a great deal of emphasis is placed on helping the addict learn new productive behavioral patterns or reestablish old ones. However, the ambulatory methadone detoxification technique, more than any other, requires the patient to assume the largest share of responsibility for treatment and rehabilitation success. The physician's role is decidedly more passive than in inpatient detoxification; he or she can administer medication and provide supportive services only if the addict-patient decides to come to the clinic. During the course of withdrawal, the patient must make a series of decisions to come back for treatment. In this sense, ambulatory detoxification becomes a social interaction and motivational process, whereas inpatient withdrawal is more of a medical process.

Addicts seek treatment when they can no longer cope with the drug-induced depression, when they are arrested, when they can no longer afford their drug habits, or for a number of other reasons. Upon commencing treatment, if withdrawal has begun, the individual will appear weak, anxious, nauseated, and/or tremulous. These symptoms signal the danger of convulsion and/or psychosis. If the patient does not yet show these symptoms, a careful vigil is kept so that he or she can be treated immediately upon their onset. In the first 8 hours after abrupt withdrawal, signs of intoxication decline and the patient's condition actually appears to improve. However, after 8 hours the symptoms just described occur, perhaps accompanied by muscle twitches, impaired cardiovascular responses, headaches, and vomiting. These signs and symptoms increase in intensity for the next 8 hours (until about 16 hours after withdrawal from the drug) and become quite severe after 24 hours. Untreated, these conditions will likely develop into grand mal–type seizures between the thirtieth and forty-eighth hours. These convulsive seizures have been seen as early as the sixteenth hour and as late as the eighth day after abrupt withdrawal (Stimmel, 1983).

During the following 2 days there may be a recurrence of insomnia culminating in delirium (much like delirium tremens), hallucinations, disorientation, and marked tremors. The delirium typically lasts about 5 days, ending with a long, deep sleep. The whole withdrawal process is self-limiting, even if untreated. However, death is a real danger in uncontrolled, untreated withdrawal, especially withdrawal from sedatives (Woody et al., 1983). Treatment usually consists of administering a short-acting barbiturate to allay the first symptoms of withdrawal and then tapering off either with the same drug or, more often, with decreased doses of a long-acting drug such as phenobarbital. Because there is a cross-tolerance with many of these drugs, theoretically any of them could be administered during the withdrawal process. Phenobarbital is the barbiturate of choice in many withdrawal treatment programs because it provides a low fluctuation level (Stimmel, 1983).

In addition to hospital treatment during withdrawal, first-aid measures are often necessary, especially in cases of drug overdose. A close watch is still kept on the patient because apprehension, mental confusion, and mental incompetence will likely occur during treatment. Since barbiturates, nonbarbiturate sedatives, and tranquilizers are often abused, because the various kinds may be taken at the same time and may be taken with alcohol, overdoses are not uncommon. In a victim of barbiturate overdose, for example, coma, flaccidity of the muscles, and respiratory depression are generally apparent. The treatment to follow is (1) open the airway and clear out the oral cavity, (2) give mouth-to-mouth resuscitation if breathing has stopped, and (3) check the pulse. If there is no pulse, one should perform cardiopulmonary resuscitation (CPR) procedure (Stimmel, 1983). Perhaps the most important help one can give is to call for emergency medical assistance as quickly as possible. This treatment is combined with supportive measures such as vitamin administration, restoration of electrolyte balance, and proper hydration.

Cocaine Detoxification

Detoxification is also the first step in the treatment of cocaine-dependent persons. Often this step is quite difficult because the patient has a tremendous craving to resume the use of cocaine, and the presence of severe depressive symptoms makes participation in an overall rehabilitation program limited. The antidepressant drug desipramine has been reported to decrease cocaine craving on a long-term basis (Gawin & Kleber, 1984, 1985). In a double-blind outpatient study, Tennant and Tarver (1984) found many dropouts and no better overall results with desipramine than with placebo during the withdrawal phase. Lithium was found to decrease cocaine craving and use in some patients (Gawin & Kleber, 1986). It has been theorized that cocaine-dependent patients suffer from a dopamine depletion syndrome, and thus the dopamine receptor stimulant bromocriptine has been tried to relieve withdrawal symptoms (Dackis & Gold, 1986). Results are positive, but much more research is needed to confirm the utility of this treatment. Other drugs are also being tried to treat cocaine abuse (e.g., neurotransmitter precursors, vasopressin, calcium channel blockers), but controlled studies remain to be done. Desipramine has helped addicts abstain from cocaine for significantly longer periods than those who took a placebo. Researchers believe that this antidepressant may help cocaine users get past the depression that commonly accompanies efforts to go cold turkey. The antidepressants also are thought to restore a vital brain chemical that is depleted by cocaine use. Flupenthixol acts as an antidepressant at low doses. This antipsychotic is available in Europe for treatment of schizophrenia. In a preliminary study in the Bahamas, cocaine addicts who were given flupenthixol were able to stay off cocaine for an average of 6 months, compared with 2 months without the medication. Carbamazapine may reduce the seizures associated with long-term cocaine use and reduce the craving for the drug. Buspirone relieves the depression and anxiety accompanying alcohol withdrawal. Researchers are looking into its effects on cocaine withdrawal as well.

Treatment of cocaine toxicity is accomplished on a symptomatic basis. Drug-induced anxiety can be medically treated with sedatives such as diazepam (Cohen, 1982). Hospitalization with respiratory assistance is recommended for severe overdose. After recovery, psychological support is important. If the individual suffering from overdose is not breathing, immediate CPR is the only first aid that the lay person should administer. It is important that additional drugs be given only in a hospital setting. The cocaine user often has taken other drugs in addition to cocaine; administering additional depressants may exacerbate his or her condition. Signs of cocaine abuse may include gregariousness, hyperactivity, loss of appetite, rapid heart rate, racing thoughts, and euphoria. Anxiety and agitation may also be present. As cocaine dependence has emerged recently as a chronic, endemic problem, some attempts have been made to provide symptomatic withdrawal and psychological treatment for it (Cohen, 1982). Skilled psychotherapists, multiple and varied treatment contacts, and efficient selection of behavioral techniques have been found to increase the probability of drug abstinence (Van Dyke, 1981). In addition to psychotherapeutic and behavioral modalities, the pharmacological approach to the treatment of long-term cocaine use is also being studied. Tennant and Tarver (1984) reported that desipramine, a tricyclic antidepressant, given every 4 to 6 hours for 1 to 3 weeks after the last dose of cocaine is taken helps the long-term user to suppress drug craving and depression to the point where the patient can nearly always remain in long-term treatment. Desipramine and other drugs will continue to be researched now that neurotransmitter enhancement and antagonist administration are becoming treatment possibilities in stimulant and hallucinogen dependence.

PCP Detoxification

It has been well documented that treating PCP abusers is often a complicated and frustrating experience. The unpredictable effects of PCP vary with dose and with the biological and psychological characteristic of PCP users. Even relatively low doses (5 to 20 milligrams) can cause a state of acute confusion lasting several hours. Higher doses have been associated with serious neurological, cardiovascular, and psychotic reactions. PCP psychosis resembles a schizophrenic reaction, and some PCP users have been known to develop classic schizophrenia. Psychoses can occur because the drug effects interact with a vulnerable personality; for example, the user may have underlying borderline personality organization. Because of the behavioral toxicity of PCP, the drug poses a significant health problem, with the potential for death from drug-induced violence, accidents, and suicides. The dangerous, bizarre, disruptive behavior associated with PCP use necessitates that emergency treatment for intoxication be carried out at a medical facility. An initial evaluation can determine the level of care needed and the most appropriate treatment setting. PCP toxicity can result in highly varied and confusing behavior patterns that are difficult to diagnose. Occasionally, the patient may appear lethargic and calm at some times and disoriented and agitated at other times, social one moment and extremely hostile the next (Fram & Stone, 1986).

PCP also produces medical complications such as vomiting, seizures, and high blood pressure. It can act as a depressant, stimulant, hallucinogenic, analgesic, or anesthetic. A patient who presents to the emergency room with paranoia, distorted perception, nystagmus, and hypertension may be evidencing PCP intoxication. Urine assays for PCP as well as other drugs of abuse should be done upon admission to the emergency room. Management of PCP intoxication requires close monitoring of the patient because clinical symptoms tend to fluctuate over a period of hours as well as days. The treatment of PCP toxicity will depend on an assessment of the patterns of intoxication and the physical and psychological state of the patient. Once the diagnosis is made, staff should direct their efforts toward calming the patient, ensuring the safety of the patient and the staff, and treating any medical complications that may arise. Placing the patient in a quiet, dimly lit room may help control hypersensitivity to light and noise. Attempting to "talk down" the patient may increase agitation. Management of violent behavior may require restraint. The increased strength of the PCP-intoxicated patient may necessitate additional staff. Patients presenting with severe agitation and/or psychosis may require antipsychotic medication (typically haloperidol). Muscle spasms and seizures may have to be treated with intravenously administered diazepam, and severe hypertension may require short-term use of antihypertensive drugs (McCarron, 1986).

PCP toxicity of short duration may be treated symptomatically. Vital signs (pulse, blood pressure, respiration, body temperature) should be monitored. Most patients show improvement within several hours of PCP ingestion. However, the patient should be observed until his or her vital signs are stable and the patient is no longer agitated or violent. Following emergency care, PCP users may still exhibit impulsiveness and resistance to treatment, and therefore they need a highly structured setting. Psychotropic medication is not typically recommended during the first 48 hours. Rather, the client should be placed in a quiet, secure environment with few people. The initial treatment, lasting from 2 to 4 weeks, should generally include regular individual therapy and educational sessions.

Opiate Antagonists

Other pharmacological substances have also been tried in an attempt to find a more practical pharmacological deterrent to heroin dependence than methadone. Nalorphine, naloxone, cyclazocine, and naltrexone are a few of the drugs classified as opiate antagonists. These are less objectionable than methadone from a moral standpoint, for they are antinarcotic and block the effects of morphine. Because of their toxic effects and their inability to relieve the craving for heroin, however, the antagonists are not as popular as methadone with patients.

Treatment with cyclazocine first necessitates withdrawal from heroin. Then cyclazocine is administered in increasing doses until tolerance develops. The usual dose at which tolerance develops is about 4 milligrams per day. This level will block the subjective effects of 20 to 25 milligrams of heroin for a period of 20 to 26 hours. The user is usually tranquil and free of anxiety, without any appearance of sedation or mental disturbance. Most important is the absence of the drive to find heroin, which allows for social rehabilitation and increased productivity.

Nalorphine is too short-acting to be of much clinical value; it is used more to detect the use of heroin and to counteract the effects of overdose. Naloxone must be administered in massive doses to achieve heroin blockage, and because its supply is limited its use is also limited. At this time there is very limited use of the antagonists in treatment programs because (1) they have unpleasant and disturbing side effects, (2) they must be administered daily, and (3) heroin-dependent individuals do not find these drugs helpful. Naltrexone is another antagonist drug that has demonstrated a potential for usefulness in the treatment of heroin dependence In the presence of a sufficient dose of naltrexone, heroin and other opiate drugs will have no effect. It is theorized that naltrexone's blocking effect is due to its structural similarity to the opiates. Naltrexone molecules, through a process that is poorly understood, competitively displace opiate molecules at opiate receptor sites in the body. Through this displacement, the narcotic effects are blocked by an agent that itself is essentially neutral.

Naltrexone is nonaddicting, and there are no withdrawal symptoms associated with its discontinuance. It is nearly pure antagonist with no euphoric effects, and therefore it has no street value and does not stimulate any illicit activities in the community. Naltrexone's side effects are minimal. For many individuals there are no side effects, but in some cases relatively minor reactions occur. These include nausea and mild stomach pain and a slight increase in blood pressure. Gastrointestinal reactions are usually relieved by taking the medication after eating a meal. Elevations in blood pressure are generally not clinically significant; blood pressure tends to return to normal as treatment progresses (Brahen et al., 1977).

Naltrexone is taken orally (it has an extremely bitter taste) in a variety of different dosage patterns. Individuals who are physically dependent on opiates must first be detoxified before induction to naltrexone. A dose of 50 milligrams normally lasts for about 24 hours, and doses of 110 and 150 milligrams last 48 hours and 72 hours, respectively. Induction usually begins at 10 milligrams and increases by 10 milligrams per day until the maintenance dosage level is achieved. One of the more common treatment regimens is 50 milligrams daily for an initial period of several weeks followed by a routine of three doses a week—100 milligrams, 100 milligrams, and 150 milligrams on Monday, Wednesday, and Friday, respectively. In certain cases, twice-a-week doses of 150 milligrams on Tuesday and Friday may be prescribed (Landsberg et al., 1976).

Unlike the alcoholic receiving disulfiram (Antabuse), there is no unpleasant reaction if the naltrexone-treated patient takes an opioid. There is only a feeling that he has wasted his money because the effects of the heroin or other opiate have been neutralized. Naltrexone is the product of many years of both NIDA-funded research and pharmaceutical industry investigations in pursuit of the "perfect antagonist." Naltrexon fits this definition in many ways in that it is effective against all opioids, is not itself addictive, is relatively long acting, and has few side effects. Unfortunately, such a drug appeals only to highly motivated patients who sincerely wish to give up experiencing opiate-induced euphoria. This describes only a minority of drug-dependent individuals. Despite this limitation, naltrexone has become the drug of choice in many centers for physicians, nurses, and white collar workers with opioid dependence problems. Physicians who must constantly be exposed to the temptation to return to opiate use seem to benefit from this treatment.

METHADONE MAINTENANCE PROGRAMS

Trade and generic names for methadone (diphenyldimethylaminoheplanone) include methadone hydrochloride, Adanon HCI, Dolophine HCI, Althose HCI, and Amidone HCI. Like morphine, methadone is an analgesic drug, but it has a different chemical structure. This completely synthetic substance does possess pharmacological characteristics much like those of morphine but has many practical advantages over the opiates. Methadone maintenance is an ambulatory treatment for opiate dependence. A daily oral dose of 30 to 100 milligrams of methadone hydrochloride yields a very stable level of active metabolite. Once adjusted, the dose produces neither subjective intoxication nor clinically detectable behavioral impairment. Toxic side effects during long-term treatment are rare, and general health improves markedly as compared with taking heroin daily. Methadone can be taken orally mixed with drinks such as orange juice; its metabolism is sufficiently slow to prolong its action for 24 hours; it is less likely than morphine to cause toxic side effects; and, most important, it suppresses the desire for heroin, primarily by blocking heroin euphoria and abstinence symptoms.

Methadone is a narcotic, and it does produce tolerance and physical dependence. Although the mechanism of its action is poorly understood, the theories resemble those put forth for morphine. One of these theories hypothesizes a selective depression of interneurons of the spinal cord and postganglionic neurons of the autonomic system. Although its primary involvement seems to be with the cholinergic system (the system of nerve fibers activated by acetylcholine), findings of both increases and decreases in acetylcholine obscure exact evidence of its depressive mechanism. Depression of selected reflexes indicates action on the spinal cord, decreases in respiration rate indicate action on the medulla, and decreases in body temperature indicate action on the hypothalamus. Involvement with the hypothalamic–pituitary–adrenal axis may be indicated by the suppression of the release of ACTH (adrenocorticotropic hormone, the pituitary hormone responsible for initiating the stress response in the body) and could be responsible, therefore, for generally suppressed stress reactions. The suppressed production of sex hormones could also be responsible for the menstrual problems of the female and the loss of libido experienced by both sexes (Cushman et al., 1970). Both mental and neuromuscular functions appear to be normal. Patients perform well at jobs and in the classroom. In fact, researchers have not been able to find a medical or psychological test, except urinalysis, that can distinguish methadone patients from normal individuals. Patients in methadone maintenance programs become much more amenable to counseling, environmental changes, and support services. In this way methadone maintenance contributes not only to social factors but to psychological factors as well.

In the methadone maintenance program, the user's cycle of hustle, fix, hustle, fix is broken, and the search for drugs is ended. In essence, he or she is stabilized in a state of blockade, between euphoria and withdrawal. Patients have shown that they soon begin to tolerate frustrating situations without feeling the hunger for heroin. Their dreams and conversations about drugs begin to subside, and often, when busy, they even forget periodic medication (Dole & Nyswander, 1966, 1967). For those individuals dependent upon opium, methadone has had a tremendous positive impact since its introduction in the 1960s. Patients who have been unable to completely stop heroin and detoxify or who relapse shortly after detoxification can be transferred to a maintenance dose of oral methadone. Urine test results show that patients on methadone reduce or eliminate their use of street drugs. Best results are seen in programs that utilize contingency management along with methadone. Methadone is well accepted by most patients, and it enables them to turn their attention to social and occupational rehabilitation. Studies have shown that 65 to 85 percent of patients remain in methadone treatment for 12 months or more and that during this time there is a dramatic reduction in crimes committed and an increase in gainful employment. Some patients remain on methadone for many years; it enables them to function well and in many cases make significant contributions to society. Studies of long-term cases have failed to find evidence of toxic effects from long-term methadone ingestion (Kreek, 1983). Success rates for stopping methadone and remaining drug-free are reasonably good when both patient and therapist feel that the patient has made sufficient progress that he or she is now ready to stop.

Unlike some of the self-help programs, methadone maintenance per se does little for psychological and social development. Indirectly, however, it does allow ex-users to stay off heroin, to get steady jobs, to support their families, and to get a start on the way to becoming productive members of society. There are a number of drawbacks to and criticisms of the methadone maintenance program:

1 Even though the daily cost to the addict is roughly that of a cup of coffee, the total treatment costs to society are substantial.

2 Doctors are justifiably reluctant to start young patients on a treatment that could keep them dependent for life.

3 Maintenance ties the patient to a daily ritual of receiving the medicine at an outpatient clinic.

4 Methadone maintenance is at best an incomplete cure.

5 The giving of an addictive drug to drug users is contrary to prevalent morality.

6 Some methadone eventually finds its way into the street market.

Paradoxically, the most severe criticisms of methadone clinics stem from problems peripheral to the heroin problem. Many heroin users are also alcoholics and pill users. Methadone clinics can be gathering places for boisterous drunks, drug dealers, and unemployed loiterers. Yielding to the community's concerns, many clinics have closed and funding has been reduced. This, of course, is like the old saying of throwing out the baby with the bath water. For no other program, drug-free or maintenance, has had better results than methadone maintenance in long-term care of heroin addicts. Tens of thousands of previously intractable heroin-dependent individuals, most of whom had previously failed in various abstinence-directed treatments, have been restored to living normal lives (Dole & Nyswander, 1983).

Since American scientific technology has advanced more rapidly than social conditions, it would appear that the psychological circle would be the more profitable of the two on which to work, even if such work were only a stopgap measure. Programs based on this premise are called maintenance programs. Although they are now being used in many countries of the world, the program in use in England has received the most publicity and is known as the British system. In this program, the heroin user receives a regular daily supply of opiates free or at minimal cost. He or she is under the supervision of a knowledgeable and ethical physician who supplies the maintenance needs. The program is in the hands of a specialized individual in each area, thus reducing the corruption that once plagued the system. While the British have not legalized heroin possession, its use under a physician's care is legal. The drug culture there remains basically stable, and little crime is attributed to opiate-dependent individuals. A user who is involved in this program does not spend his or her life seeking heroin or the means to pay for it.

REFERENCES

Brahen, L., et al. (1977). Naltrexone and cyclazocine: a controlled study. *Archives of General Psychiatry*, 34:1181–1184.

Chambers, C. D., and Brill, L. (Eds.). (1973). *Methadone: Experiences and Issues.* New York: Behavioral Publications.

Charney, D. S., et al. (1982). Clonidine and naltrexone: a safe, effective, and rapid treatment of abrupt withdrawal from methadone therapy. *Archives of General Psychiatry*, 39(11):1327–1332.

Cohen, Sidney. (1982). Health hazards of cocaine. *Drug Enforcement*, Fall, pp. 10–13.

Cushman, P., et al. (1970). Hypothalamic–pituitary–adrenal axis in methadone-treated heroin addicts. *Journal of Clinical Endocrinology*, 30:24–29.

Dackis, C. A., and Gold, M. S. (1986). Bromocriptine as treatment of cocaine abuse. *Lancet*, 8438:1151–1152.

Dole, V. P., and Nyswander, M. E. (1966). Narcotic blockade. *Archives of Internal Medicine*, 118:204–209.

Dole, V. P., and Nyswander, M. E. (1967). Heroin addiction—a metabolic disease. *Archives of Internal Medicine*, 120:19–24.

Dole, V. P., and Nyswander, M. E. (1983). Behavioral pharmacology and treatment of human drug abuse—methadone maintenance of narcotic addicts. In J. E. Smith and J. D. Lane (Eds.), *The Neurobiology of Opiate Reward Processes*. Amsterdam: Elsevier Biomedical Press.

Fram, D., and Stone, N. (1986). Clinical observations in the treatment of adolescent and young adult PCP abusers. In *Phencyclidine: An Update*. NIDA Research Monograph 64. Rockville, Md.: National Institute on Drug Abuse, pp 204–214.

Gawin, F. H., and Kleber, H. D. (1984). Cocaine abuse treatment: open pilot trial with desipramine and lithium carbonate. *Archives of General Psychiatry*, 41(9):903–909.

Gawin, F. H., and Kleber, H. D. (1985). Cocaine use in a treatment population: patterns and diagnosis distinctions. In N. J. Kozel and E. H. Adams (Eds.), *Cocaine Use in America: Epidemiologic and Clinical Perspectives*. NIDA Research Monograph 61. Washington, D.C.: U.S. Government Printing Office, pp. 182–192.

Gawin, F. H., and Kleber, H. D. (1986). Abstinence symptomatology and psychiatric diagnosis in cocaine abusers: clinical observations. *Archives of General Psychiatry*, 43(2):107–113.

Glassman, A., et al. (1984). Cigarette craving, smoking withdrawal and clonidine. *Science*, 226:864–866.

Gold, M. S., et al. (1980). Opiate withdrawal using clonidine. *JAMA*, 243:343–346.

Kreek, M. J. (1983). Health consequences associated with the use of methadone. In J. R. Cooper, F. Altman, B. S. Brown, and D. Czechowicz (Eds.), *Research on the Treatment of Narcotic Addiction: State of the Art*. NIDA Research Monograph. DHHS Pub. (ADM) 83-1291. Washington, D.C.: U.S. Government Printing Office, pp. 456–494.

Landsberg, R., et al. (1976). An analysis of naltrexone use—its efficacy, safety, and potential. In D. Julius and P. Renault (Eds.), *Narcotic Antagonists: Naltrexone Progress Report*. NIDA Research Monograph 9. Rockville, Md.: National Institute on Drug Abuse.

McCarron, M. (1986). Phencyclidine intoxication. In *Phencyclidine: An Update*. NIDA Research Monograph 64. Rockville, Md.: National Institute on Drug Abuse.

Senay, E., Dorus, W., Goldberg, F., and Thornton, W. (1977). Withdrawal methadone maintenance: rate withdrawal and expectation. *Archives of General Psychiatry*, 34:361–367.

Stimmel, B., Goldberg, J., et al. (1977). Ability to remain abstinent after methadone detoxification. *JAMA*, 237:1216–1220.

Tennant, F. S., Jr. (1983). Treatment of dependence upon stimulants and hallucinogens. *Drug and Alcohol Dependence*, 11:111–114.

Tennant, F. S., and Tarver, A. L. (1984). Double-blind comparison of desipramine and placebo in withdrawal from cocaine dependence. In L. S. Harris (Ed.), *Proceedings of the 46th Annual Scientific Meeting, The Committee on Problems of Drug Depen-*

dence. NIDA Research Monograph 55. Washington, D.C.: U.S. Government Printing Office, pp. 159–163.

Van Dyke, Craig. (1981). Cocaine. In J. H. Lowinson and P. Ruiz (Eds.), *Substance Abuse: Clinical Problems and Perspectives.* Baltimore, Md.: Williams & Wilkins.

Woody, G. E., Luborsky, L., McLellan, A. T., O'Brien, C. P., Beck, A. T., Hole, A., and Herman, I. (1983). Psychotherapy for opiate addiction: does it help? *Archives of General Psychiatry,* 40:639–645.

COMPULSORY TREATMENT

The concept of compulsory treatment was first proposed in the United States shortly after the passage of the Harrison Narcotics Act of 1914. As early as 1919, the Narcotics Unit of the Treasury Department urged Congress to set up a chain of federal narcotics farms where heroin users could be incarcerated and treated for their addiction. The first serious attempt to rehabilitate the heroin user became a reality with the opening of two federal hospitals at Lexington, Kentucky, and Fort Worth, Texas, in 1936 and 1938, respectively. The emphasis was on the withdrawal procedure followed by an attempt at psychological and vocational rehabilitation.

In 1936 the first annual report of the Public Health Service hospital at Lexington stated that treatment of voluntary patients had not been very effective because most of them had left before treatment was complete. Although the hospitals were established primarily to care for narcotics addicts convicted of federal law violations, they were also authorized to admit and treat voluntary patients. Most admissions to both hospitals were voluntary from 1935 until 1968, when admission of voluntary patients ceased. Approximately 70 percent of the voluntary patients signed out against medical advice before completing treatment. Most of those who remained to complete treatment had the legal pressure of probation from a state court (Maddux, 1988).

The hospital programs were designed to treat not only withdrawal illness but also the drug-using habit and associated mental problems. The treatment programs included four fairly distinct elements: drug withdrawal, residence in a drug-free environment, psychotherapy, and supervised activities. The recommended duration of hospital treatment was 6 months, but this was later reduced to 4 months. The supervised activities included vocational training, remedial education, and recreational activities. Medical care, dental care, social services, and religious services were provided. Nearly all of the professional staff viewed drug withdrawal as a preliminary or minor aspect of treatment, with the important therapeutic work to come later. Consequently, the departure of most voluntary patients during or shortly after withdrawal became a source of continuing frustration for the staff. With major emphasis on the medical aspects and minor emphasis on the psychosocial elements, the failure of these federal narcotics hospitals was not surprising. The return rate varies from report to report, but approximately 95 percent of those treated eventually returned to drugs, 90 percent within 6 months after their release. Supporters of this program were quick to point out such obvious factors as forced confinement and quick release as major contributors to failure (Maddux, 1988).

Using the California and New York State compulsory court-ordered treatment and civil commitment alternative to incarceration programs (California Civil Addict Program, New York State Civil Commitment) as models, the federal Narcotic Addict Rehabilitation Act (NARA) was enacted at the federal level in 1966. This legislation established a close linkage between the health care system and the criminal justice system and provided a civil commitment to keep addicts in treatment beyond withdrawal. NARA also included community-based follow-up care after detoxification, similar to that initially provided at the Lexington and Fort Worth hospitals. Later, NARA inpatient treatment facilities were established in several major cities. NARA also set the stage for community treatment of narcotics addicts and subsequently other drug abusers by providing initial funding and developing a group of treatment experts in drug abuse. The focus of civil commitment procedures has been on compulsive drug abusers, especially antisocial addicts responsible for committing large numbers of criminal acts. Another major effort in the drug abuse criminal justice area was the Treatment Alternatives to Street Crime (TASC), which was established in 1972 by the Special Action Office for Drug Abuse Prevention (SAODAP) and was modeled, in part, on the court referral program developed in Washington, D.C. TASC is essentially a diversionary program for drug abusers. The program identifies clients, refers them to treatment, and monitors their adjustment. It serves an "outreach" or "case-finding" function for treatment agencies (Cook et al., 1988).

Although the federal and state civil commitment programs were in full operation for about a decade, 1965 to 1975, and were replaced by a system of community drug treatment programs, the desire of community programs to induce larger numbers of addicts into treatment and the large number of prisoners with addiction history has fueled a reexamination of civil commitment options (Leukefeld & Tims, 1988a).

THERAPEUTIC COMMUNITIES PROGRAM

In the years 1965 through 1975, large numbers of drug abusers were court mandated to therapeutic communities as an alternative to federal and state treatment programs operated under civil commitment legislation. Since 1975, the civil commitment programs have been largely replaced by community-based treatment centers that have included therapeutic communities, and civil commitment procedures were replaced by the less uniform set of activities termed "legal referral." Legal referrals to therapeutic communities have varied over the years. More than 40 percent of admissions to Phoenix House in 1970 were legally referred, compared to fewer than 20 percent in 1985. Other therapeutic communities have informally reported a similar decreasing trend in legal referrals even though some therapeutic communities serve criminal justice clients almost exclusively. Admissions to therapeutic communities now include significantly fewer opiate users and increasing numbers of nonopiate abusers. This change in admissions to therapeutic communities may reflect an actual decrease in the number of new heroin abusers, or it may indicate a shift to other treatment modalities. Generally, the pervasive use of drugs at all levels of society has resulted in more users who are minors or who have noncriminal backgrounds. As a result, there has been less need for therapeutic communities to recruit clients from the criminal justice system. Younger clients are more likely to be legally referred than adults. Nearly half of all male adolescent admissions to drug-free residential and outpatient programs were legally referred. Approximately 40 percent of the adolescent admissions to Phoenix House are legally referred, compared to fewer than 20 percent of adult clients (DeLeon, 1988).

Program Objectives

The objectives of civil commitment are to contain objectionable persons and to change the objectionable behavior of these individuals. Most nations of the world have some form of civil commitment, although different countries have very different ways of implementing programs. Effectiveness of civil commitment programs is measured by the reduction of community disruption, and costs can be measured as the toll on civil liberties. In democratic countries, a massive campaign against drug abuse requires evidence of public support. For a major intervention program to be successful, especially with reliance on compulsory treatment, the problem must be isolated and enlarged, in certain circumstance even created. Civil commitment in other countries reports similar objectives if not similar programs. Of the 43 countries studied by Porter and associates (1986) 27 had civil commitment practices. Implementation of civil commitment procedures differs markedly according to whether it comes under mental health legislation or under separate legislation specific to drug abuse. If covered under legislation specific to drug abuse, the rationale for civil commitment may be limited to evidence of dependence and/or addiction and the need for treatment. Reporting for the World Health Organization, Porter and associates (1986) made the following recommendations regarding civil commitment:

1 Persons who need a short-term emergency commitment for incapacitation due to drug dependence should be immediately released from detention on completion of treatment, that is, completion of detoxification.

2 Compulsory civil commitment for other than emergency care is justified only when an effective treatment program as well as adequate and humane facilities are available.

3 The period of confinement should be limited, and a person's involuntary status should be subject to periodic review.

4 The person concerned should be afforded substantive and procedural rights during the commitment proceedings.

The primary goal of rehabilitation is to facilitate the development of a drug-free, prosocial lifestyle. This goal is achieved through social learning methodology that fosters maturation, skills training, insight, and personal growth. The process of change is an interplay of client factors such as motivation and treatment influences: compliance, which is adherence to the rules and regulations and avoidance of discharge or reincarceration; conformity, which is adherence to the expectations of the group or community; and commitment, which is a personal resolve to change one's lifestyle.

Unfortunately, many compulsive users of psychoactive substances enter treatment only under legal coercion. Even those who enter voluntarily do so under some form of social or pharmacological coercion, such as pressure from family or friends, the perception of imminent arrest, loss of regular drug-selling connection, or inability to pay the cost of an increasing daily dosage. With or without external coercion, nearly all users seem to have an ambivalent attitude toward their substance dependence. They want to free themselves of the burden and consequences of substance dependence, but they also want the effects of the substance. At different times, one desire or the other becomes dominant. Among contemporary opioid users, two other personality attributes adversely affect engagement in treatment. The first, variously labeled psychopathy, psychopathic deviance, sociopathy, antisocial behavior, or antisocial attitude, has been reported as a noteworthy personality feature of opioid users. The other, variously labeled impulsivity, low frustration tolerance, or inability to delay gratification, has also been frequently reported among opioid users (Maddux et al., 1986). An ambivalent attitude toward the drug dependence, together with an antisocial attitude and a low tolerance for distress, create a conflict-ridden and unstable motivation for treatment. This unstable motivation has represented a major problem in the treatment of opioid dependence and consequently a major focus for treatment (Maddux, 1988).

Treatment Effectiveness

NIDA has sponsored research that suggests that treatment for drug abuse is effective (Tims, 1981; Tims & Ludford, 1984). Clients entering drug-free outpatient (counseling) programs, drug-free residential (therapeutic community) treatment, and methadone maintenance treatment generally experience dramatic reductions in drug use and associated criminality. Many studies also show improvement in employment status and other behavioral outcomes among treated drug abusers. The question of which treatment is superior becomes clouded by the prevailing pattern for clients who have multiple treatment experiences, often in more than one type of program, before becoming abstinent from their principal drug of abuse. This pattern of multiple treatments is reflected in a study by Simpson and Sells (1982), in which opioid addicts were followed over a 6-year period after admission to treatment. By the sixth year, 61 percent of these addicts were opioid abstinent and had been so for at least 1 year. Treatment figured prominently in the attainment of stable abstinence patterns, with about 80 percent of those abstinent having achieved this status directly in connection with a treatment episode. In addition to the 61 percent who were abstinent, 18 percent had given up daily opioid use but had other problems such as occasional opioid use, heavy use of nonopioids or alcohol, or long-term incarceration. Thus, even though a significant number of clients had other problems, only one-fifth of those treated continued their pretreatment levels of opioid use at 6 years after leaving treatment.

The greatest risk of relapse after leaving treatment occurs during the first 90 days, at a time when clients are exposed to drug-related stimuli without the support of a structured program to help resolve their conflicts. For this reason, aftercare programs have been developed to follow up individuals in the community and to provide a resource to assist in maintaining the client's commitment to abstinence. Aftercare models include self-help groups such as Narcotics Anonymous and approaches that stress the acquisition of drug-free living. Using sample data from the Treatment Outcome Prospective Study (TOPS) at 12 months, as well as at 24 and 48 months, the major conclusion reached was that virtually all economic measures show that crime is lower after treatment than before treatment. This finding varies by the measurement used. In addition, when TOPS criminal justice referrals are compared to self-referrals receiving treatment, a significant reduction of primary drug use is seen among criminal justice system referrals for residential treatment. However, alcohol remains a problem for groups studied, with drinking reported to be heavier than or at the same level as before treatment. This finding corresponds with other studies that show positive cost/benefit effects of treatment, especially residential treatment, which has a high cost/benefit ratio.

There is considerable research that demonstrates a direct relationship between retention and posttreatment outcomes. Numerous studies have identified time in treatment as the most consistent predictor of positive outcomes (Simpson & Sells, 1982; De Leon, 1984; Holland, 1983; Barr & Antes, 1981). Because of its obvious importance, retention has increasingly become the focus of investigations in therapeutic communities especially with regard to outcomes between legally referred clients and those referred through other channels (De Leon, 1985). Improvements in criminality, drug use, and employment occur for both groups and are directly related to time spent in treatment. Time in program is the largest and most consistent predictor of treatment outcomes, and legal referral relates significantly to retention. In general, clients referred by the criminal justice system to therapeutic communities (as well as to other modalities) remain in treatment longer than do voluntary clients. On the whole, the findings suggest that retention in treatment is the best predictor of outcome, and legal referral is a consistent predictor of retention. Thus, there is an indirect relationship between legal referral and outcome that appears to be mediated through retention in treatment. Research has shown that the more criminally involved client has a less favorable posttreatment outcome.

AIDS AND COMPULSORY TREATMENT

The Public Health Service and the National Institute on Drug Abuse (NIDA) have identified intravenous drug abusers as a major source of the spread of AIDS to the heterosexual population. The relationship of intravenous drug use to AIDS is well established, with 25 percent of all AIDS cases related to intravenous drug use. AIDS is spreading among intravenous drug abusers through sharing of needles contaminated with the human immunodeficiency virus (HIV). Through this sharing of needles, it is believed that the vast majority of needle-using addicts are at risk for contracting AIDS. Since many intravenous drug abusers are sexually active, and since many female abusers resort to prostitution to support their drug habits, the potential for the spread of AIDS from intravenous drug abusers to the general population is considerable. This potential is of serious concern for health care delivery and drug abuse treatment programs, and for the criminal justice system as well.

Concern about the spread of AIDS among intravenous drug abusers and from intravenous drug abusers to their sexual partners and children has given renewed impetus to an examination of the concept of civil commitment as a form of AIDS control. The concept has been suggested as a "treatment modality" for users of intravenous drugs, who are at risk for contracting and transmitting the AIDS virus and who are unwilling to enter treatment voluntarily. In this case, *compulsory treatment* is defined as activities that increase the likelihood that drug abusers will enter and remain in treatment, change their behavior in a socially desirable way, and sustain that change. However, it is questionable whether the threat of AIDS has the potential to muster enough popular support for civil commitment of drug addicts in the United States. Brown (1988) cites constraints on national policy in a democracy and notes that the health risk is not viewed as a sufficient threat to the heterosexual population.

FUTURE DIRECTIONS AND RECOMMENDATIONS

A review of the literature reveals a consensus among experts in the drug abuse treatment field regarding recommendations related to the future direction of compulsory treatment. It is recommended that the term "compulsory treatment" rather than "civil commitment" be uniformly adopted and that candidates for compulsory treatment receive appropriate legal protection. Compulsory treatment should be reserved for long-term drug abusers and, more specifically, the drug-abusing offender who would benefit most from treatment. Compulsory treatment has proven effective in reducing drug abuse and especially intravenous drug abuse; nonetheless, it should be recognized that dependence is chronic, and repeated interventions will probably be needed for most clients.

Research has shown that the length of time in treatment is related to treatment success and that long-term client aftercare and monitoring is an essential part of treatment. In addition, research has indicated that compulsory treatment in the form of civil commitment increases treatment retention for intravenous drug abusers. Urine testing is an important tool for identifying and monitoring drug use for both the criminal justice system and treatment programs and should be used liberally. The efficacy of methadone treatment needs to be more clearly presented to personnel in the criminal justice system, because there seems to be a bias against methadone as a treatment approach. The therapeutic community approach has a unique role for clients receiving long-term mandatory treatment and should remain an attractive treatment alternative for the judicial system. Discussion of compulsory treatment must include the impact of such a policy on the nation's treatment network. Treatment slots must be readily available, and the treatment offered should include the range of existing treatment modalities—methadone treatment, therapeutic communities, and drug-free outpatient treatments. The criminal justice system is important for client identification and retention. A strong link needs to be developed at all levels between treatment programs and the criminal justice system. And finally, compulsory treatment cannot be considered a panacea for dealing with the AIDS problem among intravenous drug abusers.

REFERENCES

Anglin, M. Douglas. (1988). The efficacy of civil commitment in treating narcotic addiction. In C. G. Leukefeld and F. M. Tims (Eds.), *Compulsory Treatment of Drug Abuse: Research and Clinical Practice*. NIDA Research Monograph 86. Washington, D.C.: U.S. Government Printing Office, pp. 8–34.

Barr, H., and Antes, D. (1981). Factors Related to Recovery and Relapse in Follow-up. Final report of project activities under National Institute on Drug Abuse grant No. H81-DAO1864, 150 pp.

Brown, B. S. (1988). Civil commitment—international issues. In C. G. Leukefeld and F. M. Tims (Eds.), *Compulsory Treatment of Drug Abuse: Research and Clinical Practice*. NIDA Research Monograph 86. Washington, D.C.: U.S. Government Printing Office, pp. 192–208.

Cook, L., Foster, R., and Weinmen, Beth A. (1988). Treatment alternatives to street crime. In C. G. Leukefeld and F. M. Tims (Eds.), *Compulsory Treatment of Drug Abuse: Research and Clinical Practice*. NIDA Research Monograph 86. Washington, D.C.: U.S. Government Printing Office, pp. 99–105.

De Leon, G. (1984). *The Therapeutic Community Study of Effectiveness*. NIDA Research Monograph 58. DHHS Pub. (ADM) 85-1286. Rockville, Md.: National Institute on Drug Abuse.

De Leon, G. (1985). The therapeutic community: status and evolution. *International Journal of Addiction*, 20(6/7):824–844.

De Leon, G. (1988). Legal pressure in therapeutic communities. In C. G. Leukefeld and F. M. Tims (Eds.), *Compulsory Treatment of Drug Abuse: Research and Clinical*

Practice. NIDA Research Monograph 86. Washington, D.C.: U.S. Government Printing Office, pp. 160–177.

Holland, S. (1983). Evaluating community based treatment programs: a model for strengthening inferences about effectiveness. *International Journal of Therapeutic Communities*, 4(4):285–306.

Leukefeld, C. G., and Tims, F. M. (1988a). Compulsory treatment: a review of findings. In C. G. Leukefeld and F. M. Tims (Eds.), *Compulsory Treatment of Drug Abuse: Research and Clinical Practice.* NIDA Research Monograph 86. Washington, D.C.: U.S. Government Printing Office, pp. 236–251.

Leukefeld, C. G., and Tims, F. M. (1988b). An introduction to compulsory treatment for drug abuse: clinical practice and research. In C. G. Leukefeld and F. M. Tims (Eds.), *Compulsory Treatment of Drug Abuse: Research and Clinical Practice.* NIDA Research Monograph 86. Washington, D.C.: U.S. Government Printing Office, pp. 1–7.

Maddux, J. F. (1988). Clinical experience with civil commitment. In C. G. Leukefeld and F. M. Tims (Eds.), *Compulsory Treatment of Drug Abuse: Research and Clinical Practice.* NIDA Research Monograph 86. Washington, D.C.: U.S. Government Printing Office.

Maddux, J. F., Hoppe, S. K., and Costello, R. M. (1986). Psychoactive substance use among medical students. *American Journal of Psychiatry*, 143:187–191.

Porter, L., Arif, A. E., and Curran, W. J. (1986). *The Law and the Treatment of Drug and Alcohol Dependent Persons—A Comparative Study of Existing Legislation.* Geneva, Switzerland: World Health Organization.

Simpson, D. D., and Sells, S. B. (1982). Effectiveness of treatment for drug abuse: an overview of the DARP research program. *Advances in Alcohol and Substance Abuse*, 2(1):7–29.

Tims, F. M. (1981). Effectiveness of Drug Abuse Treatment Programs. NIDA Treatment Research Report. Washington, D.C.: U.S. Government Printing Office, 84–1143.

Tims, F. M., and Leukefeld, C. G. (Eds.). (1986). *Relapse and Recovery in Drug Abuse.* NIDA Research Monograph 72. DHHS Pub. (ADM) 8-1473. Washington, D.C.: U.S. Government Printing Office.

Tims, F. M., and Ludford, J. (1984). *Drug Abuse Treatment Evaluation: Strategies, Progress and Prospects.* NIDA Research Monograph 51. DHHS Pub. (ADM) 8413. Washington, D.C.: U.S. Government Printing Office.

DRUG-FREE
RESIDENTIAL TREATMENT

THERAPEUTIC COMMUNITIES

The primary residential treatment model is the therapeutic community, which emphasizes a self-help approach, frequently using formerly drug-dependent individuals as counselors, administrators, and role models. The atmosphere in the programs is highly structured, especially for newer members. Clients progress through the program in clearly delineated stages. Each succeeding stage usually carries more personal freedom and responsibility. Group counseling or therapy sessions, which are usually confrontational in nature and stress openness and honesty, are a cornerstone of the therapeutic communities approach to treatment.

Therapeutic communities involve 9-to-18-month courses of treatment, followed by continuing contact during a variable period of reentry into society. Programs are designed for people with major behavioral and social impairments, including a history of serious criminal behavior. Therapeutic communities involve highly structured blends of psychotherapy, behavioral modification, an internal hierarchy of jobs and progressive responsibilities, and a variety of medical, educational, and vocational services. The core features include strict prohibitions against drugs and violent behavior during treatment, enforced by close supervision, drug testing, and expulsion on detection. Attrition and early discharge from therapeutic communities are typically high; about 15 to 25 percent of those admitted complete the full course. Behavior among those in therapeutic communities (avoiding drugs and crime and holding employment) is much better during treatment and after discharge than before admission and much better than among people who contacted the community but did not enter treatment. Dropout rates are usually significant. In seven programs surveyed by De Leon and Schwartz (1984), retention rates for a 12-

month treatment stay ranged from 4 to 21 percent. In follow-up evaluations, improvements in drug use, employment, criminality, and psychological well-being were noted both for the graduates and for the program dropouts. In general, those patients who remain longer in therapeutic communities have the better outcomes (De Leon, 1984; Simpson & Sells, 1982). The minimal retention necessary to sustain improvement after leaving treatment is at least 3 months (Gerstein & Lewin, 1990).

During the late 1950s and early 1960s, the concept of group therapy was growing in popularity throughout the country, and as therapeutic communities developed, they too adopted the concept as a major technique. The growth of therapeutic communities also paralleled the growth of communes, and some of the cooperative spirit of the communes was incorporated into the therapeutic communities. The idea of a group of people living and working together for their mutual benefit was, and still is, a basic tenet of the therapeutic community. In past years a majority of therapeutic community clients were dependent on heroin, but cocaine dependency now predominates in many programs. Therapeutic communities originally adhered to rigid designs and relied extensively on staff who were recovering "graduates," but they have become more flexible and multidisciplinary.

The primary aim of therapeutic communities is an overall change in lifestyle of the substance abuser. This includes abstinence from illicit substances; elimination of antisocial activity, especially crime; employability; and prosocial attitudes and values. A critical assumption for therapeutic communities is that stable recovery depends upon a successful integration of both social and psychological goals. Rehabilitation, therefore, requires multidimensional influences and training, which for many substance abusers can occur only in a long-term residential setting. The therapeutic community provides a 24-hour-a-day learning experience in which individual changes in conduct, attitudes, and emotions are monitored and mutually reinforced daily. Therapeutic communities offer a systematic approach to achieving maintenance of a drug-free existence. In therapeutic communities the priority is the person, not the drug. Addiction is seen as a symptom, not the essence of the disorder. Physiological dependency is secondary to the drug use behavior, and chemical detoxification is a condition of entry, not a goal of treatment. Drug abuse is viewed as a disorder of the whole person; rehabilitation focuses upon maintenance of a drug-free existence; and the treatment is the community itself, which consists of peers and staff who, as role models of successful personal change, serve as guides in the recovery process (De Leon, 1988).

In therapeutic communities the aim of rehabilitation is to change the negative patterns of behavior, thinking, and feeling that predispose an individual to drug use and to develop a responsible drug-free lifestyle. Healthy behavioral alternatives to drug use are reinforced by commitment to the value of abstinence. The acquisition of vocational or educational skills and social productivity is motivated by the values of achievement and self-reliance. Conduct, emotions, skills, attitudes, and values must be integrated to ensure enduring change. Recovery depends upon both positive and negative pressure to change.

Some drug abusers seek help, pushed by stressful external pressures; others are moved by more intrinsic factors. For all, however, remaining in treatment requires continued motivation to change. Thus, elements of the rehabilitation approach aim to sustain motivation or to detect early signs of premature termination. The influence of treatment depends upon the individual's motivation and readiness to change; however, change does not occur in a vacuum. Lifestyle change can occur only in a social context. Negative patterns, attitudes, and roles were not acquired in isolation, nor can they be changed in isolation. This assumption is the basis for the community serving as the teacher. Even though in most therapeutic communities programs last 2 years, that is a relativity short span of time to compete with the influences of the years before and after treatment. Unhealthy outside influences must be minimized until new habits have formed and the individual is better prepared to engage these influences on his/her own. Thus, life in therapeutic communities is necessarily intense, its daily regimen demanding, and its therapeutic confrontation unmoderated (De Leon, 1988).

Programs and Structures

Recovery is facilitated through the social organization, staff, and daily regimen of the therapeutic community. The treatment process takes place in a series of highly structured and stratified communities composed of peer groups that are led by staff through which the individual must pass to progress through treatment phases. The operation of the community itself is the task of the residents, working under staff supervision. Work assignments are arranged in a hierarchy according to seniority achieved by progress and productivity. The new client enters a setting of upward mobility, where job assignments begin with the most menial task, like mopping the floor, and lead vertically to levels of management. Indeed, clients come in as patients and can leave as staff. This social organization reflects the fundamental aspect of the treatment approach: mutual self-help, responsible performance, and learned success. Key staff members, who are recovered addicts, are visible role models who illustrate real personal change. Their successful rehabilitative experience qualifies them to teach and to serve as guides.

Within its structure, the therapeutic community prescribes explicit stages that are sequenced to achieve incremental degrees of learning. Each stage prepares the individual for learning at the next. Some of the specific techniques are adaptations of those used by Phoenix House and described by Dr. George De Leon (1988).

Stage I, *induction*, months 1 and 2. The main goals of this initial phase of residency are the assessment of individual needs and orientation to the therapeutic community. Important differences among clients generally do not appear until the new residents have experienced some reduction in the circumstantial stress that is usually present at entry and have had some interaction with the treatment regimen. Thus, observation of individuals continues during the initial residential period to identify special problems in their adaptation to the therapeutic community. The goal of orientation in the initial phase of residency is to assimilate the individual into the community through full participation and involvement in all of its activities.

Stage II, *primary treatment*, months 3 to 12. During this stage, the main objectives are socialization, personal growth, and psychological awareness. Primary treatment actually consists of three phases separated by natural landmarks in the socialization and development process. Phases within stage II are marked by plateaus of stable behavior, which signal further change. In each phase, the daily regimen of meetings, work, and recreation remains the same. Progress, however, can be seen in a client's profile at the end of each phase, in terms of three interrelated dimensions: community status, developmental change, and psychological change.

Stage III, *reentry*, months 13 to 24. Reentry is the stage at which the client must strengthen skills for autonomous decision making and the capacity for self-management, with less reliance on rational authorities or a well-formed peer network. There are two phases in the reentry stage. *Early reentry* is months 13 to 18. The main goal during this phase is preparation for healthy separation from the community. Emphasis upon rational authority decreases under the assumption that the client has acquired a certain degree of self-management. Emphasis is also placed on more individual decision making about privileges, plans, and life design. The group process involves fewer leaders, fewer encounters, and more shared decision making. There are instructional sessions on independent living skills such as budgeting, job seeking, use of alcohol, sexuality, parenting, and use of leisure time. This stage leads to *late reentry*, months 19 to 24. The goal of this phase is to complete a successful separation from residency. Clients are on a live-out status, are involved in full-time jobs or education, and maintain their own households, usually with live-out peers. They may attend such aftercare services as Alcoholics Anonymous (AA) and Narcotics Anonymous or take part in family or individual therapy. This phase is viewed as the end of residency but not the end of program participation. Contact with the program is frequent at first and is only gradually reduced to weekly phone calls and monthly visits with a primary counselor. Completion marks the end of active program involvement.

Therapeutic Techniques

Therapeutic communities attempt to deal with the psychological causes of addiction by changing the addict's character and personality. The techniques used were modeled upon those of Alcoholics Anonymous, which involve repeated confessions, group interaction, and mutual support among the members. Although therapeutic communities are often managed by former users and do not usually have mental health professionals on their staffs, the treatment method is based on two techniques of group psychotherapy. The first technique is confrontation, or encounter group therapy, in which the addict is forced to confess and acknowledge his or her weakness and immaturity. The second technique is milieu therapy, in which the addict lives and works within a hierarchical social structure and may progress upward in status as he or she demonstrates increased responsibility and self-discipline. The principles of behavior modification, or conditioning, are constantly applied within the community in the form of reinforcement of good behavior and punishment of bad behavior. The time period for treatment varies from one therapeutic community to another. Most therapeutic communities require members to stay for 1 or 2 years. The programs also vary in selectivity. The older programs screen applicants rigorously, accepting only the most highly motivated individuals. These programs also continue to be completely drug-free, whereas some of the newer programs use methadone maintenance or both methadone and drug-free therapy.

In its approach and daily regime, the therapeutic community has adapted familiar behavioral training methods and techniques based upon a view of the client and the recovery process previously discussed. These focus on behaviors, particularly characteristic of addicts, that must be modified in the rehabilitation process. The first skill to be learned, and one of the most essential, is awareness, which refers to the addict's recognition or understanding of the relationship between himself (his conduct, attitudes, and feelings), his environment, and other people. The second is tolerance. It has been recognized since the early days of addict rehabilitation that addicts exhibit a low tolerance for frustration and discomfort (Chein, 1964). Low tolerance may be a cause or a consequence of chemical abuse, or it may be due to a biological or personality predisposition or poor upbringing. The addict's characteristic inability to delay gratification increases his or her difficulty in tolerating the tension or uncertainty associated with life's ordinary stresses. Addicts have developed a set of complex skills and behaviors, some socially acceptable and others not, which effectively avoid or reduce discomfort. The most prominent and problematic behavior is drug use. Tolerance training involves raising the individual's tolerance levels through activities such as changing response thresholds and developing alternative behaviors for reducing or avoiding discomfort through positive or less self-defeating responses. This training effort is directed toward making the individual aware of the chain of cognitive and behavioral events that reflect poor tolerance. Any social, interpersonal, or environmental cue for discomfort can trigger sequences of behavior that lead to reduction or avoidance of the discomfort. Most often the avoidance behavior is drug taking.

Encounter groups or peer discussions retrace thoughts to a moment of discomfort—usually a particular criticism, injustice, provocation, uncertainty, interpersonal hurt, or disappointment—and focus on what triggers the negative thinking or behavior that often leads to drug taking. Isolating these typical patterns of response chains that arise from poor tolerance is an essential first step leading to alternative ways to cope with the moment of discomfort. A primary technique for increasing tolerance is to delay expected outcomes or rewards. This technique aims to teach an individual to cognitively accept disappointment, frustration, and uncertainty. Alternative behaviors are suggested, reinforced, and practiced. Tolerance training also teaches residents to cope with their drug-craving experiences.

The cornerstone training method in the therapeutic communities is the encounter group. The group collectively presents their observations and reactions concerning a resident's behavior and attitudes. The group confronts the individual with how he or she is perceived by others. It is used to initially raise client awareness and then offer concrete suggestions for positive alternative behavior. The group also provides support for change. Through this process, behaviors and attitudes are gradually modeled in stages to ensure sequenced and incremental learning toward a stable recovery.

Although behavioral science principles and methods are the mechanisms for understanding change in therapeutic communities, social learning occurs within the context of everyday life as it is perceived and experienced by members of the community. Embedded in the routine activities of community life are social and psychological factors known to strengthen the learning process. Delivery of reinforcements becomes less regular over time in the program, which prepares them for society. The progression up the hierarchy of job functions is much like the movement up the occupational ladder in the "real world." The resident begins at the bottom, and advancement requires hard work, discipline, good work, and social skills. For the resident, upward mobility is capable of imparting behavioral skills needed to successfully assimilate into mainstream society.

Effectiveness

For traditional long-term therapeutic communities, national surveys indicate that 30 percent of clients achieve maximally favorable outcomes (no crime, no illicit drug use, and prosocial behavior), and an additional 40 percent reveal moderately favorable outcomes (Simpson & Sells, 1982). Representative results are reported for Phoenix House. Five to seven years after treatment, success (no crime and no drug use) rates among graduates exceed 75 percent. Among dropouts, success rates average 31 percent, but the percentages relate directly to time spent in treatment. About 50 percent of those who remained in residence for 1 year or longer were successful across 3 to 6 years of follow-up, compared to about 25 percent who stayed less than 1 year (De Leon, 1984; De Leon & Jainchill, 1986).

The problem with therapeutic communities as a treatment method is that they appear to be suitable for very few people. About 75 percent of those who enter them drop out within the first month. Some critics feel that the treatment of residents in a demeaning or punitive way, which is characteristic of many communities, is contrary to the principles of supportive psychotherapy. Because they are residential, therapeutic communities are more expensive to operate than drug-free outpatient programs, even though many are operated entirely by members. In terms of results, however, therapeutic communities do not appear to be more effective than other drug-free methods of treatment.

Since Synanon served as the model for such programs, a few specific words on that program are warranted.

SYNANON: THE EARLY MODEL

Endore (1968) states that society prepares the crime, while the criminal merely executes it; he goes on to say that Chuck Dederich, the founder of Synanon, designed a new society for drug-dependent individuals in which they no longer have to be junkies. In recent years the reputation that Synanon once enjoyed has eroded substantially, as it has been referred to as a religious cult and a private army. The Synanon family structure has as its patriarch the charismatic figure Chuck Dederich. Devotion to him is a crucial element in the rehabilitation program. This transference to and absolute reverence of Dederich serves to keep the addict at Synanon. One of Synanon's key ingredients is a powerful reward system that provides jobs, status, and recognition in a step-by-step, achievable pattern analogous to that of society at large. A basic strategy of Synanon is behavior shaping. The approach uses confrontation, frustration, and attack. A great deal is said about the small-group sessions in Synanon, but even its founder cannot fully explain them. They are dynamic encounters in which all the fury, frustration, and other deep emotions of one individual are pitted against the feelings of all the others in the group. The only restraint is the basic rule of no physical violence. No one can hide from the truth, for other members turn their full vehemence on anyone who even appears to be deviating from the truth or hiding behind a lie. Since Synanon members live together within the organization's community, they relate to each other constantly, with all participants learning more and more about themselves, others, and the nondrug life in general.

Drug users have been likened to children who have not had a chance to mature or learn to live in a loving, caring, protecting world. Nearly every user has lacked these qualities in his or her life, and at Synanon each is finally given the experience of knowing them. One cannot rule a child with punishment and hostility, because a child does not come into this world equipped with a sense of moral responsibility. To continually punish children for a reason they do not understand is to place on them a guilt for which they know no cause, and thus their development is arrested. At Synanon, residents are given the rest of their lives—if they wish to stay that long—to develop these missing characteristics. No specific time frame can be set on a cure for addiction. Some members move out of the Synanon community when they feel confident enough about their new nondrug life, but a large majority of the ex-drug-dependent individuals remain within the organization (Deitch & Zeuben, 1981).

Therapeutic communities have claimed the highest cure rate of any rehabilitation program to date. Many people argue that this is due to the high degree of motivation of the members of these communities. People who voluntarily enter a program that they know will involve difficult problems of readjustment are obviously motivated toward cure, and this is an important variable. But the most important fact is that drug-dependent individuals have been transformed into complete human beings once again. This transformation has involved a change in all of the factors of addiction—social, psychological, physical—and the chemical has been eliminated. We have seen that other treatment programs may attempt to change one or more of these factors, but unless all are ministered to, cure rates will continue to be low. The ex-addict must live a totally new life, totally different from the life of drugs, or he or she may be led back to the drug by old habits.

HALFWAY HOUSES AND OTHER REHABILITATION CENTERS

The most common approach to the inpatient treatment of alcohol dependence is the "Minnesota model" or some variation of it. It is called the Minnesota model because it evolved from three treatment centers in Minnesota—Pioneer House, Hazelden, and Willmar State Hospital—which were founded in the late 1940s and early 1950s. In its simplest form, treatment consists of assessment and admission to a residential treatment facility for 3 to 6 weeks followed by intensive attendance at AA (Cook, 1988a, 1988b). The inpatient phase consists of intensive counseling, lectures, and group therapy. The content is based on the principles of AA, and the goal is abstinence. The staff includes both recovered persons and professionals.

There are other programs in the United States that offer the opiate-dependent individual a place to reconstruct his or her life. The services offered by halfway houses range from full-time residency, as at Daytop Village, to mere visits for counseling. The various programs throughout the nation are supported by many different institutions or organizations, and management and philosophy differ from program to program. Most of these programs treat users who have come to them from the courts, and the program is designed to enable each participant to reenter society. Halfway houses will most likely enjoy limited success because of their inability to minister to all of the many factors that cause addiction.

Treatment is a critical part of the solution to the nation's drug problem, and drug abuse treatment facilities are as essential to the health and well-being of the community as fire stations, schools, and hospitals. However, communities often resist the establishment of local treatment centers because they lack a clear understanding of the problem of addiction, the nature of treatment, and the fact that treatment works. Stereotypes about drug abusers and drug abuse treatment abound, as market research has found. Research shows that some people think abusers are criminals or at least very different from themselves. Others view drug treatment centers as places where people "on drugs" go, not where people getting "off drugs" confront their addiction and return to productive lives. So when it comes to dealing with the placement of new facilities in their neighborhood, local people are concerned about property values, safety, and crime (*NIDA Notes*, 1990).

PRIVATE RESIDENTIAL TREATMENT

The increased abuse of cocaine has led to the emergence of a large number of very expensive private treatment programs for middle and upper class drug users covered by insurance. The cost of these programs can easily exceed $1,000 to $3,000 per week. A variety of private programs housed in special wings of hospitals and private psychiatric hospitals have been designed to meet unique needs and social status. Such treatment regimens are a far cry from those offered in the typical outpatient drug clinic in the inner city. At the luxurious extreme, treatment may take place in a resortlike atmosphere and include such amenities as hot baths, swimming pools, and elaborate exercise and recreational facilities. The typical patient admitted for cocaine dependency at these centers is a male college graduate in a professional or managerial position. Ages range from 17 to 64, with a mean of 30. Most patients are daily users, although a significant percentage use drugs two to three times a week or less. Freebase smoking is the predominant mode of use, with snorting preferred by a significant number. Although most of the patients have used other drugs, cocaine dependency is their primary reason for seeking admission. Most have never been treated for drug dependency and have had no previous psychiatric treatment (Schnoll et al., 1985).

These treatment programs generally treat small numbers at any one time, and there are few research data indicating that a treatment format specific to cocaine abusers is appropriate.

Therapeutic Techniques

Many long-term cocaine abusers are unable to become drug-free and are committed to rehabilitation without being confined for a period of time in a setting in which they cannot obtain the drug. As with other types of stimulant abuse, cocaine abuse can result in severe physical debilitation and malnutrition requiring inpatient treatment. Whatever the context of treatment, its psychotherapeutic aspects generally emphasize three essential elements (Kleber & Gawin, 1984):

1 Helping abusers recognize the serious effects cocaine is having on their lives and the need to stop using

2 Helping in the management of impulsive behavior and, in particular, cocaine use, and helping the abuser to learn to avoid situations that are conducive to continued use

3 Helping abusers to understand the role cocaine plays in their lives and to meet those needs in other ways

Treatment usually consists of inpatient treatment including detoxification; day treatment, where patients stay in the inpatient treatment track but return to the family at night; and extended treatment. Most recovery programs are based on the philosophy that chemical dependency is a chronic, progressive, and sometimes fatal disease that affects the physical, emotional, and spiritual aspects of the lives of addicted persons and their families. Treatment emphasizes replacing the person's dependency on drugs and/or alcohol with close, trusting relationships with other people. The development and implementation of each therapeutic treatment program is a continuous and ongoing process.

The initial steps are to identify the patient's problem, assess the problem, and formulate an individualized treatment plan, which is then carried out by a treatment team of professionals.

The treatment team may include substance abuse counselors, staff nurses, social workers, psychologists, occupational therapists, stress management therapists, a physician, and recreational therapists. The treatment team continually reassesses patient needs and updates each treatment plan accordingly. The treatment approach usually includes group, family, and individual therapy; special education and vocational counseling; physical conditioning; leisure planning; activities therapy; and participation in support groups. Virtually all clinicians stress the value of group therapy and recovery groups, which have an essential role during and after formal treatment. Participation provides models for a drug-free lifestyle and peer assurance that long-term abstinence is possible. Since the resumption of cocaine use is a constant temptation, groups also provide peer pressure and support not to do so. Individual psychotherapy with cocaine-dependent individuals can be useful. Emphasis is placed on the difficulties of establishing basic trust and on interpersonal and intrapsychic factors that directly contribute to the need to use cocaine. Topic-specific groups (e.g., anger management, communication, relapse prevention) are essential, and patients are assigned to these groups as their needs indicate. Complete abstinence from all mood-altering substances and the adoption of a drug-free lifestyle are generally advocated as primary treatment goals. Mandatory urine screening to test for ingestion of drugs of abuse is the usual means of objectively evaluating treatment progress and promoting self-control. Since habitual cocaine abusers are likely to be abusers of other substances as well, urine monitoring is a means of identifying those who are having problems remaining drug-free.

Contingency contracting is another technique often used with the more responsible patients. This is usually an arrangement between the patient and the therapist that stipulates that a failure to remain drug-free will have certain agreed-upon negative consequences. An example would be the therapist holding a letter from the patient in which she notifies a professional board that she resigns a license to practice her profession should urine testing indicate continued drug use. Contingency contracting can employ consequences that range from moderately serious to those having an enduring impact.

The value of physical exercise demanding enough to have positive mental health effects is also stressed. This is a means of improving the positive self-image of the patient and reducing "cocaine hunger." Vigorous exercise also increases the natural endorphin level, which contributes to achieving a "natural high." Many long-term abusers are poorly nourished because of cocaine's appetite suppressant effect. The patient may also be debilitated as a result of sleep loss. Adequate nutrition and the development of affirmatively good health habits are an essential part of the program. Even when treatment is primarily on an outpatient basis, provision for possible hospitalization is necessary. Cocaine abusers may require it because of their serious psychiatric symptoms or because of a medical emergency related to their cocaine abuse.

REFERENCES

Chein, I. (1964). *The Road to H: Narcotics, Delinquency and Social Policy*. New York: Basic Books.

Cook, C. C. H. (1988a). The Minnesota model in the management of drug and alcohol dependence: miracle, method or myth? Part I. The philosophy and the programme. *British Journal of Addiction*, 83:625–634.

Cook, C. C. H. (1988b). The Minnesota model in the management of drug and alcohol dependence: miracle, method or myth? Part II. Evidence and conclusions. *British Journal of Addition*, 83:735–748.

Deitch, D. A., and Zeuben, J. E. (1981). Synanon: a pioneering response in drug abuse treatment and a signal for caution. In J. H. Lowinson and P. Ruiz (Eds.), *Substance Abuse: Clinical Problems and Perspectives*. Baltimore, Md.: Williams and Wilkins.

De Leon, G. (1984). *The Therapeutic Community: Study of Effectiveness*. NIDA Research Monograph 86. DHHS Pub. (ADM) 85-1286. Rockville, Md.: National Institute on Drug Abuse.

De Leon, G. (1985). The therapeutic community: status and evolution. *International Journal of Addiction*, 20(6/7):823–844.

De Leon, G. (1988). *The Therapeutic Community and Behavioral Science*. NIDA Research Monograph 84. DHHS Pub. (ADM) 88-1576. Rockville, Md.: National Institute on Drug Abuse.

De Leon, G., and Jainchill, N. (1986). Circumstance, motivation, readiness and suitability as correlates of treatment effectiveness. *Journal of Psychoactive Drugs*, 18(3):203–208.

De Leon, G., and Schwartz, S. (1984). Therapeutic communities: what are the retention rates? *American Journal of Drug & Alcohol Abuse*, 10(2):267–284.

Endore, G. (1968). *Synanon*. Garden City, N.Y.: Doubleday.

Gerstein, D. R., and Lewin, L. S. (1990). Special report: treating drug problems. *New England Journal of Medicine*, 323(12). pp. 14–18.

Kleber, H. D., and Gawin, F. H. (1984). Cocaine abuse: a review of current and experimental treatments. In J. G. Grabowski (Ed.), *Cocaine: Pharmacology, Effects, and Treatment of Abuse*. NIDA Research Monograph 50. Washington, D.C.: U.S. Government Printing Office, pp. 111–129.

NIDA Notes (1990). *Research Advances*. NIDA Research Report, Vol. 5, No. 4. Washington, D.C.: U.S. Government Printing Office.

Schnoll, S. H., et al. (1985). Characteristics of cocaine abusers presenting for treatment. In N. J. Kozel and E. H. Adams (Eds.), *Cocaine Use in America—Epidemiologic and Clinical Perspectives*. NIDA Research Monograph 61. Washington, D.C.: U.S. Government Printing Office.

Simpson, D. D., and Sells, S. B. (1982). Effectiveness of treatment for drug abuse: an overview of the DARP research program. *Advances in Alcohol and Substance Abuse*, 2(1):7–29.

DRUG-FREE OUTPATIENT TREATMENT

The treatment method that offers drug-free services on an entirely outpatient basis is referred to as either drug-free outpatient, ambulatory drug-free, or outpatient abstinence treatment. The outpatient drug-free modality subsumes a wide variety of approaches to treatment. There are many differences among programs with respect to the scope or level of treatment they provide, but they usually include some or all of the following services: group or individual psychotherapy, vocational and social counseling, family counseling, vocational training, education, and community outreach. Programs also differ in the degree of patient involvement in treatment. Some programs are social or "rap" centers where patients drop in occasionally. Others are free clinics that provide a wide range of health services. Some programs provide structured methadone detoxification and monitor patient drug use by urinalysis throughout treatment. Little evaluation has been done on this method of treatment because program records often omit data on patients who drop out of treatment early. Most experts believe that these programs do help some people but that the attrition rates are very high. It appears that drug-free outpatient treatment may be more effective with youths who are experimenting with drugs than with hard-core drug-dependent individuals.

In large surveys of treatment, this is the most popular modality, accounting for nearly half (48 percent) of all patients in treatment. Programs vary widely from drop-in "rap" centers to highly structured programs, most providing counseling or psychotherapy as the treatment mainstay. Simpson and Sells (1982) reported improvements in the opioid abusers who received treatment in outpatient drug-free programs. Daily opioid use declined from 100 percent pretreatment to 44 percent at the end of the first year and 28 percent in the third year. Arrests also showed a significant decline, and employment increased after treatment. However, because individuals entering outpatient drug-free treatment have not been adequately described on a variety of severity variables, the significance of these findings is not clear.

PCP OUTPATIENT TREATMENT

Some hospitals have drug abuse outpatient aftercare services to help ensure continuity of care following inpatient or emergency treatment. PCP abusers can be treated in an outpatient treatment program lasting about 6 months. This allows ample time to address underlying problems, especially the depression, the sense of alienation, and the hopelessness commonly experienced by these patients. These programs involve regularly monitored urine testing, because the patients are likely to be tempted to use drugs to overcome negative feelings. Family involvement is encouraged, especially for younger clients. A structured individual counseling component is essential to guide and support therapeutic efforts. No matter what other treatment approaches are used, PCP abusers still need an opportunity to express and explore feelings, doubts, and concerns in complete confidentiality. They need ongoing support and help in coping with pressures, exploring attitudes, resolving conflicts, and solving practical problems. When clinicians help clients set limited, short-term goals (30 days or less), it increases the likelihood of holding clients in treatment and helps them succeed. Most of these clients are easily frustrated and need to see some early signs of progress. Success in achieving realistic goals helps build self-confidence and trust in the therapeutic relationship. In addition to regular individual counseling sessions, a group therapy program that meets at least twice weekly is recommended. Many PCP users feel coerced into treatment because they lack insight into their drug use and do not see it as a problem. Participating in a group helps penetrate their defenses and helps them progress beyond the denial stage. Treatment also assesses the vocational status of clients and develops a plan to enhance their skills.

Aftercare sessions are planned so that the therapeutic relationship is not abruptly ended. After PCP abusers complete formal treatment, they will most likely go back to the same social and family situations they were in when they were using drugs. By that time they should know that they have someone to consult if the need arises and that returning for help shows strength rather than weakness. An established aftercare program with regularly scheduled group meetings is useful for many individuals who need additional support (Fram & Stone, 1986).

COCAINE OUTPATIENT TREATMENT

Many long-term cocaine abusers are also unable to become drug-free and committed to rehabilitation without being confined for a period of time in a setting in which they cannot obtain the drug. As with other types of stimulant abuse, cocaine abuse can result in severe physical debilitation and malnutrition requiring inpatient treatment. Since cocaine abusers are vulnerable to relapse and need constant reinforcement and support, emphasis is also placed on the period that begins after formal treatment ends. These programs focus on developing a rewarding lifestyle so that the temptations to resume cocaine or other drug use are minimized. As with other drug abuse, there is a consensus that once compulsive use has occurred any subsequent attempt to return to more controlled use will fail. Self-help groups such as Alcoholics Anonymous and Narcotics Anonymous can be helpful in maintaining abstinence when groups such as Cocaine Anonymous are not available. Support groups ensure continued participation in essential aftercare. Even when treatment is primarily on an outpatient basis, provision for possible hospitalization is necessary. Cocaine abusers may require it because of their serious psychiatric symptoms or because of a medical emergency related to their cocaine abuse.

FAMILY THERAPY

Drug abuse emerges from a variety of social interaction patterns involving the family, the peer group, the school system, the legal system, and the community at large. While it is important to note that family patterns do not cause adolescents to abuse drugs, an adolescent's drug abuse problem may be partially caused by problems within the family (Joanning, 1991). From a treatment perspective a teenager can be isolated and detoxed in a hospital and treated individually, but if the family is not included in the treatment, and if the family environment has not changed when he gets out, the adolescent may return home and resume the same roles that led to drug abuse—it's just a revolving door back. The family therapy approach is based on the premise that if someone—particularly an adolescent—is doing something undesirable, you look to the whole family system. Dysfunctional behavior in an individual is often associated with a dysfunctional family system. Family therapy doesn't just provide treatment, it also can prevent non-using siblings from becoming addicted, because the family's actions that may have facilitated drug use in one child will have been changed (Lewis et al., 1990, 1991).

Family therapy has become an increasingly popular concept in the treatment of alcoholism and other chemical dependencies because of the recognition that all members of the family are affected. For example, when one member of the family drinks excessively, a higher level of anxiety develops in the other family members. They adjust their roles within the family in an attempt to adjust to the imbalance (Figure 23).

In addition to the expected dynamics that occur, there are specific rules for the family's behavior, and the children and spouse often assume certain characteristic roles (Figure 24). Although each of these roles allows the individual to survive the present situation, the role may become very destructive to the individual's future mental and emotional development. Without help, these dynamics, rules, and roles may significantly determine the future adult lives of

THE ALCOHOLIC'S FAMILY IS LIKE A MOBILE
ALL MEMBERS ARE AFFECTED BY THE DISEASE.

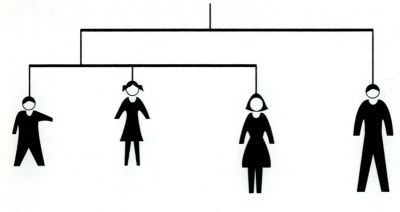

EACH ASSUMES NEW ROLES TO SURVIVE.

FIGURE 23
The alcoholic's family.

the family members. Children often grow to adulthood maintaining the life scripts they learned while living with the alcoholic. Spouses, after divorcing an alcoholic, often marry another alcoholic or create a similar family dynamic with the new spouse.

Treatment for alcohol and substance abuse using family therapy techniques fall into two categories, based on two different theories: family systems theory and family behavior theory. Each has a slightly different focus, but both have been shown to provide excellent treatment options, especially for the adolescent. Bry (1988) provides an excellent review of the research findings on the effectiveness of these techniques.

Family Systems Theory

The family systems concept is based on the idea that relationships between family members constitute a system of dynamic and recurring patterns of interaction. This concept has developed from a general systems conceptual framework that proposes that human behavior is determined by systems of reciprocally interdependent interactions and that behavior problems can best be understood by studying the structures and processes of systems within which behavior occurs (Bry, 1988; Bertalanffy, 1981; Miller, 1978). Adolescent

FIGURE 24
Roles assumed by the family of an alcoholic. (Adapted from Houston Regional Council on Alcoholism, Inc.)

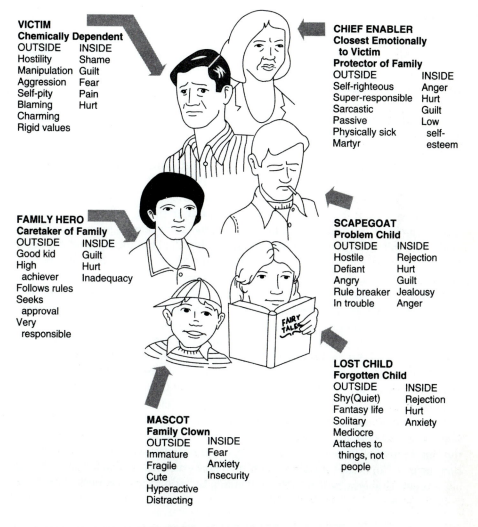

VICTIM
Chemically Dependent

OUTSIDE	INSIDE
Hostility	Shame
Manipulation	Guilt
Aggression	Fear
Self-pity	Pain
Blaming	Hurt
Charming	
Rigid values	

CHIEF ENABLER
Closest Emotionally to Victim
Protector of Family

OUTSIDE	INSIDE
Self-righteous	Anger
Super-responsible	Hurt
Sarcastic	Guilt
Passive	Low
Physically sick	self-
Martyr	esteem

FAMILY HERO
Caretaker of Family

OUTSIDE	INSIDE
Good kid	Guilt
High	Hurt
achiever	Inadequacy
Follows rules	
Seeks	
approval	
Very	
responsible	

SCAPEGOAT
Problem Child

OUTSIDE	INSIDE
Hostile	Rejection
Defiant	Hurt
Angry	Guilt
Rule breaker	Jealousy
In trouble	Anger

LOST CHILD
Forgotten Child

OUTSIDE	INSIDE
Shy(Quiet)	Rejection
Fantasy life	Hurt
Solitary	Anxiety
Mediocre	
Attaches to	
things, not	
people	

MASCOT
Family Clown

OUTSIDE	INSIDE
Immature	Fear
Fragile	Anxiety
Cute	Insecurity
Hyperactive	
Distracting	

problems such as substance abuse can best be understood by studying the characteristics of the family system, such as boundaries, flexibility of interactions, closeness, autonomy, and interdependence (Foote et al., 1985). To reduce adolescent problems, family systems therapists attempt to change some of these family characteristics. Working with the adolescent, the family therapist must first acknowledge the child's often long ignored unhappiness. The therapist's aim for parents is to rekindle the parental love and commitment they once had for their child. Parents who repeatedly fail to deal with their children's behavior often come to the conclusion that they'll never make a difference and give up trying (Liddle, 1991; Liddle et al., 1991).

Typically, the introduction to treatment occurs when one family member seeks help. This is most often motivated by a combination of personal dissatisfaction with one's behavior, a sense of powerlessness to help change this behavior, and a fear of negative consequences of the behavior. Adolescents typically enter treatment after a mother makes the initial telephone call in search of a therapist to whom the family can transfer full responsibility for helping their adolescent. Gaining access and influence in the family system is the most difficult step in developing an effective family therapy situation. Foote et al. (1985) reported that only 15 percent of the family members who called their clinic about adolescent problems actually entered famiy therapy.

Techniques Since the family is viewed as a system, the family systems therapist must join the family physically, empathetically, and contractually. This takes the form of sitting in between them in therapy sessions, demonstrating and accepting each family member's goals and values, and promising that if the family will engage in therapy for a specified, limited period of time, the therapist will help it reach those goals (Kaufman, 1984). The therapist observes and interacts to discover recurring behavioral patterns, alliances, and unspoken family rules that may be maintaining the adolescent's problem. Often a family will initially appear to agree about family rules, but focusing on concrete behavior can reveal hidden disagreements and dispel the myth of family harmony (Stanton & Todd, 1982). Family systems therapists can direct family members' reactions during a session or between sessions in ways that are contrary to their usual interactions. This direction, and the new behavioral sequences that occur in the family as a result, may be sufficient to break recurring dysfunctional patterns. The therapist can use reframing techniques or explain a behavioral sequence or family characteristic in a new, more positive way that is compatible with the family's value system. This often develops from evoking minor emotions that everyone in the family acknowledges, such as irritation over unmet expectations (Szapocznik et al., 1984).

If the foregoing techniques have not reduced the adolescent's drug use, larger societal systems are used in an attempt to interrupt the family's destructive interactions. These involve teachers, school officials, police, and probation officers in supporting the family's goals in the interactions with the adolescent. Sometimes this includes placing the adolescent on probation if the drug use continues, and home detoxification where the adolescent is watched 24 hours a day to ensure that no drugs are taken.

Behavior Theory

Behavior theorists view all behavior as a function of the behavior plus its consequences. Drug use is also seen as a function of past and present environmental and genetic variables. To reduce substance abuse problems, behavior therapists select one target problem behavior that is measurable and appears to be modifiable, analyze that behavior and its consequences, record its frequency, work to change the environment, and finally record the impact of changes on the targeted behavior.

Techniques   Target problem behaviors of adolescents are selected during interviews with both the parents and the adolescent. Behavioral and reinforcement checklists are constructed during observations at home and at the adolescent's school. Parents and adolescents typically begin by discussing only nonbehavioral problems and blaming each other. Unseen problem behaviors, such as stealing and drug taking, can be redefined so that they are observable. Stealing can become "taking or being in possession of something that does not belong to you." Drug use can become "money disappearing unaccountably," "sleeping at unusual times," "smelling pungent," "not making focused eye contact," "possessing paraphernalia," or "being in the company of known drug users" (Chamberlain & Patterson, 1984). Another approach to analyzing unseen problem behaviors is to substitute functionally dependent behaviors that are observable. Since drug use often lowers school performance, measurements of school performance can be useful indicators of unseen heavy drug use (Pandina & White, 1981).

Family behavior therapists work more directly on parental behavior than on adolescent behavior, not because they assume that parents cause adolescent problems, but because parents can readily observe many family-related antecedents and consequences of the adolescents' behavior (O'Dell, 1985). After selecting target behaviors, therapists choose methods that will influence parental behavior. Giving parents books and brochures and monitoring subsequent behavior has proven effective in reducing children's antisocial behavior (Green et al., 1976). In combination with other methods, informal instruction and modeling are probably the most commonly used behavioral change methods in behavior therapy (O'Dell, 1985). Shaping and behavioral rehearsal are also commonly used techniques. While parents are interacting with their adolescents in the therapist's presence, the therapist can prompt and shape the parents' behavior by coaching and praising successful interactions (Gordon & Davidson, 1981).

Family attendance at therapy sessions and completion of homework are extremely important for effectiveness; however, few families comply automatically. The therapist can provide positive and negative consequences to increase or decrease specific parent and adolescent behaviors. Positive reinforcement improves session attendance and homework completion (Szykula et al., 1982). Most parents initially assume that the adolescent is the sole cause of his or her own problems, so the first concept taught is that most behavior is learned through interaction with the social environment, which leads to a reinterpretation of the cause (Nichols, 1984). Once it is clear that the family behavior therapist is not going to "fix the child" but instead help the parents to "fix the environment," parents ask what they can do to change the situation.

Communication training and problem-solving skills are another aspect vital to the success of family therapy. Communication skills teach people to gain control over what had previously been reflexive interpersonal behaviors. Parents are taught to state the new rules to the adolescent in a calm, matter-of-fact manner; to reduce the frequency of their demands, commands, and general nagging; to consistently praise or provide a tangible reward for desirable behavior; and to be consistent in the punishment or withdrawal of rewards for undesirable behavior (Gordon & Davidson, 1981).

Once parents and adolescents have communicated what they want from each other, whole-family problem-solving skills can be addressed. Then both the parents and the therapist can model them for the adolescent in everyday life. Families are taught to reach an agreement about a specific problem by defining the problem (as a dissatisfaction) concisely and without accusations, "brainstorming" a variety of alternative solutions, negotiating a solution that maximizes benefits and minimizes costs for everyone involved, and specifying the details of the implementation of an agreement, including what will happen if difficulties arise (Robin & Foster, 1984).

A major reason for training parents to change their children's behavior is to enhance the possibility that these behaviors will continue to be used after therapy and with other siblings. However, empirical evidence indicates that transfer of treatment effects seldom occurs without specific programming. Consequently, variables outside the therapy must be influenced. Family-based reinforcement teaches spouses to reinforce each other's new child management behaviors in the same way that they were taught to reinforce their child's positive behaviors (Gordon & Davidson, 1981; O'Dell, 1985).

Another reinforcement possibility is the school. Positive changes in an adolescent at home do not necessarily correlate positively with change at school (Forehand et al., 1981). Therapists can hold school conferences and arrange for weekly report cards or progress reports, with teachers sending parents regular reports about targeted school behaviors. Alternatively, school personnel can be trained to provide consequences for targeted behaviors in school with the knowledge and support of parents (Bry et al., 1986; Bry, 1982; Bry & George, 1979, 1980). Family-based interventions have also included coordinated job training, job placement, and social reinforcement for good performance.

Effectiveness Over the past 20 years, our knowledge has increased about family systems and behavior therapy techniques. Proponents of both systems agree that the family and greater social context play important roles in determining adolescent substance use. They also concur that successful interventions to change adolescent behaviors include (1) targeting behaviors appropriate for the adolescents' developmental status, (2) recognizing that adolescents are seldom self-referred, and (3) utilizing the fact that parents still potentially control much in the life of the adolescent. Research into family systems interventions focuses primarily on family systems characteristics and secondarily on the behavior problems of individual family members, while behavior therapy research focuses on parenting behaviors and the manner in which they affect child behavior.

Research from the family systems perspective has produced evidence that such interventions can be more effective than traditional individual approaches in changing both family function and the dysfunctional behavior of an individual member. The results indicate that a great deal of outreach effort must be expended to gain access to the family system of a client with substance use problems. Behavioral research has determined that parental participation in treatment; concurrent personal, family, and community problems of the parents; and parents' failure to discriminate between problem and nonproblem behaviors in their children are determinants of successful treatment.

Kaufman (1985) points out that many theory-based questions remain. It is not known whether the observed differences between families with and without substance abusers precede or follow the substance abuse. Many of the effects that family systems therapy is assumed to have upon family characteristics are yet to be demonstrated, and many of the postulated interconnections between family characteristics and adolescent substance use have yet to be validated. Few studies have experimentally investigated the assumed functional relationships between discrete changes in parent-initiated antecedents and consequences and adolescent problem behavior. Theoretical differences lie in choice of technique; however, both theories are currently generating knowledge on how to reduce adolescent substance use.

Family Outpatient Therapy

The family of the person abusing cocaine and other drugs must not only be involved in treatment, they must also seek professional help for themselves. The family needs support to regain its emotional health and stability; the substance abuser needs treatment to end his or her addiction. It is important to remember that while the family can help provide the substance abuser with opportunities for recovery, the drug abuser is ultimately responsible for his or her own life. The families of drug abusers must take care of themselves emotionally and physically.

Reaching outside the family to seek support is an important step in breaking out of the destructive environment the drug addiction has produced. Sometimes a telephone call to an anonymous service like the nationwide hot line run by the National Institute on Drug Abuse (1-800-662-HELP) can be a first step. For many years, self-help groups such as Al-Anon, Ala-Teen, and Adult Children of Alcoholics (ACoA) have existed for the families and friends of alcoholics. These groups, which have no dues or fees, can also help families of drug abusers. Support groups patterned after those serving the families of alcoholics have been formed specifically for the families of drug abusers, Nar-Anon is for people whose lives have been affected by a drug abuser; Families Anonymous focuses on the families of drug abusers as well as those concerned about runaways and delinquents. COCANON family groups are for people whose lives have been affected by a friend or family member's cocaine habit. These groups are organized into local chapters, which are often listed in the phone book. They exist to help the families of drug users rather than to address the needs of the users themselves. In these groups, members share experiences and common concerns and work to increase their understanding of how the drug abuse problem affects them. The anonymity of all participants is protected and respected.

Local chapters of the following groups can usually be found in the phone book. If no number is listed, contact the national headquarters to locate a nearby group. The alcohol-related groups can also offer support for families of someone addicted to cocaine or other drugs. Do not hesitate to call them if none of the other groups holds meetings close to your community.

COCANON Family Groups
P.O. Box 64742-66
Los Angeles, CA 90064   (213) 859-2206

Families Anonymous
P.O. Box 528
Van Nuys, CA 91408   (818) 989-7841

Nar-Anon Family Group Headquarters
World Service Office
P.O. Box 2562
Palos Verdes Peninsula, CA 92704   (213) 547-5800

Adult Children of Alcoholics (ACoA)
Central Service Board
P.O. Box 3216
Torrance, CA 90505   (213) 534-1815

Al-Anon/Ala-Teen
Family Group Headquarters, Inc.
7th Floor
1372 Broadway
New York, NY 10018-0862   (212) 302-7240

REFERENCES

Bertalanffy, L. V. (1981). *A Systems View of Man*. Boulder, Colo.: West Press.
Bry,, B. H. (1982). Reducing the incidence of adolescent problems through preventive intervention: one- and five-year follow-up. *American Journal of Community Psychology*, 10:265–276.

Bry, B. H. (1988) Family-based approaches to reducing adolescent substance use: theories, techniques, and findings. In E. R. Rahdert and J. Grabowski (Eds.), *Adolescent Drug Use: Analysis of Treatment Research*. NIDA Research Monograph 77. Washington, D.C.: U.S. Government Printing Office.

Bry, B. H., and George, F. E. (1979). Evaluating and improving prevention programs: a strategy for drug abuse. *Evaluation and Program Planning*, 2:127–136.

Bry, B. H., and George, F. E. (1980). The preventive effects of early intervention upon the attendance and grades of urban adolescents. *Professional Psychology*, 11:252–260.

Bry, B. H., Conboy, C., and Bisgay, K. (1986). Decreasing adolescent drug use and school allure: long-term effects of targeted family problem-solving training. *Child and Family Behavior Therapy*, 8:43–59.

Chamberlain, P., and Patterson, G. R. (1984). Aggressive behavior in middle childhood. In D. Shaffer, A. A. Ehrhardt, and L. L. Greenhill (Eds.), *The Clinical Guide to Child Psychiatry*. New York: Free Press, pp. 229–250.

Foote, F. H., et al. (1985). One-person family therapy: a modality of brief strategic family therapy. In R. S. Ashery (Ed.), *Progress in the Development of Cost-Effective Treatment for Drug Abusers*. NIDA Research Monograph 58. DHHS Pub. (ADM) 85-1401. Washington, D.C.: U.S. Government Printing Office.

Forehand, R., et al. (1981). Predictors of cross setting behavior change in the treatment of child problems. *Journal of Behavior Therapy and Experimental Psychiatry*, 12:311–313.

Fram, D., and Stone, N. (1986). Clinical observations in the treatment of adolescent and young adult PCP abusers. In *Phencyclidine: An Up-Date*. NIDA Research Monograph 64. DHHS Pub. (ADM) 86-1443. Rockville, Md.: National Institute on Drug Abuse, pp. 204–214.

Gordon, S. B., and Davidson, N. (1981). Behavioral parent training. In A. S. Gurman and D. P. Kniskern (Eds.), *Handbook of Family Therapy*. New York: Brunner/Mazel. pp. 517–555.

Green, D. R., et al. (1976). Training parents to modify problem child behaviors. In E. J. Mash, L. C. Handy, and L. A. Hamerlynch (Eds.), *Behavior Modification Approaches to Parenting*. New York: Brunner/Mazell, pp. 3–18.

Kaufman, E. (1984). *Substance Abuse and Family Therapy*. Orlando, Fla.: Grune and Stratton.

Kaufman, E. (1985). Family systems and family therapy of substance abuse: an overview of two decades of research and clinical experience. *International Journal of Addiction*, 20:897–916.

Joanning, H. (1991). Integrating cybernetics and construction into structural/strategic family therapy for drug abusers. In E. Kaufman and P. Kaufman (Eds.), *Family Therapy Approaches with Drug and Alcohol Problems*, 2d ed. New York: Simon and Schuster.

Lewis, R. A., Piercy, F. P., and Sprenkle, D. H. (1990). Family-based interventions for helping drug-abusing adolescents. *Journal of Adolescent Research*, 5:82–95.

Lewis, R. A., Piercy, F. P. and Sprenkle, D. H. (1991). The Purdue brief family therapy model for adolescent substance abusers. In T. Todd and M. Selekinan (Eds.), *Family Therapy Approaches with Adolescent Substance Abusers*. New York: Allyn and Bacon.

Liddle, H. A. (1991). Engaging the adolescent in family systems therapy. In T. Nelson (Ed.), *Interventions in Family Therapy*. New York: Haworth.

Liddle, H. A., Diamond, G., and Arroyo, J. (1991). Multidimensional family therapy: the initial phase of treatment with adolescent substance abusers. In E. Kaufman and P. Kaufman (Eds.), *Family Therapy Approaches with Drug and Alcohol Problems*, 2d ed. New York: Simon and Schuster.

Miller, J. G. (1978). *Living Systems*. New York: McGraw-Hill.

Nichols, M., (1984). *Family Therapy: Concepts and Methods*. New York: Gardner Press.

O'Dell, S. L. (1985). Progress in parent training. In M. Hersen, R. M. Eisler, and P. M. Miller (Eds.), *Progress in Behavior Modification*, Vol. 19. Orlando, Fla.: Academic Press, pp. 57–108.

Pandina, R. J., and White, H. R. (1981). Patterns of alcohol and drug use of adolescent students and adolescents in treatment. *Journal of Studies in Alcohol*, 42:441–456.

Robin, A. L., and Foster, S. L. (1984). Problem-solving communication training: A behavioral-family systems approach to parent-adolescent conflict. In P. Karoly and J. J. Steffens (Eds.), *Adolescent Behavior Disorders: Foundations and Contemporary Concerns*. Lexington, Mass.: D.C. Heath, pp. 195–240.

Simpson, D. D., and Sells, S. B. (1982). Effectiveness of treatment for drug abuse: an overview of the DARP research program. *Advances in Alcohol and Substance Abuse*, 2(1):7–29.

Stanton, M. D., and Todd, T. C. (1982). *The Family Therapy of Drug Abuse and Addiction*. New York: Guilford Press.

Szapocznik, J., et al. (1984). One person family therapy. In B. Lubin and W. A. O'Connor (Eds.), *Ecological Approaches to Clinical and Community Psychology*. New York: Wiley, pp. 335–355.

Szykula, S. A., Fleischman, M. J., and Shilton, P. E. (1982). Implementing a family therapy program in a community: relevant issues on one promising program for families in conflict. *Behavior Counseling Quarterly*, 2:67–78.

BEHAVIORAL APPROACHES TO TREATMENT

Behavioral interventions are usually integrated into a treatment package of specialized programs to meet the needs of special populations. Individuals tend to do better in programs when they are placed in a group with peers who have a similar cultural background and/or social status, and in programs that use some form of counseling or psychotherapy according to the needs of the client.

PSYCHOTHERAPY

Psychotherapy forms the basis for many programs that operate on the assumption that drug abuse is (1) a psychoneurotic behavior that offers escape from grief, pain, anger, and guilt; (2) a release from anxiety, hostility, or feelings of inferiority; or (3) a means of dealing with unresolved feelings of sexual inadequacy, social weakness, or general rejection. Clinicians used to believe that there was no point in attempting psychotherapy with drug abusers because they were all "psychopaths" and none of them would respond to psychotherapy. In recent years, it has been found that substance abuse and alcoholism are the most common psychiatric diagnoses and that only a minority of these patients, even among the street drug abusers, are "psychopaths" (people with an antisocial personality disorder). A number of clinical researchers have studied the efficacy of psychotherapy in using random assignment between treated and control groups. Most have found that the patients receiving psychotherapy do significantly better than the control group. The largest of these studies was conducted in a methadone maintenance population (Woody et al., 1983). It compared drug counseling with cognitive behavioral psychotherapy and supportive expressive psychotherapy. These investigators found that both types of psychotherapy administered by psychiatrists or psychologists were significantly more effective than drug counseling alone. However, results were dependent on the severity of psychiatric symptoms in the patients. Those whose symptoms were of low severity did equally as well with the nonprofessional drug counselors as with the psychologists and psychiatrists. Major differences were seen, however, in both the mid-severity patients and the high-severity patients. The middle-level patients showed significantly more improvement with psychotherapy than with the control counseling, and the high-level patients showed virtually no improvement with counseling and significantly more change with psychotherapy.

In addition to the use of psychotherapy, treatment modalities may involve the use of behavior modification. Aversion therapy is an example of how behavior modification is used in the treatment of alcoholism. It involves teaching deeply relaxed patients to visualize themselves drinking, becoming sick, and eventually vomiting, or to first visualize distasteful scenes, then think of drinking. Later, they are taught to visualize feelings of well-being and associate these with being sober. Hypnosis may be used, especially with subjects who find drinking euphoric and pleasurable. In some cases, effective use has been made of posthypnotic suggestions such as, "I will never drink another drop in any form, for alcohol is meaningless and I am indifferent to it and to people who use it." Electrotherapy is also used as a conditioning device in aversion therapy. Techniques vary, but one common practice is to attach electrodes to the subject's fingers or ear. Then, in a barroom setting, the patient is allowed to drink at will but receives shocks when he or she does so; the shocks continue until the drink is rejected.

A more popular reeducation program involving aversion therapy is conducted with the help of the drug Antabuse (disulfiram). This drug interferes with the metabolism of alcohol; after the alcohol is converted to acetaldehyde, further breakdown is blocked. The toxic acetaldehyde causes flushed face, headache, increased heart rate, heart palpitations, nausea, vomiting, and breathing difficulty. When this drug is used in treatment, the alcoholic knows that ingesting alcohol will make him or her physically ill. It is in a sense a chemical conscience for the alcoholic.

The idea of gaining power and control over one's self is an ego-building experience that helps reinforce self-control. Biofeedback instrumentation has been used in this manner as patients are taught to control brain waves (alpha, beta, theta states) at will, reduce muscle tension, or voluntarily change the temperature of a particular body site. This not only aids in reducing anxiety and tension but also gives a feeling of self-control that has been found to carry over into those situations that previously led to drinking.

Exercise programs have also been successful in the treatment of alcoholism. The alcoholic individual develops poor health habits, is out of touch with his or her body, and forgets what it is like to feel good physically. Exercise increases fitness, develops self-confidence, and reduces tension and anxiety. The importance of reducing tension and anxiety cannot be overemphasized—it is the reason most programs use tranquilizing drugs in some part of their treatment regimen.

A related behavioral approach uses social and vocational skills training (Hall et al., 1984). This technique focuses on specific behaviors that often need attention when former abusers in a rehabilitation program attempt to obtain work. These behaviors range from dressing appropriately for a job interview to more subtle interpersonal behaviors such as being polite and controlling such emotions as depression and anger. It has been shown that patients who complete the course have an increased chance of obtaining and continuing in meaningful employment. Contingency contracting is another technique that has been shown to be one of the most promising behaviorally based treatments. This treatment involves setting up an explicit contract between the patient and therapist that requires specific behaviors from each (Crowley, 1984; Dolan et al., 1985; McCarthy & Borders, 1985).

Not all psychological treatment is on an individual basis. Group therapy is also a widely accepted treatment modality. It is usually less expensive and gives the patient a chance to develop the skills for dealing effectively with social situations. Psychodrama, role-playing, and sensitivity group interaction break down defense mechanisms and allow patients to see themselves in a more positive light and to analyze their relationships with the rest of society, especially their families. Family sessions help to reestablish communication and to analyze problems that caused frustration, which are then worked out with the help of a therapist.

HEALTH BEHAVIOR CHANGE THERAPY

This section provides an example of the use of selected health counseling or health behavior change procedures in a clinical program for substance abuse. This is a skills development program that has educational, behavioral, and counseling components (Girdano & Dusek, 1988). The success of this type of program can be greatly enhanced by a process that screens clients to establish a "fit" between program capability and client needs. This approach has three primary elements:

1 Motivation to change
2 A program of action
3 Reduction of blocks to success

Generally the program components include

1 Intake—general assessment and orientation
2 Condition-specific assessment
3 General education
4 Individual counseling
5 Program of action
6 Posttreatment assessment and follow-up

The first element is that of motivation. Some clients are highly motivated, whereas others are somewhat reluctant even though they have come to the program. The level of motivation is increased through the use of comprehensive assessment and orientation. One of the most important motivational procedures is to establish attainable, measurable behavioral outcomes that are unique to each individual.

The second element of the clinical program is an effective plan of action. Action is the key, as people change only when they can experience their outcomes. The positive experiences will be reinforced, and the negative ones will be extinguished. The extinguishing process is called protection. We all act to protect ourselves from experiences that do not feel good, do not meet our needs, and do not achieve outcomes.

A change program can be packaged—that is, it can be similar for a large number of people. However, within the uniform structure it must be individualized to fit each client's needs and readiness. A critical element in behavioral change programs, besides effective strategies, is outcome setting. The procedure for instituting a change plan includes

1 Assessment.
2 Outcome or goal setting.
3 Strategies.
4 Constant monitoring.
5 Periodic evaluation referenced to outcomes.
6 Flexible scheduling, especially with termination, which should be based, not on time or mastery of technique, but on the experiencing of outcomes. In other words, success is doing rather than just knowing how to do.
7 Reinforcement, relapse training, follow-up.

The third element in the clinical model is a reduction of blocks to success. Even though the current success rate for health behavior change programs is between 5 and 25 percent, these programs can work. A variety have been successful. Often, when they are not, it is because individuals who usually appear to be trying to succeed are actually actively involved in sabotaging their own programs. This occurs out of an unconscious fear of success. "What will happen when I no longer have this crutch? How will I get along without it?"

Blocks to program success are often seen as factors contributing to a poor health condition—factors such as lack of self-esteem, anxiety, stress, anger, the inability to express feelings, lack of assertiveness, personality behavioral traits such as those associated with Type A behavior, poor self-control, and what is generally termed lack of readiness. These factors are assessed and often call for a change program within the larger behavior change program. The objective is to eliminate the blocks to success that often defeat an otherwise effective behavioral change program.

The assessment, education, and counseling parts of clinical programs are used to diagnose and treat the blocks to success. Success is evaluated both independently and within the larger context of the health behavior change program. As was previously mentioned, behavior change programs have a better chance of success when the change feels positive. If blocks are reduced and fear is eliminated, the chance of these positive feelings emerging is greatly enhanced.

A SMOKING CESSATION PROGRAM

Smoking cessation provides a good example of how behavioral change programs can be utilized (Dusek & Girdano, 1987).

Program Orientation and Intake

The individuals who come into smoking cessation counseling may enter through many kinds of referrals. Self-referral occurs in response to advertising, word of mouth, and individual response to lifestyle inventory assessments at work, school, or other organization. Second, physicians may refer patients with heart disease, hypertension, or other related disease as a supportive measure for their medical treatment. A third means of referral is through established groups such as business and student groups.

Information Gathering Intake Interview

In addition to the gathering of biographical data and explanation of program protocol, questions that pertain specifically to smoking behavior are asked in the initial session. These questions include the following:

How long have you been smoking?
Do you know what motivates you to smoke? If yes, explain.
How many cigarettes do you usually smoke per day? What kind?
What activities of yours are related to smoking?
Have you tried to stop smoking before? If yes, what prompted you to start again?
On a scale of 1 to 10, how stressful do you feel your life to be? (1 is low stress)

At the end of the intake session, the client is rated on persistence, supportive environment, and realistic thinking.

Screening

After the medical history is examined, the client may be referred to other health care personnel. Conditions that may affect the smoking cessation program include alcoholism or other drug-dependency problems, serious personality disorders, and stress-related illness.

Goal Setting

The goal-setting procedure has two basic components: (1) goal setting through the use of assessment inventories and (2) goal setting through the use of diagnostic counseling.

Assessment Inventories Assessment is both general and condition-specific and identifies some of the characteristics that are appropriate for a smoking cessation program. Routine intake assessment includes measuring the client's weight, skin folds (body composition), height, blood pressure, and resting heart rate. Except for height, these are parameters that may change with smoking cessation. Eating and exercise behavior may be of interest owing to the weight gain seen in some individuals as they stop smoking. The Horn (1979) inventory (in Section 2.2) gives behavioral, psychological, and emotional information and thus directs treatment modality. The psychological/emotional assessment and inventories suggested here elicit information that has been statistically related to smoking behavior, the ability to quit smoking, and the subsequent maintenance of nonsmoking status.

Diagnostic Counseling The obvious outcome for the client in a smoking cessation program is to quit smoking. Few internalize that stopping smoking is just the first part of the process, that the real outcome is to become a non-smoker for a long period of time. This is merely a "first things first" phenomenon. Most smokers suspect that the process of stopping is not going to be easy, and many have not fully committed themselves to the idea of quitting when they come into the program. The ambiguity of wanting to stop but also wanting to smoke is natural. Those who still strongly prefer to smoke but come to the program because of pressure from others must have some internal interest in the program or their likelihood of success in stopping smoking over a period of time will be very small.

There are a number of predictors for success in smoking cessation that the counselor should keep in mind during the outcome-setting process. These predictors include various aspects of stress: stressful life events within the last 12 months, Type A behavior, and level of anxiety. In addition to the stress-related items, depression, personal security, and locus of control are also predictors. Personal security reflects, to some degree, stress and locus of control and is related to various aspects of self-concept. Any or all of these predictors may show up as blocks, along with others such as anger/hostility and lack of energy.

Smoking behavior, especially if the person has smoked for many years, is a very convoluted health problem, making it difficult to attack from just one direction. Individuals start smoking for one reason (or perhaps many reasons), and continue to smoke for other reasons. All of those reasons have positive intent, so there are many intents that must be separated from the behavior of smoking. Alternative behavior must be found for each intent before the individual can easily become a lifelong nonsmoker. It is no wonder that the success rate (1 year maintenance) from most smoking cessation programs is only 6 to 25 percent.

If it is found that the client is hyperstressed, that client should immediately be referred to a stress management clinic or class before he/she attempts to stop smoking (or at least the client must work on stress management concurrently with the smoking cessation program).

The outcome model serves as the basis of information gathering in order to set outcomes, develop resources, and diminish the negative effect of blockers. The questions are (Girdano & Dusek, 1988)

1 What outcomes do you want from this program? What do you want that you do not have now? [Besides the obvious desire to stop smoking, clients may have outcomes such as wanting to be able to exercise longer and harder without panting and puffing. They may want to get rid of the smell of smoke on themselves and around the house (and in the car), they may want to be more acceptable to their friends and family, and so on.]

2 How will your life be better or different when you achieve these outcomes? How do you want to feel? [Each outcome should be a motivator for a more desirable lifestyle. This question helps to clarify how they are feeling now about their lifestyles and what changes they would like to make to feel better. Clients should be asked to visualize themselves as nonsmokers and to get a very clear picture of how life will be as a nonsmoker.]

3 What will you accept as proof that you are meeting your outcomes? [Filling out forms or keeping a diary noting how many cigarettes were smoked each day (if using the tapering-off method), smoking lower tar and nicotine cigarettes, and other changes in behavior give them easily defined proofs. Each proof must be reduced to measurable units rather than subjective feelings, although subjective rating scales can be used.]

4 What resources do you have to help you attain your desired outcomes? [This includes all personal, interpersonal, and physical resources that will help improve the chance of success.]

5 What has kept you from reaching these outcomes before? [These are blockers that usually revolve around the inability to manage stress. If so, stress management should become the immediate target outcome.]

6 What is your plan of action? [The plan of action is a joint contract between the client and the counselor. The client must be willing to work in the necessary areas with guidance from the counselor, but the program prescription must be tailored to (a) the client's stated outcomes, (b) contraindications, (c) time and other resources available, (d) the client's beliefs and readiness, and (e) the results of assessments. The program will consist of three main areas: education, behavioral intervention, and counseling.]

Program Plan

Because the phenomenon of smoking initiation (i.e., learning to habitually take hot smoke filled with tars, gases, and nicotine into the lungs) is due to a variety of motivations, including social, physical, and psychological/emotional, the program plan for smoking cessation must also be multidimensional. The composite model is endorsed here and is supported by many approaches to smoking cessation, which combine education, behavior modification, coping techniques, stress management, and so on. The Horn (1979) inventory, which is recommended for use to ascertain the smoker's motivation for smoking, ad-

INTERVENTION GRID FOR THE VARIOUS MOTIVATIONS FOR SMOKING

Motivation	Intervention techniques
Stimulation	Behavioral intervention (develop skill in activities that increase energy and enthusiasm).
Handling	Behavioral intervention (develop skill in manual activities that fulfill manipulation needs).
Habit	Behavioral intervention (recognize behavior, learn new nonsmoking behaviors, make old behavior difficult, reward new behaviors).
Pleasure	Counseling (identify intent, reframe and use intent for resource state, collapse association, collapse anchor and/or polarity integration, visualize outcome, learn cognitive restructuring techniques).
Negative affect	Counseling (identify blockers, find intent, and attenuate blockers). Behavioral intervention (stress management skills, assertiveness, anger management, reality therapy). Education (study appropriate reading material).
Addiction	Same as for negative effect. Tapering process; nicotine substitute.
All the above	Counseling (find resource states). Learn behavioral intervention skills (stress management, physical activity, healthy eating behavior). Education (learn about goal setting, health aspects).

Source: Girdano & Dusek, 1988.

dresses six categories of smokers (see self-test in Section 2.2), those who smoke for

Stimulation
Manipulation of cigarettes, lighter, matches, etc.
Habit
Pleasure (positive affect)
Negative affect reasons (anxiety, anger, fear, etc.)
Addiction

Education

From the available literature regarding smoking cessation it appears that information may be helpful for the smoking cessation client. Education can be done effectively with groups.

Behavioral Intervention

Skill development in several behavioral areas is known to be helpful in the smoking cessation process. These areas include (1) stress management, (2) smoking behavior change (behavior modification), (3) assertiveness training, (4) cognitive/rational techniques, and (5) anger management.

Counseling

The outcome model presented earlier is a means of assessing the outcomes of the client. If progress is not being made, outcomes must be redefined. Each problem or blocker within the program may produce new outcomes. Part of the counseling procedure is to identify resources. Those of specific concern in a smoking cessation program are external social support and motivation, personality characteristics that will aid in progress, control over exercise and eating options, time to contribute to the program, and the desire to succeed (which includes a high degree of readiness).

Blockers vary among clients, but the literature regarding smoking cessation suggests that the counselor examine such possibilities as Type A personality characteristics, anxious reactivity, locus of control, lack of energy, and a grouping of recent stressful life events as likely blockers. Counseling techniques can also be used to work on assertiveness skills, overcome low self-concept, identify specific stress areas, and combat anger and other specific negative states and/or beliefs.

Progress is monitored for each of the outcomes for client, counselor, and program. The client should have visible proof of progress in the form of charts, journal entries, and other written homework. It is important to divert the focus from refraining from smoking to other important outcomes such as immediate positive outcomes in self-concept enhancement, stress management, physical activity progress, and so forth. During the program the client is monitored for side effects such as depression, lethargy, fatigue, weight gain, anxiety, grief, anger, and fear. Any of these conditions (or others) may be related to smoking cessation secondary to change in lifestyle. Especially if the client has been smoking for many years, there may be a sadness due to the absence of an old friend (cigarettes) and also anticipated grief and fear of going into various situations without the help of the old friend.

The client who "finishes" the program and who has made successful progress toward the stated outcomes is prepared through fading techniques to become internally motivated and supported. When the program is over, however, the weekly "boost" is gone, and unattended clients are highly vulnerable to recidivism, especially in the 3 to 6 months following exit from the program. Follow-up may be in the form of return visits at 1 month, 3 months, 6 months, and 1 year. These visits are helpful in researching the long-term effect of the program. In addition to the personal check-in, letters and/or telephone calls can be used to support the client; however, the effectiveness of calls and letters has been found to vary according to the type of smoker the client was (Shipley, 1981).

Many behavioral change programs offer a weekly or bimonthly group for clients who have exited a specific program. This provides social support at the same time for a number of people who are experiencing similar problems. This group is especially helpful during the 3-to-6-month period of great vulnerability after the program is over. Other forms of ongoing support are calendars of activity drawn up by clients at their last session, self-evaluations to be sent in at specific times, and materials such as motivational audio and video tapes that can be checked out. Evidence shows that this phase can decrease the magnitude of recidivism. Most people who quit smoking and then start again do so within a few weeks of quitting (there is a 60 to 70 percent failure rate in the first 3 months after quitting). Follow-up data indicate that many programs lose 50 to 80 percent of their successful participants during this critical period. It makes little sense to allow this to occur when recidivism could be reduced through attention and support in the form of relapse training and support groups.

Relapse Training

Two important factors are related to relapse. First, the need to smoke is still felt. Even though the smokers have changed their overt smoking behavior, they either did not successfully eliminate the triggers, or cues, to smoking or they did not establish a new behavior that acts as a substitute for smoking when the triggers occur. Second, the all-or-nothing attitude of smokers tends to make them feel like total failures if they have one or two cigarettes after the program is over. This undermines their self-image, and a vicious cycle is initiated that further increases the motivation to smoke. Relapse control consists of

1 Not adopting an all-or-nothing attitude
2 Examining each relapse situation as a separate incident to identify triggers, feelings, emotions, etc., and finding new ways to handle them next time
3 Reviewing the motivation and commitment portion of the program

Support Groups

Successful programs often establish "smokers anonymous" meetings that offer ongoing support for ex-smokers for up to a year after the program ends. In addition to providing a forum for talking over common problems, these meetings encourage the development of positive lifestyle skills. They also create a new social circle, which fills the needs of many individuals.

REFERENCES

Crowley, T. (1984). Contingency contracting treatment of drug-abusing physicians, nurses and dentists. In J. Grabowski, M. Stitzer, and J. Henningfield (Eds.), *Behavioral Interventional Techniques in Drug Abuse Treatment*. NIDA Research Monograph 46. Washington, D.C.: U.S. Government Printing Office, pp. 68–83.

Dolan, M. P., et al. (1985). Contracting for treatment termination to reduce illicit drug use among methadone maintenance treatment failures. *Journal of Consulting and Clinical Psychology*, 53:549–551.

Dusek, D. E., and Girdano, D. A. (1987). *Becoming a Nonsmoker*. Winter Park, Colo.: Paradox.

Girdano, D. A., and Dusek, D. E. (1988). *Changing Health Behavior*. Scottsdale, Ariz.: Gorsuch-Scarsbrick Press.

Girdano, D. A., and Dusek, D. E. (1988). *Changing Health Behavior*. Scottsdale, Ariz.: Gorsuch-Scarsbrick Press.

Girdano, D. A., Everly, G. S., Jr., and Dusek, D. E. (1990). *Controlling Stress and Tension: A Holistic Approach*, 3d ed. Englewood Cliffs, N.J.: Prentice Hall.

Hall, S. N., Loeb, P. C., and Allen, T. (1984). The job seekers' workshop. In J. Grabowski, M. Stitzer, and J. Henningfield (Eds.) *Behavioral Intervention Techniques in Drug Abuse Treatment*. NIDA Research Monograph 46. DHHS Pub. (ADM) 84-1284. Washington, D.C.: U.S. Government Printing Office, pp. 115-130.

Horn, D. (1979). *Why Do You Smoke?* Department of Health, Education and Welfare, U.S. Public Health Service, National Institute of Health, Pub. 79-1822. Washington, D.C.: U.S. Government Printing Office.

McCarthy, J. J., and Borders, O. T. (1985). Limit setting on drug abuse in methadone maintenance patients. *American Journal of Psychiatry,* 142:12.

Shipley, R. H. (1981). Maintenance of smoking cessation: effect of followup letters, smoking motivation, muscle tension, and locus of control. *Journal of Consulting and Clinical Psychology*, 49(6):982–984.

Woody, G. E., et al. (1983). Psycho-therapy for opiate addiction: does it help? *Archives of General Psychiatry*, 40:639–645.

PERINATAL SUBSTANCE ABUSE—TREATMENT AND PREVENTION

Increasing numbers of women are abusing drugs during pregnancy and thus endangering their own well-being and lives as well as the well-being and lives of their children. The spreading abuse of phencyclidine piperidine (PCP) and cocaine and its potent form "crack," added to the more established drugs alcohol and nicotine and narcotics such as heroin, has intensified concerns about the implications of maternal drug use for unborn children (Gittler & McPherson, 1990). According to the National Institute on Drug Abuse (NIDA, 1989), approximately 8 to 13 percent of all pregnant women, nationwide, are substance abusers, which increases the incidence and prevalence of low-birth-weight infants and premature infants and the perinatal problems of high-risk infants.

Nationally, the substances most frequently abused are alcohol, tobacco, marijuana, cocaine, valium, and barbiturates (Chasnoff, 1988). Women who abuse one substance tend to be multi-drug abusers. In addition, substance-abusing women may be intravenous drug users or live with a partner who is an intravenous drug user, making this population at higher risk for infection by the AIDS-related human immunodeficiency virus (HIV).

Smoking during pregnancy is a significant cause of infant mortality, with 40 percent of the low-birth-weight infants in 1987 having had mothers who smoked. Fetal alcohol syndrome (FAS) is one of the top three known causes of birth defects with accompanying mental retardation. Nearly 5,000 babies are born with FAS every year, and FAE (fetal alcohol effects) may affect an additional 36,000 newborns each year (NCADD, 1990a).

Recent studies suggest that pregnant women who smoke marijuana are frequently at higher risk of stillbirth, miscarriage, and having babies of low birth weight and/or with fetal abnormalities, especially of the nervous system. Women who use marijuana during pregnancy also deliver infants five times more likely to have features like those with FAS (OSAP, 1989). Heavy cocaine use has been linked to higher rates of miscarriage and premature onset of labor. Infants born to women using cocaine often experience painful withdrawal from cocaine at birth. These infants can even suffer prenatal stroke because of the fluctuations in blood pressure that cocaine can produce (OSAP, 1989).

There has been a great deal of denial about the extent to which women experience alcohol and other drug problems, and this denial is more profound when pregnant women are concerned. This country has made progress in expanding prevention and treatment efforts to include women, but our social and medical institutions have not responded effectively to the needs of pregnant women who are alcoholic or have other drug dependencies (NCADD, 1990b). Furthermore, in cases where substance abuse has been identified in the prenatal period, the prevailing attitude has been to first treat the pregnancy, then treat the substance abuse problem. The common practice is to hospitalize the woman prenatally, deliver a "healthy" infant, and deal with substance abuse in the postpartum period. Pregnancy and the postpartum period represent a golden opportunity for chemical dependence intervention. However, many women do not follow up, and a valuable "window of opportunity" is lost. Pregnancy is a time of intrinsic change for women, and the potential price of failure to change chemical use is high: possible fetal damage, loss of custody, and another generation of family dysfunction. The problems surrounding alcohol and drug abuse treatment in general are greatly compounded by pregnancy. The treatment issues surrounding alcoholic and drug-abusing pregnant women and mothers are numerous. They include punitive attitudes; lack of access to prenatal, pediatric, and general health care; reimbursement issues, particularly problems in Medicaid reimbursement; discrimination against accepting pregnant women into many substance abuse treatment facilities; liability concerns in treating pregnant women and women with children; controversy and misunderstanding surrounding the detoxification of pregnant women; and a host of legal issues such as whether, how, when, and for what purpose toxicology screens should be performed, whether child abuse or neglect is occurring, and whether the pregnant woman is in an abusive relationship.

BLOCKS TO TREATMENT

Numerous barriers exist that prevent women from seeking treatment. Foremost among them are stigma, denial, and lack of gender-specific services for women.

Stigma

A substance-abusing woman has two strikes against her in our society—she is a woman, often considered a second class citizen, and she is seen as sexually promiscuous, weak-willed, shamefully negligent of her children, and irresponsible in her "decisions" to bear more children. For women, alcoholism and other drug abuse remain very much a moral issue, with female substance abusers viewed as "fallen women," "whores," and "lushes." In the presence of this rejection and blame, profound feelings of guilt, shame, and low self-esteem emerge. This low self-esteem is too often coupled with depression and can have an immobilizing effect on a woman. Lower social tolerance of addiction in women also leads to increased isolation. Studies show that women who have problems with alcohol or drugs tend to drink or use drugs alone, whereas men are more likely to drink socially and in bars. In addition to the stigma attached to going into a substance abuse treatment center, these women have other barriers such as lack of local support groups to attend, lack of employment, lack of assertiveness skills, lack of autonomy skills, relationship problems, and perhaps even psychiatric disorders.

Denial

Shame and guilt lead to high denial of drinking/drug problems on the part of both the woman herself and family members and friends, who tend to conceal substance abuse problems from outsiders and protect the female substance abuser. Women are more likely than men to encounter opposition to treatment from friends and families. Women are also less likely to be identified and referred for treatment by professionals, including physicians and social service workers (Beckman & Amaro, 1986). In general it appears that alcoholic and drug-abusing women are frequently blamed for their disease and its consequences on the one hand and infrequently referred to treatment on the other hand.

Lack of Gender-Specific Treatment Services for Women

The reasons substance-abusing women are not identified or do not get proper representation and treatment are often based on the lack of gender sensitivity in our institutions. Many treatment facilities will not take pregnant women. Most treatment centers are geared for men who have been sent there by the law. Women are rarely sent by the law; they go into clinics and medical centers for symptoms other than overt substance abuse. Since most treatment programs were designed initially by and for men, and women were admitted as an afterthought, little attention has been paid to specific women's treatment issues including the different emotional, social, and economic realities of women's lives. Many women have child-rearing responsibilities, and many are single parents by the time they reach a treatment agency. Since the majority of pregnant women currently seeking treatment are also mothers of young children, the treatment of pregnant addicts must also involve services for mothers.

Only a few prevention and treatment efforts have focused specifically on pregnant alcoholic and other drug-dependent women. There are tremendous fears among service providers about liability problems associated with the treatment of pregnant addicted women. There is a great need to train treatment providers in how to proceed with safe detoxification and treatment. To date, much of the reaction to treating pregnant women with alcohol and other drug dependencies has been dominated by fear, lack of knowledge, and lack of experience. The irony is that pregnancy offers an opportunity to intervene and provide treatment at the time that the least amount of treatment is available.

These are the problems of pregnant women who are identified as substance abusers. Other problems include denial and lack of screening for substance abuse in pregnant women. Although pregnant substance abusers have more physical illness and will ask for help sooner than men, they are misdiagnosed more often than men in regard to substance abuse. In addition, there may be a resistance by a woman's doctor to screening for and identifying drug abuse— for financial reasons, lack of knowledge of appropriate screening techniques, ignorance about alcohol effects, denial that there could be a substance abuse problem in his/her patients, or other reasons.

PRENATAL SCREENING

Screening of the pregnant woman can occur during regular prenatal visits to the physician. Through the use of written drug use pattern checklists, observation, and key questions, clinic staff may identify "red flags" that warn of high or medium risk. Pregnancy risk factors that might be considered "red flags" include heavy smoking patterns, use of psychoactive drugs, anxiety and/or depression, stress-induced problems, poor nutrition, and increased proportion of drug-taking days and amount per session.

"High-risk" clients include those who have used one or more drugs heavily together, continue to use drugs heavily after pregnancy is suspected or confirmed, are not concerned about the risks, and have no plans to stop use during pregnancy. These are the women who are already at risk for low-birth-weight babies because of other factors (such as poor nutrition) and have had some recent problems related to drug use.

"Medium-risk" clients include those who used drugs heavily in the past but quit or cut back before or just after the onset of pregnancy, reported past problems from drug use but none in the last 2 years, have a family history of substance abuse problems, used an abusable prescription drug or illicit drug in the last 2 months, and continue light to moderate drug use during pregnancy without apparent concern.

"Low-risk" women include those who report no previous use or only occasional use of alcohol, cigarettes, or marijuana and no use of other abusable drugs; stopped using drugs altogether either before conception or immediately after pregnancy was suspected; and express their concern about possible problems connected with drug use during pregnancy.

Women at risk have been identified by a common set of psychosocial characteristics. They

- Suffer greater personal distress than comparison women
- Have lower self-esteem
- Have fewer social supports
- Have fewer personal resources and skills for coping with emotional distress or practical problem situations
- Believe that people look down on them

- Rate themselves low on masculine traits associated with ego strength, effectiveness, and self-esteem
  - Lack self-discipline
  - Perceive that they cannot control their lives
  - Demonstrate low self-expression and lack assertiveness
  - Are angry
  - Are self-absorbed

PREVENTION

Drug abuse exacerbates the "normal crisis" of pregnancy and magnifies the helplessness and hopelessness of the mother-to-be. Prevention and intervention efforts need to focus on skill building in the areas of self-esteem, self-discipline, self-expression, assertiveness, anger, relationship skills, interpersonal communication, and other risk factors that "set the woman up" for drug abuse. All females who are of childbearing age should have information regarding the effects of substance abuse on the fetus. The women who need the critical help are those who are abusing either licit or illicit drugs while they are of childbearing age.

Education programs might be considered a preventive intervention treatment. There are three tiers to prevention that might be used in this situation: (1) primary prevention, (2) secondary or targeted prevention, and (3) preventive treatment.

Primary Prevention

Primary prevention helps promote the involvement of a number of community organizations in producing a mass education campaign similar to the national campaign against drinking and driving. The effort puts educational materials in the offices of health care providers, provides curriculum materials and lectures for the community schools, and supplies lecturers for community groups.

Secondary or Targeted Prevention

Secondary or targeted prevention includes prevention activities (education and prenatal counseling) targeted to women, especially pregnant women, at schools, prenatal classes, and caregivers offices. This is designed to increase the availability and accessibility of prevention and early intervention services for pregnant women.

Preventive Treatment

Preventive treatment includes aspects such as screening, health behavior change, support groups, and referral, all of which are designed to increase the availability, accessibility, and effectiveness of treatment services for pregnant women. Although there may be an initial increase in referred cases, these activities should ultimately result in a decreased prevalence of substance usage among pregnant and postpartum women and move toward the final outcome of healthy babies. Another result should be an increase in referrals for pregnant substance-abusing women to treatment centers and to physicians.

LEGAL ISSUES

Each day more children and fetuses are endangered as drugs compound family violence problems and interfere with the ability of a mother or pregnant woman to parent properly. The financial and personal magnitude of the problem are great—estimates for initial hospital treatment and drug withdrawal are about $6,000 per infant. One-third of these babies go into intensive care, which raises the cost to approximately $60,000. If the infant is born prematurely, the stay in the hospital is much longer, and the cost can run as high as $250,000.

To protect society from these expenses and the infant from medical problems, there has been a trend toward prosecution of drug-using pregnant women in order to force treatment. However, this has led to a clash between the government's legal apparatus and the medical community. The current climate of punishment and blame of substance-abusing women involves complicated issues concerning conflicting rights and responsibilities.

Some medical and social workers view increased prosecution as the problem despite the enormous costs imposed on communities to support drug-addicted babies. This causes widespread reluctance to cooperate with the criminal justice system or to undertake radical responses. Some medical and social work professionals erect barriers to prevent prosecutorial involvement. There is a view that criminal prosecution of chemically dependent women will deter such women from seeking prenatal care and chemical dependency treatment. This may result in increasing rather than preventing harm to children and to society as a whole. Those individuals opposed to prosecution are lobbying states and local governments to avoid any measures that define alcoholism or other drug use during pregnancy as prenatal child abuse and to avoid prosecution, jail, or other punitive measures as a substitute for providing effective health services for these women.

Few authorities flatly favor punishment by itself as the alternative, as it has been shown that criminal justice sanctions alone have little value in reducing the criminality of drug-involved offenders. Most knowledgeable individuals believe that sanctions can, however, serve a powerful role by facilitating effective drug treatment. There are a variety of pressures that bring drug abusers into treatment. Parents, employers, loved ones, and friends may all apply psychological and social pressures. The most powerful pressure may be the threat of legal sanction—the threat of arrest and conviction and, most important, the threat of incarceration. The leverage created by this threat, and by the sanction itself, permits serious abusers to consider treatment as a viable option. The belief is that many drug-addicted women are in a high state of denial while pregnant and will remain so after the birth of their child. The only time they may seek treatment is when some prosecution is involved.

The middle ground in this issue is that in some instances legal sanctions may be necessary for the treatment program to be meaningful but that they should not become a substitute for adequate treatment programs. Deferred prosecution is also an option, with treatment made a condition of probation. The prosecution/medical model must encourage, not discourage, treatment. Prenatal care should require cocaine testing for purposes of medical attention. The positive results would not necessarily have to be reported. Most existing child abuse reporting laws do not require that the government be informed of a positive drug test. If a mother tests positive early in her pregnancy, then treatment and intensive counseling could be undertaken.

The most significant problem that exists is the absence of adequate treatment and evaluations of successful treatment strategies. Treatment, which would be a condition of an enforced agreement by a prosecutor, should be available and include postdelivery substance abuse treatment when the mother tests positive for drugs. To turn the drug-using mother and child back out into the community with no treatment harms the child and inevitably increases the costs to society (Keith et al., 1989).

SPECIAL TREATMENT ISSUES

Most studies indicate that a high percentage of alcoholic and drug-abusing women have grown up in substance-abusing families. A significant number of alcoholic and drug-abusing women are involved in intimate relationships with other substance abusers. Research suggests that women's drug and alcohol abuse is dependent on the encouragement of other people, especially their husbands or partners. Likewise, among illicit drug users, women are most likely to be introduced to and supplied illicit drugs by men as part of an intimate or sexual relationship. A study of drug use among adolescent mothers found that the most significant factor in an adolescent mother's own drug use was her partner's drug use. Adolescent mothers who had drug-using partners were more likely to be involved with partners who used drugs more frequently and in greater quantity as well as to be at greater risk for escalation of their own drug use (Amaro et al., 1989).

Women frequently start using illicit drugs within the context of a relationship with a male partner. However, although it may start in a connected relationship, illicit drug use often ends by destroying the woman's capacity for relationships. A woman usually enters treatment with a history of failed and abusive relationships that often include violence and abandonment. Therefore, treatment issues include examining sexuality and sexual preference issues, developing comfort in close relationships without alcohol or other drugs as a balm or buffer, and developing trusting and mutually supportive networks with other women (Finkelstein et al., 1990).

Many substance-abusing women's lives include battering, child abuse, rape, incest, and violence. Many have been victims of violence throughout their lives, beginning with early childhood physical abuse and incest. This violence often continues into adulthood in relationships with abusive partners and extending to the abuse or neglect of their own children.

Violence, incest, and sexual abuse should be recognized as important realities in the lives of many substance-abusing women. Sometimes women repress prior incest experiences and find that the drugged state facilitates the suppression of painful memories. Current violence must always be dealt with, and treatment should consider the possibility that there was some form of violence in the past and that denial contributes to further helplessness, despair, and escalating violence (Finkelstein et al., 1990).

The special treatment needs of alcoholic and drug-abusing women include, first of all, an understanding that substance abuse in women is surrounded by a number of individual, interpersonal, familial, and social issues that require many different levels of intervention and treatment. The social and economic context of the lives of many substance-abusing women is one of inadequate financial resources, lack of affordable housing, and a lack of marketable job skills. Many are single parents, socially isolated and without adequate support systems. Substance-abusing women should be viewed within the context of their relationships with others. Women's lives are, by and large, intimately entwined with others—their families, their children, and their friends, as well as therapists, doctors, social agencies, courts, child welfare organizations, and children's schools. They are extremely affected by what happens to them in their relationships and how they in turn affect other people (Finkelstein & Derman, 1990).

REFERENCES

Amaro, H., Zuckerman, B., and Cabral, H. (1989). Drug use among adolescent mothers: profile on risk. *Pediatrics*, 84(1):76–85.

Beckman, L., and Amaro, H. (1986). Personal and social differences faced by females and males entering alcoholism treatment. *Journal of Studies on Alcohol*, 45:135–145.

Blocher, D. H. (1980). Some implications of recent research in social and developmental psychology for counseling practice. *The Personnel and Guidance Journal*, 58(5):334–336.

Chasnoff, I. J. (1988). Drug use in pregnancy: parameters of risk. *Pediatric Clinics of North America*, 35:1403–1412.

De Leon, G., and Jainchill, N. (1986). Circumstance, motivation, readiness, and suitability as correlates of treatment tenure. *Journal of Psychoactive Drugs*, 18(3):203–208.

Finkelstein, N., and Derman, L. (1990). *Single Parent Women: What a Mother Can Do (Alcohol and Drugs Are Women's Issues)*. New York: Scarecrow Press.

Finkelstein, N., Duncan, S., Derman, L., and Smeltz, J. (1990). *Getting Sober, Getting Well: A Treatment Guide for Caregivers Who Work with Women*. Cambridge, Mass.: The Women's Alcoholism Program of CASPAR, Inc.

Gittler, J., and McPherson, M. (1990). Perinatal substance abuse: an overview of the problem. *Children Today*, 19(4):3–7.

Keith, L., MacGregor, S., Friedell, S., Rosner, M., Chasnoff, I. J., and Sciarra, J. J. (1989). Substance abuse in pregnant women: recent experience at the perinatal center for chemical dependence of Northwestern Memorial Hospital. *American Journal of Obstetrics and Gynecology*, 73:715–720.

NCADD. (1990a). *NCADD Fact Sheet: Alcohol-Related Birth Defects*. Washington, D.C.: National Council on Alcoholism and Drug Dependence.

NCADD. (1990b). *Women, Alcohol, Other Drugs and Pregnancy: NCADD Policy Statement*. Washington, D.C.: National Council on Alcoholism and Drug Dependence.

NIDA. (1989). *NIDA Capsules: Drug Abuse and Pregnancy*. Rockville, Md: National Institute on Drug Abuse.

OSAP (Office of Substance Abuse Prevention). (1989). *The Fact Is . . . Alcohol and Other Drugs Can Harm an Unborn Baby*. Rockville, Md.: National Clearinghouse for Alcohol and Drug Information.

SELF-HELP MODALITIES

Two of the most widely known, effective, and highly subscribed self-help groups in the United States are Alcoholics Anonymous and the Adult Children of Alcoholics.

ALCOHOLICS ANONYMOUS

Alcoholics Anonymous is perhaps the most successful of all group treatment modalities. This organization's basic aim is to help alcoholics stop drinking. Through group discussions with others who have similar problems, the alcoholic can come to realize that his or her problem is not unique and that other individuals have met the challenge of alcoholism successfully. Alcoholics Anonymous offers group identity, status, and prestige, qualities sorely lacking in the life of the alcoholic. With self-identity restored (or gained for the first time), the nonpracticing alcoholic is able to work toward regaining a normal life.

Since AA was founded in 1935 it has provided help for hundreds of thousands of people (Beattie, 1990). The first step, that of admitting powerlessness over alcohol, is a difficult one and is often taken only after other forms of individual treatment have been exhausted. But once this is achieved, the alcoholic usually is able to refrain from taking the first drink, while each day of sobriety adds to his or her self-confidence. AA does not demand any long-term "I will never drink again" pledges. Forty years of accumulated wisdom has shown the folly of such gestures. Instead, AA follows what it calls the 24-hour plan. It encourages the alcoholic to concentrate on not drinking for 24 hours, to take each day, each 24 hours, one at a time. This is but one example of the realism, honesty, and simplicity that spell success for this unique treatment.

Unique is an understatement, for in this day of government subsidies, political activism, and programs that change with each new research report, AA stands as a model. There is only one requirement for membership—a desire to stop drinking. There are no dues or fees for AA programs. AA is not allied with any sect or religious denomination, although many of its doctrines rely on a "Power" greater than the drinker alone. As a group, it does not engage in research or medical or psychiatric treatment, nor does it endorse any causes or engage in any controversy. Its single purpose is to help members remain sober. Its methods, support, and fellowship from others with similar problems sound too simple to be effective until you take a closer look at the basic underlying causes of alcoholism. The now famous Twelve Steps of AA further describe their approach (see box).

AA is a way of life for the nonpracticing alcoholic; a club- or fraternity-like atmosphere develops, and most social activities of AA members revolve around that group. Members become dedicated to helping others remain sober, which becomes a form of egotistic altruism. By helping others they help themselves. In addition to the help given the alcoholic, AA offers aid in understanding the alcoholic mate or parent through its Al-Anon and Ala-Teen groups. Here, nonalcoholic family members may learn about the disease of alcoholism and, more important, that the nonalcoholic is not responsible for the actions of the alcoholic. Guilt is an emotion common to family members of

---

TWELVE STEPS OF ALCOHOLICS ANONYMOUS

We: . . . admitted we were powerless over alcohol and that our lives had become unmanageable.

. . . came to believe that a Power greater than ourselves could restore us to sanity.

. . . made a decision to turn our will and our lives over to the care of God as we understood Him.

. . . made a searching and fearless moral inventory of ourselves.

. . . admitted to God, to ourselves and to another human being the exact nature of our wrongs.

. . . were entirely ready to have God remove all these defects of character.

. . . humbly asked Him to remove our shortcomings.

. . . made a list of all persons we had harmed, and became willing to make amends to them all.

. . . made direct amends to such people wherever possible, except when to do so would injure them or others.

. . . continued to take personal inventory and when we were wrong promptly admitted it.

. . . sought through prayer and meditation to improve our conscious contact with God, as we understood Him, praying only for knowledge of His will for us and the power to carry that out.

. . . having had a spiritual awakening as the result of these steps, we tried to carry this message to alcoholics, and to practice these principles in all our affairs.

alcoholics, because they are apt to feel that they are the cause of the situations that drive the alcoholic to drink.

ADULT CHILDREN OF ALCOHOLICS (ACoA)

Many adults who grew up in households with an alcoholic mother and/or father share a certain set of characteristics that become more and more problematic in adulthood. The Adult Children of Alcoholics organization is widely spread throughout the United States and is responsible for helping thousands of adults modify behaviors that resulted from growing up in a dysfunctional alcoholic family. Realizing the common characteristics of adult children of alcoholics, the ACoA organization has helped provide answers and resolve the emotional problems of many adults who grew up in alcoholic homes.

Since a positive self-concept is formed early in life by interacting with caring adults, the child of an alcoholic is more likely to miss out on the positive early development that children of nonalcoholic parents experience. Children of alcoholics (regardless of age, order of birth, sex, occupation, or religion) have been shown to have lower self-esteem than children from homes where alcohol is not abused (Woititz, 1983). Since self-esteem or self-empowerment is the basis from which individuals generate their successes, it is understandable that children of alcoholics have issues to confront as adults that they did not have the opportunity or the experience to confront as children.

To understand some of the dilemmas that ACoAs must face, it is important to look at the childhood experience of survival when one's mother or father is an alcoholic. If the mother is the alcoholic, the child often becomes the caretaker because there is no one else to take care of the home, the other children, and the mother (the father is often absent—has left or seldom comes home). When the alcoholic mother is sober she usually tries very hard to "make up for" the abandonment during her binges, and this honeymoon period is warily enjoyed by the child, waiting for the relapse. When the relapse comes, the child often feels that "if I would have been better, quieter, worked harder, loved her more, etc." Mother would not have gone back to drinking. The child is alternately shown affection, then scorn; loved, then abused—which unwittingly teaches the child an approach–avoidance kind of relationship.

If the father was the alcoholic, the child may have been abused while the father was drunk and treated in a caring way while he was sober, being plied with promises that were never kept. The mother was likely codependent, trying to control her husband's actions so he wouldn't make a fool of himself and the family. No one was allowed to talk about the alcoholic outside of the family, which gave the message that it is not all right to talk about your problems. The secret of alcoholism that the child must keep out of loyalty to the family often keeps the child from forming childhood friendships.

If both parents were alcoholic, life for children in the household was even more chaotic, unpredictable, and volatile. No one knew what would happen next!

From these common childhood experiences come some basic characteristics that may be generalized to most adult children of alcoholics (Woititz, 1983):

1 ACoAs do not know what normal, mentally healthy behavior is; they have no norms upon which to base their behavior. They have learned not to ask, so they can only guess at appropriate behavior. They continue through life feeling that they are different from everyone else.

2 ACoAs lack the ability to see a project through from start to finish. Starting is the easy part; following through is the difficult part.

3 ACoAs learned lying as a basic form of communication. Childhood life was built on lies, fantasy, and unkept promises. Even when telling the truth would be easier, the ACoA often makes up a story out of habit.

4 ACoAs are their own most critical judges. No matter what the child of the alcoholic did, it wasn't right or it couldn't fix the problem, and self-criticism became ingrained.

5 ACoAs take themselves and life seriously. Truly self-abandoned play is a luxury not known to many children of alcoholic parents.

6 Relationships are difficult for ACoAs. Again, the early dysfunctional relationships that served as models for the child remain as models for the ACoA. New models based on unconditional positive regard for another person must be learned as adults—many times through self-help groups and therapy.

7 ACoAs hate situations where they are not or cannot be in control. In order to survive as children, they had to be in control because they couldn't trust anyone else. As adults, these individuals retain that learned behavior until they learn to let go and trust.

8 ACoAs have a deep need for external recognition and approval. Still wanting to please the parent(s) who could never be pleased, these individuals are more motivated by others than by their own needs and desires.

9 ACoAs are either very responsible or very irresponsible. In some alcoholic families the child will become an early adult, taking care of household duties, siblings, even parents. In other families the child acts out in rebellion, blaming the world for his/her problems, and learns irresponsibility.

10 ACoAs exhibit extreme loyalty, even if it hurts. Loyalty patterns arise early in every family and culture. To be part of the group, one must be loyal. To be loved, one must be loyal. When ACoAs succeed in finding a relationship, they may be so grateful that they would rather take verbal and physical abuse than end the relationship.

11 ACoAs tend to be impulsive—they start off on a track not knowing where it will take them or what the full consequences of their actions will be. They soon feel caught up in the process and out of control; they want out but don't know how to get out.

These are the basic problematic behaviors that ACoAs bring into self-help groups, and by sharing their experiences they find that they are not alone, different, or undesirable just because they grew up in an alcoholic household. In the group they learn new behaviors that help them empower themselves, enjoy healthy relationships, and change the behaviors that are no longer working for them.

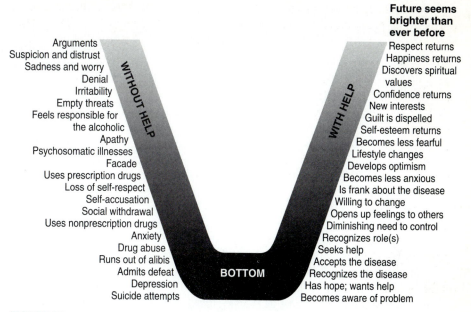

Future seems brighter than ever before

WITHOUT HELP

Arguments
Suspicion and distrust
Sadness and worry
Denial
Irritability
Empty threats
Feels responsible for
the alcoholic
Apathy
Psychosomatic illnesses
Facade
Uses prescription drugs
Loss of self-respect
Self-accusation
Social withdrawal
Uses nonprescription drugs
Anxiety
Drug abuse
Runs out of alibis
Admits defeat
Depression
Suicide attempts

BOTTOM

WITH HELP

Respect returns
Happiness returns
Discovers spiritual
values
Confidence returns
New interests
Guilt is dispelled
Self-esteem returns
Becomes less fearful
Lifestyle changes
Develops optimism
Becomes less anxious
Is frank about the disease
Willing to change
Opens up feelings to others
Diminishing need to control
Recognizes role(s)
Seeks help
Accepts the disease
Recognizes the disease
Has hope; wants help
Becomes aware of problem

FIGURE 25
Alcoholism: progression and recovery of the family with and without help. (Adapted from Care Unit Hospital, Kirkland, Washington.)

REFERENCES

Beattie, M. (1990). *Codependents' Guide to the Twelve Steps*. Englewood Cliffs, N.J.: Prentice-Hall.

Woititz, J. G. (1983). *Adult Children of Alcoholics*. Hollywood, Calif.: Health Communications.

INDEX

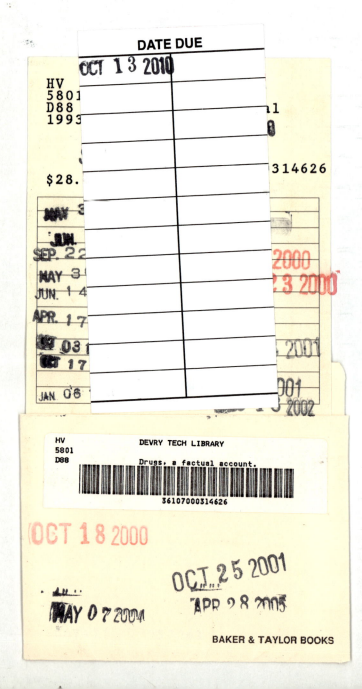